THE MAMMOTH BOOK OF
GANGS

James Morton

ROBINSON

RUNNING PRESS
PHILADELPHIA · LONDON

Constable & Robinson Ltd
55–56 Russell Square
London WC1B 4HP
www.constablerobinson.com

First published in the UK by Robinson,
an imprint of Constable & Robinson Ltd, 2012

A copy of the British Library Cataloguing in Publication
Data is available from the British Library

UK ISBN: 978-1-78033-088-4 (paperback)
UK ISBN: 978-1-78033-089-1 (ebook)

1 3 5 7 9 10 8 6 4 2

First published in the United States in 2012 by Running Press Book Publishers,
A Member of the Perseus Books Group

Books published by Running Press are available at special discounts for bulk
purchases in the United States by corporations, institutions, and other organizations.
For more information, please contact the Special Markets Department at the
Perseus Books Group, 2300 Chestnut Street, Suite 200, Philadelphia, PA 19103, or
call (800) 810-4145, ext. 5000, or e-mail special.markets@perseusbooks.com.

US ISBN: 978-0-7624-4436-6
US Library of Congress Control Number: 2011930512

9 8 7 6 5 4 3 2 1
Digit on the right indicates the number of this printing

Running Press Book Publishers
2300 Chestnut Street
Philadelphia, PA 19103-4371

Visit us on the web!
www.runningpress.com

Printed and bound in the UK

Contents

Introduction

What is a gang? What is organized crime? What is a criminal, even? Sociologists have wasted thousands of acres of trees trying to put together satisfactory definitions or at least one on which they can agree. Generally they have failed.

Defining a criminal is relatively easy. In the years before his death the Chicagoan journalist and playwright Ben Hecht, who wrote *The Front Page*, was working on a biography of the Californian mobster Mickey Cohen. He wrote, in what would have been the foreword:

Out of my contacts has come what I think may be a major piece of anthropological lore. The criminal has no hates or fears – except very personal ones. He is possibly the only human left in the world who looks lovingly on society. He does not hanker to fight it, reform it or even rationalize it. He wants only to rob it. He admires it as a hungry man might admire a roast pig with an apple in its mouth.

I was pleased to find this out, for I have read much to the contrary. Society does not, as sociologists and other tony intellectuals maintain, create the criminal. Bad housing, bad companions, bad government etc., have little to do with why there are killers, robbers and outlaws. The criminal has no relation to society to speak of. He is part of man's soul, not his institutions. He is an old one. A thousand preachers, summer boys' camps, plus a congress of psychiatrists can barely dent even a minor criminal. As for the major criminal, he cannot be touched at all by society because he operates on a different time level. He is the presocial part of us – the ape that spurned the collar.

The criminal at the time of his lawlessness is one of the few happy or contented men to be found among us. While he remains a criminal he is as free of conscience pangs as the most right-doing of bookkeepers. He eats well, sleeps well, lives well, and his only disadvantage is that he may die ahead of his time from an enemy bullet, the gas chamber or electric chair.

Not even the latter two nowadays.

As for organized crime? Perhaps as good as any definition are two North American offerings. The first, by the Canadian police, is "two or more persons consorting together on a continuing basis to participate in illegal activities, either directly or indirectly, for gain". An unnamed American organized crime boss thought it was "just a bunch of people getting together to take all the money they can from all the suckers they can. Organized crime is a chain of command all the way from London to Canada, the US, Mexico, Italy, France, everywhere".

If that is organized crime what, then, is a gang? When I first began researching my book *Gangland*, a north London solicitor told me he did not act for gangs: "I act for families." And if those families find they need a little help from friends and acquaintances does that make them into a gang? Surely gangs were for little boys giving secret passwords and meeting in the same shed every Saturday at teatime? Gangs were for American television films, said Reggie Kray.

It is really a question of semantics. A gang does not necessarily require a paid-up subscription, although members are often required to contribute a certain amount of their weekly take, or maintain a list of members, as does the Garrick or any other gentleman's club. It is, however, a clearly recognizable floating body with the equivalent of a chairman, members of the board, officers of the club and members who come and go for a variety of reasons. Some are in prison, some die, some retire and, just as some football players may leave Chelsea for Liverpool (but rather more dangerously), some may join another gang. But for a period of time they are members in one form or another.

Gangs do not always need to have machine-guns to qualify for the name. There have been many successful gangs of shoplifters, such as London's all-women Forty Thieves and the Australian Kangaroos who looted shops in Europe in the 1960s and 1970s. The latter is a good example of members coming and going, being replaced by newcomers as they returned home, often linking up to carry out a couple of jobs and then moving on to another team. But they were regarded as "the shoplifters' shoplifters", the crème de la crème of thieves. The story may not even be true but it is said that some Kangaroos stole a chimpanzee to order from the zoo that was then on the top floor of Harrods, the ritzy department store in Knightsbridge, London. The animal was stuffed in a baby carriage, given a dummy and wheeled out.

Some of the most dangerous gangs have been those whose members use the pen and the tongue as opposed to the sword. Blackmail – the so-called murder of the soul – does not require a large team. Two, perhaps three, are all that are needed: one to lure the victim into a compromising position and the other, and possibly a mate, to take advantage of the man with his trousers around his knees.

Apart from a time in the United States in the 1920s and 1930s when there was something of a cachet to being a gangster, underworld characters have been keen to present themselves as a collection of friends rather than as members of a gang. It may be that the word itself, with its resonance of organization, brought heavier punishment from the judge.

When, in the 1940s, the killing of a waitress took place as the result of a protection racket in Melbourne, the defence tried to portray it as a domestic dispute. A similar thing happened a few years after the Second World War when an Italian was stabbed over ninety times and it was suggested the attacker had been protecting his sister. In fact, it was over control of Melbourne's fruit and vegetable market. Over the years gang shootings, knifings and beatings have been projected as personal disputes rather than group activities.

Eddie Richardson, one of the brothers convicted in the so-called Torture Trial of 1966, argued that the friends of the Hayward family who fought with him in Mr Smith's Club in March 1965 were "a group". In the "villain business", they are not called gangs, wrote bank-robber, later supergrass, Maurice O'Mahoney. Adhering to the business and sporting similes, he thought of his associates and rivals as teams. In the past decade or so things have changed. The black street-gangs' use of the word "posse" seems to be in decline and now they are happier to be known as gangs. Another decade and it will no doubt change again. What's in a name anyway? It's the activity that counts.

A word about the distaff side. In the western world there have been few female gang-leaders. There was Billy Hill's sister, Aggie, who led the Forty Thieves, and in Sydney in the 1920s the English-born Tilly Devine and her New South Wales counterpart Kate Leigh certainly ran chains of brothels. But this was more because it was an offence for men to control prostitution while this was not so for women. In Miami, Griselda Blanco undoubtedly led a team of drug-runners but she used men to do the killing for her. One woman who was quite definitely at the coalface was Montreal's Monica Proietti, known as "Machine Gun Mollie". She was from a criminal family. Her grandmother, who was thought to be running a crime school for children, was sentenced to twelve years, at the age of sixty, for receiving. Proietti, one of eight children, four of whom died in a fire in 1958, married Anthony Smith, a Scottish gangster, at the age of nineteen. When he was deported in 1962 their two children were sent to Britain to live with him. She then took up with Viateur Tessier, who four years later went down for armed robbery. The next in line was Richard Blass, a rival to the Montreal Mafia, and after Blass's death in January 1975, when he was killed by police shortly after he had herded thirteen people into a storeroom in a bar and set fire to them, Proietti was protected by the drug-trafficker Roger "Le Gros" Provencal.

Her team of robbers included her own brother Mario and brothers Gérald and Robert Lelièvre who were killed in 1984 when a bomb was detonated in a downtown Montreal building as a revenge for the killing of West End gang-leader Frank "Dunie" Ryan. The jobs Proietti and her team pulled were relatively small-time and it is doubtful if they grossed much over $100,000 in total. Thinking of starting a new life in Florida, she went for one last job to add to the twenty or so banks she had robbed. On 19 September 1976, aged twenty-seven, she died when she was shot by an undercover officer after crashing into a bus during a high-speed chase through the north end of the city.

It is rarely possible to provide a complete and accurate account of the comings and goings of the gangs. For a start they are naturally secretive and, for obvious reasons, those who have written their memoirs, or had them ghosted, will try to cover their tracks, play down their parts in their less heroic exploits and enhance their roles in the greater coups. For example, unsurprisingly Billy Hill's escape from Portland Borstal differs very substantially from the newspaper accounts and he is by no means the only gangster who has viewed his life through more rose-tinted spectacles than the police and public have done. For libel and other purposes many memoirs and biographies, for example those of Charles Sobhraj, have used aliases for the characters. Some are more easily decipherable than others but, as the years pass, contemporaries die and memories fade, they will be forever lost. Very often Jack Spot's rivals were the alliterative "Newcastle Ned", "Manchester Mike" and so on. Seemingly some writers do not bother with research. One recent book has Spot killed in a club fight in 1960 when in fact he lived until the mid-1990s. Errors have been repeated over the years until the legends have become the facts. Nevertheless, I have tried to find a path through the tangle of these myths and legends to produce as accurate a version of gang-members' lives and misdeeds as possible.

My thanks go to my publisher Duncan Proudfoot and then, in strictly alphabetical order, to Harold Alderman, the late Mickey Bailey, Marcel Berlins, J. P. Bean for his help over the Sheffield Gang Wars, Anne Brooke, Carl Chinn, Andrew and Jean-Ann Hyslop, Paul Donnelly, Peter Donnelly, James Dubro for his help and advice regarding Rocco Perri and the Canadian gangs of the 1930s, Frank Fraser, Barbara Levy, Susanna Lobez, Adrian Neale, Sybil Nolan, Gerry Parker, Nipper and Pat Read, Adam Shand, Adrian Tame and Russell Robinson. They are also due to the staff at the British Library, the British Newspaper Library at Colindale, the State Archives of New South Wales and Victoria, the New York Public Library, the Miami Public Library, the Calgary Public Library and the Musée d'Espionnage, Paris.

Once more, this book could not have been begun, let alone completed, without the constant help, research and advice of Dock Bateson.

1

Marm Mandelbaum

The old phrase loved by judges, "If there were no receivers there would be no burglars", may not be wholly true but it certainly applied to Fredericka Mandelbaum from the Lower East Side, New York, who was the greatest fence of her day. From the middle of the 1860s the seriously overweight "Marm" Mandelbaum, described as a "bustling Israelite" and "as adept in her business as the best stockbroker in his", had her office at her home at 79 Clinton Street in what was then known as Little Deutschland. She also maintained representatives along the eastern seaboard, Chicago, Mexico and Europe. She graduated from being a small-time receiver to the queen of criminal society, holding splendid dinners at which her favourite thieves, such as the bank robber "Western George" – George Leonidas Leslie – sat at her right hand. George Walling, one-time police chief of New York, thought:

> As a handler of stolen goods Marm Mandelbaum had no peer in the United States ... Suppose you are a burglar and last night's efforts have resulted mostly in jewellery and silver-ware, you would have neither the time nor the plant to melt the silver and disguise or unset the stones. "Mother" Mandelbaum would attend to all that for you on about a 5 per cent commission.

Born Fredericka Goldberg, she came to the United States from
Germany and took a position as cook to the dyspeptic Wolfe
Mandelbaum, a pawnshop owner and haberdasher. A little
good home-cooking goes down well and, following the maxim,
the way to Wolfe's heart was through his stomach. Given that
she had by far the stronger personality of the two it is fair to
say she married him rather than the other way about. On his
death she took over the business. Pledging stolen goods was
a standard receiving practice with the clients never intending
to redeem them while giving the receiver the rudiments of a
defence if charged. The scope of her dealings was immense.
Sophie Lyons, one of her most talented suppliers, thought she
alone may have made up to 500 transactions, big and small,
with her.

Marm took care never to have the goods initially brought
to her home. Instead, a messenger would call and she would
send a trusted representative to examine the stolen goods and
report back to her. Her integrity was described as absolute. She
established what was referred to as a Bureau for the Prevention
of Conviction and would lend money to those who needed
defending, but woe betide those who could not or would not
repay her the fees advanced.

Although Sophie Lyons wrote that Marm never stole
anything herself, she was a regular visitor to Tiffany & Co.
to examine its collections of diamonds, her own preference.
It was there that the idea occurred to her to set up a robbery
and to this end she employed a Chicago shoplifter, Mary
Wallenstein, and a pickpocket, "Swell" Robinson. He was
the first into Tiffany's to examine some diamonds and
reject a number. Before he left one was found to be missing.
Robinson was also a talented conman and angrily rejected
suggestions that he had the diamond. He demanded to be
searched and when none was found he was released. In
comes Wallenstein who looks at a few diamonds, rejects
them and goes out.

The next morning chewing gum with the imprint of a diamond was found on the underside of the rim of the counter. If Lyons is correct this was the first recorded example of what was known as pennyweighting. She said that the trick was not worked again because jewellers' associations alerted their members but she was wrong. It was certainly worked in 1905 in London by the highly talented Annie Gleason, posing as the daughter of Ulysses S. Grant.

Marm was also credited with running the Grand Street School, one of the numerous schools of crime in New York towards the end of the nineteenth century at which small boys and girls were taught the art of pickpocketing and sneak theft. Older and more talented pupils learned safe-breaking and burglary, as well as, for women pupils, the very skilled art of blackmail.

Over the years Mandelbaum's weight bulged to over 200 pounds and she was described in the files of the Pinkerton National Detective Agency as "a gargantuan caricature of Queen Victoria with her black hair in a roll and a small bun hat with drooping feathers". Apparently, however, she was not vain enough to wear corsets.

Not all her vendors were as faithful to her as she to them and one Mike Kurtz, known as Sheeny Mike and Mike Sheehan, was a good example. On 2 March 1877 he was arrested in Baltimore and taken to Boston charged with robbing Scott & Co. of bundles of silk. On 29 March that year he was sentenced to twelve years' imprisonment. Now, it was a question of devising his release. It took him a year and a half.

During that time he drank soap-water and as a result lost weight by the stone. He also cut his side and, it appeared, pus began to flow. With his wasting coupled with the wound, the prison doctors believed he would not live a month and there was a discussion about his pardon. Then, as now, rehabilitation cannot occur without a confession of past sins and Kurtz told the authorities that he had indeed stolen the silk and sold the whole parcel to Marm Mandelbaum.

With Kurtz' rehabilitation complete he was pardoned by Governor Butler on 19 October 1880. The wound miraculously healed; he began to put on weight and was well enough to travel to New York where the good Mother M. seems to have forgiven him his lapse of conduct if indeed she ever knew he was her betrayer. She, poor woman, was sued in the civil courts and was ordered to pay $6,666 by Judge Van Vorst for acting as a receiver when Scott's brought an action in 1877.

Superintendent George Walling, who later became Police Commissioner, said after the case, in which he described Marm as having grown "greasy, fat and opulent":

> we even hired rooms on the opposite side of the street from her store for the purpose of obtaining such evidence as would lead to her arrest and conviction as a receiver of stolen goods. Mrs Mandelbaum is a very sharp woman, however, and is not often caught napping. Whenever she buys goods off thieves she appoints a place of meeting where she can confer without suspicion. She will not allow them to come to her store under any consideration. Whenever any of the men from whom she buys stolen goods is arrested, she advances money for their defence and compels them to pay a good round sum for her trouble and the use of her money. I am glad that for once the old lady has been outwitted and made to suffer for her violation of the law.

Worse, in the July of 1884 she was very badly betrayed. There are a number of differing accounts of her downfall but it was almost certainly Mary Holbrook, aka Mollie Hoey and who at the time was working as Lizzie Wiggins, who did the deed. For once Marm Mandelbaum would not provide the services of her retained lawyers, the splendidly corrupt William Howe and his partner Abe Hummel, and when Hoey went to prison for five years she squealed.

Mollie Hoey had had an interesting career. She had lived with George "Buck" Holbrook, a gambler and thief who had run a sporting house and a roadhouse in Chicago. He was arrested for a bank robbery in Illinois in 1871 and was sent to the state prison from where, with two colleagues, he tunnelled out. As soon as he put his head above ground he was shot. Sensibly his fellow escapees backed down the tunnel.

What was a girl to do in the circumstances? The now common-law widow was arrested in Chicago in January 1872 and charged with stealing $40 from her landlady. She was able to put up $1,200 bail and fled to New York where she met and then married Jimmy Hoey. She was caught at the badger game – the extortion scheme whereby the victim is lured into a compromising position and blackmailed – in 1874 where she had relieved a man of $25,000. Taken back to Chicago – via Canada for some reason – she managed to persuade a passing policeman that she had been kidnapped and had her escorting officer arrested. She was discharged and was not rearrested until two years later. From then on she was in and out of prison, very often in Boston, and in March 1884 she peached on Marm Mandelbaum in order to obtain her release.

On Hoey's information, Mother was finally entrapped by Detective Frank over some silks coming from a burglary on West Fourteenth Street, New York. The *grande dame* was not pleased and said to Frank, "So you are the one who is at the bottom of this, you wretch you." She had hit him on her arrest and he wanted to prefer an assault charge but was told to wait. On 23 July she was produced in the court in Harlem much to the protest of her lawyer William Howe who had wanted the case heard in one of the more sympathetic regions of Manhattan.

The courts may not have been sympathetic but the *New York Herald* was:

When a man who has lost a $50 watch went to the police station and offered "$25 and no questions asked" for its recovery what could be more profitable for the time consumed than for a detective to go to "Mother Baum" and buy for $15 an identical ticker for which the shrewd woman had paid no more than $10?

To now have to run about among a lot of minor fences in search of stolen property that once could be confidently looked for at the Mandelbaum place will be very annoying to detectives whose habits have become fixed. It is no wonder that Mother Baum had never before been troubled by detectives. Shall a man quarrel with his own bread and butter, particularly when the person who provides it gives him occasionally a new dress for his wife and diamond studs to illuminate his own official front?

In July 1884 a grand jury returned a bill against both her and her son Julius along with Herbert Stroub, described as a clerk but possibly an unofficial replacement for the now deceased Herr Mandelbaum. She had trouble raising bail of $100,000 and three sureties were turned down before she was eventually released. A date in December was fixed for her reappearance. The *New York Herald* reported:

Rows and rows of stiff backed, rusty seats were crowded with people who had come to see Mother Mandelbaum, the protectress of thieves, brought to the bar of justice. There were bankers and bank burglars elbowing each other in the eager chattering throng. Bewhiskered policemen and dusty old-court loungers were jammed together. Lawyers, actors, pickpockets, clergymen, merchants and clerks by the score strained and jostled and whispered in the most democratic fashion.

And in the midst of it all sat lawyer Howe with his legs crossed and a look of peace in his eyes.

There were only three empty chairs in the courtroom and when one man tried to take one he was smartly told it was for one of the defendants. Detectives Frank and Pinkerton lolled sleepily in their chairs. The District Attorney and his assistants were brimming with enthusiasm.

But yet the lawyer with the sparkling diamonds looked happy. Nor could all the detectives and District Attorneys disturb the beautiful serenity of his rosy countenance.

The case was called.

Lawyer Howe arose and looked around the court carefully. His eyebrows went higher and higher up his peaceful brow as his gaze wandered back to the troubled visage of the District Attorney. Then a very red hand, that glimmered and shone with jewelled gold, was swung on high. "I am forced to confess that the defendants are not here," he said. "No, they are not."

The authorities were right to have been wary of letting the woman out of their sight. Despite being under watch by Pinkerton agents who rented a house opposite hers, she had escaped. The neighbours who had let out the house to the Pinkertons also told Marm whenever the detectives were on the premises. She sent out a heavily veiled servant who was about the same build as her and, while the agent was decoyed away, she and the others left the house and were driven to New Rochelle, where they boarded a train to Chatham Five Corners and from there rode to Canada.

When she fled she took with her jewels said to have been stolen in Troy by two of her best clients, Billy Porter and the redeemed Kurtz. She was arrested and held in Montreal, from where the New York District Attorney prophesied the speedy return of her and the jewellery to the United States. Howe did not think so and, as was so often the case, he was proved correct. Abe Hummel, his junior partner, was immediately dispatched to deal with matters, something he did completely successfully. Marm remained unmolested north of the 48th parallel.

It was supposed that the authorities would at least pick up the $100,000 forfeited bail but even this went wrong. Hummel had arranged a string of interlocking sales and mortgages so that the poor bondsmen were quite unable to pay the court and, better still, because of the complexity of the deals, no further action was taken. Overall it was an outstanding triumph for Howe and Little Abe Hummel.

Safe in Canada, Marm Mandelbaum opened a clothing shop for ladies and children. She also bought a handsome house in Victoria Avenue North, Montreal, where she lived with her daughter, Mrs Sarah Weill. She seems to have pined for New York and through Hummel attempted to settle the charge against her. She failed, although her son Julius eventually returned in June 1888 when Moss, one of Hummel's staff, confidently and accurately predicted an acquittal. Back in Canada, Marm was generally resentful of her situation, telling a journalist, "The *World* drove me out of New York and I'll have nothing to say to its reporters."

Before she left for Canada, Howe had described her as: "A lady the peaceful rectitude of whose life has been broken in upon by the rude acrimony of official strife."

She may have pined in Canada, and the shop may not have been an unqualified success, but she was still making a decent living buying and selling stolen silk and jewels. In October 1886 an undercover police officer nearly lured her across the border claiming he was looking for a bargain in diamonds but her antennae still twitched. She gave the officer a stone telling him to take it home and send her the price agreed upon. The next day he discovered he had been given paste. During her time in Canada she was twice acquitted of smuggling lace and jewellery.

She did once return to New York. One of her daughters, the teenaged Anna, had remained in Clinton Street and in November 1885 she contracted typhoid pneumonia. Mrs Mandelbaum was reported to have visited her before she died, with the connivance of the authorities turning a blind eye, and to have watched her funeral at a distance. The route she travelled in disguise to the funeral was arduous – Montreal to Rouse's Point, Rome, Watertown, Ogdensburg on to Utica then the Erie Road to New York.

Mother Mandelbaum died in Hamilton on 27 February 1894. She had been suffering from Bright's disease. She had, it was said, begun attending the Anshe Synagogue to which she made substantial bequests but had not been allowed her own pew. Her body was returned to New York for burial. Like so many figures – Robin Hood, Lord Lucan, Elvis, JFK and Robert Maxwell amongst them – people were not prepared to accept her death and six months after her burial there were reports that it was another body in the grave. It was thought that with the bribes paid and Howe and Hummel's fees, her escape from justice cost her \$125,000. Overall it was probably not a heavy price.

As for Mollie Hoey, after her piece of bad behaviour she was pardoned but such credibility as she had in the underworld was gone. She was arrested again in Canada and once more in Chicago and took to visiting Detroit to see her husband. Hoey himself never amounted to much, contenting himself with fencing some of the property his wife stole. Mollie was a woman of some undoubted courage. In 1886 she was jailed in Cleveland and dug her way out of jail with a pair of shears. Her face and hands were badly bruised and scarred by the effort and when questioned by a cab driver she told him she had been beaten by her husband. Later, in a house-to-house search, she was almost arrested but, disguised as a man, she took a boat to Detroit. She was thought to have eventually made her way to London.

Marm Mandelbaum probably had no rival worthy of the name but there were several other women who were major receivers of the time. The foremost was, perhaps, "Black" Lena Kleinschmidt who, along with her sisters Amelia Levy and Mary Anderson, known as Mother Weir, visited nearly every prominent city east of the Missouri. Black Lena had a penchant for the upper echelons of society. During one of her more successful periods she moved, under an assumed name, to Hackensack, NJ, where she gave dinner parties. These came to an end when one of her guests saw her own ring now adorning Black Lena's finger. Mother Weir was another of those who ran a pickpocketing school and was also the head of one of the larger organized gangs of thieves. It was a family business because one of Mary's sons would act as their coachman.

In 1883, only two months after finishing a prison sentence, Black Lena and Mother Weir were arrested in Chicago with large bunches of ostrich feathers under their cloaks. When their room was searched Saratoga trunks filled with assorted goods were discovered. For this Lena received eight years in Joliet prison. She was discharged in June 1889 and went straight back to work in Chicago but her skill was passing and in 1894 she could be found in the workhouse in St Louis.

Sophie Lyons believed that Marm's male counterpart was John D. Grady, who was known as "Supers and Slangs" and specialized in diamonds. It was in his offices that the failed robbery of the Manhattan Bank was planned. Grady also traded out of a satchel, visiting thieves at night. It seems that he was only once sandbagged and robbed of around $7,000 of diamonds, something which he good humouredly put down to his own foolishness. The story of his death is, in a contorted way, rather romantic. He fell in love with the widow of a socialite and together they worked a series of confidence tricks and robberies. She apparently despised him but could not live without the work he provided. When it came to the pass, under increasing pressure, she agreed they would go away together. At the rendezvous to which he had brought his collection of diamonds, she gave him poison. Although he saw her eyes flicker at the wrong moment and suspected her, he nevertheless drank the poison. She fled leaving the diamonds behind.

O'Grady had not had all that much luck with women. Earlier he had fallen foul of the highly talented swindler Ellen Peck who persuaded him to hand over cash against a compartment in a safe full of imaginary diamonds.

Another of the great receivers, and one of Howe's best clients, was Marm's friend, "General" Abe Greenthal, who in his younger days had been an expert pickpocket. He was known throughout the States as the man who led the Sheeney Mob. The General was born in Prussia in 1831 shortly before his father began a fifteen-year sentence for robbery. Greenthal received two years for the theft of a gold watch at the age of eighteen and on his release teamed up with his father and another man, who was later replaced by the General's brother, in a nationwide series of thefts. It resulted in a seven-year sentence for all. Later the General escaped with the help of his wife while being transferred between prisons. She had been allowed to walk part of the way with him and they took the opportunity to make off. He fled to Berlin where he bought papers that enabled him to get to Liverpool. On the day his wife arrived in England they left for New York where they again took up pickpocketing. A passionate gambler, he served a three-year sentence, again for theft, in 1864 and then became a high-class receiver.

On 19 April 1877, with his brother Harris and son-in-law Samuel Casper also in the dock, he received twenty years for robbery in Rochester but was pardoned in the spring of 1884. The General was arrested again, this time with Bendick Gaetz, known as the Cockroach, for pickpocketing on a crosstown horse-car in Williamsburg and received five years. On his release, following the disappearance of Marm, he took over a large part of her business.

2

The Foster and Stander Gangs

Armed robbery in South Africa in the twentieth century can be neatly bookended between two gangs. The first, the Foster Gang, was led by Robert William Foster who was said to have been born either in Birmingham, England, or in Pretoria, South Africa. Educated by the Marist Brothers, he was popular at school and a good sportsman. His biographers Henry May and Ian Hamilton painted a positive picture of him as a schoolboy:

> William as a boy was lively and attractive, with strong features, bright grey eyes, and a ready smile. He held his head high and his shoulders straight, and when he walked he gave an extraordinary impression of electric energy, as if his body and limbs were tautened by some strange inner force.

After he left school Foster, who had four false teeth, two of them gold, in his upper jaw, took up photography in Johannesburg. However, he soon went off the rails acquiring a number of minor convictions – drunkenness, resisting arrest and stealing donkeys for which he received six months. In 1909 when he had finished his sentence he returned to Johannesburg where he again worked as a photographer and where he fell in love with the red-haired Peggy Korenico. A quick robbery is often more productive than long-term saving and, in an effort to put together sufficient money to marry her, William, his brother Jimmy and Fred Adamson robbed the owners of the American Swiss Watch Company in Longmarket Street, Cape Town, on 19 March 1913. One of the owners was bound and hooded while the other was made to open the safe. The raid itself was a total success and they made off with £5,000 worth of jewellery.

They left the stolen jewellery in a suitcase at the left luggage office at Cape Town station but a clerk became suspicious because of its weight. The trio were arrested when they went to collect it. They had also given their landlady a pair of cufflinks made from Krugerrands, which were easily identified. They all received twelve years. The getaway driver, the American "Cowboy" Jack Martin, a former circus worker better known as John Maxim, was never charged. Independently he received nine months for selling liquor to black Africans. While awaiting trial Foster married Peggy Korenico in prison.

Two years into his sentence on 27 February 1914 Foster, now also known both as Jackson and the self-commissioned Captain White, broke out of Pretoria jail. He had become friendly with the prison tailors who made him a suit. When his fellow prisoners staged a fight, he cut his way through a wire fence during the distraction, put on the suit and was off.

Now he joined up with Maxim and Carl Mezar, also known as Smidt (who could be identified by the lash marks on his buttocks), and pulled off two post office robberies. The first, in April, was at the Roodepoort Post Office on the West Rand where £1,876 in gold coins and notes was taken. In the Vrededorp Post Office burglary several hundred pounds of revenue stamps were taken.

In the investigation that followed it was discovered that the postmaster had lent himself £72 from the post office, when he had found himself short after buying a new car. In view of his thirty-three-year-long service he was given a suspended sentence but, ruined, he committed suicide.

Things went wrong for the trio on 17 July that year when they attempted a robbery on the National Bank in Boksburg North. A clerk slept on the premises overnight and when he heard the sound of drilling he went for help from people in the hotel across the street. The barman, Alexander Charlson, and another man ran across the road and the fleeing bandits shot both of them. In the case of Charlson, he was shot again when he was lying on the ground. He died within the hour but the second man survived. A third man was pistol-whipped when the robbers stole his car. Wanted notices were posted with a reward of £3,000 on offer.

Just as American bank robbers dreamed of a life below the border in Mexico, Foster's aim seems to have been to raise enough money to pay the fares for himself, Peggy and their small daughter to get to what is now Maputo in Mozambique and then sail for Europe. Meanwhile, he rented an empty house in the Regents Park district of Johannesburg and stocked an underground cave with provisions. The burglaries and robberies continued including one on the National Bank in the Cleveland suburb of the city which pulled in £4,500.

In a police sweep of Marshall Square, described then as the crime centre of Johannesburg, Albert Jenkins, Harry Fisher, his brother Snowy and an Australian called George Riordan were rounded up. All were charged with conspiracy to rob and murder. Now the names of Foster, Maxim and Mezar surfaced but they had disappeared completely. The witnesses against the men in the dock were not of the highest quality. They included prison snitches and one, Isabella Eichorn, who had kept four revolvers they had given her under the mattress, admitted under cross-examination her ear had been bitten off by a man in Kimberly. The committal proceedings dragged on for weeks; witnesses disappeared; the prosecution wanted an adjournment to find them; and Riordan applied unsuccessfully for his discharge.

Then on 13 September 1914 Foster, Maxim and Mezar failed in an effort to rob the Big Bottle Shop in Fairview. They disturbed a nightwatchman sleeping on the premises and when he alerted a police officer the constable was knocked unconscious.

Some hours later the police found Mezar with a loaded gun sitting on a bench by the Imperial Bottle Store in the same town. While he was being questioned an explosion went off in the shop. When the police went into the premises to investigate, one of them, Sergeant Neil McLeod, was shot and killed. The gunmen put Mezar on the back of a motorcycle and rode off. Soon afterwards the body of Sergeant Robert Mansfield was found shot in a nearby street.

An elderly lady who lived next door to Foster and his family at the corner of Bob Street and South Road, Regents Park, recognized them from photographs in the morning paper and telephoned the police. On 15 September Sergeant Mynott saw Peggy Foster get into a car while William Foster turned the crank handle to start it. He called on him to stop and Foster shot and killed him. The Fosters, Mezar and Maxim drove off, stopping to hijack a car. When they broke down they abandoned it and told Peggy Foster to make her way to Germiston by bus. The three men headed for the caves at Kensington, seven miles east of the city centre, where they holed up. The next day they were tracked down by Bantus working with the police.

Reinforcements were called up; the entrance to the cave was sealed off and the robbers were surrounded. Now the public began to arrive to watch the proceedings. Despite a blustery wind hundreds were still there at 11 p.m. that evening. An attempt to force the men out using gas canisters failed because of the wind, which blew the gas towards the spectators, and the police settled down for a siege.

The next day, at around 11.45 a.m., the police and the crowds who were arriving on every available tram heard a shot from inside the cave. A little later Foster called out that he would not surrender until he saw his wife. The police went to Germiston where she had taken a room under the name Doyle and brought her back, with their baby, to the cave. At 2.30 p.m. she was allowed into the cave. Next Foster wanted to see his family, and his father, mother and two sisters went in. At 4.30 the family and the baby left the cave leaving Peggy Foster behind. Within minutes a series of gunshots was heard and when the police entered the cave they found Peggy Foster with the top of her head blown away. Foster was lying dead across her body and Maxim was dead nearby. There was also a suicide note from Mezar who had been shot by Maxim. That was the shot heard shortly before midday.

There were three more casualties of the siege. The first was Dr Gerald Grace, the brother of the celebrated cricketer W. G. Grace. He was shot in the neck and killed when on 15 September he failed to stop at a police roadblock. His wife was shot in the arm. There was a high wind blowing and it was thought he had not heard the orders. Another casualty was General Jacobus de la Rey. Again it was thought neither he nor his driver had heard the order to stop. Ironically, shortly before Dr Grace was shot the Fosters had driven through the roadblock unchallenged. Inspector Ernest Leach, who had allowed Peggy Foster to see her husband in the belief that she could talk him into surrendering, shot himself a few days later.

Foster's parents said that he had blamed the carnage on the judge who had sentenced him and his brother to twelve years for the American Swiss Watch Company robbery in 1913. There were, however, suggestions, never substantiated, that some time earlier Foster had killed another of his sisters. Peggy and Robert Foster are buried in the same grave alongside Mezar at the Braamfontein Cemetery. Maxim is buried in the general section.

The case had a curious sequel in 1936 at a time when annually £2 million was being stolen in gold from the South African mines. Twenty-one-year-old Andries Stephanus du

Plessis went on trial for killing five people in cold blood. The married bricklayer had fallen in love with Helena Breitenbach, the wife of a police constable, and they had set up house in Strubenvale, together with his mother, his child and Helena's child.

His criminal record began in February 1934 when he was convicted of theft after snatching a handbag from a woman. He was again convicted in October 1934 for housebreaking and theft. A report suggested that du Plessis had developed into "a desperate character and a criminal not averse to robbery with violence".

The first two counts of an indictment against du Plessis alleged the murder, in the early morning of Thursday, 29 October 1936, of two Greeks named Spiros Paizes, the owner of the Waldorf Café, Modder Road, Brakpan, and Pericles Paxinos, his assistant. The medical evidence showed that Paizes was shot through the head and neck with a revolver, while the skull of Paxinos had been extensively fractured by a blow or blows from a heavy blunt instrument. Both bodies were dragged into a gully near the Jubilee Road, two miles from Brakpan, and set on fire after petrol or some similar fluid had been poured over them.

The "Sandspruit murders", which constituted the charges in the remaining three counts, consisted of the murder of Samuel Berman, Barney Liebowitz and Essie Liebowitz, who were all killed with revolver shots in the early evening of Monday, 2 November 1936, at a wayside store and house adjoining a railway station, known as Sandspruit, some ten miles west of Volksrust. They had been having an evening meal when a masked gunman broke in and shot Barney Liebowitz and Samuel Berman and then chased Essie Liebowitz into a bedroom where he shot her. He then opened the safe and stole money and documents. Forensic evidence showed that the same gun had been used at both the Sandspruit and Brakpan murders.

Du Plessis maintained that he had been forced to be the driver in both sets of murders and two other men were responsible but the evidence against him was overwhelming. His car was identified and grease on his glove matched candles at the Berman home. The trial judge believed there was something more to the murders than simple robberies but tried in vain to get an explanation. There was no evidence against Helena Breitenbach and she was acquitted.

Du Plessis was sentenced to death and appealed to the Supreme Court where the case was heard by Acting Judge-President B. A. Tindall with two assessors. Tindall thought there was nothing worthwhile in du Plessis's defence:

> The second point raised is that he was a member, and an insignificant member at that, of a gang operating in the East Rand area in housebreaking and theft. In a letter of 8th February 1937, the attorney for the prisoner first raised the point that a jeweller named Heyman was the head of this alleged gang ... Heyman is alleged to have been the receiver of the proceeds, particularly jewellery, of the housebreaking and thefts indulged independently by members of the gang. Except in the case of Tommy van Schalkwyk, there is no evidence except the word of the prisoner that any of these [seven other] persons engaged in housebreaking and theft ...
>
> But in any case, even if we accept that Heyman was a receiver – there is evidence that he was the subject of a trap for illicit gold buying – it does not follow that he was present at the murders and committed them or even that he instigated them, or in any way coerced the prisoner into committing them. And if Heyman was not present at Brakpan or Sandspruit the theory of gang coercion falls to the ground.
>
> There is nothing impossible in one man being responsible for the murders and burglary at Sandspruit;

the circumstances connected with the Brakpan murders suggest strongly that more than one person committed the murders, but who the assistant was is known to the prisoner alone. He must be shielding someone, and the probability is that that person is Mrs Breitenbach.

Du Plessis was hanged on 17 June 1937.

After the case Helena told a police officer that in fact they had killed eight people in total and she had fired the gun killing the last. She also maintained she was the daughter of Robert and Peggy Foster. There was no evidence to support her confession and she was released.

Fifty years later Police Captain Andre Charles Stander had apparently everything going for him. The handsome son of retired police officer Major General Frans Stander, he had been Pretoria police college's student of the year and, as captain at the CID branch of Kempton Park police station, he was destined for a career which might have led all the way to the top. But then he took to robbing banks after, he claimed, he was sickened when he shot up to twenty-two unarmed demonstrators in the Tembisa township uprising of 1976. Others say he had never been at Tembisa and that, forced into the police by his father, he had resented the discipline required when he joined the drugs squad.

The first robbery seems to have been after he gave out the morning assignments to his staff and then drove to Jan Smuts Airport, catching a plane to Durban where he hired a car. He put on a wig and a false beard then drove to a bank. South African banks in the late 1970s were open plan with little security.

Stander approached a cashier, sat down and quietly pulled a gun on her, asking her to fill a bag with money. Terrified, she did. Stander took the money, left the bank before anyone realized what had happened, got in his car and drove back to

Louis Botha Airport, peeling off his disguise on the way. Then he flew to Johannesburg in time for an afternoon's work.

Very often he would carry out a robbery in his lunch break and return later in the day as the investigating officer. His colleague, bank robber George Allan Heyl, would later say, "He held the whole regime in contempt and thought banks were the very symbol of greed, duplicity and exploitation. I hated the South African system and, as we were both bank robbers and both set on a campaign of defiance, we were ideal company." Others suggest, more prosaically, that Stander was in debt.

Money was laundered through a souvenir shop he opened in Durban with a police friend, Carl van Deventer. At a party in late 1979 Stander, drunk, told van Deventer about the robberies and asked him to take part. He claimed he had a stolen car parked at Jan Smuts Airport. When his friend refused Stander laughed off the confession as a joke. But it was enough for van Deventer to worry and he approached a senior officer in the Bureau of State Security (BOSS), South Africa's secret police. They investigated the stolen car and found wigs, fake beards, a balaclava and a false number plate in the boot.

The car was staked out. On 3 January 1980 Stander visited the vehicle to remove some items and caught a flight to Durban where he robbed another bank. He was arrested in the Jan Smuts arrival lounge on the return trip, with 4,000 rand and a revolver in his suitcase.

On 6 May 1980 he received a sentence of seventeen years for a total of fifteen bank robberies and possessing illegal weapons. In prison he became friendly with the car thief and bank robber Heyl, who had once started a teacher training course, and another car thief and bank robber, the balding Paul McCall, known as Lee. Three years later, on 11 August 1983, after complaining of back pains Stander and McCall along with five other prisoners were taken from Zonderwater Maximum Security Prison to physiotherapist Amelia Grobler's consulting rooms near Cullinan. Stander and McCall overpowered the guards, stole their guns and her car keys and fled. The other prisoners refused to go with them.

The pair took a local farmer and his son hostage and had him telephone the police. Only one officer arrived and he was grabbed and put in the back of his police van. Another car was hijacked, the driver was put in the van and off they went, clear and away.

While on the run they robbed the United Building Society of 13,000 rand (around £7,000), disguised themselves with tracksuits, gym bags and squash rackets and went to stay in a Holiday Inn. On 31 October 1983 the pair returned to Zonderwater to free Heyl who had been taken to the Olifantsfontein facility for a trade test. They forced five guards to lie on the floor, called to Heyl and all drove off in a Cortina.

When Heyl had been free for only three weeks, Stander got up one morning, put on his black wig and stick-on Freddie Mercury moustache and asked if Heyl was ready to go to work. "The first bank set the trend for non-violence, and was only remarkable because no one, apart from the tellers, knew we had robbed it: the security guard even opened the door for us," said Heyl later. During the next three months the trio carried out around twenty bank robberies, sometimes three in a single afternoon, netting between US$400,000 and US$500,000. It was a technique that gave them the nickname of Bank Hoppers and the public took to them; men began growing horseshoe moustaches in tribute. When, in an effort to discredit him, the police put about the story that Stander had raped a teenage model, the public ignored it. His popularity increased when the gang raided a highly guarded bank at Jan Smuts Airport. When they raided a bank directly below the offices of Brigadier Manie van Rensburg, who had been put in charge of a special taskforce to arrest them, they achieved folk-hero status.

The gang had a series of safe houses and led, for those twelve weeks, something of a charmed life. It helped that Stander was a master of disguise. On one occasion, under the name of Mark Jennings, on crutches and with his legs apparently in casts, he was in a video store when the police came to check for pornographic material. On another occasion the police called at their safe house in Lower Houghton to warn the occupants of burglaries in the neighbourhood. Again as Jennings, Stander thanked them for their help. Once, he was recognized by a fellow diner at a fashionable restaurant and fled. McCall meanwhile was becoming more and more nervous. On one raid he shot and wounded Marlene Henn, the owner of a gunshop in Randburg.

It was, perhaps, Stander's penchant for disguise that led to his ultimate capture. Posing as an effeminate man in Cape Town, in the space of just one afternoon he bought a yacht, the fifteen-ton *Lily Rose* for $200,000, had it provisioned and hired a delivery crew to take it to Fort Lauderdale, Florida. The salesman thought that the plan may have been to use the yacht for drug smuggling and reported the purchase to the police.

On 27 January 1984 Stander flew to the United States to make berthing arrangements using a fake Australian passport in the name of Peter Harris. Heyl saw him off at the airport but when he returned to the Houghton safe house, with its swimming pool and tennis court, a servant told him the police had been there shortly before asking for a "Mr Stander". One of the call girls they had brought to the house had recognized the gang from newspaper photographs and turned them in. Heyl drove off and phoned McCall to warn him but his fellow bank robber shrugged it off as a routine house-to-house enquiry and refused to leave.

Two days later the police staked out the house but only McCall was there. At 6.30 on the morning of 30 January they called on him to surrender. He declined and began shooting. In response, during a ten-minute siege the police lobbed tear gas and grenades into the house as well as riddling it with bullets and killing the naked McCall. A more romantic version of the tale is that, unwilling to face a lengthy prison sentence to add to the one he should have been serving, McCall turned the gun on himself. Of Stander and Heyl there was no sign. Stander was believed to have dyed his hair red and to be driving a yellow Porsche. The *Lily Rose* was confiscated.

Now in Fort Lauderdale, still using the name of Peter Harris and posing as an Australian author, Stander led a quiet life dating a stripper, Ayten Kiles, who lived next door. Stander had bought a Ford Mustang from a car dealer, Tony Tomasello, and on 10 February he was stopped by the police for running a red light. He gave the name Harris, producing a fake licence. He was arrested but released on a $100 bond. That night he returned to the police lock-up and took back his impounded car. On 13 February he returned to the dealer to have the car resprayed but his luck had run out. Tomasello was reading an article in the local paper in which it said the man stopped could possibly have been Stander. Tomasello asked, "Is this you?" Amazingly Stander admitted it was. Instead of cutting and running perhaps Stander hoped Tomasello would not report him but he did.

At 10.30 that night Stander was seen riding a bicycle several times around a block cordoned off by the police. Called on to stop he shouted, "I give up," raising his arms as he did so. But it was a ruse. He snatched Patrolman Michael Von Stetina's shotgun and pointed it at him. Von Stetina closed on him and in the struggle shot him three times with his pistol. Stander died before the ambulance arrived. Tomasello received a $64,000 reward.

The South African papers received many calls about his death, almost all in favour of the man who had become a folk-hero. "We were all rooting for him," said one grandmother of five. "He had style." His father said he wished he had not forced his son to be a police officer.

Immediately after McCall's death Heyl had fled to the Greek island of Hydra, followed by Spain and then England. The following year at Winchester Crown Court, in the name Philip John Ball, he was sentenced to ten years for a wage snatch. On his release he was extradited to South Africa to serve a thirty-three-year sentence in Krugerdorp, before finally being paroled in May 2005. During his time in South African jails he attained a bevy of certificates in such diverse subjects as the Management of Change, Emotional Intelligence Seminar, Listening Skills Course, Jealousy Management, Investment in Excellence, Anger Management, Adult Education and Tutors Course Level 4. He is now a motivational speaker.

In October 1992 Stander's former wife committed suicide. Marlene Henn, the gunshop owner shot at by McCall, was murdered three years later in a home invasion.

3

The Ashley–Mobley Gang

Had they come from the Midwest there is little doubt that the now half-forgotten Floridian Ashley–Mobley Gang could have claimed its rightful place as one of the major gangs of the early part of the twentieth century. It is estimated that apart from its smuggling operation the gang stole up to $1 million and was involved in forty robberies. Certainly, even allowing for lax prison security, its members were some of the greatest escapees of the time. At least ten people including gang-members were killed as a result of their activities.

John Ashley was born in the Everglades, Florida, on what his biographer describes as a cracker farm. His father Joe had come from the Fort Myers area to work on Henry Flagler's Florida East Coast Railway which was being built from St Augustine to Miami and eventually through the Keys. John Ashley's bid for fame and riches began impressively when at the age of eighteen, efforts were made to arrest him for the murder in 1911 of a man known as "the Osceola Tiger" near Fort Lauderdale, following the theft of otter hides worth over $1,000. The Tiger, found shot in the back in a canal at Lake Okeechobee in the Everglades, was the son of a Seminole Indian chief, Tom Tiger Tall. The evidence was strong against Ashley. He had been the last white man to be seen with the Indian and he had sold the skins in a Miami store.

Palm Beach sheriff George B. Baker sent deputies to find Ashley but, in turn, they found they were being tracked by him and his brother Bob, who sent them back to Baker with a warning that he should not send any more "chicken-hearted men" as they might get hurt next time. Baker took the insults personally and Ashley fled to New Orleans, up to Washington State and into Canada where he is said to have robbed a bank.

Apparently missing his family, he was back in Florida in the autumn of 1914 when he robbed a Florida East Coast train. The next year, on 23 February, Ashley, his father Joe, his brother Will and two others arrived in Stuart, a small town approximately halfway between Miami and Cape Canaveral. At the time, their bank-robbing style left something to be desired. At first they did not use a car, simply because they did not know how to drive one. It was easier to kidnap a bank employee who had a car parked outside the bank and turn him loose when they were well out of town. Later the gang-members drove Model T Fords.

Unfortunately as they sped away from the Stuart bank, firing at their pursuers, Ashley was shot in the jaw by fellow gang-member Kid Lowe from Chicago when a bullet ricocheted. The bullet exited near his eye. The gang made off with $4,500 but Ashley, in excruciating pain, was found lying on a palliasse at the roadside. His brother and father were also captured. His eye was replaced with a glass one and he invariably wore a patch. Lowe and the others escaped and Ashley claimed Lowe had shot him so he could get a bigger share of the proceeds.

Ashley was put on trial for both the bank robbery and the killing of the Tiger but there were serious problems in selecting a jury and a mistrial was declared. Then the prosecution asked for a change of venue.

On 2 June 1915, with the family dithering about an attempted rescue, Ashley's brother Bob set out on a lone effort to free him. It was the wrong decision. Deputy Wilber Hendrickson stood in front of the open door to the jail and before he could move, Bob Ashley shot him in the chest, killing him. As Bob snatched the deputy's keys, Hendrickson's wife grabbed a rifle and pulled the trigger as he went out the door but the rifle failed to fire.

As the shooting had alerted people in downtown Miami, Bob Ashley fled, dropping the jailer's keys in the street. He quickly commandeered a passing delivery truck, threatening the driver with a gun to his head. T. H. Duckett, the driver, deliberately stalled the truck as Officer John R. Riblet, who had also commandeered a vehicle, approached from the rear. As Riblet called out to Bob Ashley to give himself up, Ashley swung around and shot the officer in the head. The officer was also struck near the heart and Ashley was hit twice – once in the body and the second through the head.

Both Riblet and Bob Ashley were rushed to hospital where Riblet died. Miami had lost its first police officer killed in the line of duty. A mob gathered at the hospital and as it grew and became more menacing, the Sheriff wisely moved John Ashley to the county jail for safekeeping. The Sheriff also took him to identify the dying man to make sure it was indeed his younger brother Bob.

Now it was time for a plea bargain over the Osceola Tiger. The murder charge was dropped; John Ashley pleaded guilty to manslaughter and was sentenced to seventeen and a half years' imprisonment. He went to the state penitentiary on 23 November 1916 where he behaved so well that on 31 March 1918 he was sent to a road camp. He duly rewarded the authorities by escaping that June with a bank-robber, Tom Maddox.

One of the reasons for his survival outside jail was his relationship with Laura Upthegrove, described as "dark, unkempt, weather beaten, and [most usefully] a skilled driver". Known as the Queen of the Everglades, Laura was every bit as resourceful as Bonnie Parker and the Dillinger Gang's women twenty years later, if not more so. She had first married a man called Colliers and they had a daughter, Vera. She later married Edgar Tillman, a marine engineer with whom she had two more children, Clarence and Sidney, while living at Pahokee in Palm Beach County. She seems to have met John Ashley near Gomez and left her family to live with the most dashing and best-dressed member of the gang – the others wore cheap collarless shirts and rough trousers stuffed in high boots.

Along with his brothers Ed and Frank, and Kid Lowe who seems to have been forgiven for his careless marksmanship, now Ashley went into rum-running. He was recaptured when he was found delivering a truckload of liquor in Wauchula, Dade County. This time he gave the name of Davis and all would have been well had he not been recognized by a black prisoner with whom he had been serving before he escaped. In June 1921, he was sent to Raiford prison and sometime during that year his brothers Ed and Frank died. They had been continuing the family business of rum-running, alien-smuggling and a spot of piracy. It is possible they drowned on their way back from Stuart Harbour. Their bodies were never recovered and Ashley became convinced that they had been killed by Jim White, Bo Stokes and Alton Davis, all well-known runners and hijackers. Ashley escaped prison again and very shortly afterwards all three men disappeared.

In the unavoidable absence of the Ashleys, the pimple-faced Clarence "Roy" Middleton from Chicago had taken over running the gang, sharing the leadership with Roy Matthews and later with Hanford Mobley, Ashley's seventeen-year-old nephew. It was he who, disguised as a woman, led the second raid on the Bank of Pompano in Stuart in 1924 when the haul was $4,000 cash and $5,000 worth of Liberty bonds. The gang fled to Lakeland where Mobley and Middleton were arrested. Matthews had gone to buy cigarettes and watched the capture. He then caught a train and disappeared before being arrested some weeks later.

In the Palm Beach county jail Mobley and Matthews were given the run of the jail by the jailer, W. W. Hicks, and not surprisingly took advantage of their freedom by escaping. Matthews was thought to have been killed later in a gang quarrel. Mobley went to California. Middleton, who had declined to escape with them, was transferred to Raiford where he met Ray Lynn, John Ashley and Joe Tracy. Tracy was released and it was only a matter of time before Ashley and Lynn escaped from a road gang and headed back to the Everglades.

They then continued their profitable bank-robbing and rum-running until, at around 2 a.m. on 9 January 1924, the police raided their camp. Sheriff Bob Baker and four deputies, armed with a warrant to arrest father Joe Ashley for highway robbery, found the camp where the Ashleys ran a still three miles deep in the Everglades, twenty-six miles north of Palm Beach. In the shoot-out Deputy Sheriff Fred Barker was shot in the right lung and killed by Albert Miller, a lookout who was himself wounded. Thinking he was outgunned, Sheriff Baker went back to Stuart for reinforcements but by the time they returned to the camp the gang had fled. Nonetheless, among those arrested were Wesley Mobley, the father of Hanford; Hanford's wife, Mary; and Laura Upthegrove who had been shot in the leg – other less gallant reports say the buttocks – and also had a scalp wound. Miller and Joe Ashley had been shot dead in the earlier gunfight. Now several hundred citizens took revenge on the Ashleys, burning Joe Ashley's home and Albert Miller's grocery store.

The Ashley Gang had taken to piracy, raiding rival rum-running concerns operating out of Bimini, a chain of islands in the westernmost part of the Bahamas around fifty-three miles west of Miami. Outside American territorial waters, ships loaded with bonded whisky would unload their cargo on to packet boats which would bring them to mainland Florida. That year John Ashley launched a lightning attack on the harbour at West End, Grand Bahama, stealing £8,000 in cash and destroying the storage buildings and the docks. It was the first attack by an American privateer, if that is not too grand a description, on a British crown colony. After the raid, coastguards were employed and this signalled the end of Bimini as a safe haven for smugglers, for the time being at least.

On 12 September the gang again robbed the Bank of Pompano, calling out "We got it all" as they drove down the town's main street before disappearing back into the Everglades.

At the end of October 1924 Sheriff Bob Baker heard that the gang proposed a raid on a bank in Jacksonville and on the night of 1 November a six-man posse, including Deputy Sheriff Oren Benton Padgett, set up a roadblock at Sebastian River Bridge. A chain with a red lamp was run across the bridge and when at around 10.30 p.m. two youths, Williams and Miller, stopped at the bridge and went to inspect it they were hurried to one side by the officers. Behind them were the Ashley Gang with nineteen-year-old Mobley at the wheel and Clarence "Bob" Middleton sitting up front with him. Ashley and Ray "Shorty" Lynn were in the back seat. Mobley stopped and apparently the men did not realize that Baker and other deputies had emerged from the mangroves where they had been hiding.

What happened next is a matter of conjecture. The official version is that the quartet tried to escape and were shot. Williams and Miller said they had seen the men being handcuffed before they were gunned down. In support of that there were handcuff marks on the bodies. The inquest was adjourned and Will Fee, to whose funeral parlour in Fort Pierce the bodies were taken and laid out on the pavement for the public to see, gave evidence at the second hearing that there were no handcuff marks. Representing the family, Alta Adams, who later became the chief justice of the Florida Supreme Court, asked that the bodies be exhumed but his request was denied. On 8 November the coroner's jury returned a verdict of justifiable homicide. Later Deputy Sheriff Oren Benton Padgett said that after the gang was arrested he had heard Henry Stubbs suggest to Elmer Padgett, another of the arresting officers, "Elmer, do you want to kill John?" Elmer said, "Might as well and get it all over with."

Baker is said to have taken Ashley's glass eye to put on his watch chain but, following death threats by Laura, he returned it to her saying, at least according to legend, "I knew I'd have to kill her if I kept it so I sent it back."

One gang-member who missed the killing was Laura Upthegrove's half-brother Joe Tracy who some weeks earlier had given himself up at Kissimmee on a Florida East Coast branch line train. In 1926 he took police and prison guards through the Everglades in a search for bonds worth in the region of $110,000 and said to have been buried by the gang. Only some $32,000 was found and on the way back to prison Tracy took the opportunity to escape near St Cloud but was soon recaptured. In 1935, still serving life for a murder in Orange County and fifteen years for robbery, Tracy received something of a belated reward in the form of parole. He quickly broke the terms and was send back to Raiford from where he was released in 1947.

Laura Upthegrove went to Okeechobee where she was repeatedly in trouble for drunkenness, bootlegging and gambling. She then moved to Canal Point in the Everglades and operated Upthegrove's Gas & Service station at Sand Cut, living on what was described as her father's plantation but which in reality was far removed from the antebellum establishments of *Gone with the Wind*. On 10 August 1927 during a fight over change for a pint of liquor she seems to have gone for a knife. She was disarmed and, when Elza Padgett, Oren's brother, and Deputy Sheriff Brownlee went to question her she drank a bottle of lysol, in what appears to have been an act of desperation, and died. Her mother is said to have told

Padgett that no attempt should be made to revive her and it was better this way. She was thirty years old. One story is that it was she who tipped off the Sheriff that the Ashley Gang was heading north without her. John Ashley's sister, Daisy, said to be the best looking of the family, also killed herself.

Those whose lives touched the Ashley Gang seem to have had poor fortune. In 1925 the jailer W. W. Hicks was convicted of killing Clarence Barber in Fort Lauderdale and was sentenced to life imprisonment. Frank Coventry, a customer in the Stuart bank when it was first robbed, was killed in 1925 by a Jesse Quinn who received a ninety-nine-year sentence.

On 7 October that year Charles Heisley, who had reported the Ashley Gang to the authorities in the Bahamas, was found near his garage door at the rear of his house at 434 S. Colorado St, lying on his left side. His wife, Gladys, was not home at the time. He had been shot in the back at close range.

On 6 November 1925 Oren. B. Padgett, the deputy involved in the final shoot-out at the bridge on 1 November the previous year, now police chief, was involved in a car accident when he hit a vehicle driven by an Evelyn Christopher in which her mother broke her neck and died. He was charged with manslaughter and resigned.

The Martin County sheriff's department had been carrying out ongoing raids on the illegal rum-running activities around Stuart and evidence started to come to light about former Police Chief Padgett's involvement. By 18 December Padgett now faced a charge of trafficking in liquor. There was worse to come.

On 11 January 1927, three people were charged with the murder of Charlie Heisley – Gladys, her brother Louie Gray and Oren Padgett. Gladys and her brother were kept in the West Palm Beach jail and Padgett in the Okeechobee jail, all without bail. Charges were dropped against Gladys and her brother but Padgett, who had been seen driving away from the shooting, went on trial alone. Heisley had been shot because of his treatment of Gladys and the evidence was that Padgett had offered a junior police officer $500 to kill him. It did not help him that he had sent a telegram from his cell to Gladys in the West Palm Beach jail telling her to "Keep mouth shut" and "Tell them to go to hell."

He was sentenced to life imprisonment on 9 February 1928. All appeals and applications for a new trial were refused, but in March 1934 he was granted a conditional pardon followed the next year by a full pardon, with his rights of citizenship restored, by Florida Governor David Sholtz. For the remainder of his life he worked steadily in the construction industry, continuing his bootlegging operations as a profitable sideline.

In January 1948 the now paroled Joe Tracy, said to have been the last member of the Ashley Gang, went to jail on a charge of robbing the Perkins State Bank in Williston. He was offered parole in return for telling the authorities where he had hidden the stolen $23,700. This time he refused to do so and died, still in prison, on 31 August 1968 at the age of either seventy-eight or eighty-three.

Cashing in on the success of Bonnie and Clyde, in 1971 *Little Laura and Big John* was released starring Frankie Avalon and Karen Black. It is generally considered to rank among the worst B-movies ever made.

Of course, the Ashley Gang was not the only one operating in Florida at the time. James Horace Alderman was known as the King of the Rum Runners or the Gulf Stream Pirate. He also smuggled aliens into Florida.

Born around 1882 near Tampa, Alderman spent several years in the Thousand Islands area of southwest Florida as a farmer, fisherman and field guide. With his wife Pearl and three daughters, Bessie, Ruby and Wilma, he lived variously in Chokoloskee, Caxambas, Palmetto and Tarracia Island before settling in Fort Myers around 1911. After the First World War and the passing of the National Prohibition Act, Alderman began his smuggling operations from Cuba and the Bahamas to Florida; in the 1920s he set up a base of operations in Miami.

On 7 August 1927 his boat, crammed with liquor, was stopped thirty-five miles off the coast from Fort Lauderdale and "King" Alderman was arrested. He managed to snatch a gun from one of the men guarding him but while he debated out loud whether to make his captors walk the plank, fire his own boat and set them adrift in it or scuttle the cutter with all hands on board, American secret service agent Robert Webber and two coastguards, Sidney Sanderlin and Victor Lamby, rushed him. He shot and killed all three before he was disarmed.

He was hanged on 17 August two years later in a metal hangar at the US coastguard station near Fort Lauderdale with a bare number of officials present. Although Alderman wanted a public execution so his friends could attend, the trial judge had effectively imposed a blackout on all reporting and one newspaperman had his camera smashed as he tried to take a picture of Alderman arriving in Fort Lauderdale before his execution. The Broward County commissioners had refused to sanction his hanging, insisting it must be carried out on United States property. "A singing sea breeze through the shed swayed his body at the end of a rope as justice was done for all good U.S. people," wrote *Time* alliteratively.

In the two years between the shooting and his execution, Alderman had become a popular figure, possibly because the principal witness against him, one of his crew, Robert Weech, had received only a twelve-month sentence. Ten members of the jury and the trial judge had recommended a commutation of the sentence but President Herbert Hoover would have none of it. Before his burial 2,000 people passed Alderman's bier.

4

Johnny Torrio and Al Capone

There have always been gangs that have preyed on other criminals. In Australia in the 1920s Melbourne's Safe Protection Gang was run by Snowy Cutmore; forty years later in Sydney the well-named Toecutters snipped off extremities to persuade their victims to hand over a share of the profits. But the first two decades of the twentieth century in the United States belonged to the Black Handers who, with letters signed with a picture of a Black Hand, dripping knife or exploding bomb, extorted relatively small sums of money from their fellow immigrant Italians but even high-quality operators such as "Big" Jim Colosimo, the first of the great Chicago-based crime bosses, were not always immune.

Colosimo had arrived with his father from Palermo in the 1870s – and had grown up on the Levee, joining the rackets before he was in his teens. He had worked in the traditional way as a newsboy and bootblack until he was a better than average pickpocket and was spotted as potential talent by two mob politicians, Michael "Hinky Dink" Kenna and "Bathhouse" John Coughlin. Colosimo became what is euphemistically called a collector.

In 1902 he met and married the dumpy and middle-aged madam, Victoria Moresco, taking over her brothels and adding the fabric and stock to his own. She loved his looks; he loved the properties she owned. Prices were raised and from every

$2 earned by a girl he took $1.20. By 1908 he controlled literally scores of brothels as well as an illegal wine-making business with an income said to be nearly $500,000 a year. He owned the fashionable Colosimo's Café frequented by opera singers such as Enrico Caruso and Amelita Galli-Curci, and entertainers and actors like Al Jolson and John Barrymore. He also faced a problem. Now he became the target of Black Handers. It was no use his being able to protect his interests through political pay-offs; the Black Handers required cash and he suffered a total humiliation when he was beaten up and threatened with permanent violence unless he increased his contributions. Victoria sent for her young cousin, Johnny "The Fox" Torrio.

For Torrio most of the Black Handers presented no trouble. He flushed a number of them out and had them killed but not the Cardinellis, run by the eponymous Sam, aided and abetted by Frank Campione, Nicholas Viana – known as the Choirboy and aged eighteen when sentenced to death at which time he was believed to have killed some fifteen men – and Thomas Errico as his chief henchmen. They certainly survived Torrio's cleanout and, by the beginning of Prohibition, were sufficiently strong to be able to control an area of Chicago that even Torrio did not dare to challenge.

The end came for the Cardinelli mob when Campione shot Albert Kublanza during a pool-room hold-up on 14 October 1919 in which Andrew Bowman, the owner, was killed. The getaway driver, Santo Orlando, was found shot dead in a drainage ditch ten days later. Errico, Campione and Viana were sentenced to death but were initially reprieved before that decision was reversed. Cardinelli had been convicted in a separate trial and, when he refused to walk to the gallows, was hanged in a chair on 15 July 1921. An attempt by his friends to revive him in an ambulance after the hanging was discovered and aborted. During his career he was thought to have organized the murder of over 100 men. There had been considerable pressure on Viana to give up the secrets of the gang in exchange for a reprieve but he did not do so. Apparently the fear of the hold the gang had on his family kept him from squealing.

Judge Scanlan thought:

> I tried Cardinelli and I know something of the character of the man. He was the greatest bandit we ever had in Chicago and the case tried before me showed that he had sent out men who had murdered at least four persons and the police claimed that he was the cause of twenty others.

Torrio may have thought Colosimo would show his gratitude but he was wrong. Instead of receiving the reward of a place high in the Colosimo machine, he was given a job as the manager of the Saratoga, absolutely on the bottom rung of the vice stable where the girls charged the few customers $1 a trick. Torrio, described by writer Herbert Asbury as "the nearest thing to a mastermind", turned the joint around with a lick of paint and the unpleasant if lucrative idea of dressing the girls in children's clothes. He raised the prices and business flourished. He was promoted to a position more in keeping with his abilities and now began to attract the company of men such as Jake "Greasy Thumb" Guzik and Charles "Lucky" Luciano, who would not only help him during his long and distinguished career but would be significant figures in organized crime for decades to come. It was they who suggested that he should hire at $35 a week the young Alphonse Capone as a bouncer for the Four Deuces, so called because it was at 2222 South Wabash. Described as a one-stop "vice centre", the Deuces had a saloon on the ground floor, gaming on the first and second floors, and a smart brothel on the top.

Capone was born in Brooklyn on 17 January 1899, the son of hard-working Italian immigrants, Gabriele and Teresa, who had arrived in the United States from Naples six years earlier. Neither spoke English and Gabriele began work as a barber in Park Avenue, Brooklyn. They had nine children, of whom Alphonse was the third. The first, Vincenzo or James, became a law officer working in the southwest. There was also an elder brother, Salvatore, anglicized as Frank, and a younger, Ralph, known as Bottles because he once worked in a bottling plant. Those two joined their more famous sibling in the rackets, loyally supported by their sister Mafalda. By the age of eleven Capone had joined the Bim Booms and the James Street gangs before progressing to the Five Points Gang while still regularly attending school and, it seems, doing well in his grades. He also was a competent sand-lot baseball pitcher who wanted to play in the major leagues but whose arm control was never good enough. Nor was his control of his temper. When he was publicly lectured for truancy, while in sixth grade, he knocked down his female teacher. He was then thrashed by the headmaster and suspended, never again returning to school. He became a clerk in a sweet shop and later a pin-setter in a bowling alley, a pool hustler and, tutored by the gangster Paul Kelly and Torrio, an expert knife-fighter.

It was while Torrio was still in New York that he recruited Capone as an enforcer for his debt-collecting and prostitution businesses. Late payers and girls who were thought not to have accounted for the whole of their earnings were beaten. The girls were also served by Capone and it may have been then that he contracted the syphilis which, untreated sufficiently early, led to his eventual insanity. Other versions suggest that he caught the disease in Chicago much later from a Greek girl who had worked in a brothel. He had installed her in the Hotel Lexington on Michigan where he and his entourage had fifty-four rooms. Equally, he may have caught it from a girl at the Roamer Inn in 1925.

Al Capone took his nickname "Scarface" from the scar that ran down the left-hand side of his face from his eyebrow to his chin. Again various stories were put about as to exactly how he acquired the injury. The most attractive was that it was the result of shrapnel while fighting in the so-called "Lost Battalion" of the 77th Division while in France during the First World War. Sadly, it is not correct; Capone didn't fight in the First World War. The most usual, and likely, version is that he was cut in a fight in the Harvard Inn when working as a bouncer. He had insulted the girlfriend or sister of Sicilian Frank Galluccio. In later life, so the legend goes, Capone forgave him, offering him a job.

On 12 September 1918 he married an Irish girl, May Coughlin, known as Mae. She was seven months pregnant at the time and the reason for the marriage may have been not only to give a name to the child but, more cynically, to enable Capone to avoid the call-up. Albert Francis, known as Sonny, was born on 4 December. Johnny Torrio was the godfather.

Part of the Capone legend is that he fled to Chicago to avoid a murder charge but according to one biographer, Laurence Bergreen, he had moved away from the New York rackets and was working as a bookkeeper in a construction company in Baltimore. It was only after the death of his father on 14 November 1920 that Capone returned to New York briefly before going west. The other version of Capone's flight is that he had fought, and left for dead, Arthur Finnegan, a member of the White Handers, and that his departure was to avoid revenge at the hands of William "Wild Bill" Lovett. Whichever version is correct, when Capone came to Chicago along with his brother Ralph he first managed mid-level brothels until he was promoted to manager of the far grander Four Deuces.

Meanwhile, Torrio had the sense to branch out of prostitution. He would never abandon that lucrative field but there were rumblings over the white slave trade and in 1910 Congress had passed what was the first of the three major pieces of social reform, the so-called Mann Act. Now it was punishable by a five-year sentence, a fine of $5,000 or both to transport a woman across a state line for "immoral purposes". As is the case with so much hastily put together legislation, it was an ill-drawn Act and in no way could stop women working in a brothel as was proclaimed on its behalf.

So, from 1910 to 1920, while the boss of the Chicago underworld was Big Jim Colosimo (sometimes known as "Diamond" as a tribute to his penchant for the gems that he wore on every finger and that he carried in his pocket to distribute to police and politicians alike), the brains behind the throne were those of Torrio. Colosimo was content to leave things in the hands of his wife's cousin while he toyed with his own merchandise and generally displayed himself about town, finally leaving the elderly and increasingly fat Mrs Colosimo for a young singer, Dale Winters. She and Colosimo dreamed of her performing grand opera. Caruso was invited to hear her sing and, with a favourable report from both him and the conductor Cleofonte Campanini, she enrolled in the Chicago Musical College. Colosimo married her in April 1920 in French Lick, Indiana. The former Mrs Colosimo received $50,000 in the divorce settlement about which she claimed to have heard nothing until it was already final. Two weeks after the divorce she married Antonio Villani, a small-time criminal twenty years her junior.

By 1919 Torrio, adopting the principle that it is necessary to change in order to maintain the status quo, was keen to take advantage of the forthcoming Volstead Act which brought with it Prohibition. Curiously, he had difficulty in explaining the benefits to the besotted Colosimo. It appears he eventually persuaded him to take an interest but now the great man's heart belonged not in business but to Dale. He would allow Torrio only to acquire sufficient liquor to stock their own brothels and speakeasies rather than deal on the open market. He was becoming an encumbrance.

On 11 May 1920, four months after Prohibition came into force, Torrio arranged for Colosimo to be at his café to receive a shipment of whisky. An unknown man leaped from the checkroom and shot Colosimo twice in the back of the head.

On hearing the news, Torrio, who had a cast-iron alibi, was suitably upset. "Big Jim and me were like brothers," he is reported to have said. He arranged the funeral with a silver and mahogany casket costing $7,500, and those who were to act as honorary or active pall-bearers included two congressmen, three judges, one federal judge designate, ten aldermen (including Bathhouse Coughlin who led the prayers) and a state representative. The Mayor of Chicago, William "Big Bill" Thompson, had the sense both to be occupied and to send personal representatives. Mr Coughlin paid tribute to Colosimo's charity: "You know what he did? He fixed up an old farmhouse for broken-down prostitutes. They rested up and got back into shape and he never charged them a cent."

Police inquiries into the murder latched on to Frankie Yale, brought by Torrio from New York for the purpose. Indeed, a waiter who was an eyewitness travelled to New York, to which Yale had returned, to identify him. On the journey the waiter sensibly changed his mind and went back to the Midwest leaving Colosimo's death unsolved.

Also unsolved was what happened to his fortune. He had left home on the day he was shot with $150,000 to pay for the whisky, but when his estate was inventoried only $675,000 in cash, $8,894 in jewels and fifty-four barrels of whisky could be traced from the millions he had undoubtedly made. Because she had not been Colosimo's wife under Illinois state law, which required a year's interval between divorce and remarriage, the new Mrs Colosimo could not inherit. She was given $6,000 in diamonds and bonds by the family. The former Mrs Colosimo was allowed double. For a short time after Colosimo's death Dale Winter tried to run the café but eventually she returned to the stage and took over from Edith Day in the hit musical *Irene* on Broadway. In 1924 she married actor Henry Duffy in San Francisco and toured in stock theatre until the 1930s.

As for the Colosimo empire, that was now Torrio's and he made good use of it. It was not for nothing he was known in underworld circles as "The Brain". To him goes the credit for the concept of a confederation of gangs in Chicago and ultimately nationwide. He did not survive in office to see it come to fruition but there is little doubt that the idea was his. It was a short step for Capone to go into partnership with Torrio. Capone was made. He received 25 per cent of the profits from prostitution and 50 per cent from bootlegging. It is estimated that in his first month as a partner he made $275,000.

At the time of Colosimo's death the West Side was run by the Irish brothers Bernard, Myles and William "Klondyke" O'Donnell, none of whom could abide the Italians and who were in opposition to the Jewish Herschie Miller and Samuel "Nails" Morton. Son of a small shopkeeper, Morton was born in Chicago in 1894. In his teens he joined the Miller Brothers Gang led by boxing referee Davy "Yiddles" Miller, who later also joined Dion O'Bannion. Morton became a street-fighter, earning his nickname for being as hard as nails. He was arrested in 1917 for assault and, given the option of prison or the Army, he chose the latter and served bravely, being awarded the Croix de Guerre for service in France. Later he became a receiver of stolen cars and dealt with Dion O'Bannion after he pulled off what was possibly the first recorded Chicago hijack – a lorry full of whisky outside the Bismark Hotel on the Loop – on 30 December 1919.

On 13 May 1923 Morton was kicked to death by his hired horse on the Lincoln Park Bridle Path. When O'Bannion and gunman Louis Alterie heard this they rented the horse and shot it – a scene re-enacted in the 1931 film, *The Public Enemy*. Morton was thought to have killed at least eight men including two policemen in the Beaux Arts Club, although he was acquitted of the charges. Regarded as something of a hero by the Jewish community, whom he championed, his funeral was suitably splendid.

On the South Side, in what was Little Italy, the Gennas – Sam, Vincenzo known as Jim, Pete, Angelo, Tony known as "The Gentleman", and the youngest, Mike, known as "Il Diavolo", held sway. The Gennas were all born in Marsala, Sicily, and came to the United States in 1910 when their father was able to obtain employment as a railway construction worker. Their passage had been sponsored by "Diamond" Joe Esposito, a republican ward boss who was later machine-gunned to death, almost certainly on the orders of Capone, on 21 March 1928 outside his home as his wife and children watched. By 1910 Sam, Angelo and Mike were involved in Chicago Black Hand operations and brother Jim ran a brothel with help from Tony and Pete.

By 1919 they were a strong enough faction to have carved out a territory for themselves in Little Italy, employing a workforce of hundreds of Sicilians. The men gave up their labouring jobs and operated stills at the substantial weekly wage of $15. Costing 40 cents a gallon to produce, the liquor was sold on for $2 to Torrio and Capone, who then retailed it to the saloons at $6. It was a high-risk industry for the workforce. Apart from the risk of a raid by the police (unlikely) and a raid by opposition forces (highly likely), homemade stills were quite likely to explode, maiming or killing their operators. As befitted caring employers, the Gennas provided a fund for the burial cost of those killed.

Next door to the Gennas, on the way to Cicero, south of the Eisenhower Expressway, was the fifty-plus strong Valley Gang, basically an Irish street-gang, originally from Fifteenth Street, led by the staunchly Catholic Terry Druggan and Frankie Lake who ran a North Side cabaret, Little Bohemia, and a hijacking business to go with it. It is said that on one occasion they hijacked a beer lorry in front of a church. In the front seat were two Jewish gangsters whose misfortune was compounded by being told by Druggan, "Hats off, you Jews, when you're passing the House of God or I'll shoot 'em off!"

On the Southwest Side was the Saltis–McErlane Gang, which before Prohibition had devoted much of its time to labour racketeering. Joe Saltis was of only marginal intelligence and is said to have clubbed to death a woman owner of an ice-cream parlour because she would not convert it to a speakeasy. Despite his limited intellect he had the wit to buy himself a summer estate in Wisconsin on his bootlegging proceeds. Frank McErlane, known as Dingbat after a cartoon character, was an alcoholic. Built like a Japanese wrestler with a red face and the beady eyes of a wild boar, he was said by the Illinois Association for Criminal Justice to be "the most brutal gunman who ever pulled a trigger in Chicago". He is said to have shot a customer in a bar in Crown Point, Indiana, as part of a bet and it was he who would introduce the "greatest aid to bigger and better business the criminal has discovered in this generation" – the Thompson submachine gun.

The South Side, where the stockyards were situated, was under the control of the Ragen Colts, now a collection of racist bootleggers who included among their number James Ragen who went on to found a racing wire-service that would lead to gang warfare in the middle 1940s.

On the far South Side lived another set of O'Donnells, brothers Steve, Walter, Tommy and Ed, who was known as Spike. Sadly, Spike was currently in the prison at Joliet serving a sentence for a $12,000 bank robbery and the brothers were in some disrepair, acting as little more than Torrio's gofers.

Perhaps the most powerful of all the gangs was that run by Charles Dion "Deany" O'Bannion on the North Side. A handsome man, with his left leg shorter than his right as the result of a fall from a streetcar, he had been brought up in Aurora, Illinois. After his mother died when he was five the family moved to a flat on the North Side's Little Sicily, which had previously been the Irish shanty-town, Kilgubbin. He had sung at Holy Name Cathedral in the choir but was quickly enveloped into a gang, the Market Streeters. By the age of sixteen he was a singing waiter and jack-roller in McGoven's Saloon. The next year he was part of the strong-arm team on the side of the *Herald-Examiner* in one of the perpetual newspaper circulation wars of the time in which rival vans were overturned and their contents burned, and newspaper vendors were beaten up and robbed. From there it was a short step to his own gang of robbers and burglars.

He was said to have killed twenty-five people and was unwilling to shake hands because it would leave him vulnerable. His specially tailored suits concealed three extra pockets for firearms. One was under the left armpit of the coat jacket, another on the outside left and a third as a sort of codpiece on the trousers. He could shoot accurately with either hand. He possessed a reckless and murderous temper and on one occasion shot "Yiddles" Miller and his brother Maxie in the foyer of the LaSalle theatre. No charges were brought and O'Bannion shrugged off the incident as "just a piece of foolish hotheadedness". His legitimate business was as a flower shop proprietor and he owned a half share in William Schofield's business at 738 North State Street, sensibly positioned opposite Holy Name. All tributes for gangland funerals, irrespective of the allegiance of the deceased, had to be ordered through him.

His wife described him in the proper terms reserved for gangsters:

Dean loved his home and spent most of his evening in it. He loved to sit in his slippers, fooling with the radio, singing a song, listening to the piano player. He never drank. He was not a man to run around nights with other women. I was his only sweetheart.

To his credit he does seem to have distributed some of his wealth over and above the amount needed to keep the support of the community, visiting the slums with his car laden with food and clothing, and giving money to the poor and orphaned.

His second-in-command was the fearsome Earl Wojciechowski, known for convenience as Earl Weiss. It was he who is sometimes credited with coining the phrase "a one-way ride". The first recipient, in July 1921, was Steve Wisniewski who had hijacked an O'Bannion beer truck. He was lured into a car and his body was found near Libertyville, some twenty-five miles out of central Chicago.

The non-smoking, non-drinking, non-womanizing, dapper little Torrio appears to have been both master and teacher who endeavoured, and sometimes succeeded for lengthy periods, to persuade rivals that there was more profit in cooperation than in fighting. Immediately after Colosimo's death he managed to structure peace in Chicago. He called a meeting attended by all the gang-leaders with the exception of Saltis and the absent Spike O'Donnell; with their grudging approval, he divided the city into territories. He and Capone held the South Side; the Bannion–George "Bugsy" Moran alliance had the North; and the remainder had the leftovers. The Bannion–Moran/Torrio–Capone sections were divided by Madison Street. There was to be no crossing into another's section. The peace was to hold for three years, by which time, in 1923, it was estimated that, overall, the police officers in Chicago were actually working as bootleggers rather than merely turning a blind eye. Ranged against them was the Chicago Crime Commission, founded by a group of private citizens in 1919 and determined to "keep the light of publicity shining on Chicago's most prominent, well-known and notorious gangsters to the end that they may be under constant observation by the enforcing authorities".

And eventually its light would shine on Torrio, whose peace was still more or less holding. As part of his efforts in that direction he had secured the services of Governor Len Small, a puppet of the Bill Thompson administration. Soon after he had become governor in 1921 Small had been indicted and charged with embezzling $600,000. With Torrio's assistance, a bribed and frightened jury acquitted him. Favours could now be called in and they were. In three years Small pardoned over 1,000 convicted felons. In 1923 the Chicago Crime Commission announced a list of twenty-eight persons "who are constantly in conflict with the law". This was soon translated into "Public Enemies". Capone topped the list followed by his bodyguard, and then his brother Ralph Capone.

It was now that Torrio's peace structure started to unravel. Part of the problem was the reappearance of Spike O'Donnell, now released from Joliet. Until then many of the smaller gangs had been content with subservient but profitable roles in the overall scheme of things. The Valley Gang and Claude Maddox of the Circus Gang along with Ragen's Colts were happy or, at worst, prepared to deliver beer and sell it. Now in 1923 Spike O'Donnell began leading his brothers on raids on Torrio's beer trucks and on the Saltis–McErlane operations. In their condemnation of the O'Donnell raids there was at least unity. Over a two-year period, in which Torrio's men were helped by McErlane as well as "Machine Gun" Jack McGurn, eight of O'Donnell's men were killed. Spike narrowly escaped and left Chicago.

There was also a certain amount of internal trouble. The Gennas were causing difficulties. They wanted extra territory in which to expand, including O'Bannion's North Side. The Klondyke O'Donnells also wanted more space and the increasingly difficult O'Bannion was organizing the hijacking of Torrio's shipments from Detroit's Purple Gang.

More trouble, however, came from the new mayor, William E. Dever, elected on a Democratic reform ticket. He instructed his Chief of Police Morgan A. Collins to enforce the Prohibition Act and he did so. Offered a $100,000 bribe by Torrio he replied by closing down the Four Deuces. When

Collins was then offered $1,000 a day to permit the movement of 250 barrels of beer, he responded by raids on breweries, brothels and blind pigs (drinking dens). Over 100 men were locked up and Mont Tennes, who had run the city's racing-wire service for years, decided that he should now retire.

As a result Torrio moved the centre of his operations to the western suburb of Cicero, in Klondyke O'Donnell territory. In the middle of 1923 there were slot machines and beer joints, the proceeds of which were shared by the O'Donnells, a lightweight fighter, Eddie Tancl, who ran the bars, and Eddie Vogel, the political boss of Cicero. Tancl, who had killed an opponent, Young Greenberg, in the ring, had immediately retired. Now he ran the Hawthorne Park café, the scene of a number of deaths.

In October 1923, to the fury of the neighbours, Torrio opened a brothel on Roosevelt Road, furnishing it with twenty women. It was raided and closed down as was a second one that had been opened immediately after the first. Two days later the Torrio-owned sheriff of Cook County, Peter M. Hoffman, moved in and confiscated all the slot machines in Cicero. Negotiations were undertaken and Torrio was allowed into the town on condition he did not bring in prostitutes. He would operate the one-arm bandits and have the beer franchise, ceding a small portion to the O'Donnells. He would also have his offices in town. Now Torrio set up the Hawthorne Smoke Shop next door to the Hawthorne Inn. Unsurprisingly, the one man seriously unhappy with the arrangement was Eddie Tancl, who continued to buy his liquor from whichever source he chose. His end came when Myles O'Donnell and a drinking friend, Jim Doherty, arrived at the Hawthorne Inn one Sunday morning following an all-night drinking spree. After breakfast they complained about the bill. In the ensuing fight Tancl's head bartender, Leo Klimas, was shot dead while bravely, if foolishly, trying to separate the men. Tancl also died but O'Donnell and Doherty survived.

In 1923, with his operation established, Torrio set sail with his wife for a well-deserved holiday in Italy, leaving his understudy, the legendary Al Capone, in charge.

Once Torrio was safely on the way to Italy, Capone effectively took over Cicero. He moved into Anton's Hotel and opened a series of drinking clubs including the Cotton Club of Cicero. Through his brother, Frank, he was able to renegotiate the position on prostitution and it was agreed that in exchange for his muscle at election time there would be no further raids on the brothels. Subsequent elections at Cicero were celebrated with a show of force by the Capone team. There was intimidation of voters, ballot boxes were seized, emptied and re-filled, and there was double- and treble-voting.

Meanwhile Frank moved his operations to the Stockade, a new brothel in Forest View. The Chief of Police, who objected, was pistol-whipped and so withdrew his complaints. With Greasy Jake Guzik and Ralph Capone acting as enforcers and hardmen and Al Capone as Mr Nice Guy, the operation rolled smoothly along.

On 1 April 1924, in another poll-rigging operation, Frank Capone was killed. Alphonse had been promoting Joseph Z. Klenha as his stooge and was fighting the reform candidate William K. Pflaum. Frank Capone led an attack on Pflaum's headquarters and later during polling the candidate's supporters were abducted and, in one case, shot in the legs as a deterrent. A squad of seventy detectives sworn in by the Cook County judge, Edward K. Jarecki, found Frank Capone together with his cousin Charles Fischetti outside a polling station by the Western Electric Plant. Accounts vary as to whether Frank Capone drew on the police mistaking them for rival gangsters or whether they merely thought he was trying to draw a gun. The then pro-Capone *Chicago Tribune* noted that the $20,000 funeral was fitting for "a distinguished statesman". As a mark of respect the all-night saloons in Cicero were closed for two hours on the night of his burial. Frank's death was not in vain. He would have been pleased to know that Klenha won by a landslide.

By 1924 Torrio was back from his vacation and facing increasing difficulties. Within the prevailing climate he was undoubtedly a man of peace and he spent considerable energy in trying to placate Capone who wanted him to move against O'Bannion. In his turn O'Bannion was becoming more and more daring, repeatedly breaching the territorial divisions and encroaching on the lethal Gennas. Now Angelo Genna went to Torrio to ask his permission to murder O'Bannion and was told to wait. Then Capone, who had been called a "dago pimp" by O'Bannion and whose team had been constantly and successfully sniped at by the Irish mob, asked the same thing. He, too, was told to remain calm.

The finale began in May 1924 when O'Bannion came to Torrio to say he was retiring. He wanted to sell his interest in a gambling resort, the Ship, as well as what was considered to be the best brewery on the North Side, Sieben's Mid-City Brewery. He was, he said, worn out by the fighting with the Gennas and was going to buy a spread near that of "Two Gun" Louis Alterie in Colorado.

Capone argued that O'Bannion could not be trusted but he was overruled. A price of $500,000 cash was paid and on 19 May 1924, when Torrio went to meet with O'Bannion and Earl "Hymie" Weiss to inspect his new property, he heard the buzzing of police sirens. It was a set-up. Although all were arrested, O'Bannion and Weiss had no previous convictions so their maximum sentence would be a fine. Torrio, however, had a previous conviction for violating the Volstead Act and was now liable for an automatic prison sentence. O'Bannion, who had never taken an interest in brothels, arguing that the Italians were taking advantage of "diseased women", now said, "I clipped the pimp for $500,000 and then dumped him in the can."

Torrio, out on $7,500 bail, recruited Albert Anselmi and John Scalise, two professional killers who mistakenly believed that if they dipped their bullets in garlic and failed to kill their targets outright, infection would nevertheless set in. Frank Yale was brought over from New York and on 10 November 1924 the three went to O'Bannion's flower shop on North State Street. It was a propitious time. Mike Merlo, president of the Unione Siciliane, had died and there was the usual scurry to outdo each other with the size and cost of the floral tribute. All the Italians had ordered their flowers from O'Bannion and shortly before the visit Torrio had telephoned the shop to see when his would be ready. With Yale shaking hands with O'Bannion and holding him so he could not pull one of his three guns, Scalise and Anselmi shot the diminutive Irishman. The identity of the killers was an open secret but no charges were ever brought.

O'Bannion's solid silver coffin cost $10,000 and was followed by twenty-six lorries carrying flowers worth in excess of $50,000. It is estimated that 20,000 people watched the procession.

The price Torrio paid for the flowers was a high one. He was sent to prison for nine months following his conviction and while on bail pending his appeal he began to rein in his interests, depositing large sums in New York and European banks. On 24 January 1925 as he and his wife, Anna, climbed out of their chauffeur-driven limousine in front of their South Shore apartment building, Torrio was shot by Bugsy Moran and Earl Weiss. His chauffeur, Robert Barton, fired on the men and was, in turn, shot in the leg. Moran stood over Torrio and saying, "This is for Deanie O'Bannion, you dago bastard," pulled the trigger. Amazingly, he had miscounted and the gun was empty. Torrio managed to drag himself into the apartment building and, shot in the neck and believing the garlic story, yelled that his wounds be cauterized.

On 9 February 1925, with his wounds healed – he had appeared at a press conference within a week of the shooting – Torrio had his appeal dismissed and was sent to Waukegan County jail where there was also a friendly sheriff who allowed Capone to protect the prisoner. Torrio served his sentence in some comfort and towards the end he called in Capone to say he would retire to Italy if he could get out of Chicago alive.

Capone promised that he would and he kept his promise. Torrio was escorted in Capone's armour-plated car to the railroad and put on a train east. Gangsters patrolled the Gary, Indiana, depot and Capone personally saw Torrio into his compartment. "I'll never be back," Torrio is reported to have said. Now Capone was the boss of Chicago.

The suggestion has often been put that Capone was behind the attack on Torrio. There is some evidence for this. Capone, almost alone, would have known the timing of his partner's shopping expedition. Torrio's immediate gift of his empire is indicative that he thought he would not be safe with Capone. Also, why did he think that Irish gunmen would use garlic-dipped bullets?

Torrio never returned to Illinois. First he went to Florida, to which he was traced by Weiss, and then he went to Naples where he rented a villa for three years. In 1928, hassled by Benito Mussolini, he returned to the United States and lived in New York. There he bought into property and, along with Lucky Luciano, Abner "Longy" Zwillman and Meyer Lansky, established a liquor distribution system which ran from New York to Florida; he became a valued and venerated adviser to the New York mob. After the repeal of Prohibition his liquor distribution chain was even more successful but, as with so many gangsters, he attracted the attention of the Inland Revenue Service. He was arrested for tax evasion on 22 April 1936 and bail was set at $100,000. Within hours, his wife appeared carrying new dollar bills wrapped in paper.

Torrio eventually paid $86,000 in back tax and served a thirty-month sentence. He was paroled in 1941 and immediately went into semi-retirement. On 16 April he suffered a fatal heart attack in the barbershop he had visited for years. His funeral was attended by only a couple of dozen people and the press were not notified until he had been buried for three weeks.

5

The Lewis–Jones Gang

At midday on 8 August 1918 a grey Hudson speedster with Iowa licence plates stopped outside the doors of the South Side State Bank of Indianapolis, half a mile outside the city's business district. Three men got out of the car; two went into the bank and the third stayed outside the front door. One employee was knocked unconscious with a blow from a revolver and the others were covered. A customer who came in was pushed into the circle of employees and guards, and all were made to lie on the floor. Counter drawers and vaults were cleaned out. It took less than five minutes before the pair, carrying pillow cases with an estimated haul of $18,000 in cash and gold, joined the third man. The bank had been held up by the little-known but thoroughly professional Lewis–Jones Gang, sometimes regarded – rather than the German-born ex-officer Herman K. Lamm who a decade later developed a meticulous style of robberies – as responsible for mastering the art of the automobile getaway.

The hunt for the South Side robbers was on within half an hour but there was no trace of them. Later, it was learned that they had rented a garage three blocks from the bank and had parked the Hudson there and driven off in a Packard with one of the trio, Dale Jones, wearing a dress, hat and veil. The Packard had been stolen a few days earlier in Columbus, Ohio, forty-five miles away. The Pinkerton National Detective Agency was called in and staff were asked to look at photographs of men with criminal records. Frank Lewis and Roy Sherrill, the son of a minister, were picked out the most often. Both were wanted in connection with the hold-up of the Kansas City and Denison Railway Post Office at Kick Siding, near Paola, a week earlier.

Just who the robbers were became clearer four days later when David Wolf, a cab driver from Terre Haut, was hired to drive to the local country club to meet a lady. Near the club he was told to turn down a lane and when he refused, the passenger pulled a gun on him saying he was taking the car. Wolf fought him with a tyre wrench and was shot in the chest. The man ran away leaving bags from the South Side bank containing $200 and clothing stolen from the Plymouth Clothing Company store in Quincy, Illinois. Wolf, who survived, identified the man who shot him as Sherrill. The owner of Plymouth Clothing picked out both Sherrill and Frank Lewis as well as the baby-faced Dale Jones, who was missing the middle finger of his right hand.

Dale Jones, known also as Denver Dean and half a dozen other aliases, had begun his career as a car thief in 1916. One story about his first appearance in court is that he refused to give his antecedents so as not to shame his parents. For his decency he was given a suspended sentence. Another is that he started his career in Nevada, Missouri, where he was taken under the wing of J. B. Johnson, a prosecutor who tried to reform him. At one time he had been a member of the Kansas City YMCA. Yet a third is that Jones fell into bad company and was a member of the gang that shot a constable called Queen at Rich Hill, Missouri, when the officer started out for Butler in order to lodge a robber, John Shead, in the prison there. Later Jones helped Shead escape from the Butler jail. Along with Charles Tully Lane he was wanted for a robbery at the Culver City Bank in December 1917. The Lewis boys, Frank and his brother Roy, had lived in Nevada, Missouri, as children before moving to Sedalia and then to St Louis.

Around 11 p.m. on 6 September, Frank Lewis and Sherrill held up George Cook and took his Marmon automobile leaving him on the city limits to find his own way home. The Pinkertons heard that the Lewis–Jones Gang had left for the West in Cook's car and tracked them through Kansas. At the same time Lewis's mother, Martha Babb, headed for Denver by rail with a heavy trunk. The gang was under surveillance from the moment they arrived and met her in Mile High City two days later.

In early September Dale Jones, his twenty-year-old girlfriend Margie Celano, also known as Jewell Dillon, along with Roy "Roscoe" Lancaster, known as Kansas City Blackie, drove to Denver where they rented an apartment in a high-rise district and joined up with the others. One version of Celano's life is that she spoke French, Italian and Spanish fluently and had been born in a ghetto in Paris, France, in 1896. As a young girl she emigrated to New York and quickly turned to shoplifting. She left New York for Chicago, where she was convicted of stealing diamonds from a jewellery store. While serving out her sentence at Joliet Penitentiary she met Eva, the girlfriend of Frank Lewis.

In Denver members of the gang were spotted by a Pinkerton man who told the police where they could be found. On 13 September 1918 they were followed when they drove in the Marmon to Frank Henderson's gas station in Colorado Springs. The tail lost them on the way but wanted posters had been sent to filling stations and Henderson recognized them. After telephoning the police, he deliberately took his time over refuelling. Meanwhile, a Mrs Harmon had driven into the gas station, effectively blocking the gang's exit. The police arrived and a shoot-out took place in which Chief of Detectives John W. Rowan was killed outright with a bullet hitting his shoulder and exiting through his stomach. A second bullet hit his watch, stopping it at 3.10 p.m. Patrolman Luther McMahill was also shot and died from his injuries the next day. Lancaster was shot in the leg and body, and a bullet ploughed through his scalp. With the windscreen of Mrs Harmon's car shattered, Frank Henderson drove the petrified woman out of the filling station, thereby giving Margie Celano, at the wheel of the Marmon, an escape route. She and Jones then drove the badly injured Lancaster to Kansas City. The Marmon was later found dumped in the Kaw River near the town. A reward of $2,000 was posted for Jones's capture.

That evening, Frank Lewis and Sherrill held up a man and his female friend on the outskirts of Denver, took their car and left them with a fifteen-mile walk back to town. Once in Denver the car was recognized and two more officers were shot and wounded when they tried to make arrests. During the night Lewis and Sherrill drove to a house at 16th and Colorado Boulevard to collect Eva before heading west. All three were captured in a gunfight in which Sherrill, on his 21st birthday, was seriously wounded and one Denver officer was killed.

Lewis and Sherrill did what they could to divert the Pinks from the trail of the others. The men gave detailed and totally false stories about where Jones, Celano and Lancaster might be, saying Roy Lewis was dying in Pueblo nursed by Margie Celano and that Dale Jones, who was with them, always carried a vial of nitroglycerine to blow up himself and anyone else within range if he was captured. Extensive research by the Pinkertons failed to find any sign that they had ever been in the town. It was thought Margie Celano was pregnant and might be found attending a hospital. Rewards totalling $3,000 were posted for their arrest. Both she and Jones were described as "particularly desperate characters".

On 24 September Roscoe Lancaster was found with his brother Warren on the second floor of a rooming house at 1904 Montgall Avenue in Kansas City. There was never any chance he would surrender and he barricaded himself in his room and began shooting. During a two-hour gun battle, just before he died, he said that Dale Jones had planned a job in Minnesota. It was another of the gang's diversionary tactics. Some reports have it that Jones and Margie were there and managed to get away. Warren Lancaster was also arrested. There is also a story that Roscoe Lancaster told the police, "Jones is nuts! He wants to get in the movies," and this inadvertently led the Pinkertons to search for the pair in California, where one account has them tracked because a Mrs Forbes regularly bought a favourite perfume from Celano.

Meanwhile, Celano and Jones had moved to a house on Sierra Madre Avenue in Arcadia in the San Gabriel Valley, around twenty miles outside Los Angeles. They are said to have married in the Methodist church at San Bernadino and by early November there were regular reports of sightings. It was their inability to change their habits that did for them. Every evening they stopped at the White Oaks garage to fill up their Cadillac.

On 19 November police officers and Pinkerton men staked out the filling station. The Cadillac appeared and was driven 100 yards past. Jones returned and checked the garage for a trap but he missed seeing the deputies and signalled Margie to pull in. Accounts of what followed vary but certainly Deputy Sheriff George Van Vliet called on the pair to hold their hands up. Jones replied, "You got me," but when he raised his hands he was holding a Luger and a Smith and Wesson. He shot Van Vliet in the face, killing him. Margie Celano then hid behind the car, emptied her pistol and grabbed a rifle. Other accounts have her crouching behind the steering wheel firing a .30-30 Winchester carbine that had a sort of machine-gun swivel and which could be dropped into a slot on either side of the car. As she began to fire Deputy Sheriff William Anderson shot her dead with a shotgun and his last bullet killed Jones as he poked his head out from behind the car. An innocent bystander, Private Albert Brock of the 52nd Balloon Company who was waiting for a lift into town, was shot in the back by a stray bullet.

A search of Jones's house turned up a complete arsenal of weapons and dies for changing the numbers of automobile plates but there was no nitroglycerine. Jones's father, Paul, refused to send funds for his burial. Rather contradicting the exotic upbringing of Margie Celano, her mother Joan, interviewed immediately after the shooting, said her daughter was a "home girl" who had left home seven months earlier saying she was going to Albuquerque. The papers thought that Margie had actually married Charles Tully Lane who was wanted for the 1917 Culver City Bank robbery. This would have made her the sister-in-law of Ray Niemeyer who was also wanted for that raid.

As for the remainder of the gang, Frank Lewis died from pneumonia in Topeka jail before his trial, Eva received five to seven tears for highway robbery, and Frank's brother, Roy, went to the Missouri penitentiary. Roy Sherrill and another gang-member, Thomas Knight, were sentenced in November 1918 when they drew twenty-five years.

6

Rocco and Bessie Perri

In popular culture Rocco Perri was the nearest Toronto had to a major gang-leader in the 1920s. In fact, the credit should probably go to his common-law wife, Bessie. He may have been called the King of the Mob; she was genuinely the Queen.

Gangsters are often diminutive men and Perri was no exception, standing a mere five foot four inches and in later life weighing in at 174 lbs. Sometimes known as Little Caesar after his resemblance to Edward G. Robinson in the 1931 film of that title, Perri came to Canada from Plati, Calabria, at the age of thirteen in 1903. Working in the Dundas stone quarry and then on the Welland Canal, he was also a Black Hand extortionist and part-time arsonist until 1912, when, while working as a macaroni salesman, he had an amazing stroke of fortune. He took lodgings with Bessie, then married to Harry Tobin with whom she had two daughters and ran a rooming house. Perri clearly had some charm with women. Despite being penniless he persuaded the thirty-year-old woman to leave her husband. They went to live in St Catherines and he continued to work as a travelling pasta salesman. Bessie was born Besha Starkman. Her parents were among the thousands of destitute Polish Jews who arrived in Toronto at the end of the nineteenth century. Bessie learned Italian and she and Perri opened a grocery store in Hamilton, which had a long history of Black Handers, who had initially been led from the turn of the century by John

Taglerino, who was also involved in smuggling immigrants to Detroit. When the immigrants were safely in place and earning then came the time to blackmail them.

On the romantic front fidelity was not Perri's strong suit. Using the freedom of his position as a travelling salesman, he had two children by Olive Rutledge, a farm-girl from Bancroft, who committed suicide by throwing herself from her lawyer's seventh-floor office when she discovered that Perri would neither marry her nor pay for their children's upkeep. On the face of it this extramarital liaison did not seem to faze Bessie who clearly adored her husband. She also dabbled in the white slave trade. In March 1917 she was fined $50 with an alternative of two months in prison after a house in Caroline Street North, of which she was the registered owner, was raided. She paid up.

The Perris's bootlegging business took off when the Ontario Temperance Act came into effect on 16 September 1916 restricting the sale and distribution of alcohol. They did even better when Prohibition was declared in Canada on 23 December 1917 and the hat-trick was completed for them in April the next year when it became illegal to transport alcohol in Canada. Finally, in 1920, the Eighteenth Amendment prohibited sale and consumption of alcohol in the United States.

There was also a resurgence of black-handing in the 1920s followed by a string of bomb attacks on property as well as a bootleg war. The once pre-eminent gang of bootleggers, the Basile family, had been wiped out over a ten-year period. Peter Basile was killed in Lockport in 1914; his sister Consima and her husband Patsy Bane died in 1918; and his brother Joseph was shot in Buffalo in 1924. With that family out of the way, the road was clear for Perri who had begun by selling bootleg whisky at 50 cents a shot and by the mid-1920s was selling an estimated 1,000 cases a day.

In due course Perri and Bessie expanded the business to the Niagara frontier and the Buffalo area. They specialized in exporting liquor from old Canadian distilleries, such as Seagram's and Gooderham's, to the United States, and helped these companies obtain a large share of the American bootleg market – a share they kept after Prohibition ended. Bootlegging was still profitable. With Canadian taxes so high on liquor it was always worthwhile to drive a lorry load across the border.

Undoubtedly Bessie was the brains behind the business, keeping eight bank accounts, one of which housed half-a-million dollars. With this money behind them she and Perri became what passed for high society, buying a nineteen-room house in Hamilton and later one in Toronto. Mostly they looked after their employees and, over the years, one or other of the Perris would appear to post bail for unfortunates caught with whisky in the back of their cars. In September 1923 when the police found a crew unloading whisky near Leslie Street, Toronto, shots were fired and John Gogo of Hamilton was killed. Perri was put on trial as being in charge of the operation but was triumphantly acquitted.

The next few years were punctuated by police raids and increasing competition. In November 1924 when Joe Boitvich and Fred Genesee were killed in part of the Italian–Ukrainian feud running at the time, the Perris had a double act going with the newspapers explaining that their men were not allowed to be armed. "I won't stand for guns," Perri lied to the *Toronto Daily Star* in November that year. He was also careful to denounce moonshine whisky as a dangerous poison.

People either did not read the papers or failed to heed his warning because in 1926 thirty-five people died in one night throughout the Niagara Peninsula, poisoned by bad liquor. Perri surrendered to a warrant and, once more, was acquitted. As with other mobsters, the only way the authorities could get at the Perris was through their financial accounts and in 1928 he served six months for perjury when it was proven that he and Bessie had been less than forthcoming.

With the end of Prohibition in sight it was time to expand and the Perris moved into drugs. By 1926 the Royal Canadian Mounted Police (RCMP) had some evidence he was supplying "an Italian dope-peddling ring" in Pennsylvania. Perri was running drugs from South Ontario into the United States and his men were returning with raw opium that could be processed into either smoking opium or morphine. The gang was also smuggling drugs using a seaplane that landed on Lake Ontario near Burlington or dropped packages on disused airfields near Hamilton.

By 1929 the RCMP regarded the Perri outfit as "very shrewd" and if they suspected the police were on to them they would "close down temporarily rather than take any unnecessary risks". The police had no doubt that while Perri may have had the Italian connections, Bessie was the real brains. That year the RCMP tried to infiltrate the organization. Mountie Frank Zaneth went undercover trying to buy morphine from Perri dealers, particularly Tony Roma who dealt out of the grandly named Marathon and Enosis Club, a gambling hall east of Yonge in Toronto. He also managed to identify Francesco Rossi, known as Frank Ross, as a main dealer who kept drugs in Hamilton at the home of another Perri man, Nazzareno Italiano. On 20 June 1929 raids took place throughout Toronto and Hamilton. Italiano was in the process of being arrested in his Dundas Street home in Hamilton when Bessie arrived and was stopped and searched. Although she was carrying hundreds of dollars none of them were the marked notes that had been used for undercover purchases and she was released.

On 23 September Italiano and another man received six months; a third was sentenced to half that. Tony Roma absconded and he was not arrested until July 1936 when he was found in California. He was sentenced to two years and deported to Italy. Although Bessie was repeatedly mentioned in the case, with reports that she had been visiting Italiano, she was never charged. Perri himself was keeping a low profile.

Bessie's career ended, and to all intents and purposes Perri's with it, when she was shot to death in her garage at 166 Bay Street South, Toronto, on 13 August 1930. On the evening of her killing, she telephoned her maid shortly before 11 p.m. to ask her to make up her room and then drove with Perri to their luxurious home. Their practice was for Bessie to open the garage, turn on the lights and then go indoors leaving Perri to put their car away and lock up.

According to Perri this is precisely what happened at about 11.35 p.m. except that when Bessie went into the garage she was shot twice by men with shotguns. Perri panicked and ran for help. A third shot was fired. The police were called immediately and when the area was searched, shells designed to cause the maximum possible damage were found.

When her husband, Harry Tobin, whom she had left along with their two daughters in 1913, was told of her death he was less than sympathetic. "I can say, 'Thank God'," he told the *Toronto Star.* "She dies as she deserved to die."

Perri announced that the motive for the killing was robbery but this was not an explanation accepted by everyone. For a start none of Bessie's expensive jewellery had been touched. There was a number of more attractive theories. The first was that the killing had been carried out by underlings in the Perri Gang. While Perri was always happy to look after those who went to prison on his behalf, Bessie was made of sterner stuff and the payments to wives and children had not always gone through. Another was that the killing was over a bundle of drugs for which Bessie was refusing to pay, telling New York State gangsters that they could sue her. Her killers could have been members of the rival Rochester organization. It is possible, too, that Rocco Perri knew it was likely to take place but was powerless to prevent it.

Her funeral was in the best gangster tradition. Her casket was bronze and steel with a silver trim, and covered in white lace. Standing over it was a silver candelabrum.

Perri's fortunes sank, rose and sank after Bessie's death. For a time he worked with another Jewish woman, the handsome, silver-haired Annie Newman, who also became his constant companion, but with Bessie's death he seems to have become more vulnerable. In March 1938 there was an attempt to dynamite his home on Bay Street South. He was out at the time. In December he was in his car outside 499 Hughson Street North when he turned on the ignition to get his cigar-lighter working. Although power lines were knocked out in the subsequent explosion he was not even hurt. He later claimed insurance for his destroyed car.

In May 1940 a prosecution against Perri and Annie Newman alleging they had corrupted customs officials in Windsor collapsed when witnesses disappeared. The next month, however, Perri was less fortunate. Mussolini declared war on England and Perri, described as "an important member of the Fascio who are naturalized and whose internment is recommended," was interned as an enemy alien.

Annie Newman, like her predecessor twice the man Perri was, continued the good work running a high-grading scam with gold stolen from the mines at Kirkland Lake in Northern Ontario and smuggled across the border to Buffalo and New York. By the time arrests were made in October 1941 it was alleged she and her co-conspirators had smuggled over $850,000 of gold. In June 1943 she was sentenced to three years' imprisonment with an additional year if she did not pay a fine of $5,000. She did.

By now the balance of power had shifted away from the independent dealers such as Perri into more structured but less autonomous groups who were subservient to Mafia families in the United States. The new Calabrian bosses in Ontario, Anthony "Tony" Sylvestro, Cologero Bordonaro aka Charles

Bardinaro, and Santo Scibetta, collectively known as the Three Dons, effectively reported to Buffalo's Magaddino crime family run by Stefano Magaddino, who looked like Nikita Khrushchev and was said to be just as ruthless. Known as The Undertaker because he ran a funeral parlour, he is one of a number who have been credited with inventing the double-coffin burial in which a victim is placed under the body of a genuine customer.

Scibetta was thought to have been a made member of the family before he arrived in Hamilton to join his brother Joseph, an old-time Black Hander. He, along with Bordonaro, was thought to have been behind extortion-related bombings in the 1920s. Sylvestro went to Guelph where he ran a high-grading racket. In the 1940s and 1950s he became one of Magaddino's biggest heroin distributors.

In 1943, when Italy left the Axis alliance with Germany, detainees were released and in October that year Perri began to plan a campaign to regain his territory lost to the Magaddino family. In the meantime he worked as a doorman at the Metro Theatre on Bloor Street. It was owned by Annie Newman who had paid $15,000 for it and the position was purely a nominal one to cover the terms of his licence. For the moment he lived with Annie's sister Leah in what was then the largely rural West Hill, Toronto. Annie herself was still in jail serving her sentence.

It seems that on 20 April 1944 he went to stay with his cousin, Joe Serge, in Murray Street, East Hamilton. According to Serge, three days later at around eleven in the morning, Perri complained of a headache and said he was going out for a walk. He left wearing a blue-striped suit, black oxford shoes, a light-brown overcoat and the gangster's obligatory light-brown fedora. And vanished. His cousin reported him missing that evening but his body was never discovered. Almost certainly he was murdered and possibly he was fitted with cement shoes and thrown into Hamilton harbour.

Suspicion fell on his one-time lieutenant, Antonio "Tony" Papalia, but no charges were ever brought. Another version of Perri's disappearance is that he took himself off to Cuba and another that he went to Mexico. Yet another is that he went to live in upstate New York. Indeed, the crime authority Antonio Nicaso claimed he had seen a letter dated 10 June 1949 from Perri to Joe Serge saying he was alive and well. However, the RCMP had a rather more sanguine attitude, saying in 1954, "We won't find his body until the Bay dries up." A long-running joke was that a man was so old he could remember when the water was so clear he could see Perri's body. If, which is doubtful, Perri did live on, he certainly never sent for Annie Newman when she was released later from prison. She sold her house in Bay Street and married twice before her death in 1974. She was aged eighty-five.

And if the Lord Lucan/JFK survival theory of immortality needs testing, there was a clearout of Perri associates of the time. John Deluca was disembowelled and on 15 January 1949 liquor-runner and high-grader Louis Wernick disappeared. He had dinner with his family and then put on a hat and left. His wife did not report him missing for eight days because she was afraid "what the gang downtown might do to the children". His body was found in a snowbank in Islington on 29 January. Wernick had been buying drugs from Frank Lojacono who had represented the same group that supplied the Perris, and it was thought he had been killed by what was described as the "Buffalo Dope Syndicate". Other Perri associates Paul Doneff and Giovanni (John) Durso disappeared about the same time.

Perri may have been the most significant Canadian mob figure of his time but when Al Capone was asked if he knew Perri he is said to have replied, "I don't even know what street Canada is on."

As for Stefano Magaddino and the Buffalo mob, they took Tony Papalia into their organization. Papalia's son Johnny "Pops", who was heavily involved in the heroin trade, maintained something of a stranglehold on Hamilton crime until 31 May 1997 when he was shot dead outside his home by hitman Ken Murdock who claimed he had been paid a mere $2,000 and forty grams of cocaine for his efforts.

7

The Purples

It was Prohibition that turned organized crime into a nationwide operation and to protect their interests the leaders employed two killing machines to eliminate the opposition across the United States. First came the Purple Gang from Detroit followed a little later by Murder Inc. As the years have gone by there has been a tendency to downgrade the Purples but their activities should in no way be underestimated.

Jazz clarinettist Mezz Mezzrow, who played in Detroit during Prohibition, recalled them: "The Purple Gang was a lot of hard guys, so tough they made Capone's playmates look like a kindergarten class, and Detroit's snooty set used to feel it was really living to talk to them hoodlums without getting their ounce-brains blown out."

The nucleus of the gang came from the Hasting Street neighbourhood known as Paradise Valley in Detroit's Lower East Side and many attended the Old Bishop School on Winder Street. There is considerable dispute as to how the Purples acquired their name. A Detroit Divisional Detective Inspector, Henry Garvin, claimed to have named them himself, saying it came from the nickname of an early leader, Sammy Cohen, known as "Sammy Purple". Other suggestions were: that the members wore purple swimsuits; that when Eddie Fletcher, a run-of-the-mill featherweight from New York arrived in Detroit to join them, he boxed wearing a purple jersey at the

Fairview Athletic Club or that he wore purple shorts; and, the most popular, that someone described them as not being quite straight, rather like bad meat, "They're a bit purple."

Whatever the origin of their name they were the amalgamation of two sets of second-generation Jewish immigrants from Detroit's East Side. The first was the Oakland Sugar House Gang whose leaders, shortly after the First World War, were Harry Fleisher, Henry (Harry) Shorr, who was the financial man, Irving Milberg, Harry Altman, Morris Raider and Phil Raider.

The other gang, the Purples, was based on the talents of Sammy Cohen until the Bernstein brothers, Abe, Isidore and Ray, took over control from him. By 1923 they had been joined by Eddie Fletcher, Abe Axler and a number of dissatisfied members of Dinty Colbeck's Egan's Rats, the St Louis-based operation that was at the time in disarray.

The amalgamation was almost certainly as a result of the predations waged upon the Sugar House Gang at the beginning of Prohibition by the Italian mob led initially by Sam Giannola. The Black Handers had operated in Detroit through the first two decades of the century and within the Detroit police there was a Black Hand squad. In the early 1920s the Italians were under the control of Sam Catalonotte who had kept the peace between the various rival Sicilian factions with an iron, if not black, fist until his death. Almost certainly at the time the Sugar House Gang was at war with the Sicilians, something that resulted in the death of Sol Conrad in a drive-by shooting in which Italian Chester Le Mare was spotted behind the curtained windows of the car. Another Sugar House man, Isadore Carter, fled to New York but he was shot to death there. It was probably this above everything else that brought about the amalgamation of the Sugar House Gang with the Purples.

There is disagreement as to who was the actual leader of the Purples. Some say it was the short, slightly built, Ray Bernstein but, more likely, it was his brother, Abe, described as "small and dapper with the soft hands of a woman and a quiet way of speaking".

The brightest of all the Purples, if only a relatively short-lived member, was undoubtedly Morris "Moe" Dalitz. He was born in Boston to Jewish immigrant parents on 24 December 1899, and the family then moved to Ann Arbor where they owned a laundry.

Dalitz went to Central High School, Detroit, where he lodged with relatives. He was regarded as academically poor and did not complete his eleventh grade. Together with his elder brother, Louis, known because of his looks as The Chinaman, they opened their own laundry, Detroit Supply Systems in 1920. In 1924, at the height of the Cleaners and Dyers War in Detroit, it became a limited company, finally becoming Michigan Modern Overall Cleaners. For a time he was a member of the Little Jewish Navy, bootleggers who ferried alcohol from Canada, and then more or less drifted into the Purples.

Later when Dalitz went to Cleveland he built up a similar empire. A man with great foresight, during Prohibition when the Canadian authorities tightened controls and so slowed the flow of bootleg liquor down the Detroit river, he had the wit to ship the imports to Galveston, Texas, and then send them by rail to Cleveland. He was also keen to reverse the trend that had excluded Jewish and Italian gangsters from working together. When he joined the Army in 1942 he listed his religion as "Preferably Jewish".

It is not exactly clear why Dalitz left the Purple Gang. One suggestion is that they were becoming too violent, a second that he had married and needed a quieter life. A third is that he was never an original Purple and once he lost the battle for the gang's leadership he left Michigan. It is also possible he had fallen foul of the Italians, now led by Joseph Zerilli. At the Senate Hearings on Organized Crime in 1951, Senator

Estes Kefauver asked Dalitz about his wealth: "Now, to get your investments started off, you did get yourself a pretty good little nest egg out of rum running, didn't you?"

"Well, I didn't inherit any money, Senator," was his reply.

On his move to Cleveland he made up the collection of four financially astute Jewish entrepreneurs known as the Cleveland Syndicate which consisted of Dalitz, Morris Kleinman, Lou Rothkopf and Samuel Tucker, and which lasted until the death of Rothkopf in 1956.

As the years passed the activities of the Purples expanded from shoplifting and extortion through bootlegging to include kidnapping, fraud, drug dealing and contract killing. They were by no means the most scrupulous of contractors, however, and their employers regularly found themselves having paid for unfinished business and, because of the power of the gang, unable to do anything about it.

The first of their best-known contract killings occurred in 1927 when local gamblers employed them to dispose of members of the re-formed Egan's Rats who were muscling in on local interests. There had been a number of kidnappings including in March 1926 that of Meyer "Fish" Bloomfield, a croupier at the Grand River Athletic Club, which was owned by Charles T. "Doc" Brady. Clearly the Purples were involved but on which side is more obscure. There is no doubt, however, that in March 1927 Eddie Fletcher and Abe Axler rented a suite at 106 East Alexandrine Avenue and invited over Frank Wright, Reuben Cohen and Joseph Bloom for what were said to be peace negotiations.

Wright was possibly the principal target. He was said to have killed Johnny Reid, a friend of Abe Bernstein, on 27 December 1926. At the time he was wanted for a $100,000 diamond robbery in Chicago in the previous May and it was thought he had been involved in the killing of Adolph E. Fisher, a diamond merchant. He was a known close associate of Eugene "Red" McLaughlin, who was later murdered in June 1930.

Wright, Cohen and Bloom were found machine-gunned to death just outside the doors of the rented apartment. Fred "Killer" Burke, a defecting Rat, was arrested along with Axler and Fletcher.

By 1927 the Purples were thought to be between forty- and fifty-strong and were in almost sole control of the 25,000 drinking clubs known as blind pigs – 150 of them in one block – throughout the city. On 15 June, Axler undertook a contract on the St Louis gunman, Milford Jones, who had imprudently sat with his back to the door of the Stork Club at 47 Rowena Street. There were no witnesses.

On 13 August that year, Axler and Irving Milberg, together with their girlfriends, came into a black-and-tan cabaret at 1708 St Antoine, quarrelled with two black players, Geoffrey Quales and Hobart Harris, and shot them dead. They claimed self-defence and again, in the absence of witnesses to say otherwise, were released without charge.

Even at their height the Purples were not invulnerable. In 1928 they attempted to move into bootlegging in Rochester, New York, and found themselves thwarted by the Staud Brothers, Midge, George, Karl and Ed, who originally came from Cleveland. Ed had been a rustler in Nevada where he had killed a man and had his thumb blown off in a gunfight. According to a report on the abortive Purple invasion, the brothers had thrown two of them from the seventh storey of the Seneca Hotel and the invaders had retreated in some disarray.

As for their women, their taste ran to teenage showgirls, beautiful and quotable. "The wops finally got him," lamented one of them of a former boyfriend. On the other hand beauty was not always an essential requirement. One member of the organization, known as Tiny Sam because he weighed 300 pounds, had a sister who seems to have acted as book-keeper for the organization and "made Bonnie Parker look like a girl scout. She was a Polish Jew. She wore a butch haircut and if anyone got out of line she could handle it".

Apart from their other activities the Purples also took an interest in the film industry, hijacking films of prize-fights and ordering local cinemas to rent them. In 1928 members were cleared by the police of the kidnapping of Max Rubin of the Motion Picture Operators Union. Union members implored J. Edgar Hoover to have his FBI intervene but he did nothing. Nor were the Purples averse to recruiting specialized talent to work for them and Morris "Red" Rudensky, the celebrated safe-breaker, fondly remembered working for them at fees ranging from $5,000 to $15,000 depending on the quality of the job.

They were also involved in what was known as the Cleaners and Dyers War, which lasted for two years in the mid-1920s. Even without the intervention of the Purples the almost wholly Jewish-owned garment-cleaning industry was in turmoil and Al Capone apparently sent an envoy, Harry Abrams, from Chicago to try to sort out the warring parties. He negotiated a settlement between Charles Jacoby of Jacoby's Cleaners and Dyers and Frank X. Martel, the president of the Detroit Federation of Labour.

It did not last long and Jacoby turned to his brother-in-law, Abe Bernstein, for a more permanent solution. The war resulted in the deaths of Sam Polakoff, the president of the Union Cleaners & Dyers, and of a cleaner, Sam Sigman, whose premises were bombed. The Purples' interest in the affair ended with the arrest of a number of members including the Bernsteins, Irving Shapiro, Irving Milberg, Harry Keywell and Eddie Fletcher along with Jacoby, and charges of conspiracy to extort $12,000 at $1,000 a week over a three-month period. The defence was that it was all the fault of Martel, described in a closing speech as "ruler of stench bombers, window breakers and perjurers who has duped the prosecutor's office". There may have been something in this. One of his men was Louis Green who sadly had been killed when he ran into the path of a car as he was fleeing from the stench-bombing of a barber's shop. There may also have been some help from members of the Purples not under arrest as the ten were triumphantly acquitted. Jacoby announced he was going to sue for $1 million for pain and suffering and for damage to his business. The Purples must have thought enough was enough. There is no further record of their interest in that particular industry.

On 28 October 1929, Ziggie Selbin was shot to death in a shebeen on 12th Street. One of the less attractive of the Purples, Selbin specialized in robbing the customers of blind pigs of their wallets and jewellery. On one occasion, when he took a fancy to a ring that his victim refused to hand over, he cut off the man's finger to take it. Eventually his activities interfered with the Polish Hamtramck mob who were seeking an alliance with the Purple Gang. Part of the price of the merger of interests was the death of Selbin who was caught without his gun in a doorway on Detroit's west side.

Hamtramck, situated wholly within the boundaries of Detroit, was then the seventh largest city in Michigan. Over 50 per cent of its population was Polish. The city was controlled by regulating vice rather than prohibiting it. In 1934 the chief of police was found dead drunk on the street, unable to walk. The following year the city's first mayor, Peter Jezewski, along with thirty-one other defendants, was indicted on bootlegging charges and sentenced to two years' imprisonment.

Purples could be hired out as contract killers and there is little doubt that members were actively involved in the St Valentine's Day Massacre of the Bugsy Moran mob in Chicago in 1929. Quite apart from the fact that they were contract killers, they had a personal interest. Their willingness to assist came from the hijacking by Moran's men of a shipment of the Purples' "Old Log Cabin Whiskey".

Around 10.30 on the morning of 14 February a fake Chicago police car drew up outside Moran's headquarters at the SMC Cartage Company at 2122 North Clark Street. Fred Burke and another Purple, Fred Goetz, dressed as police officers, got out and walked inside. They lined up and shot and killed six members of the Moran Gang as well as a Dr Rheinhardt Schwimmer who had stopped by for a game of cards. Moran survived because when he arrived at his headquarters, he saw the police car. His antennae twitched and he waited in a café until it was all over. Apart from Burke and Goetz, three other Purples, George Lewis and Phil and Harry Keywell, were identified from photographs but never charged.

By the end of the 1920s the gang was quite clearly under siege, both internally and externally, from the Italian criminal element in Detroit, which was growing progressively stronger. The great Collingwood Massacre of 1931 would soon take out three key players. The years from 1929 to 1937 show the terminal decline of the Purples.

On 24 July 1929 Abe Axler, Irving Milberg, Harry Sutton and Eddie Fletcher each received twenty-two months and $5,000 fines for liquor offences. Three days later the body of twenty-three-year-old Irving Shapiro was found on Taylor Avenue. A $50 bill and his watch had been left on his body but the labels of his suit had been cut out. He had been shot in the back of the head and dumped from a car.

One reason advanced for his killing was that it was feared the police were leaning on him to become an informer. Another is that he wanted an unacceptable increase in his share of the profits. A third was a variation. He had been freelancing and so cutting across the gang's operations. The first may have been correct. There is no doubt the Purples were highly sensitive to outside interest in their activities.

On 15 December 1929 Fred Burke shot and killed a patrolman, Charles Skelly, who was called to a traffic accident in St Joseph, Michigan, where Burke was refusing to pay a farmer $5 for a dented bumper. He was arrested six months later at his father-in-law's farm at Milton, Missouri, where an arsenal of weapons was found. Tests showed they included a gun used in the St Valentine's Day Massacre and also one which had been used to kill the New York mobster Frankie Yale in July 1928, as well as his sidekick Frank Marlow in Queens a year later. Burke may have been fortunate. He was sent for trial in Michigan where circuit judge Charles E. White ruled he had been intoxicated at the time he shot Skelly and so lacked the premeditation that would have turned the killing into a capital offence. He was sentenced to life and died in the state prison in Marquette on 10 July 1940.

Fred Goetz went on to work with the so-called Ma Barker Gang, acting as the go-between in the kidnapping of millionaire Edward G. Bremer. He was killed on 20 March 1934 in a drive-by shooting outside the Minerva restaurant in Cicero, Illinois. As is often the case there are rival theories of who had him killed. Suggestions include the Barkers who feared he knew too much, Capone gunmen who believed he would tell who was with him in the Chicago massacre and the Bugsy Moran Gang seeking revenge.

Joe "Little Joey" Bernstein had been in New Orleans in 1927 when Ted Werner, his partner in a roadhouse operation, was shot dead, unfortunately in the apartment they shared. Bernstein was held for several months before being released. Little Joey was nearly killed himself in May 1930 when Harry Kirschbaum, whom he was trying to wean off opium, shot him in the spleen. He retired from the rackets and went into the oil business at which he was a notable success, becoming treasurer of the Garfield Oil Company. He and his brother, Abe, along with Moe Dalitz, give the lie to the story that the Purples were simply strong-arm men, all brawn and no brains. It was clear that the Bernsteins as a family, if not the Purples as a whole, had extensive and nationwide interests, some of which were even legitimate.

In July 1930 Phil Keywell killed a black youth, Arthur Mixon, who he thought was spying on the warehouse and liquor-cutting business he ran at the rear of Jaslove's butchers shop. The boy turned out to be seventeen and he may have been backward. His story to Keywell was that he had been playing with a ball that had run under a door, but his responses were not deemed satisfactory and he was shot. The police charged Keywell and Morris Raider, who was said to have a perfect alibi that he did not use. The first jury disagreed but the second convicted Keywell inside ninety minutes. Raider received twelve to fifteen years with Keywell getting life imprisonment. All the defence witnesses were charged with perjury but only one was tried and he was discharged on the direction of the judge. The first Purple to be convicted of a murder charge, Keywell served thirty-two years, becoming a prison trusty before his release.

Indeed, July 1930 proved to be a particularly hard month for the gangs and the citizenship in general. In an eleven-day spree ten gunmen died. Mayor Charles Bowles commented, "It is just as well to let these gangsters kill each other off, if they are so minded. You have the scientists employ one set of parasites to destroy another. May not that be the plan of Providence in these killings among the bandits?" It was not an attitude that appealed to the voters who two weeks later dismissed him.

One of the deaths that July had been that of the radio commentator Gerald "Jerry" Buckley who was killed in the lobby of the La Salle and the Detroiter Hotel off Woodward and Adelaide. On 22 July 1930 Buckley had voiced his opposition to Bowles whom he accused of being in cahoots with the underworld. The next evening he was shot after receiving a call from an unknown woman. Buckley may not have had spotless hands. In those days it was not uncommon for reporters to have unhealthily close links to crime – Chicago's Jake Lingle's ties to Al Capone is a good example. It was clear that this time the police thought the Italians rather than the Purples had been responsible. Following newspaper headlines of indictments and arrests and grand juries returning true bills (that is, agreeing that there is enough evidence that an accused should be indicted), three Italians were charged but there were no convictions.

The Collingwood Massacre took place on 16 September the next year. The three men who died, Herman "Hymie" Paul, Joseph "Nigger Joe" Lebovitz and Joseph "Izzy" Sutker, were all originally out of Chicago and were part of the bootlegging Little Jewish Navy. They were one-time members and then later rivals of the Purple Gang, who correctly believed they were hijacking shipments of alcohol destined for Chicago. In an apparent effort to sort out the dispute and restore peace, Ray Bernstein invited local bookmaker, Solomon "Sollie" Levine, to take the Little Jewish Navy members to Apartment 21, 1740 Collingwood Avenue. Once the men were in the apartment Bernstein said he was going out to see his bookmaker. In reality, he left to start the getaway car and give the signal for the killings. The sailors were shot to pieces by Irving Milberg, Harry Keywell, aged only eighteen, and Harry Fleisher. To eradicate fingerprints they dropped their guns in a pail of green paint left in the kitchen. Numbers on the guns had already been filed off. They took Levine with them as Bernstein drove away, almost knocking down a young boy. In a matter of minutes they had made two serious errors. The boy gave evidence against them and, worse, they released Levine after a couple of hours. He was promptly arrested and became a believable principal prosecution witness. Keywell and Bernstein were arrested the day of the killings and Milberg was caught four days later. Of Fleisher there was no sign.

On 17 November 1931 the three Purples were found guilty and were sentenced to life imprisonment. Judge Donald Van Zile said: "The crime which you have committed was one of the most sensational that had been committed in Detroit for many years. It was, as has been said, a massacre." Van Zile had been prepared to send Keywell to a less severe prison than the others but he opted not to be separated.

Naturally newspaper reporters were there to watch them go to prison together. They duly recorded that the men played pinochle, munched corned beef sandwiches and that Bernstein had given the man who brought them a $5 tip. They were also able to record the following tough-guy conversation:

Keywell: I suppose it will be tough at first.
Bernstein: Yeh. Like everything else you have to get settled and organized. It will be new and strange at first, but we'll get organized. We always did.
Keywell: Sure, we will.

Fleisher was later charged but not convicted. The star witness, Levine, had now disappeared, some said to France with his passage paid by the police.

It was their ruthless and ill-thought-out behaviour in the massacre of 1931 which seriously depleted the Purples, who were already under heavy siege from Italian interests.

In November 1933 Eddie Fletcher and the fearsome Abe Axler were found dead in the back seat of Axler's car in Oakland County. Whoever shot them arranged the bodies so it appeared they had been holding hands. Both had been shot a dozen times in the face. Fletcher was wearing his Purple shirt and there were no signs of a struggle. The theory was that Fletcher was shot by the driver who turned around to fire and Axler was killed by the man sitting next to him in the back seat. Their hands had been linked as a gesture of contempt for the pair who were referred to as "the Siamese Twins". They had probably known they were marked men for some time before their execution. One suggestion was that Axler had defaulted on a $30,000 contract. Another was that Axler and Fletcher had been trying to take over the gang and had double-crossed the Bernstein Brothers, Harry Millman and Harry Fleisher. Their actual killer was thought to have been Millman.

In 1936 Fleisher, who had started life as a driver for the Old Sugar House, eventually went down along with his brother Sam. He received eight years for liquor violations, and in 1944 he was convicted of armed robbery of an Oakland County gambling joint. This time he received a sentence of twenty-five to fifty years and was paroled in 1965 at the age of sixty-two.

Along the way Fleisher was suspected of a number of crimes including the murder of the financier of the Purples, Harry Shorr, who simply disappeared one day in December 1935. His body was never found but his bloodstains were found in the back of Fleisher's car and they had been seen together in a delicatessen earlier in the evening. Fleisher had an unbreakable alibi.

The last serious player of the Purples to be killed was Harry Millman who was gunned down in the early hours of 25 November 1937 in Boesky's, a restaurant cum deli on Hazelwood and 12th. He had earlier survived a bomb attack. The bomb had been placed in his car, triggered to explode when the accelerator was pressed. Unfortunately a car valet, Willie Holmes, had started the car that day. Millman's eventual killers were said to be Harry "Pittsburgh Phil" Strauss and Happy Maione of Anastasia's Murder Inc., but they were never charged. A colleague describing Millman's death put it poignantly:

> It was very simple. He was a big handsome Jewish guy. God, he was a good-looking bastard, big and handsome and well dressed and he was knocking off whorehouses and he didn't know that the whorehouses at that period were protected by the Dago Mob ... I forget the name but there was a very fancy blind pig on 12th Street and he was at the bar having a good time with some people and in walked the Dagos and shot the shit out of him.

They also "shot the shit" out of five innocent bystanders.

Finally, Purple Sidney Markman was electrocuted in New York for the robbery and murder of a Brooklyn merchant,

Isidore Frank, in 1938. Along with David Goldberg he had shot Frank dead in front of his home at 733 Alabama Avenue. Markman was later arrested in Detroit for possession of a machine-gun and was linked to Goldberg. He was executed on 18 January 1940.

Despite their loss of power to the Italians, who would rule Detroit's underworld for the next seventy years, the Purples had one last outrage to commit. It was as bold as anything they had ever previously managed. On 11 January 1945 state senator Warren Hooper, who had been due to testify before a grand jury into horserace gambling, was killed after he had left by car from his hotel. A key witness, Hooper had been given indemnity after confessing to receiving a $500 bribe for his vote on former state representative William Green's horseracing bill. Hooper's body was found on a road three miles north of Springpoint. He had been shot in the head, almost certainly by the unknown driver, who it was said had been released from prison that morning to undertake the contract. The man had not been signed out or reported missing and consequently had an unimpeachable alibi.

The story finally came out that in the lead up to the senator's death, several of the inmates of Jackson, including Ray Bernstein and Harry Keywell, were offered $15,000 to kill Hooper. The deal was struck in the office of the Deputy Warden D. C. Petit and the men were provided with $10,000 as an advance, guns, street clothes and false licence plates. The men left the prison in Petit's car and when Hooper drove past they forced his car to the side of the road and Ray Bernstein shot him. Louis Brown, the inmate who finally told the story, said that they had bragged about the killing afterwards.

On 20 April, brothers Harry and Sammy Fleisher and Detroit saloon operator Mike Selik, all former Purples Gang members, Selik's wife, Naomi, and Pete Mahoney of Detroit were taken into custody for questioning in Hooper's murder. Naomi Selik was soon released.

On 2 May the men were charged with conspiring to kill Hooper. The star witness at their arraignment was Sam Abramowitz, a career criminal who was granted immunity for his testimony that he was one of several people who had been hired at different times by these men to kill Hooper. The offers had been made by Mike Selik, then in prison, but allowed out by Deputy Warden Petit to spend his evenings in Larry "O'Larry" Pollack's bar while the warden was supplied with prostitutes paid for by Selik. The Fleishers, Selik and Mahoney were convicted and sentenced to spend between four and a half and five years in Southern Michigan Prison.

They appealed to the Michigan Supreme Court, which upheld the sentences of the Fleishers and Selik but set aside the conviction of Mahoney. Selik and Harry Fleisher both jumped their bail and remained at large for several years. Fleisher lived in Florida, working as a salesman, until he was arrested sunbathing on Pompano Beach in 1950. The next year, Selik, who had taken the name Green, was arrested in New York for a suspected burglary. No one was arrested for pulling the trigger or bankrolling the hit, and Hooper's murder remains unsolved. However, the gambling investigation snowballed after Hooper's death with sixty-two convictions, including a former lieutenant governor, twenty-three state legislators and more than thirty lobbyists, police and court officials.

Hooper was the third grand jury witness to die under unusual circumstances. State Senator Earl Munshaw was found dead in his garage with the motor of his car running two days after he testified. Harvey Bylenga of Grand Rapids, an official of the Star Transportation Co., which was also under grand jury investigation, was killed when his car was struck by a train in Grand Rapids.

Attorney General John R. Dethmers, who was investigating Southern Michigan Prison at the time of Hooper's murder, later claimed that a ring of big-time convicts virtually had their own way in the prison and came and went almost at will. Warden Harry Jackson and other prison officials were eventually ousted for corruption.

Ray Bernstein, one of the three convicted of the Collingwood Massacre, by then paralysed and in a wheelchair, was released on 16 January 1964. One of the grounds of his application for parole had been that he had tried to educate other prisoners. Another of the grounds was that he had helped them financially, a clear indication that after thirty-four years there was still some Purple money somewhere. He died two years later. His pastime in prison had been breeding and training canaries that he sent out to his friends. Milberg had died in prison in 1938 and Keywell, who had an exemplary record whilst inside, was not released until 1965. There had been efforts throughout the 1960s to obtain his release. The missing Levine had been located in Kansas City and had sworn an affidavit contradicting his earlier indictment of the Purples. Now, he said, he hadn't even been at the scene of the killing. He was not believed.

Louis Fleisher, Harry's brother, was one of the last to go. He had been wanted for arson and robbery for a year when, in 1938, he was seen driving in downtown Detroit. In the ensuing chase his wife, Nellie, threw a pistol away. It was merely a gesture. Back at his flat at Highland and Second Avenue the police found an arsenal of machine-guns. He received thirty years and was paroled in 1957. Sadly, he was a classic example of the maxim that long sentences do not prevent recidivism. The next year he was found on the roof of Dorsey Cleaners at 1348 East Seven Mile Road. A hole had been bored in the roof and a can of gasoline was next to him. His parole was revoked and he received a further five years. He died following a heart attack in prison on 3 April 1964. He had been regarded as the joker of the Purples. One of his more entertaining stunts had been to drive after friends pretending he was going to knock them down.

By the time of Hooper's death Italian interests had absolute control of major crime in Detroit. But, with their consent, Abe

Bernstein survived as a bookmaker. He lived in a suite in the Book-Cadillac Hotel, dying there on 8 March 1968 at the age of seventy-six. The Purples faded away into obscurity and perhaps now are best remembered for the line "the whole of the rhythm section was the Purple Gang" in Elvis Presley's "Jailhouse Rock".

As for Moe Dalitz, he went on to become second only to Meyer Lansky as the Mafia financial wizard, taking over the development of Las Vegas on their behalf after the death of Bugsy Siegel.

8

Gang Wars of the 1920s and 1930s

In the UK, during the fifteen months from November 1925, four men in two separate cases in Sheffield and Cardiff were hanged for the murder of victims of protection gangs. The Sheffield killing related to a tossing ring at Sky Edge which overlooked a slum area of the city. The Cardiff killing arose from the battle to control bookmakers at Monmouth horse races.

Before the First World War the Sky Edge ring, as it was known, attracted heavy gamblers from all over south Yorkshire. The tossing ring opened around 10.30 a.m. and continued until dusk, and individual bets could be as large as £50 at a time. The game developed from the children's game of pitch and toss in which the winner was the one who pitched a coin nearest a small piece of crockery or a designated coin. He, for no women played, was then entitled to toss all the loser's coins and keep those which landed heads. A tossing ring had many local variations but in principle three coins were tossed in the air either manually or off a bat and bets were placed on how many would fall either heads or tails. In Australia the game, played with only two coins, is known as "two-up". For the organizer it was an extremely lucrative business.

Sheffield has always had its share of gangs. In the 1840s men from the city joined what was known as the Northern Mob – racecourse bullies who also operated at cock prizefights. By the 1860s there were two local gangs, the Gutterpercha Mob and their rivals led by Kingy Broadhead. During the First World War there were the Gas Tank Gang of Neepsend and the Red Silk and White Silk gangs who helpfully wore coloured scarves to denote their allegiances. The Sky Edge ring, which had opened before the war, was operated by "Snaps" Jackson who also worked as a tic-tac man on the racecourses. When Jackson joined the Army in 1916 his brothers took over the ring, but by the end of the war control was in the hands of another local bookmaker, William Cowan. In the pitching game, might was right and after the war the Mooney Gang assumed control.

Led by George Mooney, who by the time he was in his late twenties had acquired a number of convictions for theft and violence, the gang specialized in extorting money from local shopkeepers and publicans. George Mooney had also been in the war, much of it spent on the run as a deserter from the York and Lancaster Regiment.

When he took over from Cowan the money was pouring into the ring; wages were good and miners were still being paid so-called Sankey money of an additional ten shillings a day (the Sankey Commission of 1919 had reported that miners' wages should be raised, following the threat of major strikes). As there was so much money being taken, there were two rings operating side by side. Mooney had to employ a dozen tollers who for £2 a day collected the ring's percentage of the bets, and numbers of touts and lookouts known as pikers. By 1920 Mooney had control of a very substantial enterprise whose men were drawn from the West Bar and Park districts of Sheffield and who included the devious Sam Garvin. They also demanded protection money from bookmakers and worked a series of scams at the races and on the trains taking the bookmakers and the public to the course. These included the Three Card Trick or Find the Lady as well as the now almost forgotten Crown and Anchor and "E and O", an early form of roulette. Even run honestly, which was seldom, there was a house percentage of 5 per cent.

It could not last and when the Sankey allowance was withdrawn miners lost over half their income. Mooney no longer needed so many helpmates and decided to dispense with the services of Garvin and others from the Park. Those who remained naturally included his brother John as well as Peter Winsey, Frank Kidnew and Albert Foster. Garvin was by no means pleased, particularly since Sky Edge was on his doorstep. Three of his men, including the ex-boxer Sandy Barlow, toured the pubs collecting a group who were willing to fight for control of the ring. Mooney was ousted.

It was not something that could be left to lie. On 23 April 1923 Park man William Furniss was attacked in his bed and beaten unconscious with pokers by Kidnew and Foster. A month later Kidnew was badly slashed. It was the beginning of a war that would continue on and off for the next five years.

The next outbreak of violence, which involved the police, was on 16 June 1923 when Park members stormed Mooney's house in Corporation Street. When the police arrived a Park man, George Wheywell (known as Ganner because he was always "ganner do this or do that"), was lying in the gutter with gun wounds to his arm and shoulder. The windows of the Mooney house had been broken and there were bullet holes in the walls. Inside, the police found a terrified Mooney and his wife along with a collection of guns and various "life preservers", which were often leather-weighted coshes but could be heavy pieces of wood studded with nails. When the Mooney brothers and their men appeared in court on a variety of charges they asked to be remanded in custody. One who did not, Tommy Rippon, was released on bail and was promptly chased by the Park team until he found sanctuary in the Central Police Office. The Park Gang, including Wheywell, who had not been that badly injured when he was shot, followed Rippon into the police office and in turn they were arrested. Possibly the Sheffield Gang Wars could have been halted there and then if the local magistrates had been stronger. Instead, modest fines were imposed on both teams and they were bound over to be on good behaviour in each case, something not worth the paper on which it was written.

To celebrate Christmas that year, the Park Gang, led by Sam Garvin, stormed Mooney's home once more. "We come to wish your father a merry Christmas," they told his terrified daughter. A trifle ignobly, Mooney saved himself by hiding in a cupboard. Soon after, he left the area, not returning until 1925. The Mooney Gang was effectively broken but there was another pre-Christmas visit in 1924 when the gang attacked former Mooney man, the attack-prone Tommy Rippon. A bullet was fired through the window and a visitor was beaten with stool legs. Five Park members were arrested and when asked what it was all about, one replied, "Old broth being warmed up."

There were reprisals the next year when the Mooney Gang was re-formed albeit without Mooney himself. It was led by George Newbould who was establishing other betting rings in the area. The Park men were not to be intimidated and on 1 March, John Towler and two others staged a home invasion at Newbould's house in Edward Street. Now, Newbould recruited Tom Armstrong, a hardman from Birmingham's Brummagem Boys. In the meantime Towler received four months but the wheels of justice ground too slowly for the Mooney Gang's liking and, to show their mettle, on 2 March they beat Park man George Butler with an iron bar outside the Edmund Road Drill Hall. He was unconscious for ten days and although witnesses were reluctant to give evidence against him this time Albert Foster was convicted and sentenced to eighteen months with hard labour.

On 28 April 1925, the day Sheffield United brought home the FA Cup after beating Cardiff City, a former boxer William Plommer, a man with neither convictions nor affiliations to either gang, unwisely intervened in a fight between Wilfred Fowler, a Garvin man, and Trimmer Welsh over an insult to a barmaid. The next night Garvin wound up his men and they went looking for Plommer. Outside his house the unarmed Plommer offered to fight them in turn. For his pains he was knocked down and while on the ground was stabbed with a sharp object. He died within minutes of being taken to hospital.

Sam Garvin, the man who did so much to incite the attack, had already left the scene. That night he and three others attacked a member of the Rippon family, Harry, outside the Bull and Oak public house in the Wicker, north of the city centre, hitting him with a cosh and cutting him with a razor. It was an ideal alibi for the murder charge that would follow Plommer's death.

A week after the murder the Chief Constable, Lt Colonel John, put together a handpicked squad of men known as the Flying Squad; it consisted of a sergeant and three constables whose instruction was to break up the gangs. No one would ask too many questions as to how they accomplished it. In particular Walter Loxley, a giant of a man who it was said could hold ten tennis balls in either hand, was particularly feared by gang-members. When Ganner Wheywell claimed three of the squad had beaten him for refusing to leave the Red House in Solly Street, the charges were dismissed and it was he who received three months hard labour. On another occasion when the defendant appeared swathed in bandages it was accepted by the magistrates that he had fallen down some stairs. His defending solicitor ironically suggested his client should have been charged with "attempted suicide".

On 28 July 1925 Sam Garvin was one of ten men who appeared at Leeds Assizes to face an indictment charging them with Plommer's death. Four days later only two brothers, twenty-three-year-old Wilfred Fowler and twenty-five-year-old Lawrence, were found guilty of murder. Three men were convicted of manslaughter: Amos Stewart and George Wills, who received ten years, and Stanley Harker, who picked up seven. The remaining five men, including Garvin, were acquitted. The Fowler brothers were sentenced to death. The next day Garvin was sentenced to twenty-one months for his attack on Harry Rippon. On the same day Mooney quarrelled with William Cowan on the train from the Worksop pony races back to Sheffield, breaking three of his ribs and biting off part of an ear. In turn, he received nine months.

On his release from his ten-year sentence Amos Stewart was said to have been a broken man. On their release Garvin and Mooney returned to Sheffield where in 1927 Mooney had one final fight with the Flying Squad, when he received a beating followed by two months imprisonment, after which he retired into respectable betting, under the name George Barratt, on northern racecourses. Garvin carried on a double life as a career criminal and the bookmaker "Captain Mee" both on racecourses and at Owlerton greyhound stadium until his death in the 1950s.

The Fowler brothers had been convicted on identification evidence by witnesses who said they had seen one or both of them with something which looked like a dagger or a short bayonet – the actual weapon was never found. Their applications for leave to appeal were turned down and an appeal for a reprieve was also rejected by William Joynson-Hicks, the Home Secretary. On the eve of Wilfred Fowler's execution on 3 September 1925 he wrote a letter accepting full responsibility and exonerating his brother but the Home Secretary would have none of it. They were hanged at Leeds prison on consecutive days with Lawrence Fowler still claiming he was innocent. They could have easily been hanged together, because Wilfred Fowler was hanged with Alfred Bostock, a married man who in May that year killed his girlfriend Elizabeth Sherrat when she told him she was expecting his child. One reason the Home Secretary may not have been disposed to allowing the brothers even this shaft of clemency was that in the previous week there had been gang-fights on northern racecourses from Haydock, near Manchester, through Ripon, Catterick and Thirsk up to Newcastle.

In 1926 Percy Sillitoe was appointed Chief Constable of Sheffield police by the Watch Committee in controversial circumstances. Sillitoe added further members to the Flying Squad and it was he who garnered the credit for breaking up the gangs when, after repeated raids and arrests, they faded away in 1928. For Sillitoe it was a stepping stone to becoming Chief Constable of Glasgow and ultimately his position as Director General of MI5.

On 29 September 1927 the former welterweight boxer turned bookmaker Dai Lewis, who ran a protection racket at the races, had his throat cut outside the Blue Anchor as he walked along St Mary Street in Cardiff's Butetown, better known as Tiger Bay. The street was one of the worst in the city of the time. In the immediate vicinity there were said to be forty-two cafés, a dozen pubs and sundry brothels.

Lewis, a lone operator, was strictly small-time compared with his rivals, the Rowlands brothers. John Rowlands, known as "Tich", and Edward worked with Danny Driscoll, the eldest of a family of twelve running racecourse protection rackets, forcing bookmakers to buy chalk from them and to use their sponges to wipe the odds off their boards. It may have only produced a few shillings a bookmaker per race but it added up to such an extent that in the 1920s Darby Sabini, the leader of a London-based gang, was said to be taking home, if not earning, £30,000 a year from this type of racket.

The day before his death Lewis had been warned that the Rowlands were looking for him and instead of going home after Monmouth races he stayed the night in what was euphemistically called a hotel in St Mary Street. In the evening he returned to the Blue Anchor where he drank all night, ignoring the Rowlands, Driscoll and their mates, John Hughes and William "Hong Kong" Price.

After closing time the men waited for Lewis to leave the pub, and then John Rowlands attacked him as the others stood around. The wound to his throat was seven and a quarter inches long and his windpipe was severed. Prostitutes in the street tore off their petticoats in an effort to stem the bleeding before he was taken to the Royal Infirmary hospital where the police were waiting to interview him.

While the police were waiting to speak to Lewis there were two calls to the hospital asking after the health of Lewis. The second was traced to the Colonial Club in Custom House Street where they found all five men.

By the early hours it was apparent that Lewis was not going to survive and the clerk to the local justices was called in to take what was known as a dying declaration that could be used in evidence. If the police thought he was going to cooperate they were to be sadly disappointed. Edward Rowlands and Driscoll were brought to the bedside to be identified but all Lewis had to say was, "I do not know how I have been injured. I do not remember how it happened. There was no quarrel or fight. Nobody did any harm to me, I did not see anyone use a knife." He said Eddie Rowlands had not been involved, adding, "We've been the best of friends." To Driscoll he said, "You had nothing to do with it either. We were talking and laughing together. My dear old pal." Lewis handed his wife £3 and five shillings, which he had left from his days at the races – the rough equivalent of two weeks wages for a labourer – and died. His funeral was attended by crowds estimated to be up to 25,000.

A week after the funeral John Rowlands told the police it was he who had cut Lewis's throat. The boxer had, he said, attacked him and in the struggle as he tried to get hold of the knife Lewis had been cut. Driscoll and Eddie Rowlands both said they had seen the fight but had taken no part and indeed had made off not wishing to be blamed for it. All five men were charged. John Hughes was found to have no case to answer and the others were committed to Glamorgan Assizes.

The trial began on 29 November with Lord Halsbury appearing for the Crown. There had been a thirty-six-hour queue to get into the public gallery and those who managed to get in were not disappointed to hear a flamboyant opening: "This was murder as cruel and beastly as you can possibly imagine, premeditated and carried out – I might almost say flaunted – in Cardiff's main street."

In fact, the evidence was muddled and contradictory. Some witnesses said John Rowlands had the knife as he approached Lewis but a police officer said that Driscoll had been holding Lewis when Edward Rowlands hit him. Driscoll called a patently false alibi that cannot have helped any of them. The jury was out only an hour before they convicted the Rowlands brothers and Driscoll. Hong Kong Price was acquitted.

Money was raised for an appeal principally on the grounds that Halsbury's opening speech had been inflammatory and had no evidence to support it. Halsbury defended himself saying he was touched that they thought a twelve-minute opening was so influential at the end of a four-day trial. A Harley Street doctor broke his holiday in France to say he thought Lewis had died from a heart attack. Three doctors who had been at the inquest agreed with him. But the convicted men were never likely to get any help from a court presided over by the hanging judge Mr Justice Avory. On the way to the Court of Appeal John Rowlands had gone berserk and was committed to Broadmoor. The court pointed out it was not concerned with his condition at the time of the appeal but at the time of the killing.

Now the efforts began to save the men. Eight members of the jury petitioned T. P. O'Connor, the Father of the House of Commons, saying that they were now worried about their decision. O'Connor went to see the Home Secretary, Sir Austen Chamberlain, but he was turned down with the words, "No regard can be paid to expressions of opinion by individual members of a jury by which a prisoner has been convicted." A Driscoll Reprieve Committee collected over 200,000 signatures.

In the condemned cell Edward Rowlands told his family, "I have told the truth all through. Don't forget me at eight o'clock tomorrow. They can break my neck but they can't break my heart." But he cracked and was taken to the gallows semi-conscious when the men were hanged together on 27 January 1928. In contrast, Driscoll, who had asked for a bottle of port the night before, was in good spirits. Confronted by the two nooses he asked, "Which one is mine?" His last words were said to have been, "Well. I'm going down for something I never done, but you don't have to pay twice." Outside a crowd of 5,000 sang the "Ave Maria". The police had been prepared for a demonstration and the entrance to the jail had been barricaded.

The case became known as the Hoodoo Murder. John Hughes, who had no case to answer, died within twelve months. One of the prostitutes who gave evidence committed suicide as did a detective in the case. Three other detectives died as young men; one from cancer, the second from tuberculosis and the third from a stomach complaint. The solicitor Harold Lloyd, who had represented Price, was sent to prison for five years after being found guilty of embezzling his client.

The view of some of the police was that if Driscoll had not called the false alibi he might have been acquitted. It is also thought that it was never the intention of Edward Rowlands to kill Lewis, but simply to cut him on the face to show others they should not meddle with the Rowlands Gang.

Four years after the death of Lewis, Percy Sillitoe, the scourge of Sheffield's gangs, was appointed Chief Constable of Glasgow. Born in 1888, the son of a south London wastrel, after an education at St Paul's choir school Sillitoe had served with the British South Africa Police and the Northern Rhodesia Police before returning to England. In 1923 he was appointed

Chief Constable of Chesterfield and then of the East Riding of Yorkshire before moving on to Sheffield and then to Scotland.

Glasgow's long history of gang problems dated back to the Penny Mob, which operated in Townhead and Glasgow's East End in the 1880s. The gang derived its name from the toll it took from local shopkeepers for protection and the fund to which they were obliged to contribute to pay any fines incurred by Penny Mob members. There were at least three other fighting gangs at the time; the Wee Do'e Hill and the Big Do'e Hill, as well as the Drygate Youths. By 1900 the gangs had coalesced into the Young San Toys and the Tim Malloys. After that came the Mealy Boys, the McGlynn Push, the Village Boys and a few years later the Gold Dust Gang. During the First World War there were the Redskins, thought to be over 1,000 strong in their prime and far superior to the local gangs such as the Kelly Boys from Govan and the Baltic Fleet from Baltic Street. Then in the early 1920s there were the Cheeky Forty and the Black Diamonds who could each muster a hundred a side. Personal participation was not deemed necessary to maintain a reputation. In one fight, two hardmen slashed at each other with razors, stopped and went to hospital together to be patched up. The loser, however, continued his quarrel but this time hired a man from the Gorbals to do battle for him. According to former Detective Chief Superintendent Robert Colquhoun, he lost no face by recruiting a champion.

The Beehive Corner Boys led by Peter Williamson, who it seems came from a respectable family, took things up a notch, moving on from being a fighting gang to a team of housebreakers, safebreakers and armed robbers. Williamson's lieutenant was Harry McMenemy who served a term of nine months while taking the rap for Williamson. His leader would more likely have drawn nine years after he and Daniel Cronin had badly beaten a man.

It was, however, in a battle between the Parlour Boys and the Bridgegate Boys, affiliated to the San Toys, that the snub-nosed James Dalziel, known as Razzle Dazzle, died. Dalziel, a Bridgegate Boy, favoured a pickshaft, three pounds in weight and three and a half feet in length, as his weapon of choice. At a time when the police were squeamish about searching women, girl gang-members known as Queens used to bring weapons into the dance halls. Dalziel thought that to dance with them would be considered effeminate and would only dance with boys.

The Bridgegate Boys' rivals, the Parlour Boys had, they believed, proprietorial rights over the Parlour Dance Hall in Celtic Street. They did not pay admission, telling Mrs Stevenson, the cashier, they "knew the boss", but they would always wipe their boots as they went in. On 2 March 1924 the Bedford Boys went to the hall, shortly followed by the Bridgegate Boys who mumbled to Mrs Stevenson that they "knew the boss", but when they failed to wipe their boots she sounded the alarm. It was too late. Before the police arrived fighting had broken out and Dalziel was stabbed in the throat. A youth called Collins was acquitted of the murder but was sentenced to twelve months for affray. Fines imposed on other participants were paid by a levy raised on shopkeepers and the convicted men were immediately elevated to heroic status.

Gang brawls were not necessarily spur-of-the-moment affairs. Rules of battle could be negotiated in advance. When a Queen belonging to a junior gang, the South Side Stickers, was injured in a fight in a cinema by a member of the Calton Entry Gang, emissaries were sent by Abraham Zemil to the Calton leader Frank Kerney to arrange the terms of engagement, which were agreed at five-a-side. Weapons used included a sword and a dagger and, in the ensuring battle, James Tait of the Caltons died. Six youths, including Zemil, were charged with the murder. Unsurprisingly no one could explain quite how Tait came to be stabbed in the back and everyone was acquitted of murder. James McCluskey pleaded guilty to mobbing, rioting and culpable homicide, the Scottish equivalent of manslaughter, and was sentenced to five years. Zemil himself received a year.

That same year the Billy Boys, one of the most enduring Glasgow gangs, were created by William Fullerton, who came from Franklin Street, Bridgeton. He was a fighting man who worked in boxing promoter Tommy Gilmour's club in Olympia Street. Named after the Protestant William IV of Orange, the Billy Boys, who at their height had over 800 paid-up members, spent much of their existence in conflict with the Catholic gangs of Bridgeton such as the Norman Conks based in Norman Street. In the 1930s the Billy Boys had a junior section, the Derry Boys, led by "Killer" McKay. In 1935 a pitched battle between the Billy Boys and the Conks took place on nearly every public holiday or major Catholic saint day. Fullerton, who worked as a strike-breaker in the General Strike of 1926, was also a member of Oswald Mosley's British Union of Fascists and it was following his marches in the East End that he took to leading the Billy Boys through the Catholic areas of the city. Curiously although bottles were thrown and excrement poured on the marchers from the tenement buildings, members of the ultra-Protestant Orange Lodges of Freemasonry obtained permission from Fullerton to march with his men. These bowler-hatted, dark-suited, sash-bedecked men walked behind the pipe bands with their bowler hats stuffed with papier-mâché to provide ad hoc crash helmets.

Once appointed Chief Constable, Sillitoe carried on in Glasgow where he had left off in Sheffield. According to John McLean, who was a constable in the city force for over thirty years, "He got together the biggest and hardest men in the force and ordered them to go out and batter the living shite out of every Ned who scratched his balls without permission." To supplement the direct confrontational method used in Sheffield, when Sillitoe's "batter gangs" heard of a gang-fight they would drive up in unmarked police vehicles and wait until the participants were tiring and then go in and give them a good beating. According to legend, on one occasion when the band marched towards Celtic Park, two officers ordered them to turn round and when they refused two police vans emptied officers, armed with long riot batons, on to the streets. The whole band was arrested and charged with a variety of assaults and disturbances. Elijah Cooper was the only man uninjured. He had jumped into his bass drum and hidden there until the fighting was over.

The end of the Billy Boys came when a drunken Fullerton, carrying a three-year-old child, was seen leading his men towards the Toll Gate. Two officers tried to remove the child but were pushed aside. They followed at a distance until they saw Sergeant Tommy Morrison, known as "Big Tom", arresting Fullerton for being drunk in charge of a child. He struck the sergeant who "drew his baton to defend himself". Fullerton received twelve months imprisonment and, when he was released, he found the Billy Boys had dispersed. With no one to fight, the Conks seem to have pined and faded away.

After the war Fullerton seems to have had something of a conversion. He worked as a ring whip for British bantamweight champion Peter Keenan, a Catholic, and actually carried Keenan on his shoulders on to the pitch at Celtic Park to receive the cheers of the crowd. Fullerton died in poverty in 1962 at the age of fifty-seven. His spectacular funeral, attended by a crowd estimated to be around 1,000, featured marching fife bands playing "Come to the Saviour" accompanying the coffin as it was taken from Bridgeton Cross to the Riddrie Park Cemetery. He is the basis of the character Johnnie Stark in Alexander McArthur and H. Kingsley Long's novel *No Mean City*.

Following his success as a gang-buster, but with nothing much else to recommend him, Percy Sillitoe was appointed head of MI5 in May 1946.

9

Ma Barker and Her Boys

The definitive image of Ma Barker is that of the cinema poster for the 1970 Roger Corman film, *Bloody Mama*, with Shelley Winters holding a machine-gun under a banner bearing the legend, "The family that slays together stays together". That was the way J. Edgar Hoover and the FBI had presented her but was it accurate?

It is difficult to know exactly what part Kate, or "Ma" as she came to be known, played in her sons' activities. Certainly she was on hand to attend police stations and plead their cause but was she, as the FBI claimed, the planner of the jobs, a machine-gun-wielding harridan who ran the operations with an iron discipline? Or was she, as her boys and others said, a dumpy and none too intelligent little lady? Almost certainly it was the latter. Not that this meant her sons were not ruthless killers who shot anyone who stood in their way during their reign of terror in the Midwest.

Arizona Clarke Barker, who soon changed her name to Kate, was born around 1871 near Springfield, Missouri. In 1892 she married George Barker from Joplin and they had four sons. Herman, Lloyd, Arthur (or "Doc") and Freddie were born between 1894 and 1902. Both Arthur at five-foot three and his brother Freddie, an inch taller, conformed to the belief of the time that their criminal activities were to compensate for their lack of height. Along with their Canadian-born partner

Alvin "Creepy" Karpis and assorted friends who came and went – imprisoned or killed – they were, said Hoover, "the toughest mob we ever cracked". Some of the men who drove with the Barkers were close to Al Capone and the mob. At least one friend, Fred Goetz – also known as "Shotgun" George Ziegler – was reliably thought to have taken part in the 1929 St Valentine's Day Massacre of members of the Bugsy Moran Gang in Chicago. Apart from his comments on the Barkers' mother, Hoover may have been right.

It was in the reformatory at Hutchinson, Kansas, where he was serving a five to ten for warehouse-breaking, that Karpis met Lawrence DeVol, who would later also become a member of the gang. Then, however, DeVol was very much the senior figure, a talented safebreaker who could handle nitroglycerine with ease. Karpis, very much in awe of him, escaped with him in 1929 and they worked their way across Kansas and into Colorado. In March the next year they were in Kansas City to rob a poolroom safe when they were stopped by the police, given a bad beating and sent back to Hutchinson from where they were transferred to the State Penitentiary in Lansing. It was there that Karpis met Freddie Barker who had been there since 1926, serving a five to ten years for safe-breaking in Windfield, Kansas.

Karpis had learned his trade at the hands of Walter Dietrich, himself a pupil of "Baron" Herman K. Lamm, a former German military officer whose precision turned bank robbery into an art form. Unfortunately Karpis did not absorb the lessons and the result of his and the Barkers' robberies was a trail of bodies and bungled jobs.

Karpis was released in May 1931 and met up again with Barker. Together they robbed a bank in Mountain View, Missouri. When Barker shot and killed Sheriff Roy Kelly at West Plains, Missouri, after a raid on a clothing store on 19 December that year, they moved on to St Paul, Minnesota, one of the so-called safe towns for criminals, where they worked hand-in-glove with the local police. On 5 January the next year they took $3,000 in a hold-up in Cambridge, Minnesota, and then in March two girls, Margaret "Indian Rose" Perry and Sadie Carmacher, were found murdered in Karpis's burned-out car near Balsam Lake. They were thought to have been about to talk to the authorities about the Cambridge raid. Karpis maintained he had loaned his car to the killer and knew nothing of the murders.

By the early 1930s George Barker had left his wife, Kate, and returned to Joplin. Now Ma was keeping company with the dapper, grey-haired Albert Dunlop whom Karpis and the others thought was both sponging off her and, more importantly, was a danger to them due to his liquor consumption.

The first serious troubles for the Barker family had come in 1910 when Herman was arrested for highway robbery in Webb City, Missouri, something he repeated on 5 March 1915, this time in Joplin. He and brother Lloyd were now thought to be part of Tulsa's Central Park Gang. On 18 July 1918, Doc Barker was arrested for stealing a car and was sent to the penitentiary in Joplin. He was there for a day over eighteen months when he escaped on 19 February 1920. At least he avoided the shoot-out following the burglary of a jewellery shop by the Central Park Gang in Okmulgee in early January 1922, which resulted in the death of Jimmy Sexton, one of the gang, and that of Police Captain Homer Spaulding. For his part Ed Lansing was sentenced to life imprisonment. Doc Barker was not rearrested for another two years when he was sentenced, along with Volney Davis, to life imprisonment for the murder of a nightwatchman in 1920.

In 1922 Lloyd received twenty-five years for a mail-truck robbery at Baxter Springs, Kansas, and was sent to Leavenworth penitentiary. For the time being, only Freddie was free. He had been paroled earlier following the shooting of an officer in a routine car theft. At the end of August 1927 the newly released Herman Barker killed himself – or was killed as some reports claim – in a shoot-out with the police as he tried to escape after the hold-up of an ice house in Newton, Kansas. He was stopped near Wichita by a patrolman who leaned into the car. Barker pulled him further in and shot him with a Luger. In the more romantic version, the officer on the other side of the car then opened fire on Barker who, badly wounded, heroically shot himself with the Luger. For a short time Herman's widow, Carol Hamilton, a full-bloodied Cherokee, took up with Alvin Karpis until she introduced him to Dorothy Slayman, whom he married before taking up with Dolores Delaney, one of a trio of gangster-loving sisters.

Freddie and Arthur Barker, together with Karpis and up to twenty-five luminaries such as Frank "Jelly" Nash, Tommy Holden and Ray Terrill, now began what was literally a reign of terror throughout the Midwest. Not only were banks robbed but, more damagingly as far as their public image was concerned, they took up kidnapping for ransom. Bank robbery could be tolerated; kidnapping fellow gang-members might just about be deemed all right; but the kidnapping of respectable citizens certainly was not.

For the moment, however, banks were the target. The Northwestern National Bank in Minneapolis was robbed in March 1932 and the next month, thanks to a tip from the corrupt St Paul police chief, Tom Brown, the gang was able to escape before the FBI found them. In a manner of speaking, Ma Barker's fancy man, Arthur Dunlop, was left behind. His body was found floating in a lake in Wisconsin, with three bullet-wounds in the back. Karpis maintained the killing had been done by Jack Peifer, St Paul's fixer and operator of the town's Hollywood Casino, as a favour to him and Freddie Barker. Ma Barker seems to have taken the loss of her paramour with equanimity. She was closer to her "boys" than any lover.

In June 1932 Karpis and Barker joined with Harvey Bailey, Machine Gun Kelly, Verne Miller and DeVol to take $47,000 from a bank in Fort Scott. Three other men – James "Frank"

Sawyer, Jim Clark and Ed Davis – were wrongly convicted of the robbery. They escaped from Lansing in a mass breakout on 30 May 1933. Sawyer was caught just over a month later and was pardoned in 1969 after an affidavit from Karpis cleared him of the robbery.

Harvey Bailey, then more of a member of the Keating–Holden Gang, who also operated out of St Paul, was captured on 7 July 1932 while playing golf with Keating and Holden in Kansas City. Jelly Nash, a poor player, trailed several holes behind and so avoided capture by FBI agents who did not realize he was part of the four-ball. Bailey was eventually paroled in 1964 at the age of seventy-six and died in 1979 in Joplin. Following his release Holden, known as Tough Tommy, became the Public Enemy No. 1 after shooting his wife and two of her brothers in a drunken argument on 5 June 1949 in Chicago. He was finally traced when a factory worker recognized his picture in the *Portland Oregonian* and he was recaptured. He died in prison two years later.

In July 1932 the gang took $240,000 in cash and bonds from the Cloud County Bank in Concordia, Kansas. Arthur Barker was released from Oklahoma State Penitentiary on 10 September that year, with a condition he leave the state. He went to join his brother and Karpis in Minnesota. Regarded as "a little light between the eyes", he had a hair-trigger temper, particularly when drinking. A fortnight later the gang relieved a Redwood Falls Bank of $35,000. At the time the Oklahoma authorities had a curious practice of allowing criminals to take leave from their sentences and, with a bribe from the Barker family, Doc Barker's boyhood friend Volney "Curley" Davis was allowed a twenty-month absence. In early November, Davis was released and never returned. Now he rejoined Arthur Barker although from time to time he also worked with John Dillinger.

On Friday, 16 December 1932, the gang raided the Third Northwestern National Bank in Minneapolis. It was a disaster.

The driver was Jess Doyle and on the raid were the Barkers, Karpis, Bill Weaver and Verne Miller. The trouble began when the raid took too long. The girl cashiers would not cooperate and nor would bank-teller Paul Hesselroth, who claimed he could not open the vault. He received a beating but he and a book-keeper managed to trip alarms. Larry DeVol was left as guard outside the front door and when a patrol car pulled up he opened fire with a Thompson machine-gun, killing officers Ira Evan and Leo Gorski as they answered the alarm call. Fred Barker then killed Oscar Erickson as the gang switched cars and changed a damaged tyre in Como Park, St Paul. Erickson had slowed down when he was driving past and Barker thought he was trying to take a note of the car plates. The proceeds amounted to $22,000 cash and around $100,000 in securities.

Two days later, brandishing a gun, DeVol, who had been drinking, walked into the wrong apartment in the Annbee Arms Apartments where he was staying, interrupting a bridge game. When the police were called they found part of the proceeds from the bank in DeVol's apartment. At the time he was wanted for the murders of Sheriff William Sweet and Marshal Aaron Bailey in Washington, Ohio, a murder in Tulsa and the killing of John Rose, a Kirksville Missouri policeman who had tried to stop DeVol after he robbed a theatre in Hannibal, all in 1930. He was also suspected of killing two men in the Severs Hotel in Muskogee in April 1930 and had escaped from the local jail where he was being held. A wanted poster described him as a "paranoid maniac" and said he suffered from persecutory delusions that made him liable to kill associates without warning. He was, of course, also wanted for killing Evans and Gorski in the Third Northwestern raid. Sentenced to life imprisonment, he was found to be insane after he claimed the guards were trying to pump poisoned gas into his cell. Transferred to a hospital for the criminally insane in St Peter, Minnesota, he remained there until June 1936 when he led a successful fifteen-man breakout. On the run for the next month, he was finally trapped in the German Village Tavern, Enid, Oklahoma, where he was shot and killed but not before he had killed one officer, Cal Palmer, and wounded another.

The gang had already been depleted when, at the beginning of April 1933, a member called Earl Christman was killed in a raid on the First Bank of Fairbury, Nebraska. But now it was time for a change of operations.

It was the St Paul gangster Jack Peifer who introduced the Barker–Karpis Gang to the rewards and troubles of the kidnap, as well as to Fred Goetz and Byron Bolton, both Cleveland Syndicate men, who would help out. His introductory fee was to be 10 per cent of the $100,000 ransom money. The first job involved Freddie and Doc Barker, the two Syndicate men, Karpis as the driver and the elderly safe-breaker Chuck Fitzgerald, whose job it was to lure wealthy brewer William Hamm into a waiting car on 15 June 1933. In fact, the whole exercise went off almost without a hitch. The gang had arranged to use the postmaster's house in Bensonville, correctly believing that no one would look for a kidnap victim in a government official's house. According to Karpis, Hamm was treated well, fed and given copies of the *Saturday Evening Post* and books to read until the money was paid. The next problem was whether the ransom money had been marked and Hamm was given some of it as his fare back to St Paul. The gang had serious problems changing the money. Launderers in Reno would not touch it and Peifer eventually cut his fee to 5 per cent. In fact, the lion's share of the $100,000 went to St Paul's police chief Thomas Brown, whose campaign for office had been financed by gangsters, including Homer Van Meter who put up $1,000. Now, he earned his money tipping off Fred Barker and his girlfriend Paula Harmon that their neighbours in Vernon Street were suspicious that they were part of the kidnap gang.

The FBI, in one of their regular blunders of the time, latched on to the gang of Roger "Tough"Touhy as the kidnappers, had them identified and put them on trial. They were all acquitted but in 1934 Touhy was convicted for the kidnapping on the false evidence of Jake "The Barber" Factor, half-brother of the cosmetician Max Factor. Touhy was released in 1959 and promptly shot to death in Chicago, probably on the instructions of Murray "The Camel" Humphreys whom he had humiliated back in 1931 and also in his autobiography, *The Stolen Years*.

The second kidnapping of the era, which came within the month, was not a Barker–Karpis operation. Not to be outdone by them, on 22 July 1933 George Barnes, better known as "Machine Gun" Kelly, along with his wife Kathryn and Albert Bates, kidnapped millionaire Texan Charles Urschel in Oklahoma City. They took Urschel and Walter Jarrett from Urschel's home, where they were playing bridge with their wives. Jarrett was left on the road outside the Urschel mansion but the oilman was taken to a farm in Paradise, Texas, where he was held for over a week, handcuffed to a child's high chair and sleeping on a quilt on the floor, before a ransom of $200,000 was paid. Urschel was then cleaned up and given ten dollars before being dropped near a gas station twenty miles out of Oklahoma City.

In all twenty-one people were convicted of participating in some way or another in the Urschel kidnapping. They included a Barker-Karpis associate, Harvey Bailey, a bank robber who was unfortunately hiding out at the farm at the time. He maintained his innocence to his death and Urschel, whose recall of detail, even to the extent of a plane flying over the farm at the same time each day, led to the arrests, never identified Bailey as one of his kidnappers. After the plane had come over Urschel would ask his kidnappers what time it was.

Born in 1895, Kelly, who once kidnapped the wrong person and had to release him, never really justified his ranking as Public Enemy No. 1. When agents broke into his room to arrest him for the Urschel kidnapping, he is alleged to have said, "Don't shoot, G-men – don't shoot," so coining a suitably attractive moniker, derived from Government men, for FBI agents generally. Kelly died in Leavenworth following a heart attack in July 1954 after, it is said, writing to Urschel, "these five words seem written in fire on the walls of my cell, 'Nothing can be worth this'." Kathryn Kelly, by far the stronger of the pair and who had actually wanted to kill Urschel, was released four years later.

Meanwhile it was back to their stock-in-trade robbery for the Barkers and Karpis. On 30 August 1933 a police officer was killed and another injured in a raid on a stockyard's payroll being delivered to St Paul; $35,000 was stolen.

The second Barker–Karpis kidnap was fingered for them by Harry Sawyer, the owner of the Green Lantern Saloon, the hangout of choice for bootleggers, robbers and killers in St Paul. The saloon had formerly been owned by "Dapper" Dan Hogan, the effective godfather of the city.

Hogan had begun his criminal career as a hotel-room thief, followed by a spell of bank robberies and fur thefts that saw him end up in prison in San Quentin, Wisconsin, South Dakota and finally, in 1909, Minnesota. It was there that he changed his unsuccessful career as a doer and began his new and wholly profitable one as an organizer.

He teamed up with the local journalist, "Big Ed" Morgan, opening a gaming house and gradually extending his contacts and political connections to the point that, under his guidance and due to his relationship with the corrupt police chief, John O'Connor, St Paul became a safe city for criminals. Hogan also planned robberies and laundered money and bonds from raids. It is generally accepted that he washed the money from both the Hamilton County Bank raid on 28 September 1922, in which securities totalling $265,000 were stolen, and the great Denver Mint robbery on 18 December of the same year in which the Oklahoman robber Harvey Bailey's gang killed a security guard.

Hogan was not completely free from the dangers of informants, but those who cooperated with the police usually either retracted or did not survive. In 1927 he was indicted for conspiracy to rob the Chicago Great Western Railway Station in St Paul in which $35,000 was stolen. He was released on $100,000 bond. Hogan was fortunate that Tommy O'Connor, one of the robbers, escaped from custody and told newspapers that his confession, which implicated Hogan, had been a pack of lies. The charges were finally dropped. John Moran, who had been due to become a prosecution witness, died in his prison cell a week after Hogan visited him. Two girlfriends of members of the Hogan organization were also killed in 1927 after they were interviewed about a mail robbery. At first a taxi driver, John L. Talty, said he had seen Hogan at their flat but sensibly changed his mind and admitted his mistake.

Then, on 4 December 1928, Hogan was blown up when he started his Paige coupé in his garage at 1607 Seventh Street, St Paul. The killing was possibly by East Coast gangsters in reprisal for the death in New York of gambler Arnold Rothstein who had fixed baseball's 1919 World Series. The theory is that the gun that killed Rothstein had been traced to St Paul and, as such, the killing must have been with the approval of Hogan, for nothing went on in the city without his knowledge. It is more probable, however, that Hogan was killed by, or on the orders of, his junior partner, Harry "Dutch" Sawyer, for the very good reason that he wanted Hogan's enormously profitable bar on Wabasha Street and the trade and power that went with it.

After Hogan's death, Harry Sawyer refined the arrangements his predecessor had set up with the police in the city and elsewhere. With police cooperation, raids were telegraphed in advance and wanted faces on posters went unrecognized. Extradition requests by outside agencies were refused. When a fugitive arrived by train Sawyer would send his errand boy, the former boxer William Albert "Pat" Reilly, to arrange a hotel room and introduce the felonious visitor to the local underworld.

By 1929 Sawyer had developed a sophisticated system by which a gangster could get the bullet holes taken out of the bodywork of their car, buy a new one, purchase an automatic weapon, launder stolen money and identify potential kidnap victims effectively without leaving his saloon. In addition there were, of course, women available on a long- and short-term basis as well as medical advice on everything from venereal disease and abortion to the treatment of gunshot wounds and rudimentary plastic surgery for faces and prints. It was, however, the fingering of a kidnap victim for the Barker–Karpis Gang that would prove to be his undoing.

During the end of December 1933 and the beginning of the New Year, the Barker–Karpis Gang thought about their next venture. One suggestion was the Commercial State Bank of St Paul but Harry Sawyer believed the kidnap of thirty-seven-year-old Edward G. Bremer, the son of Adolf Bremer, president of the Jacob Schmidt Brewing Company, would be more profitable. It is possible that his motives for fingering Bremer were not wholly financial and there was an element of revenge attached to the suggestion. There had been business dealings in the past between Sawyer and the Bremer family which had not always worked to his advantage. This time the ransom was to be $200,000. It was a curious decision. Machine Gun Kelly and his crew had been caught following their kidnapping of Charles Urschel and the penalties had been severe. The gang also wanted the help of Capone's man, Fred Goetz. He had already helped in the Hamm kidnapping but was on record as saying he did not want to take part in another. However, in the end, money overcame scruples and it was he who suggested the ransom money had to be paid in old and unmarked $5 and $10 bills. They were also assisted in their efforts by Thomas Brown, a St Paul police officer who was later dismissed from the force because of his contacts with them. Thoughtfully, he had provided them with details of Bremer Jr's movements.

The kidnapping took place on 17 January 1934 after Bremer had dropped off his daughter at school. On his way to work he was stopped at the halt sign on the corner of Lexington Avenue and Goodrich Avenue. Freddie Barker and Harry Campbell blocked his car with Doc Barker, Karpis and Volney Davis preventing him reversing. Bremer was hit with the butt of a revolver and the car door was slammed, injuring his knee as he tried to escape. The car would not restart and he was beaten until he showed the gang how to do it. Taken to Bensenville, Illinois, he was kept in a bedroom mostly blindfolded and bound tightly. He was, however, able to see and remember the pattern on the wallpaper of his bedroom and the designs on the plates on which he was fed chilli, chop-suey and fried chicken, all of which he would say were over-seasoned.

On 6 February the ransom was paid and the money hidden in the garage of Goetz's wife's uncle. Bremer was released the next day near Rochester, Minnesota, to get a bus and train back to St Paul. The $200,000 received for his ransom was perhaps the last major success of the gang. From then on they were hounded down.

Goetz would have been advised to stay in Chicago. He had acted as the go-between and indeed collected the ransom money and released Bremer. However, he began to brag about the incident and Freddie Barker came to believe his loud mouth might betray the gang. Goetz was shot to death outside the Minerva café in Cicero on 20 March 1934. Another suggestion is that he was killed as a reprisal for his part in the St Valentine's Day Massacre but given the lapse in time this is more doubtful.

It was common enough for gangs to turn on members whom they thought might betray them. For example, it was really not safe to be a member of the Tri-State Gang based in Philadelphia in the 1930s. Led by Anthony Cugino along with Robert Mais and Walter Legenza, they robbed and killed throughout Ohio, Virginia and Pennsylvania, giving them their name. Cugino, who had killed his cellmate during his imprisonment for a jewel robbery, was paranoid and in turn killed two members of the gang and their girlfriends because he feared they might give evidence to the police. He later stabbed another to death. However, he did help Mais and Legenza escape from a prison in Richmond while awaiting execution. They were later recaptured after murdering a guard. Cugino later killed yet another colleague Anthony "Musky" Zanghi in a quarrel over the division of a robbery's proceeds. He was betrayed by the underworld and arrested in New York on 8 September 1935. In questioning he had implicated himself in the death of a New York police officer, James J. Garvey, the previous year. He then hanged himself in his cell.

Just as it is desirable for a gang to have a tame lawyer on hand it is perhaps even more necessary to have a tame doctor ready to extract bullets and do general sewing without the need for the injured to go to hospital where unpleasant and difficult questions are likely to be asked. In London the Kray twins had their drunken Doctor Blasker; in Melbourne Squizzy Taylor had his more sober Dr Taylor; while in the 1930s in the Midwest one of the physicians of necessity, if not of choice, was the alcoholic Joseph Patrick Moran who had qualified with honours from Tuft's Medical School. Moran had a good track record. Before he went to prison for illegal abortions he had worked for the unrelated George "Bugsy" Moran and had looked after the girls in Al Capone's brothels. He was also the official physician for the International Brotherhood of Teamsters, Chauffeurs, Warehousemen and Helpers union. Struck off the medical register he took up with the Barker–Karpis Gang. In the 1930s, when identification was often made by fingerprints, there was a belief that these could be altered surgically. Once more hope triumphed over experience when Freddie Barker and Alvin Karpis paid Moran $1,000 for the required fingerprint and some facial surgery. Moran was drunk when he undertook the operations and not only were both men left in agony when the bandages came off but Karpis looked even uglier than before. Worse, as was always going to be the case, the men's fingerprints grew back.

As with many gangland killings there are conflicting versions of what happened to Moran. Possibly, after the Battle of Little Bohemia in April 1934, he refused to treat John "Red" Hamilton, one of Dillinger's men. This, together with his drunken unreliability, may have led to him being shot after Dillinger's death. Another version is that while drunk he was boasting in the Casino Club near Toledo, where he was last seen, that "I have you guys in the palms of my hands." Later Fred Barker is said to have remarked, "Doc will do no more operating. The fishes probably have eat him up by now." His body was apparently found on Crystal Beach, Ohio, on 26 September 1935 and identified through dental records. Karpis claimed that Freddie Barker told him that he and his brother Doc had killed Moran and buried him in lime in Michigan. The most likely version is that Fred Barker and Karpis killed him during a boat ride on Lake Erie.

Nor was it always easy for failing lawyers. In 1932 Tulsa's J. Earl Smith was retained to defend Harvey Bailey on the Fort Scott robbery charge but forgot to appear. He was found dead at the Indiana Hills Country Club on 13 August that year.

The Barker–Karpis Gang started to unravel when, on 5 September 1934, Wynona Burdette, Gladys Sawyer and Freddie Barker's mistress Paula Harmon, never regarded as reliable when drunk, were arrested on drunk and disorderly charges in a Cleveland hotel. Naturally they gave false names but, unfortunately for the gang, Francine, the five-year-old girl whom Gladys Sawyer was hoping to adopt, told the police who her mother really was. They were taken to Chicago where they were pressured into making long statements detailing the workings of the gang. It was the beginning of the end.

The next year began badly for the Barkers and got worse. On 6 January one of their peripatetic members, William B.

Harrison, was killed by fellow mobsters in Ontarioville, Illinois, but there was much worse to come. Two days later Doc Barker was captured by Hoover's one-time favourite agent, Melvin Purvis, in Chicago. Women were Doc's downfall. His girlfriend had been followed and inadvertently led the FBI to him. "This is a helluva time to be caught without a gun," he is said to have remarked. The same day Russell "Slim Gray" Gibson, who had been with the Barkers since the days of the Central Park Gang in Tulsa, was killed and Byron Bolton was captured in a separate shoot-out. Even so, it was not the FBI's finest hour. When they arrived at the apartment block they released tear gas in the wrong apartment. When the local police arrived they nearly opened fire on the FBI agents whom they took to be the gangsters. Gibson, wearing a bulletproof vest, managed to get to a fire escape but was shot and died instantly. His wife was promptly charged with harbouring. Bolton disgraced himself. He pleaded guilty to the kidnapping and gave evidence against Doc Barker and the others. In return he received concurrent three-year sentences and was released in 1938.

From notes and drawings in Doc Barker's apartment the FBI was able to work out where they could find Ma Barker who, as usual, was not far away from Freddie. The police had also been informed that the Barkers were living at a house where there was an alligator called "Old Joe". Apparently while the gang had been staying there on a previous occasion the creature had become the subject of machine-gun target practice but had survived.

At daybreak on 16 January 1935 Freddie Barker and his mother, living under the identity of Mr and Mrs J. E. Blackburn, were surprised at their cottage on Highway 27A in Lake Weir, near Ocklawaha, northern Florida. The story goes that agent Earl Connelly from Cincinnati called out for them to surrender or the shooting would start. Ma Barker is alleged to have replied, "Go ahead." Both Barkers died in the ensuing six-hour shoot-out during which the FBI fired in the region of 1,500 rounds into the cottage. When the bodies were discovered, Freddie's had sixteen bullet-wounds. His mother had either three or one depending upon the version of the story and it is also possible that one bullet was self-inflicted. It did not look as though she had been in the forefront of the battle. This left Hoover in something of a dilemma. Here was a dumpy, elderly woman shot to death by his agents. Some strategic thinking was required and in the space of a few press releases the FBI transformed her into the machine-gun-wielding harridan who, overruling Fred Goetz, had authorized the Bremer kidnapping. Close to Freddie's body was, "Ma lying on her back, with a machine-gun beside her lifeless body. The barrel was still smoking." Their bodies were put on public display and were then stored, unclaimed, until 1 October when relatives took them for burial in Williams Timberhill Cemetery, Welch, Oklahoma, next to the grave of Herman. Her marker reads, "The Darkest Night, Shall end In bright Day".

In his autobiography Karpis remembered her as a woman of no great intelligence who listened almost exclusively to country-and-western radio stations and the popular comedy duo Amos and Andy. It is doubtful if she had heard of Bremer in any meaningful way. He wrote:

> It's no insult to Ma's memory that she just didn't have the brains or know-how to direct us on a robbery. It wouldn't have occurred to her to get involved in our business and we always made a point of only discussing our scores when Ma wasn't around. We'd leave her at home when we were arranging a job, or we'd send her to a movie. Ma saw a lot of movies.

On 17 May 1935 Doc Barker and four others were convicted of kidnapping Edward Bremer, followed on 7 June by Volney Davis and another four. Harry Sawyer went down the following January. In 1955 he was found to have cancer of the spine and was paroled in February of that year. He died in June, disowned by his family and long divorced by Gladys.

Karpis, away from the Barker Gang, continued his life of robbery until, on 1 May 1936, the FBI discovered he was in New Orleans. The previous month Hoover had come under considerable criticism at a Senate committee hearing from Senator Kenneth D. McKellar of Tennessee because he had never actually made an arrest himself. The Karpis capture provided that opportunity and from then Hoover never looked back. Now he flew in to arrest him personally on Jefferson Parkway in a highly publicized operation. The FBI version is that Hoover grabbed Karpis before he could reach a rifle on the back seat of a 1936 Plymouth coupé and said, "Put the handcuffs on him." Karpis maintains that Hoover's part was less heroic, claiming there was no back seat in the coupé and that Hoover only emerged when he was already surrounded by FBI men. In fact, no one had brought handcuffs so Karpis was bound with his own tie. In any event there was so much excitement at his capture that another bank-robber, Freddie Hunter, who was with him, was able to slide out of the passenger seat and disappear.

Later Karpis was put in chains and guarded by machine-gun toting G-men until his trial when he was sentenced to life imprisonment. He was first sent to Leavenworth and then to Alcatraz and McNeil Island prison on Puget Sound, from where he was released in January 1969 after serving thirty-three years. He was deported to Canada. It is doubtful if he ever saw Dolores Delaney or his son again. He was, however, one of the few gangsters of the time to keep his money. During his career he had given the proceeds from the jobs to his nephew who had banked it for him and, on his release, Karpis was given a cheque for capital and interest.

He went to live in Spain where in 1979 he was reported to have died in Torremolinos from an overdose of sleeping pills at the age of seventy-two. Just how they came to be administered was never clear and, as befitted the old villain, rival theories, with little to support any of them, of suicide, accident and even murder were advanced. He had written the highly successful book, *Public Enemy No. 1*, followed by *On the Rock* about his life in Alcatraz.

Doc Barker was among the heavies sent from Leavenworth to Alcatraz, established in 1868 on an island in the San Francisco Bay from where escapes were almost certainly doomed to failure. First, the security and regime in the prison was tight and, more particularly, the currents in the San Francisco Bay were lethal. Successful escapes really depend on the definition. If it means getting off the island on to the mainland and getting away then probably there were none. Over the years from 1934 to 1963 when the prison was closed there were fourteen separate attempts by thirty-six men including two who tried it twice. Twenty-three were caught, six were shot and killed and two drowned. Five were reported missing, presumed drowned. In December 1937 Ralph Roe and Teddy Cole jumped into the sea but their bodies were almost certainly washed away.

On 13 January 1939, Doc Barker, who had become the boss of the prison's mat-shop after terrorizing the guard, along with kidnapper and bank robber Rufus McCain, twenty-nine-year-old murderer Henry Young, and bank-robbers Dale Stamphill and William Martin, made a break from the isolation unit after sawing through the iron cell bars. Guards found them as they reached the water. Young, Martin and McCain surrendered. Stamphill and Barker were shot. Barker died the next day saying, "I was a fool to try it. I'm all shot to hell." Stamphill, who had been shot in the legs, would later say that he was left unattended for four days in the hope he would die. Instead, he survived and, after his release from prison, he was granted a pardon and became a member of the state's counselling board.

The escape attempt was hopeless. Firstly, they had been grassed by a fellow prisoner, the fraudsman Frank Gouker. Secondly, although they planned to make diving masks they do not appear to have done so nor was there a boat near the island, merely an improvised raft. The cold conditions and currents would almost certainly have killed them in minutes. Barker's body was eventually brought back to Welch where his marker reads:

> Lord I deserve Justice
> But Mercy is what I need.
> Let me cling to thy hand, dear Lord
> Only thou knowest my need.

Young and McCain were initially placed in solitary confinement. After they were returned to the prison population, Young, who seems to have blamed McCain for the escape failure, slashed him in the stomach with a prison-made shiv on 3 December 1940. He was charged with first-degree murder but, after the jury heard the conditions on the Rock, they returned only a verdict of manslaughter. He served his sentence and then was transferred to Washington State Penitentiary to serve another sentence for a previous murder. He was paroled in 1972 but failed to report and vanished.

The death of Doc Barker left only his brother Lloyd, whose own death was not quite in the family tradition. Released from prison in 1938, he went straight, served in the US Army and was a cook in a prisoner-of-war camp during the Second World War. Afterwards he and his wife went to Colorado where he worked as the manager of the Denargo Market in Denver and where they rowed constantly. On 18 March 1949 she shot and killed him. She was sent to the Colorado State Insane Asylum.

The FBI had received criticism for the 1934 killing of Dillinger who, the public believed, had been given no chance to surrender, and there was some ridicule over the arrest of Karpis when the lack of handcuffs became common knowledge. They did, however, garner some praise for ending the run of the now largely forgotten Brady Gang which had left its own trail of destruction throughout the Midwest in the mid-1930s. Formed by Al Brady, Clarence Shaffer and James Dalhover, and temporarily featuring Shaffer's friend, Charles Geiseking, they robbed banks and stores, killing grocery-store clerk Edward Lindsay in Indianapolis. They were obviously highly regarded because it was said of them, "they would make Dillinger look like a piker". Brady had met Dalhover, a one-time bootlegger, on a farm he was visiting. The gang made a serious mistake when they robbed a jewellery store of $8,000 in Lima, Ohio, but threw away the boxes across the state line. This allowed the FBI to take an interest in them.

They were nothing if not versatile. In January 1936, when the bad weather and frozen roads temporarily put a hold on bank robberies, they organized a car theft and stripping ring. On 27 April that year the gang robbed the Kay Jewelry Store at Lima for a second time, using a DeSoto airflow sedan they had carjacked in Chicago. While Brady, Geiseking and Dalhover went into the store and held up the clerks and customers with their guns, Shaffer remained outside at the wheel of the getaway car. During the robbery, a police car drew up and parked in front of the gang's car, and one of the policemen got out and went into a store next door. Dalhover, coming out of the jewellery store with four pillow cases full of items, saw the police car but continued on his way and took his automatic rifle from the back of the gang car. Brady then walked over to the police car and held up the policeman with a revolver. Dalhover, approaching from the other side, held his rifle on the policeman and took his gun from him. While this was going on, the other officer came out of the store and started shooting at Brady and Dalhover, who returned fire. Geiseking ran out of the jewellery store and was shot in the leg. He was hustled into the gang's car and they drove away, pursued by the police car occupied by both officers. During the chase, the police car was wrecked and one of the officers was seriously injured.

The gang drove to Indianapolis where they took Geiseking to a doctor, telling him that he had been shot by a jealous husband. Later Dalhover and Shaffer decided to return to the doctor's house to ensure his silence. In the meantime, however, the physician had notified the police department of the incident, and when the bandits turned up, they were met by Indianapolis police officers. A gun battle ensued during the course of which Sergeant Richard Rivers was killed and the gang escaped, driving to Chicago to dispose of the jewellery, valued at approximately $12,000, through fences.

The agreed selling price was about $850, but the money was never received as Brady was caught by Indianapolis police on 11 May. Shaffer was arrested there the same day and Dalhover on 15 May in Chicago. They were all returned to Indianapolis to await trial for the murder of Sergeant Richard Rivers. Geiseking was arrested on 12 September at Henderson, Kentucky. He had been working with another man, holding up filling stations, and was sentenced to ten to twenty-five years for armed robbery.

On 24 September, while they were awaiting the Rivers trial, Brady, Dalhover and Shaffer were transferred to the Hancock County Jail at Greenfield, Indiana. One breakfast time the following month they attacked the sheriff, took his .38 calibre revolver and escaped in a car stolen from a man who had come to the sheriff's aid.

On 23 May 1937 they robbed the Goodland Stateland bank in Goodland, Indiana, of $2,500 and in the subsequent chase they ambushed, shot and killed police officer Paul Minneman, taking his gun. With some of the proceeds Brady bought a bar, which he operated for a short time, as well as a motor boat. Keen on roller-skating, he also bought himself a specially built pair of skates. By now there was a $1,500 reward on offer for the Brady Gang's capture. With money again running low, on 23 August they robbed the Peoples Exchange Bank in Milwaukee, snatching approximately $7,000 and a revolver.

The next day they drove to Bridgeport, Connecticut, where they rented an apartment.

The trio had a seemingly insatiable appetite for guns and on 21 September they went to Bangor, Maine, to purchase additional firearms, which they believed they could buy in a sporting goods store with no questions asked. On 5 October, the gang returned to Bangor and purchased yet another .45 calibre colt automatic while ordering various clips and asking about a machine-gun. It was their undoing. After they left, the manager telephoned the police, telling them that the men had said they would be back on either 11 or 12 October. The police contacted the FBI.

Surveillance of the store was arranged and one agent was placed in the sporting goods section where, to all intents and purposes, he was working as a clerk; another was placed behind a partition in the rear of the store and others in a building across the street.

Around 8.30 a.m. on 12 October, the gang arrived in a Buick automobile with an Ohio licence plate. After driving past the sporting goods store twice, the occupants, apparently satisfied that everything was quiet and that there was no danger, parked the car a few doors from the store. Leaving Brady in the back seat of the car, Dalhover entered the store while Shaffer remained on guard in front. Dalhover was immediately arrested.

Shaffer must have seen what had happened because he began firing through the front door of the store, hitting an agent in the shoulder. The agents inside returned fire, and Shaffer was shot dead as he ran out to the street. In the meantime, two agents approached the Buick and told Brady that they were federal officers, ordering him to get out of the car with his hands up. He did put his hands up and started to slide along the back seat crying, "Don't shoot, don't shoot, I'll get out." As he got out of the vehicle, he shot at the agents with a .38 revolver, the gun he had taken from the body of the murdered Indiana state policeman, Paul Minneman. The agents immediately shot him dead in the middle of the street. On this occasion no complaints were raised about the FBI ambush.

Dalhover was later convicted in Indiana for the murder of Minneman. On 18 November 1938, he was electrocuted at the Indiana State Penitentiary.

10

John Dillinger

Most histories of organized crime in the United States omit robbers such as John Dillinger, Bonnie Parker and Clyde Barrow, and the Barker family. Possibly this is because of the equation of organized crime with the Mafia, in which these characters played no part, and possibly because they are really examples of disorganized crime. There is certainly no evidence that the men and women who rampaged through the Midwest between the wars put their often very substantial proceeds to any better use than paying for whores and drink and, in the end, doctors and lawyers' fees. Nevertheless some of their efforts were spectacular and they and their contemporaries deserve a place in any history of world gangs. They also provide links to that home-from-home for gangsters on the run: St Paul, Minnesota.

By the turn of the century the gangs of the Old West had almost completely disappeared. The Daltons had been wiped out in Coffeyville, Kansas, in 1892. Jim and Cole Younger were finally released from prison in 1901 as old men after they had served time for the abortive Northfields, Minnesota, raid in 1876. Jesse James, shot by Bob Ford, had been dead eighteen years. Frank James, acquitted following his surrender after his brother's death, had become respectable. The last surviving members of the Wild Bunch were ending their careers. In December 1901 Harvey Logan, known as Kid Curry, was arrested in Knoxville and escaped, before being tracked down and sentenced to twenty years of hard labour for train robbery. Two years into his sentence he escaped from the Knoxville prison and rode off on the sheriff's horse. The next year he and two others robbed the Denver & Rio Grande Railroad at Parachute, Colorado. They were tracked by a posse and ambushed, when Kid Curry shot himself. In April 1902 O. C. "Deaf Charley" Hanks, another member of the Wild Bunch, was killed while resisting arrest in a San Antonio saloon. Butch Cassidy and Harry Longbaugh (the "Sundance Kid") did survive the turn of the century but were down in Bolivia when they were probably killed in 1911. If, as a version of the legend goes, Cassidy survived and returned to the States then he certainly retired. One story is that he became William Phillips, who died in Spokane, Washington, of natural causes on 20 July 1935. Longbaugh is said to have moved to Argentina with Etta Place, the soiled dove or former school teacher – accounts vary – and mistress of both men.

Although there were sporadic robberies over the years, often by old-timers, it was not until 1914 that any serious and long-lasting alliance of bank-robbers was formed. Then, Henry Starr led a gang, which for a short time included Frank "Jelly" Nash, in a series of raids on banks in Oklahoma. Beginning with the Kiefer Central Bank on 30 September, from which they stole $6,400, they moved through the territory over the next four months relieving small-town banks of their cash.

Henry Starr, born in Indian territory in 1873, was related to Tom and Sam Starr and, by marriage, to the notorious Belle, who on 3 February 1889 was shot to death near Eufaula, Oklahoma. Born in Carthage, Montana in 1848, she had been the associate or mistress of some of the most notable of the post Civil War villains in the West, having a daughter, Pearl, by Cole Younger. It is possible she was killed by her son, the eighteen-year-old Ed Reed, with whom she was reputed to have had an incestuous relationship. Reed later became a deputy marshal at Fort Smith and was shot in a barroom brawl six years later.

Tom Starr, a full-bloodied Cherokee, is believed to have killed over a hundred men. He controlled Adair County, Oklahoma, occasionally making raids into Texas. On his death in 1890 his family described him as "full of fun and eager to josh folks".

Henry Starr's criminal career began when he was charged with trading whiskey to the Indians and he never looked back. By 1892 he had his own gang of robbers and in one raid killed a deputy of the hanging Judge Parker. He was sentenced to death on 20 October 1894 but, after a series of appeals and new trials, was pardoned after he had served five years. He was finally released from prison in 1919 and, for a time, became an actor in silent Westerns. The lure of robbery proved too much for him, however, and on 18 February 1921 he was shot by banker, W. J. Myers, when he raided the People's Bank at Harrison, Arkansas. He died four days later of his wounds.

It was really the next generation of robbers and killers who swept across the Midwest and, through the cinema, became the stuff of which legends have been made. Among them was Starr's protégé, Frank "Jelly" Nash. It was to free him when he was brought to Union Station in Kansas City that, on 17 June 1933, a team including (so the FBI said) Charles "Pretty Boy" Floyd and his partner Adam Richetti was assembled by Nash's old friend, Vernon Miller. The disastrous rescue operation almost coincided with a similarly ill-fated kidnapping of William Hamm by the Barker–Karpis Gang. This, coupled with the Kansas City Massacre, brought the wrath of the public, and with it the FBI, down on the heads of the independent, non-Mafia gangs.

Frank Nash, born in 1884, was acquitted of a murder in 1913 and then promptly killed his former partner, one of the witnesses who had given evidence against him. This time he received life imprisonment and in 1918 had his sentence commuted to ten years before this was changed to a full pardon. Almost at once he robbed the Corn State Bank in

Corn, Oklahoma, and received twenty-five years for his troubles. Again, he was paroled and rewarded the trust of the prison department by robbing the mail train in Osage on 20 August 1923. Six months later he was back in prison at Leavenworth. Here he met fellow robbers Jimmy Keating and Tommy Holden who both escaped with his help in February 1930.

Apart from this small lapse Nash had become a model prisoner and, working as a house servant for the deputy warden, he simply walked out in October that year. He spent some time in Joplin and Chicago before meeting up with Holden and Keating in Minneapolis and St Paul. He married bigamously and moved to Hot Springs, Arkansas. By now he was drinking heavily and had changed his appearance, having had part of his nose removed and, less painfully, wearing a toupee. On 8 April 1931, using George "Machine Gun Kelly" Barnes and Louis "Doc" Stacci as the getaway drivers, he and Harvey Bailey stole over $40,000 from the Central Bank in Sherman, Texas.

On 16 June 1933 he was captured in St Paul by the FBI who wished to get him away from the city as soon as possible. Had he been left in the town, one of the most favourable places for criminals, he would almost certainly have been allowed to escape. Instead, the agents took him to Kansas City, but their plans had been leaked to Nash's friend, Verne Miller, to say the agents would be arriving with Nash at Kansas City station on the Little Rock Flyer, en route to prison. It is possible that Miller tried to involve the Barker–Karpis outfit to help free Nash but at the time they had their own problems with the Hamm kidnapping.

As Nash was being transferred into a police Chevrolet, Miller, and supposedly Pretty Boy Floyd and Adam Richetti, opened fire with a sub-machine-gun killing him, an FBI agent called Raymond Caffrey, the Chief of Police of McAlester, Otto Reed, and two Kansas City officers. Various other scenarios have been advanced. The first is that neither Floyd nor Richetti were at the scene; the second is that the shooting was to silence Nash rather than free him; and the third is that when Miller opened fire Nash called out for him to stop. This infuriated Miller who promptly killed his old friend.

Miller, who had himself been shot, went to Chicago with his girlfriend, Vivian Mathis. He intended to go abroad but the FBI dragnet prevented him. He had been born in 1896 in Kimball, South Dakota, and served in France in the First World War where he had perfected his technique with a machine-gun. It was said that he could shoot his initials in the gas tank of rival bootleggers. In 1921 he became a police officer and was elected sheriff of Beadle County but was sent to the South Dakota State Prison for embezzling $4,000 two years later. On his release from there it was a short step into bootlegging and then the major leagues. He worked for the Keating–Holden Gang, on one occasion breaking all the fingers of a victim's hand to show his devotion to the cause. He may have also worked as a freelancer for Lepke Buchalter of Murder Inc. and for the Purple Gang of Detroit. In 1931 he teamed up with Machine Gun Kelly in a series of successful bank robberies and the next year was suspected of killing two Minneapolis police officers.

He had a hard time surviving his friend Nash. He was now being blamed for any major unsolved crime in the Midwest – the kidnappings of Charles Urschel and William Hamm (carried out by Machine Gun Kelly and the Barker–Karpis Gang respectively), the robbery of a bank in Brainerd (by Babyface Nelson) and, more likely, the machine-gunning of Miles Cunningham, a police officer in Chicago. He was also on the run from the underworld who disliked the pressure being placed on them by the police and the FBI. Even before this, Miller had never been overly popular. Invariably he took the death of a colleague as a personal slight and would hunt down the man's killer.

His naked body, identifiable only by his fingerprints, was found in a ditch near Detroit on 29 November 1933. He had been strangled and his skull crushed. His killers, it has been suggested, were members of the Purple Gang.

Adam Richetti, who always denied being present, and Charlie "Pretty Boy" Floyd also suffered in the FBI backlash following the Union Station massacre. Richetti was captured on 22 October 1934 and charged with both the Kansas City murders and the killing of two police officers near Columbus, Missouri, on 14 June. He was sentenced to death but before his execution two brothers confessed to the Columbus killings. It did Richetti no good. On 7 October 1938 he was taken to the gas chamber in the Missouri state prison still protesting his innocence. As he was being strapped to the chair he is reported to have called out, "What have I done to deserve this?"

Floyd, of all the robbers of the time, was possibly the only one to approach the justification of a Robin Hood tag. Born in Indian territory in Oklahoma in 1901, until the decline of small sharecroppers in the mid-1920s he was regarded as a good worker. By then he was married and his wife was pregnant. He carried out an ill-executed bank robbery, receiving a three-year sentence. He served half and from then lived only by robbery. He was arrested in 1930 and sentenced to ten to twenty-five years. He threw himself off the train on the way to the Ohio State Penitentiary, linked up with Bill "The Killer" Miller and together they undertook a number of low-grade robberies of petrol stations before settling, for a time, in Mother Ash's brothel in Kansas City. It was while residing there that they killed her robber sons Wallace and William Ash in a quarrel over her daughter-in-law, Rose Ash, and her sister, Beulah Bird. Floyd Miller and the two girls then set off on a series of robberies, killing Carl Galliher, the Chief of Police of Bowling Green, Ohio. The girls were wounded in the shoot-out and Miller was killed.

It was now that Floyd obtained his reputation as a friend of the poor. When he and his new partner, George Birdwell, robbed banks he would distribute money to the townspeople and also tear up mortgages the banks held on the sharecroppers' land. In 1932 Birdwell was killed in a bank robbery on his own and Floyd attached himself to the Dillinger operation as well as carrying out his own robberies with Richetti. They zigzagged across the Midwest while his estranged wife toured the countryside promoting a film, *Crime Does Not Pay*.

In October 1934 Richetti and Floyd were seen in a wood near Wellsville, Ohio. Richetti was captured but Floyd escaped only to be shot on 22 October in a cornfield near East Liverpool. Chester C. Smith, a police officer at the scene, said that on the orders of an FBI agent, Melvin Purvis, who had been called to take charge of the hunt, he was deliberately killed as he lay against a cornstack. Floyd had also consistently denied that he had been involved in the Kansas City Massacre. Ten thousand people are said to have attended his funeral in Akins, Oklahoma.

This rather left the Barker–Karpis outfit and John Dillinger as the only major surviving Dust Bowl gangs on whom Hoover and the FBI could direct their attention.

John Dillinger, born in 1903 in Moorstown, Indiana, was perhaps the superstar of them all. A member of a youth gang called the Dirty Dozen, he majored in crime after only a short stint in the US Navy from which he simply absented himself. In 1924 he and an older and more experienced man, the web-fingered Ed Singleton, tried to rob a local grocer, B. F. Morgan. There is some evidence that Dillinger had been drinking. Certainly the grocer knew him and identified him. Dillinger, told that things would go better if he pleaded guilty, drew a sentence of ten to twenty years, the statutory minimum. Singleton did not confess and received only two years. In 1937 he fell asleep on a railway track while drunk and was run over by a train.

In his memoirs G. Russell Giradin, the lawyer who defended Dillinger, argues that this savage sentence soured the youth.

Carl Sifakis quotes the Indiana Governor's secretary, Wayne Coy, as saying, "There does not seem to me to be any escape from the fact that the State of Indiana made John Dillinger the Public Enemy that he is today." This rather overlooks the fact that Dillinger's father had already bailed him out from a number of previous thefts and assaults. He also had something of a history of enjoying forced sex.

While in prison, first in the Indiana State Reformatory and then in Michigan City, Dillinger met the men he would ultimately lead: John "Red" Hamilton, Homer Van Meter, Charlie Makley and their head at the time, Harry Pierpont. From a farming family in Leipsic, Ohio, Pierpont had been hit on the head with a baseball bat as a child and subsequently suffered from violent rages. Of the others Makley, born in 1889, was a smart talker able to argue his way out of unpromising situations and an accomplished bank-robber. Hamilton was also known as "Three Finger Jack" following a sleighing accident in Sault Ste Marie, Michigan.

Dillinger appears to have had only one flaw in the eyes of these men – he took an "old lady" prison lover, i.e. another male prisoner. In all other respects, such as trustworthiness and ability to help others, he seems to have been exemplary. He was released in 1933 following a petition signed by some 200 people from Mooresville, including his victim, B. F. Morgan. When given the news, he promised his new friends that he would work towards their escape. He returned home only to find that his stepmother, to whom he was devoted, had died hours earlier. He then began a series of small-time robberies to finance his promise.

On 26 September 1933, after an abortive attempt when guns thrown into the prison were handed to the authorities, Pierpont, Red Hamilton and eight other prisoners, armed with a smuggled gun, took hostages and escaped. Dillinger, on the other hand, suspected by Captain Matt Leach of several bank robberies, was arrested in Dayton, Ohio.

Around 6.30 on the evening of 12 October Dillinger was sprung from jail in Lima, Ohio, by Pierpont, Makley, Russell Clark and Ed Shouse. They arrived in a car driven by Red Hamilton, claiming to be officers come to take Dillinger back to Michigan City. When Sheriff Jesse Sarber asked to see their credentials Pierpont produced a gun saying, "Here are our credentials," and as Sarber went for his revolver, shot him in the stomach. Sarber's wife and a deputy, Wilbur Sharp, were locked in a cell. Dillinger's cell, where he had been playing cards, was unlocked and they were on their way to Leipsic, Ohio, where they celebrated Pierpont's birthday at his parents' home the next day. The day after Pierpont's birthday party they raided the police station at Auburn, Indiana, where they locked up the officers in their own cells and took all the guns, including a Thompson machine-gun, two rifles, four pistols and over 1,200 cartridges. A similar raid on a police station in Peru, Indiana, followed.

Now, the Pierpont Mob became the Dillinger Mob. The renaming was due to Matt Leach who spent that part of his career in hopeless pursuit of Dillinger. He hoped that by renaming the Pierpont Gang he would engender rivalry between the two leaders. In fact Pierpont did not mind at all. He was quite satisfied that Dillinger had kept his promise and had stage-managed his earlier escape.

Despite his enormous reputation, Dillinger actually operated as a robber for only a limited period. During his first run the gang undertook between ten and twenty robberies – many were falsely attributed to them and the members never actually admitted which ones they committed. There is no doubt, however, that Dillinger, Pierpont and Hamilton robbed a bank in East Chicago on 15 January 1934 when Patrolman William O'Malley was shot dead. Dillinger was given the blame for the shooting but on this occasion it is more likely to have been Hamilton.

Dillinger was arrested in Tucson in January 1934. He was taken back to Ohio where eighty-five officers met the plane.

He was charged with the murder of Sarber but, unfortunately for prosecuting attorney Robert Estill, a picture was taken of him with his arm around Dillinger. It was something that would haunt Estill for nearly twenty years. In 1951 he lost an action for defamation against Hearst Newspapers over a series of articles after the death of Red Hamilton's girlfriend Pat Cherrington which referred to the incident. For the moment Dillinger was lodged in the escape-proof prison in Crown Point.

On 3 March 1934 Dillinger escaped, possibly with the help of a wooden gun whittled whilst in prison. More likely it was with the assistance of his lawyer, Louis Piquett, who perhaps bribed an Indiana judge to smuggle in the weapon. Dillinger locked up eight deputies and a dozen trusties before escaping with Herbert Youngblood, a black prisoner. They took the car of the lady sheriff, Lillian Holley, and two hostages. Dillinger would never be in prison again. Youngblood, however, did not last long on the outside. He was killed on 16 March, shot by police officers in Port Huron, Michigan. Dying, he generously laid a trail away from Dillinger, saying they had been together the previous day.

After Dillinger's escape Eulalie Callender, an elderly deluded woman, wrote to Piquett saying it must be the hand of God that had allowed Dillinger to escape. On 7 March the lawyer, presumably with his tongue firmly cemented in his cheek, wrote back to her:

> I like you believe that it was the hand of God that enabled this young Christian soul to live on. From my experience with the party in question, I can safely tell you that he will rob no banks, it is his firm intention to travel in the path of righteousness. He is a great student of the Bible. In the last conversation I had with him he had told me that it was his intention to live the balance of his life in this world of God, and beyond any doubt your sweet prayers have had a great deal to do with this deliverance.

All successful escapees must have somewhere to go and for Dillinger it was to 901 Addison Street, Chicago, and to Evelyn "Billie" Frechette whom he had met in a nightclub in November 1933. She had been brought up on a Menominee Indian Reservation and in 1932 had married Welton Walter Spark, who drew a fifteen-year sentence for a post office robbery later that year. Two days after the Crown Point escape, Dillinger turned up at her apartment and they immediately left for St Paul.

In 1937 Frechette told *True Confessions* of her life with Dillinger:

> There was something in those eyes that I will never forget. They were piercing and electric, yet there was an amused carefree twinkle in them too. They met my eyes and held me hypnotized for an instant. John was good to me. He looked after me and bought me all kinds of jewellery and cars and pets, and we went places and saw things, and he gave me everything a girl wants. He treated me like a lady.

Now he put together the Dillinger Mob Mark II. They included Homer Van Meter, Eddie Green, who was a friend of Frank Nash, John "Red" Hamilton and Lester Gillis, who wanted to be called "Big George" Nelson but was known as "Baby Face". On 6 March they cleared $50,000 at the Security National Bank, Sioux Falls, South Dakota, where Nelson killed a police officer. Ten days later they robbed the National Bank in Mason City, Iowa, of a similar amount. Two civilians were hit and so were Dillinger and Hamilton. Pierpont, Makley and Clark were captured. When they came to trial Dillinger paid for their defence. Well, that is not strictly accurate: banks robbed by him paid for the defence but at least he did send the money to the lawyers. His financing was unsuccessful. Clark received life imprisonment, while Pierpont and Makley were sentenced to death.

Meanwhile Van Meter drove Dillinger and Hamilton to St Paul where they were met by the florid-faced underworld gopher and bootlegger William Albert "Pat" Reilly, who worked at Harry Sawyer's Green Lantern Saloon. He took them to Dr Nels Mortensen, president of Minnesota's Board of Health, to patch up their wounds. On the face of it a most unlikely underworld doctor, Mortensen always claimed that he did not know the men were Dillinger and Hamilton but he was not as squeaky clean as might have been hoped. He had given a reference for Freddie Barker when he rented a hideout in Vernon Street and had prescribed medicine to treat venereal disease for someone at that address.

Five days later Dillinger and Frechette moved to Lincoln Apartments in St Paul under the names Mr and Mrs Carl Hellman. The owner did not like the look of them and reported them to the FBI. They staked out the building and then, on 31 March, botched a raid on Dillinger. They had left the back of the building unguarded as an agent knocked on the door and was told to wait. Although shot again, Dillinger escaped with Frechette, who drove their car out of the garage and away. Within hours he was being cared for in a clinic run by Dr Clayton May, a man who specialized in abortions as well as the treatment of gunshot wounds and venereal diseases. He had been recommended by Eddie Green whom he had known since the early 1920s.

On 3 April 1934 Eddie Green was shot by the FBI as he arrived with his wife Bessie at what they thought to be a safe house in St Paul. He died nine days later and, under severe pressure, Bessie turned informer. Indictments against members of the gang were handed down on 19 May.

On 9 April Billie Frechette was arrested in her Twin Cities apartment and charged with harbouring Dillinger. Defended by Piquett at her trial she claimed that during the time she was questioned she was beaten and given no food or water for two days in an effort to get her to give Dillinger up. The

FBI maintained that this could not have happened since it was absolutely forbidden to treat a woman in this way. The story goes that Dillinger watched both her arrest and trial, where she received two years. Apparently he had to be prevented by Pat Cherrington, Red Hamilton's girlfriend, from trying to intervene when Frechette was arrested.

On 22 April 1934 Dillinger and other members of the gang were caught by the FBI at Little Bohemia Lodge, a summer resort, then closed, about fifty miles from Rhinelander, Wisconsin. Their choice of hideout was not wholly fortuitous: the owner, Emil Wanatka, was rumoured to have mob connections and, before the Depression, had owned a similarly named establishment on Chicago's North Side. Wanatka had been almost wiped out in the Depression and the lodge was his last throw.

The ensuing battle was a disaster for the FBI. Although the lodge was officially closed it was still used as a bar by Civilian Conservation Corps workers. As three of them left they were mistaken for the gang by the waiting agents who fired on them. One worker, Eugene Boiseneau, was shot dead and the shooting tipped off Dillinger and the others who left by the back door. Baby Face Nelson was in a cabin near the lodge and escaped into the woods after killing agent W. Carter Baum and wounding two other law officers. Red Hamilton was a casualty on the bandits' side, later dying of his injuries. It is said that he was shot, not at the lodge but later in a roadblock as he and Dillinger drove through the outskirts of St Paul. He was taken to the crooked doctor Joseph Moran, who had also treated him when he was shot in the January raid in East Chicago but, for some reason, on this occasion Moran would have nothing to do with him. Dillinger then took him to a Barker–Karpis hideout in Aurora, Illinois, where he was nursed by Volney Davis and Davis's girlfriend Edna Murray, known as "Rabbits" because of her ability to escape. She was also known as the "Kissing Bandit" because of her habit of kissing male victims of her robberies. It is thought Hamilton died on 30 April and he was buried with lye over his face and hands in an attempt to prevent identification. He was another in a long line of criminals who was said to have survived and there were numerous posthumous sightings of him but the FBI claimed to have identified him the next year after Murray, who had been sentenced for her part in the kidnapping of Minnesota banker Edward Bremer, took them to the grave.

Three women were captured in the battle at Little Bohemia Lodge – Marie "Mickey" Conforti, the girlfriend of Van Meter, Baby Face Nelson's wife Helen Gillis, and car thief and post office robber Tommy Carroll's girlfriend Jean Delaney Crompton, the sister of Dolores who had a son by Alvin "Creepy" Karpis. They were later released.

The only one to come out completely on the plus side was Wanatka. At least he made some money out of the whole affair. After the battle the lodge became something of a tourist attraction and, over the years, he added various Dillinger artefacts as exhibits. Little Bohemia Lodge remains open to this day.

During the early part of May, Dillinger, Van Meter and Tommy Carroll hid out in a cabin near East Chicago, in Lake County, Indiana. On 24 May, when they were stopped by police officers, Van Meter shot both officers dead. A fortnight later, on 6 June, Carroll and Jean Delaney Crompton checked into a tourist camp in Cedar Rapids. The next day a garage attendant in nearby Waterloo told the police he had seen spare licence plates in the back of Carroll's Hudson. He had parked opposite the police station and when the police went to question him, he dropped his gun and was shot and killed as he ran down an alley. Jean Crompton was captured and sentenced to a year and a day. Two days later she miscarried their child.

For Dillinger and Van Meter some change of appearance was clearly necessary and the following month, for a fee of $5,000 each, both suffered from the German-born immigrant Dr

William Loeser's "secret" formula of two parts of hydrochloric acid and one of nitro-hydrochloric acid to be used with an alkaloid. Dillinger's crooked lawyer, Louis Piquett, had gone to see him at his apartment in Wrightwood Avenue and Loeser showed him his own new fingerprints, which he said he had done in Mexico. He had fled there while on parole from a 1913 sentence for dealing in narcotics. Could Dillinger's and Van Meter's prints be changed? Certainly, for a fee of $10,000. Loeser recruited another abortionist doctor Harold Cassidy to help but the operations were not a success. First, Dillinger nearly died after swallowing his tongue under the anaesthetic. Cassidy pulled it out just in time. But, of course the repairs were useless. Fingerprints cannot be changed and the bandaged Van Meter threatened to shoot Loeser with a machine-gun. Only half the fee was paid over. Piquett kept the rest.

On 30 June Dillinger, Van Meter, Baby Face Nelson and Nelson's Californian-born friend, John Paul Chase, robbed a bank in South Bend, Indiana. In the shoot-out four bystanders were killed and Van Meter shot police officer Howard Wagner.

Now things were seriously falling apart. As has been traditional for robbers, Dillinger wanted one last big job and then to go to Mexico. There is some evidence that at one time he did go south of the border but by the middle of July he was in Chicago where, in the enforced absence of Billie Frechette, he had taken up with a waitress and probably one-time brothel inmate, Canadian-born Edythe "Polly" Hamilton and her friend Anna Sage, a Romanian brothel-keeper who had an apartment at North Halstead Street. Sage, a long-time friend of Martin Zarkovich of the East Chicago Police Department, had worked in the Guthrie Street brothel of "Big Bill" Subotich and on his death had taken over the establishment. She had also run the forty-two-room Kostur Hotel, known as the Bucket of Blood, in Gary, Indiana. Polly Hamilton had once been married to Gary policeman Roy Keele, and now combined hustling with waitressing at the S & S Sandwich shop in Uptown.

On 22 July, Dillinger, along with Hamilton and Sage, went to the Biograph Theatre to see Clark Gable in *Manhattan Melodrama*. Sage was facing her third conviction and, along with it, deportation. She had heard the stories that Dillinger, then living as Jimmy Lawrence, was telling Hamilton. Putting two and two together, she went to FBI agent Melvin Purvis to try to negotiate not only a reward, but also a relaxation of her deportation proceedings.

The legend is that, as arranged, that night Sage was wearing red to indicate Dillinger was with her – in fact, she was wearing an orange skirt but she has remained known as "the Woman in Red". According to some versions, Purvis called on Dillinger to stop and when he did not the FBI opened fire. Dillinger was hit along with two women passers-by. Hamilton and Sage simply disappeared from the scene. They were later retrieved and taken to Detroit to ensure their silence. Thousands queued to see Dillinger's body, dipping pieces of paper and even the hems of their skirts in his blood.

Sage's reward was $5,000, half the amount she anticipated. In April 1936, her appeals against deportation were dismissed. She was taken to Ellis Island where she was put on the *President Harding* and deported to Romania. She opened a bar-restaurant but was the victim of protection racketeers who thought she had more money than she did. It is suggested she actually had facial surgery, claiming she had a skin disease, and went to live in Cairo. She died in Timisoara in 1947 from liver disease. Polly Hamilton worked as a waitress under a variety of names and later married a salesman, William Black. She died on the North Side of Chicago in 1969.

Basing his theory on inconsistencies in Dillinger's autopsy report, the crime historian Jay Robert Nash argues that along with Joe Hill, JFK, Lord Lucan, Elvis Presley and Marilyn Monroe, Dillinger did not die and that the FBI were duped.

The man shot was, in fact, the small-time gangster Jimmy Lawrence, under whose name Dillinger was living. If this is correct whatever happened to Dillinger? To where did he disappear? Presumably Mexico. There is also another theory, this time that Dillinger was not shot by FBI agents but by a policeman freelancing as a hitman for the Chicago Mafia.

On 23 August 1934 Homer Van Meter was betrayed, possibly by Baby Face Nelson with whom he had quarrelled, and was shot in the now decidedly unsafe St Paul. Caught on the corner of Marion Street and University Avenue by four police officers including Chief Frank Cullen and former Chief Thomas Brown, he was literally riddled with bullets and had his fingers shot off. His family claimed he had been used as target practice. It has also been suggested he may have been betrayed by his former girlfriend Marie Comforti, on whom he was cheating, or even by the parents of his newest girlfriend, Opal Milligan. The author William J. Helmer suggests the squealer may have been St Paul crime boss Harry Sawyer, bagman to the police. This is based on the belief that Van Meter had asked Sawyer, who owned the Green Lantern Saloon, to look after $9,000, his part of the proceeds of the Sioux Falls bank raid. When Van Meter returned to reclaim the cash, Sawyer thought that it was easier to tell the police rather than pay up. There was a final suggestion that Tommy Gannon, a St Paul bank-robber, had betrayed him at the instigation of casino owner Jack Peifer. The police and Peifer kept the money and Gannon was given Van Meter's guns.

On 22 September Pierpont and Makley tried another escape from prison, this time using guns carved out of soap. They managed to overcome one guard when the riot squad opened fire on them. Makley was killed and Pierpont, paralysed in the shooting, was carried to the electric chair on 17 October. Harry Pierpont's homely looking girlfriend, Mary Kinder, who had been married to Dale Kinder, the robber son of an Indianapolis police officer, was refused permission to marry him before his execution. Kinder had the dubious and possibly unique distinction of having her brother, Earl, her husband and her boyfriend in the same prison at the same time.

The diminutive Baby Face Nelson had begun a career as a solo bank-robber before escaping on his way to prison. He then became a bootlegger and worked as a contract killer in the Midwest. Now he thought he was about to launch himself as the greatest criminal the country had known. He was wrong. On 27 November 1934 he was found by two FBI agents, Samuel Cowley and Herman Hollis, with his wife, Helen, and John Paul Chase, in a stalled car near Barrington, Illinois. His wife fled and Nelson, it seems, in the manner of a screen Western gunfight, simply walked towards the agents. He was hit several times before, in turn, he shot and killed both the men. He got into the agents' car and told Chase to drive away. His naked body was found the next day, laid out near St Paul's Cemetery in Niles Centre, twenty miles away. Helen Gillis later received a year's sentence for harbouring.

Chase went to Chicago and then to California where he was found working in a fish factory at Mount Shasta near Sacramento and sentenced to life imprisonment for his part in the killing of Cowley. Hoover directly intervened to block his 1950 parole application, describing him as "rat with a patriotic-sounding name". By then he had taken up painting at which he had some small success and he was a model prisoner. Hoover then said he would prosecute Chase over the death of the second agent, Hollis, but this was blocked by a judge on the grounds that the twenty-one-year delay violated Chase's right to a speedy trial. Over Hoover's objections, Chase was eventually paroled in October 1966 and died of cancer on 5 October 1973.

On her release in 1936 from her two-year sentence for harbouring Dillinger, Billie Frechette undertook a variety tour in the *Crime Does Not Pay* show, as did John Dillinger Sr, offering reminiscences of their lover and son respectively. Of

Dillinger, Billie said, "He liked to dance and he liked to hunt . . . I think he liked gravy better than anything else. He liked bread and gravy." She married and resurfaced briefly when her new husband, a minor criminal, was arrested in Chicago in the 1950s. Later she lived in Wisconsin where she died from cancer in 1969. She does not appear to have ever commented on the size of her lover's organ said, surely exaggeratedly, to have been twenty-three inches long.

For a time Harry Pierpont's girlfriend, Mary Kinder, also appeared in a carnival show and at the World's Fair. She died in Indianapolis in 1981. She had been suffering from emphysema and alcoholism. The somewhat overweight Pat Cherrington, Red Hamilton's girlfriend, was another who went to prison, along with her sister Opal Long. Both received two years for harbouring. On her parole she returned to working in bars, and in 1938 was accused of swindling a pool player of $8,000. She died in 1949 and was buried in Chicago. Marie Comforti served a year and a day's imprisonment and on her release was then charged with the same crime as a federal offence. She therefore served two sentences for the same crime. Helen Gillis lived quietly after her release from prison, dying in 1987.

As for the doctors and lawyers, the abortionist Clayton May was sentenced to two years in Leavenworth and his medical licence was revoked. William Loeser was given a one-day sentence and returned to prison for breach of his parole following the round-up of Dillinger's associates after his death. He had snitched on a junior doctor, Cassidy, whom he said had performed the operations. He was released on 21 September 1935. Cassidy was given a year's probation after being held in custody for eight months. In July 1946 he killed himself at his sister's home.

As for Louis Piquett, he was first charged with harbouring Dillinger. After a stormy trial in which his attorney collapsed following a heart attack during his closing speech and Piquett himself then addressed the jury, he was found not guilty. He was then put on trial for harbouring Van Meter and, perhaps surprisingly, this time lost. He was sentenced to two years' imprisonment and fined $10,000. He was also disbarred. After his release he lived quietly in Chicago, sometimes working as a bartender. He was eventually pardoned and had made an application to be allowed to practise law again when he died following a heart attack in December 1951.

11

Murder Inc.

Just how many men were killed by members of Murder Inc. is open to considerable speculation. According to a memorandum in the New York Municipal Archives a conservative estimate was that there were eighty-five murders that could definitely be laid at the doors of its members. The crime historian Carl Sifakis suggests a figure of between 400 and 500 and that "Pittsburgh Phil" Strauss may have killed between fifty and a hundred himself. Another crime historian, J. Robert Nash, suggests that Frank Abbandando himself executed half that number. There have even been suggestions that Strauss, a particularly dedicated killer, murdered up to 500 people nationwide. Certainly, the gang introduced a whole new raft of slang into the underworld and in turn the newspapers. A "contract" was a murder assignment; a "bum" (possibly signifying his low station in life) was the victim; a "hit" or a "pop" was the actual killing. Fees paid ranged from $1,000 to $5,000 and the killers were on retainers of between $125 and $150 a week. Additionally they would be given percentages of rackets such as the numbers game in a particular area. This was a time when men were machine-gunned, stabbed, ice-picked and strangled. Their bodies were burned, buried, tied to jukeboxes and sunk in lakes, and left on street corners as examples. The name Murder Inc. was invented for them by

Harry Feeney of the *World-Telegram* but they liked to refer to themselves as the Combination.

At the beginning of the 1930s, with Prohibition still in force, a group from Brooklyn at first known as the Brownsville Mob was formed and led by Abe "Kid Twist" Reles, the dapper Louis Capone (who was no relation to the more famous Al), Harry "Pittsburgh Phil" Strauss (who came from Brooklyn and merely liked the name; he was also known as Pep) and Marty "Buggsy" Goldstein. Underlings included Walter Sage (who would later be killed for skimming from his superiors), Abraham "Pretty" Levine, Anthony "Duke" Maffetore, Seymour Magoon, Jacob Drucker, Mikey Sycoff, Sholem Bernstein and Irving "Gangy" Cohen.

About a year later the Brownsville Mob formed an alliance with the Ocean Hill Mob, then led by Harry "Happy" Maione, Frank Abbandando (known as The Dasher either because of the speed he showed when he played in a reformatory baseball team at Elmira or because of the speed with which he chased one of his early victims), Angelo Julie Catalano (sometimes Catalino) and Vito "Socko" Gurino, also known as "Chicken Head" because of his habit of shooting chickens as target practice. When the mobs combined they murdered the Shapiro brothers, Irving and Meyer, and several of their associates, taking control of their rackets in Brooklyn. Shortly afterwards Albert Anastasia, who controlled the waterfront, became the boss of the combined mob.

The gangs now morphed into the notorious Murder Inc., a specific arm of the new generation crime syndicate led by Lucky Luciano, Albert Anastasia, Frank Costello, Meyer Lansky and Moe Dalitz, the least known but one of the most influential of all, once a member of the Purple Gang and later of the Cleveland Road Syndicate. The aim of the new crime syndicate was to bring order to the disorganization of Al Capone and the wars in Chicago. The rackets were to be divided in an orderly manner. The founders, quite correctly, foresaw opposition to their well-intentioned plans and Murder Inc. was to be their enforcement arm.

The rules drawn up by Lansky and Dalitz were that the members of Murder Inc. were only to be used for the most pressing of business reasons and – once more correctly seeing that the murder of public figures would only bring down the wrath of the authorities on their heads – lawyers, judges and reporters were to be inviolate. Except, of course, if those lawyers, judges and reporters mixed business with pleasure, so to speak. One of those at risk was assistant state prosecutor and later municipal judge John Sbarbaro, who had prosecuted Richard Loeb and Nathan Leopold for the kidnapping and killing of fourteen-year-old Bobby Franks in 1924. Sbarbaro's garage in Chicago was used to house illegal liquor and he doubled as the undertaker of choice to the families of dead racketeers such as Dion O'Bannion. At least Sbarbaro lived to tell the tale. The worst that happened to him was that the garage was blown up. He was mystified by this, claiming it must have been a revenge for the harsh sentences he had handed down. He lived until March 1970, dying when a plane exploded over Tell City, Indiana. In 1994 a school named after him in Chicago was renamed Arthur R. Ashe Elementary School.

As always there are conflicting versions as to how the combined Brownsville/Ocean Hill gang came to be chosen as executioners. One is that Reles was at war with the Shapiro brothers, who, according to some accounts, had raped his girlfriend and generally treated him badly. It was something of a test to see how he would deal with the problem and when the brothers were killed in the so-called Battle of Brooklyn in June 1931 his worth was realized. Irving Shapiro was killed in his flat. Meyer was killed a few days later, Joey Silver was killed shortly after that and Willie Shapiro was garrotted by Reles some years later in a bar in New York. He was then tied up, put in a laundry bag and buried in Canarsie, Brooklyn. When he was later the subject of an autopsy it was found that he had dirt in his lungs. Reles had not killed him with the garrotte; Shapiro had been buried alive.

In the meantime a bootlegger, Abe Wagner, suspected of participating in the kidnapping of the Lindbergh baby in 1932, had fallen out with the Mazza Gang, a group of up-and-comers from the East Side of Manhattan. On 22 February 1932 his car was ambushed on Sutton Street and he escaped by rolling through the passenger door. Efforts to appease the Mazzas had failed. His brother Allie and his partner Harry Brown were sent to pay off the Mazzas at the Hatfield Hotel on Upper East Side. The money was taken, Allie was shot dead and Brown sent back to Abe Wagner to tell him of the disaster.

Now Wagner fled to St Paul, staying there as a flower-seller under the name of Abe Loeb. When his whereabouts were discovered a contract was sent to hitmen George Young and Joseph Schaefer. Wagner was duly killed as he left a drugstore on University Avenue on 25 July of that year but the getaway was botched and they were both arrested immediately by a passing policeman.

It was then that Murder Inc. began what were unavailing efforts to have the pair released. Jurors were contacted and a police chief in the city turned down $25,000 to allow them to escape. Convicted, they were sentenced to life imprisonment with hard labour. An offer of $35,000 to a man to blow the prison wall went unclaimed after he had reconnoitred the site. Overall, however, Young and Schaefer's life does not seem to have been unduly hard. They had coffee, hot plates in their rooms, fresh meat and $50 a week each to bribe the guards. Schaefer, then aged sixty-five, was paroled in December 1963. On his way to the airport he said that Wagner, who had been trying to kidnap him, had been shot in self-defence. Young was released a short time later. Neither ever revealed who had paid for the contract or their living expenses.

In direct charge of Murder Inc. was Albert Anastasia, often referred to as the Lord High Executioner. He had changed the last letter of his name from an "o" to avoid causing embarrassment to his mother when she read the newspapers. Anastasia's personal principal enforcers were Jack Parisi, James Feraco and Anthony Romeo. In fact, his then superiors in the overall scheme of things were Louis "Lepke" Buchalter and Giuseppe Doto, known from time to time as Joe Dio or Joe Adonis. However, these in turn reported to the informal board of a combination of Bugsy Siegel, Lansky, Luciano, Dalitz and Costello. It was they who gave the go-ahead for the contracts that took place nationwide. Arthur Flegenheimer, known as "Dutch Shultz" and regarded as increasingly unstable, was not invited to join as his interests were under threat from Luciano.

Members of Murder Inc. received their instructions and undertook their planning at a candy store at the corner of Saratoga and Livonia Avenues in Brownsville. Run by Rose Gold, who could neither read nor write English and was then in her sixties, it was open twenty-four hours a day and was consequently known as Midnight Rose's. One reason for its importance was that, in the days when telephones were virtually unknown luxuries for the immigrant communities, the store had one and Rose Gold would take messages. When she was later arrested and refused to become a prosecution witness, she was asked, "Why do you let so many criminals frequent your store?" Her reply was, "Why don't the police keep them out?"

The weapon of choice, certainly so far as Strauss was concerned, was the ice pick, regarded as a clean and therefore favoured method of killing. As a bonus given the then limited development of the autopsy, it was not always recognizable and the medical opinion would often come out in favour of natural causes. The favoured method was to have the victim held in a lavatory or other confined space while the killer would jam the ice pick in the eardrum. Externally it would only produce a tiny hole in the ear and a very limited amount of bleeding, which could be wiped clean. The likely conclusion would be that the victim had died of a cerebral haemorrhage. However, it was not always a clean kill. If the victim struggled there would most likely be multiple stab wounds, which led to only one conclusion.

In the summer of 1937 Strauss, who took some pride in his work, was obliged to stab Walter Sage thirty-two times. Sage had been running and stealing from a syndicate coin machine racket in the Catskills and was unwilling to go quietly. Appropriately enough his body was then lashed to a pinball machine and dropped in a lake. Unfortunately the medical knowledge of Strauss and those with him was limited. Perforations by an ice pick while the victim is still alive seal quickly so, despite the weight of the machine, the gases in the body brought it to the surface within a week. Strauss is alleged to have said, "Think of that. With this bum, you gotta be a doctor, or he floats."

Strauss, in particular, was used for hits across the United States. In August 1937 Detroit's Purple Gang failed in an attempt to dispose of their renegade member, Harry Millman, with a car bomb. Ten sticks of dynamite set up to explode when Millman's car engine was switched on had merely killed Willie Holmes, a parking attendant at the 1040 Club who had gone to collect the vehicle. The Purples contacted Murder Inc. and Strauss and Happy Maione were despatched to the Midwest to deal with Millman.

From a respectable family, Harry Millman was a good-looking ladies' man and a first-class swimmer who had been to high school at a Kentucky Military Academy, from which he graduated in 1928. By the next year he had become a hijacker and gunman in the Purple Gang, and was wholly reliable until he had a drink. In November 1933 he organized the killing of senior Purples Abe Axler and Eddie Fletcher. Despite twenty-eight arrests for murder, extortion, armed robbery and assault he never spent a night in jail. Over the years, however, he became more and more of a loose cannon, targeting Mafia-protected brothels and blind pigs. He was regularly called to account by the Purple leader, Abe Bernstein, but no amount of lecturing could quieten him down.

This time there was no question of the delicate use of an ice pick. On 24 November 1937, Thanksgiving Eve, Millman along with Hymie Cooper and Harry Gross went to Boesky's cocktail lounge in Detroit. About 1 a.m. as Millman went to the bar, two men walked up and fired from point-blank range. Gross and Cooper tried to hide under a table but in turn they were shot at, as was a customer who simply got in the way. Gross died in hospital without naming his killers, if indeed he knew them. Cooper, who survived, sensibly had nothing to say.

By 1937 the racketeers Lepke Buchalter and Jacob Shapiro (known as Gurrah because of his pronunciation of "Get out of here" and no relation of the murdered brothers) had formed an alliance with Murder Inc. In turn their underlings included Charlie "The Bug" Workman, Samuel "Tootsie" Feinstein and Albert "Tick Tock" Tannenbaum.

Perhaps, however, the most important piece of work undertaken by members of Murder Inc. was the killing of the less than charismatic Arthur Flegenheimer, better known as Dutch Schultz. Regarded as a much less appealing man than Capone, he was the son of a German Jew who deserted the family, leaving young Arthur to a life of juvenile crime. Born on 6 August 1902 he grew up in the Bronx where he was a member of the Bergen Gang of pickpockets and shoplifters, and by the age of twenty he had interests in slot machines, beer joints, restaurants, taxi companies and professional boxing as well as the numbers racket. In his entire career he acquired only one conviction when in 1917 he was sentenced to fifteen months for burglary.

On his release from prison Flegenheimer announced that henceforth he would be known as Dutch Schultz in tribute to the leader of the Frog Hollow Gang of white slavers that had operated in Morrisania, New York, in the 1880s until it was broken up in 1913 when the leaders received forty-two years' imprisonment. During Prohibition Schultz had his own brewery, providing what was regarded as some of the worst beer in the Bronx, as well as an empire built on smuggling whisky from Canada and Europe. He hijacked much of his stock. In the late 1920s he had taken over a policy, or numbers rackets, in Harlem that was surprisingly run by a woman, Stephanie St Clair. He went into the slot-machine business with Costello and recruited as his enforcers Jack "Legs" Diamond and Vincent Coll – known as "Mad Dog" from his reckless use of the machine-gun when he shot and killed a five-year-old child. Diamond had been well established by this time and his smaller empire served to swell that of Schultz. Coll, along with his brother Peter, had begun his career as a beer delivery boy at $150 a week, working his way up through the ranks.

By 1930 Schultz held New York in the same way as Capone did Chicago. His rivals were simply eliminated. He was also regarded as a pathological miser. It was said that: "You can insult Arthur's girl, even steal her from him; spit in his face and push him around and he'd laugh it off. But don't steal even a dollar that belongs to him. You're dead if you do."

Both Diamond and Mad Dog Coll tried to do just that. Each had begun to hijack their leader's beer-trucks and reprisals were swift if not always certain. Finally Diamond was killed in October 1931 and Coll was assassinated, trapped in a telephone booth. His killers, who were never prosecuted, were almost certainly the brothers Abraham (known as "Abe" or "Bo") and George Weinberg.

Now with his last rival eliminated, just as Capone controlled the politicians in Cicero, Schultz had his own in New York. However, success does not appear to have brought him happiness. He became increasingly paranoid and aggressive, surrounding himself with guards he did not trust and women whom he believed were cheating on him sexually.

On 4 March 1935 he murdered Jules Mosgilewsky, known as Julie Martin, who had been his point man in his restaurant extortion racket. Schultz shot him in the back in his suite at the Haroney Hotel at Cohoes, near Albany, because he believed he had stolen $21,000 from him. The cover-up was ingenious. After the body was removed, to explain the stain Lulu Rosenkrantz was made to stand on the spot while Danny Dale broke his nose, so dripping blood on to the carpet.

Schultz was also regarded as being highly superstitious and not too worried from where his religious emblems came. During one trial it is said he accepted a rosary in the morning and a *mezuzah* in the evening. He was a social climber, constantly seeking introductions to the upper crust and the literati. He was, of course, devoted to his mother.

Now he was charged with income tax evasion. Many of his advisers were wise enough to know how to circumvent the problem. The first requirement was to move the trial out of town and it went to Syracuse, in upstate New York. The second was to create a favourable – to the defendant, that is – atmosphere. First Schultz paid a PR man $10,000 to set the scene. Then drinks were on the house for the town's children and adults alike and, before the retrial, after the jury disagreed on a cast-iron case against him, he hired a dancehall. Not guilty.

Back in town he found that Italian interests had moved in on his rackets. Luciano and Vito Genovese had taken over a large proportion of the empire and had seduced one of his more trusted lieutenants, Bo Weinberg, who was found in a river, stabbed to death, shortly after his former employer's return.

Schultz's own death followed his announcement that he would kill the special prosecutor of organized crime, Thomas Dewey, who was in the process of breaking up his slot-machine empire. When Schultz put the proposition to the syndicate, they refused to sanction it, however inconvenient the talented Michigan lawyer was becoming. When Schultz indicated that he would have the matter dealt with himself, it was he who had to go.

Schultz was killed on 23 October 1935 in the Palace Chop House, Newark. With him were his wizard accountant Otto "Abbadabba" Berman, who had devised an improved way of tampering with policy numbers payouts and who was opposed to the killing of Dewey, and gunmen Abe Landau and the broken-nosed Lulu Rosenkrantz, who were not. Their killers were Emmanuel "Mendy"Weiss, Charles "The Bug"Workman and a man named Piggy who has never been identified. The trio walked into the tavern and shot Rosenkrantz, Landau and Berman. It was, however, Workman who took most of the credit for the incident. He went to the washroom where he found Schultz urinating. He shot him, took his money and went to rejoin the others.

In fact, the murder was mishandled. When Workman came out of the restaurant he found Weiss and Piggy gone, along with the getaway car, and he began to run back to his New York flat. When he later complained to his superiors about their desertion,Weiss said that Piggy had simply panicked and driven off. He was cleared of blame as it was felt thatWorkman had, to an extent, been the author of his own misfortunes by taking the time to rob the dying Schultz. Piggy was not so fortunate. He was found some weeks later and taken to Brownsville where he was tortured and shot. His body was then set alight. Later, KidTwist Reles accepted his part in that murder and named Strauss and Maione as the gunmen.

All the victims died within hours of the Palace Chop House attack. Schultz survived the longest, dying at 8.40 p.m. after making a series of incoherent rambling statements in front of a police stenographer who was hoping he would name his killers. He is reputed to have said, "Please crack down on the Chinaman's friends and Hitler's commander ... Mother is the best and don't let Satan draw you too fast." The remarks have been variously interpreted as the ramblings of a dying man or to have some reason behind them. The gangland chronicler Hank Messik believed that Hitler's commander was the one who ordered Schultz's death but the reference to the Chinaman caused more problems. His answer is that it was Louis Dalitz, known as Louis the Chinaman, who was the brother of Moe Dalitz of the Cleveland Syndicate who were, at the time, trying to take over the Coney Island Race Track, which, despite its name, was in Cincinnati. Others suggest it was Charles "Chink" Sherman to whom he was referring in his delirium. The pair had quarrelled in a Broadway speakeasy, Club Abbey, and Sherman had shot him in the shoulder. In turn Sherman was stabbed and clubbed with a chair. However, by the time Schultz was killed Sherman was already dead and dumped. Stephanie St Clair, now back in the Harlem numbers business, sent a telegram, "As ye sow, so shall you reap."

Killings by Murder Inc. were not only for money, but as favours and importantly to prevent witnesses giving evidence. John "The Polack" Bagdonowitz was killed in 1932 as a favour to Longy Zwillman, the New Jersey boss. He had double-crossed Zwillman on a deal and was hiding out on Long Island. His killers were Vito Gurino and Joe Mercaldo from the Happy Maione section of the gang. In 1935 Abraham Meer and Irving Myron were killed as a favour to Jimmy "Blue Eyes" Alo, an associate of Meyer Lansky, because they had kidnapped Jimmy's ally, Bot Salvio. The gunmen on this occasion had been Strauss, Martin "Buggsy" Goldstein and Walter Sage.

On 13 September 1936 Joseph Rosen was killed at 725 Sutter Avenue, Brooklyn, where he had a candy store. He was found at 6.50 a.m. lying in a pool of blood. He had once owned the New York and New Jersey Clothing Transportation Company with three others, including Louis Cooper who, in turn, had been associated with Lepke Buchalter and Jacob Augen. The company had dissolved and parts had been hived off to Garfield Express Co. in which Buchalter was a silent partner.

Buchalter then employed Rosen as a manager for $150 a week. They had quarrelled and for a time Rosen had been promised that he could have work of his own. Eventually he opened a candy store but had refused to pay protection. Before the killing Buchalter had warned Rosen to leave town and when he ignored this, the instructions were given by Louis Capone. Strauss and Weiss were the gunmen who actually went into the store. It was feared that Rosen might talk to Thomas Dewey.

Hymie Yuran and Solomon Goldstein were killed in Sullivan County in 1939 and Morris Diamond in Brooklyn the same year. Goldstein was killed as a favour to Socks Lanza, the racket boss of the Fulton Fish Market in the 1930s, to prevent Goldstein from giving evidence against him.

Murder Inc. was broken in a curious way. A small-time thief, Harry Rudolph, then serving a short sentence on Rikers Island, wrote to the Brooklyn District Attorney saying that he knew about a murder in East New York and wished to speak to someone. Rudolph was not considered the most reliable of witnesses but he gave information about the November 1933 killing of his friend, Alex "Red" Alpert, a member of the squad. He named Reles, Buggsy Goldstein and Duke Maffetore as the three men involved.

Maffetore was little more than the bag boy, a man who read comic strips and was used as a driver. He rolled over into the District Attorney's arms but appears genuinely to have known little. Nor did the next convert, Pretty Levine. It was yet another turncoat, Albert Tannenbaum, who told Assistant District Attorney Burton Turkus where to find the body of the labour leader Peter Panto, who had disappeared on 14 July 1939, and from then Murder Inc. started to unravel. Strauss had wanted to help in the killing of Panto but Anastasia had already dealt with the matter.

As for Abe "Kid Twist" Reles, as the years passed he had declined in stature in the organization. In his career he had been arrested for murder on six occasions, assault seven times, assault and robbery twice and robbery or burglary a further six. He had only once been convicted – of assault. Now in 1940 he was charged with robbery, possession of narcotics and six counts linked to murder. In custody and charged with murder, unexpectedly he sent a message via his wife that he wanted to talk. He feared, probably correctly, that some of those arrested with him might endeavour to arrange a deal by informing on him and so he made sure he had the first drop on them. Reles became the canary for whom the prosecutors were looking. As a result of his information the police were able to clear up some forty-nine killings in Brooklyn alone. He named Frank Abbandando and Charlie Workman in the killing of Dutch Schultz, and his information was in a large part responsible for the conviction of his now superiors, Lepke Buchalter and Mendy Weiss. When questioned Reles said he believed that Panto's body would be found at "The Farm" where Anastasia was said to dispose of bodies in general. It was, he thought, about thirty miles out on Sunrise Highway and was owned by an Italian he knew as Jimmy. On 28 January 1941, Panto's body was found near the home of Jimmy Ferraro.

According to documents in the King's County District Attorney's Office, apart from the Rosen killing Louis Capone was suspected of taking part in nine murders, mostly in 1939 and including the killing of Irving Penn who, on 25 July that year, was shot by mistake instead of the union leader Philip Orlovsky. It was said of him that, "on all of these occasions, with few exceptions, Capone always remained in the background".

Lepke Buchalter sensibly went into hiding; one of the places being the Oriental Palace on Coney Island, owned by Zaccarino Cavitola, related to Louis Capone through marriage. It was Anastasia himself who persuaded Buchalter to give himself up to Turkus. As for Buchalter's surrender there are, as usual, conflicting stories. The one favourable to Anastasia is that he arranged it in the unfounded belief that Buchalter would only receive a prison sentence and not the electric chair. The less favourable version is that a body was needed to take away unnecessary heat from the Brooklyn mob and that from his prison cell Luciano had ordered Buchalter's surrender, with Anastasia being used as the persuader. It was said of Buchalter that he was the director of at least 250 criminal enterprises and that, at the time, he was "possibly the greatest criminal of the nation".

Who actually did the negotiating with the FBI and J. Edgar Hoover is again open to question. It may have been Frank Costello but, more probably, it was done at one stage removed through Lewis Solon Rosenstiel, who had long-standing ties with the Mafia. He had made his fortune through building massive whisky stocks during Prohibition, and it was then, like so many other liquor barons, that he had made friends in crime. He also had ties with Hoover through, it was said, homosexual orgies. Buchalter was led to believe by Anastasia and his lieutenant, Moey "Dimples" Wolensky, that he would not be turned over to the state courts and that, with a plea bargain, he would receive between ten and twelve years. The celebrated journalist and broadcaster Walter Winchell was also involved. On 5 August 1939 he received an anonymous message to the effect that Buchalter wanted to surrender but was afraid he would be shot if he did so.

Winchell knew J. Edgar Hoover well through their meetings at the Stork Club – "the place to be seen if you wish to feel important" – where he was often joined by Hoover at his favourite Table 50. It was a relationship which turned into a mutual admiration society. Quite improperly Hoover would supply Winchell with gossip from the FBI files. In return Winchell was the FBI Director's unofficial press agent and, had there been a fan club of the man, he would have been its president. He obtained assurances from Hoover that if Buchalter surrendered he would not be harmed and broadcast this over the radio.

Around 10 p.m. on 24 August 1939, Buchalter emerged from his hideout on Foster Avenue in Brooklyn and was driven by Anastasia over the bridge into Manhattan. Buchalter got out and walked to a prearranged spot where there was a parked car with Winchell in the driving seat and Hoover in the back. Together they "captured" Buchalter, who got in beside Hoover. The car was immediately surrounded by FBI agents.

It was only a short time before Buchalter discovered the depth of his betrayal. He had been condemned by Luciano from his prison cell and by Frank Costello. The electric chair was to be the end of the road for him but there were still some miles to be travelled before that appointment. First, in January 1940, he received a total of 192 years for drug trafficking, which, since most were concurrent, boiled down to fourteen years. Then Thomas Dewey prosecuted him for his bakery protection operations and in the April he received thirty years to life to begin after the fourteen. As he boarded the train to take him to Sing Sing he told reporters, "I may have done a hundred things wrong but my conscience is clear. I never did one-millionth of the things they said I did."

There was worse to come. On 28 May the King's County Grand Jury presented a true bill of murder in the first degree over the killing of Joseph Rosen and on 1 December that year Buchalter, Louis Capone and Mendy Weiss were found guilty and sentenced to death. There were still years of legal wrangling before the appeals were finally dismissed and the trio were executed at Sing Sing on 4 March 1944. They had been scheduled to die two days earlier and had ordered steak, french-fries, salad and pie for lunch and roast chicken for dinner but had been temporarily reprieved. This time they were electrocuted with Capone, who had a weak heart, going first followed by Weiss and Buchalter.

In the weeks before he died Buchalter asked to see Frank Hogan, the District Attorney of Manhattan. There was considerable speculation that, in return for a pardon, he might name names in high places, particularly in relation to the murder of Guido Ferrari, who was a casualty of the power struggle in the Amalgamated Clothing Workers Union. He did not.

Wolensky had already paid for the betrayal of his employer. Even before Buchalter died, Wolensky had been shot on a Manhattan street corner. In turn Buchalter was, without a doubt, the most senior gangster to die in the electric chair. In all probability the reason he kept his silence was for the fear of repercussions for his family.

Along with Marty Goldstein, the stone killer Pittsburgh Phil Strauss was executed on 12 June 1941 for the killing of Puggy Feinstein who had tried to muscle into loan-sharking. The normally dapper Strauss feigned insanity throughout the trial, appearing unshaven and unclean, chewing on a leather strap and remaining mute. Throughout his life he had a long affair with Evelyn Mittleman, another of the string of women in criminal history who appear to bring nothing but misfortune to the men with whom they associate, and who was known as the Kiss of Death Girl.

For a year Abe Reles was, like so many subsequent informers, held in protective custody. It was thought that he might have had tuberculosis and he was hidden out in Harbour Hospital under the name of Albert Smith at the beginning of November 1941. Then his safe home became the sixth floor of the Half Moon Hotel on Coney Island, New York, where he was kept under constant surveillance by six uniformed police officers. From time to time he, Mickie Syckoff, Sholem Bernstein and Albert Tannenbaum, all now turned State's witnesses, were taken to Heckster State Park on Long Island for recreation. It was from there he travelled to the New York courts to give his evidence. One of the problems for the prosecution was the question of providing corroboration for the evidence of Reles and the others, without which there could be no convictions. In the case of Charlie Workman it was Tannenbaum who provided the solution. As a result of a shooting, Workman had a pinched nerve in his hand and would not be able to hold a glass for any length of time. Tannenbaum suggested that, as corroboration, Workman be asked pick up a glass of water. He could not hold it and Workman received a sentence of life imprisonment for the killing of Schultz. He served twenty-four years and was released in 1956. Nothing further was heard of him.

Now Reles and Tannenbaum were to be flown to California to give evidence against Bugsy Siegel, then under indictment for the murder of Harry "Big Greenie" Greenberg, killed in 1939 to eliminate a potential witness against Buchalter.

On 12 November 1941 Reles fell from the window of his room, landing on the pavement. One of the more ingenious theories of his death is that he was playing a practical joke, climbing out of the window on knotted bedsheets and then running back upstairs to frighten the guards outside his room. Another is that he committed suicide. To do this he must have lowered himself to the third floor and then jumped. As his body was found twenty feet out into the street this seems unlikely. The grand jury, however, was perfectly happy. It found that Reles:

> met his death whilst trying to escape by means of a knotted sheet attached to a radiator in his room. We find that Reles did not meet with foul play and that he did not die by suicide. It would be sheer speculation to attempt to disarm [*sic*] his motive for wanting to escape.

The only really acceptable argument is that it was a gangland hit. At the time Reles was due to testify against Anastasia who was on trial for the Panto killing. After Reles's death the case against Anastasia was dropped and although it was reopened in 1951 no progress was made. The charges against Bugsy Siegel in California were also dropped. Lucky Luciano was later to say that the killing had been done by police officers who had thrown Reles from his room and that the contract price had been $50,000. Later Meyer Lansky said the fee paid was $100,000. Whichever, it was money well spent.

The last of the members of Murder Inc. to appear on murder charges before the courts was Jack Parisi. He had been accused of the murder of Morris Diamond in 1935 and managed to avoid capture until 1949 by hiding out in the Pennsylvania coalfields. Now Tannenbaum along with Angelo Catalano, the getaway driver, were the principal witnesses. The only eyewitness had, at first, said he did not recognize Parisi and had then undergone a series of operations on his eyes over the years.

Judge Goldstein, dismissing the charge of killing Diamond, said:

> The Court is convinced beyond any shadow of doubt that the defendant is the one who shot and killed the deceased Morris Diamond. It is indeed fortunate for this defendant that he is being tried in a state court for this case.
>
> It is my understanding that you have an engagement with the District Attorney of Bronx County on a charge of murder in the first degree. I earnestly hope for the good of the public that his office will find itself in a better position than we were to give you your just deserts.

The District Attorney also chipped in:

> I agree with you that this defendant is a most fortunate person. He is a murderer, a triggerman and deserved to go to the electric chair, but unfortunately due to the length of time or lack of evidence we were not able to accomplish that here. I wish Bronx County better luck.

Depending on one's point of view, they didn't have it. Now called Jack "The Dandy", Parisi was acquitted on 14 June that year when Chief Assistant District Attorney Edward F. Breslin threw in his hand, saying, "I know in my mind and conscience that the killer in this case is Parisi. I had an accomplice's testimony, the finest you could assemble, but I have that and nothing more. Frankly, I am not in a position legally to proceed against Parisi."

Tannenbaum survived the wrath of the mob and became a lampshade salesman in Georgia. Reles's wife changed her name.

Just how successful were the efforts of William O'Dwyer, the Brooklyn District Attorney, in clearing up organized crime in the first years of the Second World War? An internal note lists the cases against the various defendants and then adds:

> Outside of his work on the murder rings O'Dwyer appears to have accomplished little in prosecuting rackets.
>
> In addition to the Murder Ring and union extortionists, the only rackets referred to in O'Dwyer's annual report for 1940 are card swindling, shylocking around the Navy Yard and dealing in stolen cars. So far as I am aware, no action by him against any other rackets has been reported in the papers.

And just where did O'Dwyer stand in relation to those he prosecuted? Clearly something was wrong in the Brooklyn District Attorney's Office but it was never satisfactorily established just where the blame lay. When in the 1950s efforts were made to interview O'Dwyer on the subject of Reles's death he had long gone south of the border. He wrote declining to return for questioning but said he would be happy to be interviewed in Mexico.

Immediately after the death of Reles the case against Anastasia died as well. Moreover, the "wanted" cards for Anastasia, "Dandy" Jack Parisi and Tony Romeo – whose body was found in July 1942 in Delaware – had been removed from the files of the Police Investigation Bureau. A 1945 grand jury was never quite able to get to the truth but it would seem that this was done on the authority of the O'Dwyer's Chief Clerk, James Moran. Had Moran not been well over six foot and weighing 200 pounds it would be possible to call him a shadowy figure. O'Dwyer had been a magistrate in 1929 when Moran became his clerk. As O'Dwyer progressed through the judicial and political ranks so Moran came with him. Decisions in respect of cases to go before the grand jury or to be discontinued were taken by this unqualified man.

In 1945 when O'Dwyer became Mayor of New York after a bitter fight with Fiorello LaGuardia, Moran was appointed First Deputy Fire Commissioner at a salary of $10,000. In O'Dwyer's time as Mayor, political decisions of any significance had to be filtered through Moran. In 1950 just before O'Dwyer, whose mayordom had not been a success, resigned over allegations of police corruption and became the Ambassador to Mexico, he appointed Moran to be City Water Supply Commissioner in New York at the improved salary of $15,000 a year for life. Unfortunately he did not last long in office to collect his $15,000. There was evidence that he had leaned on gamblers, demanding cash contributions to help O'Dwyer's 1948 mayoralty campaign and in June 1951 he was convicted of perjury regarding his relations with numbers operator Louis Webber. He resigned.

A 1945 grand jury, sitting in secret, had fairly laced into O'Dwyer:

William O'Dwyer testified that his chief concern and paramount object was a conviction for murder of Anastasia, because Anastasia was the leader and most prominent gangster in the Brooklyn Underworld; that not a single murder in organized crime was committed in Brooklyn without Anastasia's permission and approval.

We find every case against Anastasia was abandoned, neglected or pigeonholed.

We find that William O'Dwyer as District Attorney failed and neglected to complete a single prosecution against Anastasia.

Albert Anastasia continued to run the rackets until, on 25 October 1957, he was shot to death while sitting in a barber's chair at the Park Sheraton Hotel on 56th and 7th Avenue, New York. He had been pressing for an even greater share of the rackets.

12

Prostitution in Soho – the French Gangs

By the 1920s prostitution in London's Soho was firmly in the hands of the French led by their leader, Juan Antonio Castanar. Lithe, dark and handsome, he was an accomplished tango dancer who was said at one time to have had a contract with the great ballerina, Anna Pavlova. He then opened a school for dance in Frith Street using it as a front for what was known as "white-birding" – selling women to dance troupes abroad at £50 a girl. Dance academies were popular at the time, charging up to £50 to teach girls to dance but, except for the very talented, there would be no jobs available except in clubs where they would effectively be prostitutes. There is a story that during Castanar's time in Soho he was paid a visit at his school, then in Archer Street, by Darby Sabini, the Italian gang-leader from Clerkenwell, who had come to retrieve the daughter of an fellow countryman whom Castanar was trying to lure into prostitution. He is said to have handed the girl back without demur. Given Sabini's reputation it is possibly a true story but there are other versions that Sabini then had Castanar's premises torched.

The reverse side of Castanar's business was to arrange marriages of convenience for foreign women, usually prostitutes wishing to acquire an English passport, to threadbare Englishmen. It was a trade that had been going on from the turn of the century. Generally the women, often infected with venereal disease and unable to get a certificate to work in France, would come over on a cheap day-return ticket. Once in England they would be met at the port and brought to London where they would go through a marriage of convenience and be whisked away to a flat.

One of the leading marriage experts on this side of the Channel was Archibald King who in 1924 received three years' penal servitude for bigamy. Helping out by scouring the Soho labour exchange for other suitably derelict Englishmen was George Venier, who spent much of his time at the Black Cat Café in Old Compton Street, where, according to the magazine *John Bull*, all sorts of nameless acts of vice took place. Others in Castanar's team included a former jockey, Myles Fogler, Josep Rizzo, Rene Janssens and Alfredo Sauvaget, known as Freddo, one of a number fancied for the murder of the French gangster, Martial LeChevalier, whose jugular was slashed at the corner of Air Street and Berwick Street shortly before midnight on 27 June.

Castanar's great rival was Casimir Micheletti, an Algerian known as the Assassin because of his ability with a stiletto. Micheletti, who gave his occupation as a furrier, was described as an extremely good-looking young man with dark hair, mild manners and a soft voice, who could fight with the savagery of a tiger. Both men ran strings of prostitutes. Each loathed the other and when Castanar was slashed across the face at the 43 Club in Old Compton Street, although no charges were ever brought, it was common knowledge that Micheletti was the attacker. He was also another of the suspects in LeChevalier's murder.

LeChevalier, well known in Soho, was another of the Frenchmen involved in the passport and white-slaving rackets of the time. Two months earlier he had arranged a marriage for Helen Chantenne to John Burns and was now living off the girl's earnings. LeChevalier had quarrelled with a man known as "The Algerian" in the Gordon Billiard Saloon in Frith

Street. Witnesses also suggested that he had double-crossed Freddo Sauvaget over the passport racket, and on the night of his death he was attacked by four men. Although an alert was put out to arrest Sauvaget at the ports he was never found.

The Sabini name could often be relied on to produce terror in the community even when the family had nothing to do with things. In early October 1925 Giovanni Periglione, Georges Modebodze and Wilfred Cooper were charged with demanding money with menaces from a cook, Gaston Reynaud. Periglione and Reynaud, who had lodged together in Old Compton Street, had quarrelled and fought. Later Cooper told Reynaud that Periglione was going to cut him but for £100 he would put him under the protection of the Sabini Gang of which he was "chief", something which must have come as a surprise to both Darby Sabini and his brother Harryboy. Cooper received four years' imprisonment and wrote to the police to say he could provide information about the killing of LeChevalier. He was interviewed but his story was discounted.

Micheletti was a more or less innocent witness in another murder trial. On 5 April 1926 yet another Frenchman, Émile Berthier, shot and killed motorcar dealer, Charles Baladda, in the Union Club in Frith Street, which had been wrecked the previous year by the south London villain Monkey Benneworth. The club had a wooden bar along one side, tables and chairs, a couple of fruit machines and some crude murals on the walls. When the police arrived they found Baladda sprawled in a corner, shot in the stomach. Berthier described himself as a wine merchant and indeed he had a business in Tooley Street but he was also known to be a prostitute's bully and although Baladda, described as an acrobat, had no convictions he also lived with a prostitute and thief.

According to the evidence of a Juan Gabaron, known as L'Espagnol, Berthier believed Baladda owed him money and went up to him saying, "My friends, I respect them, but those who owe me money including my partners will have to pay me otherwise I am going to settle with them. I shall do them an injury." Baladda replied, "You must not talk like that. You must do things not talk about them." Berthier then shot him with an automatic pistol. A member of the club promptly hit Berthier over the head with a billiard cue but he escaped, stopping only to have his wounds cleaned, before he caught the train to Newhaven. He was arrested when about to board the packet boat for Dieppe.

Berthier had earlier written a letter, which was produced at the trial:

> I know the Micheletti wants to kill me because I do not give him any more money. You must admit I have given him enough. See, actually that makes £1,500 all the money I owe and he is asking for more. Whilst he is away for a month I warn you that if he continues to ask me for money I shall do my best to kill him. He has killed two or three others and this man is an assassin.

That was the story according to the evidence but another version is that Micheletti had swindled Berthier out of £2,000 and Baladda, who closely resembled "The Algerian", was shot by mistake. On the other hand, the detective, Robert Fabian (known as "Fabian of the Yard") believed a feud between Baladda and Berthier had originated in Paris. At the Old Bailey Micheletti gave evidence to the effect that he was terrified of Berthier. Baladda was, he said, his friend.

The jury took only minutes to find Berthier, whose father had committed suicide by throwing himself off a building at the Lyons exhibition in 1904, guilty but insane. He was later repatriated to France.

In April 1929 both Micheletti and Castanar were deported from England but within a few weeks Castanar managed to smuggle himself back for a short period before he was once more thrown out, this time permanently. He made his way to Paris and earned a modest living as a tango dancer and running a small stable of girls. In February 1930 he and Micheletti met in a café in Paris and later that night Castanar shot his rival dead. At his trial he blamed the killing on a mysterious man known to both of them as Le Marseillais. It was he who had shot Micheletti, put the gun in Castenar's hand and ran away. The story did him no good. Castanar was not believed and was sent to Devil's Island.

1935 and 1936 saw an outbreak of murders of prostitutes and a pimp in Soho. The killing of the girls began in November 1935 when Josephine Martin, known as "French Fiffi" – the French and other foreign girls were generally known in Soho as "Fiffis" – was strangled with her own silk stockings in her flat above the Globe Club in Archer Street. In fact, she was Russian-born and had married a waiter named Henry Martin to gain citizenship. She was well regarded in the block as quiet and respectable but she was known to have acted as an agent for the dope-dealer and white-slaver Emil Allard, known as Max Kassel. A name in the frame was that of Josephine's brother Albert Mechanik, who had once run the Polyglot Club in Rupert Street, to whom she gave money on a regular basis. His argument was that since she was his sole source of income there was no reason for him to kill her. There was no evidence against him and he was never charged.

Then on 24 January 1936 Allard's body was found under a hedge near St Albans in Hertfordshire. He had been shot a number of times. Allard had been in and out of London since 1913 selling women to Latin American brothels and arranging marriages for foreign prostitutes. Although he lived in James Street off Oxford Street, he was killed at 36 Little Newport Street in a flat leased by Georges Lacroix. Also known as Roger or Marcel Vernon, Lacroix, sent to Devil's Island for robbery in 1924, was one of seven to escape in 1927, one of the relatively few to make a successful escape from the penal colony. Lacroix lived with Suzanne Bertrand who had "married" an Englishman and so obtained her passport to work the Soho streets.

The officer in the case, the slightly dubious Chief Inspector "Nutty" Sharpe who was involved in the protection of bookmakers, traced the car used to dump the body to a garage in Soho Square owned by another Frenchman, Pierre Alexandre. Through him he found Suzanne Bertrand's maid, Marcelle Aubin, who had been sent to order the car. In Little Newport Street he found pieces of glass on the pavement that matched those found in the car. In his dying struggle Allard had broken the flat window.

But by then both Lacroix and Bertrand were long gone back to France. An application for their extradition was declined and they stood trial in Paris in April 1937. It was then that at least some of the story came out. The killing had, it seems, been personal rather than business. Lacroix had been in partnership with Allard, marrying off the women. They had first met in Montreal where they were in the white slave trade together. They both were in love with Suzanne Bertrand who had been with Lacroix since he left his wife in 1933.

There was some peripheral evidence that explained rather more. Georges Hainnaux, known as Jo Le Terroir, told the tribunal that Allard had confessed to killing a white slaver, Henri Bouchier, in Montreal in 1930. Bouchier was the so-called Le Marseillais, said by Micheletti to be the one who killed his rival Castanar. Lacroix was sentenced to ten years to be followed by twenty years' banishment, and Suzanne Bertrand was acquitted. Le Terroir took the view that the killings of Bouchier, LeChevalier, Micheletti and Allard had all been part of a long-drawn-out struggle for the control of prostitution and the white slave racket in Soho and on the continent.

Le Terroir was certainly correct about the killing of the white slaver. Henri Bouchier, known as Old Martigues, the slang name for a man from Marseilles, was shot and his body dumped at Laval-sur-le-Lac, then the largest suburb of Montreal, on 1 July 1930. It is probable that both Allard and Lacroix were involved in that killing.

In April 1936, five months after the death of Allard, Marie Jeanet Cotton was strangled in Lexington Street, Soho. Born in France, she had married one Louis Cousins. A woman of some means who acted from time to time as a moneylender, she had been living with an Italian café-owner and it was in his house that her body was found. No charges were ever brought.

In the same month Constance Hind (or Bird) was strangled in her flat in Old Compton Street, this time with a piece of wire. Next, on 16 August 1937, Elsie Torchon, who adopted a French accent and was known as French Paulette or French Marie but who came from Croydon and worked in Soho's Wardour Street, was found strangled with her scarf in Bath Row, Euston. The police and newspapers were keen to play down any suggestion that the death of these three women was any spillover from the death of Allard, instead preferring to promote a "Jack the Strangler" who had killed the women after quarrels over terms and conditions.

Certainly they were correct regarding the death of Elsie Torchon. This was solved by fingerprints and had nothing to do with the earlier deaths. In fact, her killer Robert Dixon was extremely fortunate not to hang. Two months earlier he had been sentenced to ten years for manslaughter after strangling another prostitute, Catherine Chamberlain, against the wall of Fenham Barracks in Newcastle. Now he was identified from a fingerprint on the metal rim of Elsie Torchon's handbag. To avoid any possible prejudice he was tried at the Old Bailey under a different name. He claimed he had accidentally strangled Torchon when he pushed her and she fell. Again the jury acquitted him of murder. Sentencing him to sixteen years for her manslaughter, Mr Justice Atkinson commented, "It is well for you that the jury did not know of your history."

A survey of the time found that 98 per cent of prostitutes walked the streets, some earning only £1 a night. Not all the control of prostitutes was in French hands but they were the ones making the real money. In fact £1 a night was not as bad as it reads. "From personal experience I can vouch that on a steady thirty shillings a week a single man lived like a fighting cock in pre-War London," wrote the social historian Rayner Heppenstall.

There were, of course, independent owners of brothels. Among them was Queenie Gerald, who walked into restaurants with an ill-tempered parrot in her muff and who had convictions for brothel-keeping going back to 1911. In 1921 there was a fracas and she was convicted of disorderly behaviour. She was reputed to tour the lower class nightclubs in Soho recruiting girls who, rather than remain on the streets after midnight, used them to pick up clients. That was the year she featured in the exposé, *Sex Slaves in a Piccadilly Flat*, appearing on the cover of the book with a whip and cowering girls, and there were stories of girls who had been badly thrashed at her "parties". But there was never again any proof that she was operating a brothel.

Over the years she was denounced by magazines such as *John Bull*, to which she angrily replied that the real procuress of the town was Rose Phillips (also known as Heathcote, Gutteridge and Letta), variously of Great Portland, Berners, Kingley, Orchard and Panton Streets.

13

The Messina Brothers

The deportation of Juan Antonio Castanar and Casimir Micheletti and the flight of Georges Lacroix effectively signalled the end of the French control of prostitution in London's Soho. Now the Maltese Messina brothers – Alfredo, Salvatore, Eugenio, Carmelo and Attilio – took over.

Their father Giuseppe came from Linguaglossa in Sicily and in the late 1890s went to Malta where he worked in a brothel in Valetta. He married a Maltese girl and his first two sons, Salvatore and Alfredo, were born there. The family then moved to Alexandria in 1905 where he built a chain of brothels. The remaining sons were all born there, and their father ensured they were all well educated. In 1934 Eugenio, the third son, born in 1908, came to England. He was able to claim British nationality because his father had sensibly taken Maltese citizenship. With Eugenio (Gino) was his wife Colette, a French prostitute. It was on her back that Gino Messina founded his London empire.

More girls were recruited from the continent and as the empire grew he was joined on the management side by his brothers who all adopted English-sounding names. Eugenio was Edward Marshall, Carmelo was Charles Maitland and Alfredo became Alfred Martin. When they take false names most criminals stick to the same initials but Salvatore and Attilio were exceptions. Salvatore was Arthur Evans and

Attilio took the name Raymond Maynard. Properties were bought throughout the West End and the brothers turned their attention to English girls. The technique used was age-old – good-looking girls were given a good time; seduction, possibly with the promise of marriage, followed and then it became time to pay. If the good life was to continue the price for it was prostitution.

The girls were under the day-to-day charge of the French-born Marthe Watts who to obtain British citizenship had married Arthur Watts, an alcoholic Englishman brought to Paris for the purpose. Born in 1913, according to her story she had been placed in a brothel in Le Havre at the age of fifteen after lying about her age. There followed a career in the brothels of Europe ending with her marriage to Watts. From her point of view the marriage was a total success. She only saw him when she was charged with brothel-keeping in London and he was dragged to court to give evidence that he was indeed her husband and as a result she could not be deported.

In April 1941 she met Eugenio in the Palm Beach Club in Soho's Wardour Street. Within a month she became his mistress and a few weeks later she was out working the streets for him. Her loyalty seems to have been remarkable; despite regular and savage beatings – the favourite method seems to have been with an electric light flex – she stayed with the family and took charge of the new girls. As a mark of her devotion she tattooed *"L'homme de ma vie. Gino le maltais"* over her left breast – a tribute she later had removed.

After the introductory period involving fine restaurants, clubs and lavish presents, life with Eugenio Messina was no fun for any of his girls. They were not allowed out on their own; during the Second World War they could not accept American servicemen as clients; they were not allowed to smoke; nor curiously were they allowed to wear low-cut dresses or even look at film magazines where the male stars were in any sort of undress. They did not take off their clothes with the customers. Worst of all was the ten-minute rule. Clients were only allowed to stay that length of time before the maid knocked on the door. It seems to have resembled the Paris and Miami slaughterhouses where girls never leave the bed and a bell rings after fifteen minutes. The other Messina brothers seem to have been more relaxed than Gino in their attitudes, particularly over the ten-minute rule.

During the war the Messinas evaded conscription simply because they failed to report for the call-up. Warrants were issued but they were never served and they maintained a low profile as far as the authorities were concerned. Eugenio Messina, who had worked as a carpenter with his father, built himself a sort of ponce's hole, in the form of a bookcase with a removable bottom shelf in which he could hide in his Lowndes Square flat. Unknown visitors had to be cleared through a series of frontmen and frontwomen before they were allowed in to see him.

In the war years the Messina girls were regarded as a cut above other street prostitutes in the West End. Superintendent Cole thought the girls who worked around Piccadilly Circus were the "lower type of prostitute" and "persistent thieves". Girls in Glasshouse Street were a bit better but the Messina girls in Maddox Street were, "French prostitutes, a colony among themselves, clean and businesslike, who though persistent in their soliciting rarely cause trouble". It still did not stop the girls getting a whipping from the brothers.

Still, there seems to have been an amazing *esprit de corps* between the brothers and their girls. In her autobiography *The Men in My Life*, Marthe Watts tells how she serviced forty-nine men on VE night and bitterly regretted failing to find a fiftieth.

By 1946, with the Messina brothers' weekly earnings now at £10,000, the girls were taking £100 a night and being paid £50 a week. Even if takings dropped after the war the business was still a worthwhile target for other ponces.

Although most of Soho prostitution was still controlled by the brothers, other low-grade pimps were moving in on their territory, hanging out in clubs such as the billiard club at 3 Carlisle Street. There, on 15 June 1948, Amabile Ricca, known as "Ricky the Malt" and poetically, if probably inaccurately, described by the *News of the World* as "the worst Maltese in Britain", was shot and stabbed to death. Francis Xavier Farrugia and his brother Joseph were charged with his murder. In the end Joseph received a sentence of five years for manslaughter and Francis, who had thrown away the weapons, got six months. Regarded as a fearsome bully of whom the Farrugias and other Maltese were terrified, Ricca had a conviction in 1932 in Malta for discharging a firearm as a result of which a death occurred. Shortly before his death he had also served eighteen months for malicious wounding in London.

Ricca did not trespass on Messina territory but in March 1947 Carmelo Vassallo and four other Maltese had endeavoured to muscle in on the Messina enterprise, demanding protection money of £1 a girl a day. Retribution in all forms was swift. At a meeting in Winchester Court, South Kensington, Eugenio Messina took off two of Vassallo's fingertips. But it was not sufficient for the girls. Marthe Watts and two others, who claimed to be now thoroughly frightened by the rival Maltese and what would happen if they gave in to their demands, went to the police. Carmelo Vassallo and the four others stood in the dock at the Old Bailey in April 1947 charged with demanding money with menaces. All the witnesses against them staunchly denied they were "Messina girls".

One of them, Janine Gilson of Cork Street, Mayfair, admitted knowing the Messinas for three years but denied she had ever spoken to them. "I know them as diamond merchants and I know them as very wealthy people," she told the jury.

"Do you know the source of their wealth is the money they take from girls on the streets?"

"No."

"Do any of these Messina men look after you in your profession?"

"No. I don't have anybody to look after me. If I want protection I go to the police."

This sort of evidence could not possibly be swallowed by any jury. But there was a back-up. Happily the police had been on watch in Burlington Gardens, off Piccadilly, when Vassallo and the other four Maltese drew up and one shouted out to the girls, "It's better for you to give us the money, otherwise I will cut your face!"

In the car the police found a hammer wrapped in newspaper, a knife and a life-preserver. At the men's flat there were a knuckleduster and an automatic pistol with six rounds of ammunition. Convicted of demanding money with menaces, Vassallo and two others received four years' penal servitude.

However, the thwarted take-over did spell the very beginning of the end of the Messinas' reign. Eugenio Messina, who had no takers for his offer of the enormous sum of £25,000 to anyone who could smuggle him out of the country, received three years for removing Vassallo's fingertips. The Messina brothers were now known figures and questions were asked in Parliament. In view of what had emerged at the trials where Marthe and the other girls had loyally lied, denying their involvement with the brothers, would the Home Secretary appoint a commission to enquire into organized vice in London? No, replied Mr Chuter Ede:

It is a criminal offence knowingly to live on the earnings of a prostitute and the police exercise all possible vigilance with a view to the suppression of activities of this kind.

Any enquiry would not help the police because their difficulties arise from the fact that, although they may have good reason to suspect such activities, they are sometimes unable to obtain evidence upon which criminal proceedings could be based.

Then as now.

But John Foster, the MP for Norwich who was putting the questions, was not satisfied. What about an examination of the Messinas' bank accounts? Was Mr Ede aware they were popularly supposed to be making half a million a year, that they had no fewer than twenty girls working for them and that they owned a West End estate agency? But Mr Ede was having none of it and the remaining brothers continued to flourish.

All, that is, except Carmelo – Marthe Watts's favourite. Conscious of the privations Eugenio was suffering, he tried to bribe a prison officer at Wandsworth Prison, for which he received two months plus a £50 fine. There was some compensation, however. On his release there was £700 waiting for him. The girls had conscientiously been putting their money in the safe for him – watched, it has to be said, by two of the other brothers. On Eugenio's release he bought himself a Rolls-Royce. But, for the purposes of the courts, the Messinas went underground. There was no question now of having knife fights with the Maltese opposition. According to Marthe Watts complainants were simply framed:

> I am sure, from some of the remarks passed by some magistrates, that they did not believe there was such a thing as the Messina Gang. They certainly did not when Sally Wright was charged with assaulting Rabina Dickson Torrance with a knife. Sally Wright pleaded that Torrance was a Messina woman, that the whole charge had been framed by the Messina Gang, and that she was innocent.
>
> She was by no means the first person who had not been believed after pleading that she had been victimised by the Messina Gang. It seems that when anyone upset the Messinas all they had to do was enlist the aid of the Courts, apparently with police assistance, and that someone was conveniently imprisoned, and incidentally discredited for life.

It took three more years before the Messinas were exposed for what they were, and it was the work of the crusading journalist, Thomas Duncan Webb, who later caused so much trouble for Jack Spot.

Webb was a curious man. A devout Roman Catholic, he believed his mission was to clean the streets of London. After one triumph over the Messinas he put an advertisement in *The Times* offering thanks to St Jude. He had a career during which he seems to have worn both black and white hats. So far as the white hat is concerned he undoubtedly brought down the brothers. Wearing his black hat he had acquired a conviction at Plymouth Magistrates Court for communicating the movement of His Majesty's ships during the war, for which he was fined £50 on 26 January 1944. He had telephoned the *Daily Express* and spoken so loudly he had been overheard. But there again telephone lines were not what they are today.

More peculiar was his conviction at Marlborough Street on 8 August two years later. According to the evidence, Webb had picked up prostitute Jean Crews and agreed to have intercourse for £2. Mrs Crews told the court they went to her flat where he "had connections with her and then went to the bathroom to cleanse himself". He then would not leave the flat until she threatened to call the police. They left together and in the street the girl approached an actor Herbert Wadham. Webb allegedly showed him a press card, masking it as a police warrant card. He seems to have arrested Wadham and then struck him in the face. As they marched along Tottenham Court Road Wadham approached a temporary reserve police officer for help. At the police station Webb denied ever having seen Wadham before. A charge of grievous bodily harm was reduced to common assault and the magistrate dismissed a charge of impersonating a police officer. Webb was bound over under the Prosecution of Offences Act and ordered to pay two guineas costs.

On 3 September 1950 the *People* newspaper published Webb's exposure of the brothers, backing it with photographs of the Messina girls and the flats from where they operated. Eugenio and Carmelo loaded up the yellow Rolls-Royce and left for France via Dover. Although they returned using false passports, they were never again seen openly in Britain. Salvatore followed them but Attilio and Alfredo remained.

Attilio lived near Marlow, outside London, with one of the girls, the same Rabina Torrance who had brought false charges of assault against Sally Wright when the girl had tried to leave the family. Attilio completed the work of clearing up the brothers' business matters, and then he too headed for France, leaving behind only Alfredo. He lived with Hermione Hindin who worked in Poland Street as Barbara. On 19 March 1951, Alfredo was arrested at his Wembley home charged with living on immoral earnings and trying to bribe a police officer. He had offered Superintendent Mahon, one of the arresting officers, £200.

At his trial at the Old Bailey he naturally gave his employment as that of diamond merchant. No, he did not know Hermione was in fact Barbara. No, he did not know she had over 100 convictions for soliciting. When she went out in the evening he thought it was to see a relative. It was a great shock to him to learn she was a common prostitute. He had brought his personal fortune, some £30,000, to Britain at the beginning of the war and had dealt in diamonds. He had both diabetes and high blood pressure, which was why he did not really work. What on earth was this vice ring organized by his brothers? He was defended by Scott Henderson who later conducted the Rillington Place enquiry into whether John Reginald Halliday Christie had in fact committed the murder of Beryl Evans, for which her mentally retarded husband Timothy had been hanged. Henderson did his best for Alfredo but he received two years' imprisonment concurrent on each of the charges and a £500 fine. In fact, Barbara worked in the next-door flat to Alfredo's real wife, a Spanish woman who went under the name Marcelle.

For the moment it seemed the hold of the Messina brothers – with one in prison and four abroad – had been broken. It was not the case. On the face of it after their convictions and flight in 1950 the remains of the Messina empire were looked after by Anthony Micalleff. Then, with the Coronation coming up in 1953, there was a sudden surge of foreign prostitutes in the West End Central division, which covered parts of Soho and Mayfair. Spurious marriages – which would prevent any deportation of the women – were arranged by a London solicitor or, at any rate, this was the belief of the police. Now Duncan Webb set himself the task of finding out who was behind Micalleff and he discovered it was the seedy Corsican Antonio "Tony" Rossi who fronted for the Messina brothers. Rossi liked to be known as the "Lion of Montmartre" but Webb dubbed him "The Jackal of Soho".

The ever faithful Marthe Watts took over control of the ever younger girls that Eugenio was sending over from the continent, often after picking them up at tea-dances. Each girl kept her own accounts and it seems that, such was the mixture of loyalty and fear, they never tried to skim for themselves. Every thousand pounds earned meant a trip to see Eugenio in Paris. The money, however, went over by courier.

By now Attilio was back making trips to England. Alfredo's solicitors at his trial had been Webb, Justice & Co and Superintendent Mahon began to follow the firm's clerk, Watson, as he made trips to Europe. In October 1951 Watson went to his home in Chalfont St Giles for a short time, left and got into another car that drove off towards Amersham.

The car was stopped by Mahon and inside with Watson was Attilio. Charged with living off the immoral earnings of Rabina Torrance, Attilio received six months' imprisonment, the maximum sentence.

Certainly this should now have been the very end for the brothers but it was not to be so. Eugenio, Carmelo and Alfredo controlled matters from Paris until November 1953 when

Eugenio was kidnapped and only released on payment of £2,000. In some disarray the brothers moved their headquarters to Lausanne. In the meantime Attilio had completed his short stretch and had set up with Rabina Torrance again in Bourne End, outside London. Torrance leased two flats in London in her own name with payments for rent and rates being made through the Messinas' agents. Attilio, using the name Maynard, had another flat in Shepherd's Market, Mayfair, and the family had interests in a second flat there. Deportation papers were served on him in 1953 but the Italian authorities declined to have him and, once the *People* had traced him to The Hideaway, his appropriately named cottage in Bourne End, he moved to south London, reporting daily to the police as an Italian national.

But Eugenio had also surfaced again, this time buying 39 Curzon Street in Mayfair from a Mrs Augustine Johans who continued to manage it as a brothel. In September 1953 she was fined £25 but in the raid the police found £14,000 in a safe on the premises. As a result the premises were taken over by the aforementioned Hermione Hindin, who had lived with Attilio, and Mrs Johans moved elsewhere.

Home, however, is where the heart is and Eugenio yearned for England. He obtained another British passport, this time as Alexander Miller, a merchant, and yet another as Eugene de Bono. Also for the purposes of travelling to England Carmelo became a Cuban citizen under the name Carlos Marino.

By now, however, girls from respectable Belgian homes were disappearing to England and the Belgian police were actively pursuing their enquiries. Marthe Watts, who had suffered a collapsed lung, was tiring of overseeing an ever-increasing harem amassed by Eugenio. She travelled to see him in the Residence Albert in Knokke-le-Zoute in Belgium and severed her connection as Quarter Master Sergeant of the operation. She was allowed to work independently from a Messina-owned flat in Chesterfield Street, Mayfair. On 31 August 1955

Carmelo and Eugenio were arrested in the Horse's Neck at Knokke and charged with being in possession of firearms, false passports and procuring women for prostitution. It was only then that the extent of their current British empire became apparent. Title deeds to four central London properties were found in a safe-box along with long reports from Marthe Watts and Mrs Johans. One of the reports by Watts showed that one girl, a former nurse working as Therese, had earned £2,400 in six weeks. Eugenio had gone through his prospective fiancé routine before marrying her off to a stray Englishman recruited for the purpose. Eugenio received seven years' imprisonment and Carmelo was deemed to have served his sentence. He had been in custody on remand for ten months and was released. He disappeared, but not for long.

At the end of 1956 the appeals were heard in the Belgian case. Carmelo had his sentence doubled *in absentia* while Eugenio had seven months knocked off. But where was Carmelo? Back in England is the answer. In October 1958 he was found sitting in a car in Knightsbridge and arrested as an illegal immigrant. He received a six-month sentence and was deported after its completion. He died in the autumn in Sicily. But now where was Attilio?

He was working hard, or rather Edna Kallman, initially seduced by promises of marriage and the good life, was working hard for him. She had been under his control for ten years, put out to work under the tutelage of Rabina. Attilio knocked her about continually until, in sheer terror of a further beating, she managed to bring herself to go home to her parents in Derby and they called the police. He was convicted on 9 April 1959 and sentenced to four years' imprisonment. Edna Kallman had earned between £50 and £150 a week over those ten years and had been allowed to keep £7 a week for herself.

Sentencing him, the Recorder of London, Sir Gerald Dodson, commented: "You made a sumptuous but revolting living from the suffering bodies of the women you trapped, seduced and reduced to a form of slavery. You caused great suffering and it is only right and just that you should also suffer."

On his release Attilio went to Italy. Salvatore lived in Switzerland while Alfredo, who could claim British citizenship, died in Brentford in 1963.

1959 should have marked the end of the Messinas as an active force but in the late 1960s Eugenio and Carmelo were still paying the rent and rates of premises in Mayfair. Finally, Eugenio Messina went to Italy where he lived in San Remo. On 12 March 1970 he married Maria Theresa Vervaere – who worked out of Curzon Street under the name Mary Smith – and died the same day. When his brothers arrived they found his safe had been emptied. Mary Smith now wanted her share of the Eugenio fortune. She did, however, have serious problems. She had married a former Shanghai policeman, William George Smith, in August 1954 and he was still alive. She claimed that Smith had married a Russian woman and so her marriage to him was bigamous. As an alternative she claimed she had not understood that the ceremony at Paddington Register Office was in fact a marriage to Smith. Unfortunately for her it turned out that Smith had obtained a divorce from the Russian in Nevada in 1946 and the judge ruled she knew full well the significance of her marriage. On 7 May 1971 a High Court judge ruled her marriage to Eugenio was not valid and she therefore had no claim to his fortune. She appealed but on 7 March 1972 she dropped her claim.

As for the other women, Rabina Torrance opened an antique shop in the Thames Valley; in 1960 Marthe Watts wrote her self-serving book on her experiences, claiming she had left the life, sickened by the stream of young women seduced and put to work by Eugenio.

The Messinas' tormentor, Duncan Webb, died in September 1958. He had suffered from high blood pressure for some time and while researching organized crime on the waterfront in New

York he suffered a massive heart attack. He returned to England where he died in Charing Cross Hospital. He was, wrote Alan Hamilton in *The Times*, "the greatest of all crime reporters".

14

The Sabinis

London's Soho has never had a resident gang in the way that other gangs have owned their own territory. Prior to the First World War three disparate gangs fought over the area – the Elephant Boys, the Hoxton Boys or Titanics, and a team from King's Cross led by Michael Macausland.

The Titanics came from Nile Street, Hoxton, and were said to have been named after the liner because they were so smart. This cannot be correct because the first reference to them is in 1902, well before the liner was launched. They were said to be up to fifty-strong and were talented pickpockets working football crowds, the music halls and theatres, and the underground – in fact, anywhere crowds congregated. Inroads were made into the gang following arrests at a north London football match followed by a series of raids by the police. One senior member was Alf White who would, during the inter-war years, join the up-and-coming Sabinis.

The Elephant Boys, as the name implies, came from the Elephant and Castle. They were said to bite the heads off rats, were regarded as the most ferocious of the gangs and without their help between the wars it was impossible to have absolute control over Soho. Although the Sabinis did their best to disprove that theory.

The post-war gang-leader Billy Hill, who could rightly be called the Boss of Soho if not the Boss of Britain's Underworld (this slightly more grandiose title bestowed on him by the hero-worshipping journalist Duncan Webb and his publishers), thought Soho was a wonderful place in the 1920s:

> Society thought they were slumming when they rolled from Curzon Street to Gerrard Street in their then modern Rolls-Royces. The bottle party was all the rage. Every cellar in Soho was occupied and packed. Cafés and restaurants, run mostly by aliens from the Continent, flourished. Spielers turned over more ready cash than did the Riviera casinos. Every club, spieler, many small cafés, had slot machines operating in them. These slot machines, adjusted properly, would earn a fortune in one night's play. A fortune for the owners. Not the proprietor in whose premises they were installed. The owners never got their fortunes however. Darby Sabini and his boys managed to "win" too often on those machines. And if they were not paid up in hard cash the machines were wrecked along with the premises.

The Sabinis reaped the benefits of the Soho cash cow:

> From all these sources of immense wealth the Sabinis were drawing revenue. Bottle parties, clubs, public-houses, cafés, even ordinary shops, had to pay protection money to the Sabini extortionists. None dared refuse. If they did the Sabinis gave information to the police which compelled the law to act for some broken petty regulation. Individuals connected with the premises were attacked in the streets. Proprietors of businesses finished up in hospital; the streets Up West were literally paved with gold for the Sabinis.

Hill garnered all this information from the once notorious Eddie Guerin, by then very much on the slide and little more

than a hotel sneak thief. Guerin was a long-time friend of Hill's
sister Aggie:

> Burglars and thieves had no chance. If they wandered
> Up West they had to go mob-handed. And they had to be
> prepared to pay out if they were met by any of the Sabinis.
> If they went in a club it was drinks all round. The prices
> were especially doubled for their benefit. If they did go
> to a spieler they never won. They knew better than to try
> and leave while they were showing even a margin of profit.
> If one word was spoken out of place, it was all off. The
> Sabinis, who could rustle up twenty or thirty tearaways
> at a moment's notice anywhere Up West, stood for no
> liberties, although they were always taking them.

But who were the Sabinis? Although they operated principally
from Saffron Hill, Clerkenwell, and were sometimes known as
the Italians or the Raddies, the family exercised considerable
influence over the Soho underworld of the 1920s and 1930s.
Over two decades they dominated street and racecourse crime
until, at the beginning of the Second World War, the brothers,
along with their formidable friend Pasqualino Papa (who boxed
as Bert Marsh), were interned as enemy aliens, appropriately
enough at Ascot racecourse.

Just how many there were and exactly who was who is
difficult to unravel. The leader was undoubtedly Ullano or
Darby, but from time to time when it suited him, he was known
as Fred or Charles, the names of two elder brothers.

In all there were six Sabini brothers, beginning with
Frederick born in 1881, who, according to police files, traded
as bookmaker Bob Wilson at the Harringay Greyhound
Stadium and took no part in the other brothers' affairs.
Next came Charles, who was two years younger and was a
list supplier working for the bookmaker Joe Levy in what the
police thought was a protection racket. He owned shares in

West Ham Stadium and was believed to be "slightly mentally deranged". Certainly by 1940 he had spent some time in mental hospitals. Then came Joseph, who on paper was the villain of the family. He had served in the First World War in the Royal Welsh Fusiliers and then the Cheshire Regiment and had been wounded in France. Invalided out he received a 12 shillings a week pension. On 12 October 1922 he was sentenced to three years' penal servitude for his part in the shooting of Fred Gilbert in Mornington Crescent in part of the racecourse war of the time. The police thought, however, that after that he had split from his brothers and there was no evidence that he was operating behind the scenes. He traded as Harry Lake at Harringay dog track.

George Sabini was the youngest of the brothers – there was a sister who was disabled – who had no convictions and worked at both Harringay and White City tracks. He was not regarded as being any part of the gang but it was noted that his name alone would provide him with protection. Of the brothers it was Darby and Harry, known as Harryboy, who provided what euphemistically was called protection and what, in reality, was demanding money with menaces from the bookmakers.

Ullano, better known as Darby Sabini, was born in 1889 in Saffron Hill, in the western side of Clerkenwell known as Little Italy. His Italian father died when he was two and the family was raised by their Irish mother. He left school at the age of thirteen and boxed professionally from 1909. He won a novice competition that February and at one time it was thought he could, in the words of Marlon Brando, "have been a contender". It is said that while still in his teens he had knocked out the fancied middleweight, Fred Sutton, in the first round. There is no trace in Sabini's boxing records of this bout but it is possible that the contest took place at a fairground booth. Until the 1960s, when it was banned by the British Boxing Board of Control, it was common for licensed boxers to take on all-comers at booths.

Unfortunately Sabini did not like the training required and instead became a strong-arm man for the Anglo-Italian Dai Sullivan's promotions at the Hoxton Baths. In fact, he boxed over an eight-year period continuing until 1917 when he lost over sixteen rounds at the National Sporting Club.

Later, he was employed by George Harris, a leading bookmaker of the time, again as a strong-arm man. Less than middle height, Sabini always wore a shirt with no collar, along with a dark brown suit with a high-buttoned waistcoat, a black silk neckcloth and a light-checked flat cap. He had selected this outfit when he was twenty and wore it for the rest of his life – indoors, outdoors and, so it is said, sometimes in bed.

Harry, always known as Harryboy, was educated at St Peter's Roman Catholic School in Clerkenwell and then went to work for an optician. During the First World War he worked in a munitions factory. He then became a bookmaker's clerk, working first for Gus Hall and later for Walter Beresford. When the latter died he became a commission agent. By 1940 he was a wealthy man with money in bonds for his children's education, bank accounts and a number of properties. His solicitors regarded him as a "conveyancing client". He was also a Life Governor of the Northern Hospital.

After the First World War attendance at racecourses boomed, particularly at the southern tracks at which trotting was also a popular spectacle. Before the war the Birmingham gangs had established a hold on racecourse protection in the north and now they sought to advance their empire. Under the leadership of Billy Kimber, who described himself as a bookmaker and punter, and the heavy gambler Andrew Townie, they metamorphosed as the Brummagem Boys despite the fact that most of the members came from the Elephant and Castle area of London. Their organized racecourse protection racket had begun in around 1910 and for a time Kimber's mob took control of southern racecourses such as Newbury, Epsom and Kempton. There were also other gangs operating from Leeds,

Uttoxeter and Cardiff with links throughout the country. Later Kimber's men also had a loose alliance with one of the metamorphoses of the Hoxton Mob. Kimber controlled the best pitches on the courses, leasing them out on a half profit but no loss sharing basis. According to some accounts, he was well regarded and it was looser elements out of his control that terrorized the mainly Jewish bookmakers in the cheaper rings at the southern courses, an imposition they accepted fairly philosophically. It was something the Sabinis intended to redress.

In some versions of the legend the meteoric rise of Darby Sabini can be traced back to a fight he had in 1920 with Thomas "Monkey" Benneyworth, a leader of the Elephant Boys, when Benneyworth deliberately tore the dress of an Italian girl serving behind the bar of the Griffin public house in Saffron Hill. Benneyworth was knocked out and humiliated by Sabini. When his broken jaw had mended he returned with members of the Elephant Boys and they were driven out of Little Italy by Sabini with the help of young Italians who looked on him as their leader. Now, with them behind him, he saw the opportunity to muscle in on some of the smaller gangs who were providing protection around the racetracks. Although the big gangs such as the Broad Mob from Camden Town, the mainly Jewish Aldgate Mob and the Hoxton Mob could boast a membership of up to sixty, they could be spread thinly because they were obliged to operate at several tracks a day. The Sabinis moved in with force.

One explanation of their success and longevity comes from Billy Hill:

> There were more crooked policemen about than there are today. The Sabinis received protection from certain elements of the law. If a thief or pickpocket was seen on a course, a Sabini man would whiten the palm of his hand with chalk and greet the thief with a supposed-to-be

'Hello'. In doing so he would slap the thief on the shoulder, just like a long lost friend. The whitened hand-mark would identify him to the law. Then they knew without doubt that this man was safe to be nicked for being a suspected person.

Throughout the early 1920s there was a long series of battles between the Sabinis and Kimber's men from the Elephant until, after interventions by the bookmaker Walter Beresford, the Sabinis and Kimber agreed to divide the racecourses between them and the racecourse wars died down. Now, with the Sabinis controlling the south where there were more meetings, and Kimber and his friends the rest, the bookmakers were firmly in their hands.

Meanwhile, from the 1920s onwards, the Sabinis had been branching out, taking interests in the West End drinking and gambling clubs, and installing and running slot machines. One of their principal hangouts was the Admiral Duncan in Old Compton Street, Soho. They were also extending their protection racket to criminals. If a burglary took place the Sabinis would send round for their share, just as the Krays did years later.

Darby Sabini may have finally made his peace with "that fine fellow Billy Kimber", as a former police officer Tom Divall once described him, but for some time Sabini had been under threat from other sources inside his own organization. Some of the troops decided to seek a higher percentage of the takings. The four Cortesi brothers (Augustus, George, Paul and Enrico, also known as the Frenchies) were deputed to act as shop stewards to put the case. Almost immediately afterwards, part of the Jewish element in the gang, to become known as the Yiddishers, also formed a breakaway group. In true business fashion the Sabinis negotiated: the Cortesis would be given a greater percentage; the Yiddishers were given permission to lean on one, but only one, of the bookmakers under their protection.

However, peace did not last long. The Yiddishers began to side with the Cortesis and with defections amongst the troops to the Frenchies, the Sabini position was substantially weakened. In the autumn of 1922 the new team had effectively hijacked the Sabini protection money from the bookmakers at Kempton Park. Retribution was swift and as a result of the reprisals, Harry Sabini was convicted at Marylebone Magistrates Court of an assault on George Cortesi. More seriously, one of the other leaders of the breakaway group was attacked, for which five of the Sabini troops were sentenced to terms of imprisonment for attempted murder.

Then on 19 November 1922, just before midnight, Darby and Harryboy Sabini were trapped in the Fratellanza Club in Great Bath Street, Clerkenwell. Darby was punched and hit with bottles while Harry was shot in the stomach by Augustus and Enrico (Harry) Cortesi. Darby suffered a greater indignity. As he told the Magistrates Court, his false teeth were broken as a result of the blows from the bottles. He was also able to confirm his respectability:

> I am a quiet peaceable man. I never begin a fight. I've only once been attacked. I've never attacked anyone. I do a little bit of work as a commission agent sometimes for myself and sometimes for someone else. I'm always honest. The last day's work I did was two years ago. I live by my brains.

He had only once carried a revolver and that was the time he was attacked at Greenford Park. Indeed, he turned out his pockets in confirmation that he was not carrying a gun.

The Cortesi brothers, who lived only five doors from the Fratellanza, had been arrested the same night and, at the Old Bailey on 18 January 1923, Augustus and Enrico each received a sentence of three years' penal servitude. A rather sour note on a Home Office file reads, "It is a pity that the Cortesis were not charged with the murder of the Sabinis."

Meanwhile anonymous letters to the police detailed a series of incidents for which the Sabinis were said to be responsible. The principal correspondent was "Tommy Atkins" who said he had been victimized and, if the police cared to contact him by putting an advertisement in the *Daily Express*, he would reveal all. Meanwhile, he alleged that old-time villain Edward Emmanuel, who had been around since the early 1900s, and Girchan Harris were financing the Sabinis and that they had a number of members of the Flying Squad in their pay as well. The police inserted the advertisement suggesting a meeting, which was declined by "Atkins", who instead supplied details of some twelve incidents including an attack by the Sabini men, James Ford and George Langham, also known as Angelo Giancoli, on bookmaker John Thomas Phillips in Brighton. He also reported the story that the brother of George Moore had been killed and that the *Evening News* racing correspondent "JMD" had been attacked at Newmarket. There was a suggestion that racecourse man Billy Westbury had been injured so badly that he was now "mentally insane".

The police could find no trace of the death of Moore's brother and reported that poor Billy Westbury had suffered only "minor injuries". It was correct, however, that JMD had indeed been attacked.

Without their leaders, the Cortesi faction had folded, but 1925 was apparently a vintage year for gang-fighting in London. The list of incidents is formidable. According to the newspapers, on 15 February there was a razor-slashing in Aldgate High Street and another slashing took place at Euston Station on 24 April. On 21 May ten armed men raided a club in Maiden Lane looking for the Sabinis or their men. Later that night shots were fired in the Harrow Road. On 30 July, three men were wounded in a club in Brighton. There was an incident when men fought on Hampstead Heath on 3 August. Five days later a man was attacked in the Marshalsea Road in Southwark, and on 16 August twenty-four men fought in the West End's Shaftesbury Avenue. Four days after that there was a pitched battle when fifty men fought with razors on the corner of Aldgate and Middlesex Street.

The story that Darby Sabini broke his jaw may, or may not, have been true but Monkey Benneyworth remained an implacable foe. His list of convictions does not give him true credit for the mayhem he caused. He was first before the courts in July 1917 when he received probation at the County of London Sessions for theft. Then he got eight months at the Old Bailey in January 1922 for receiving. Following the Derby meeting in 1924 he collected another three months from the Epsom magistrates for being a suspected person. On 3 June 1925 he was bound over in the sum of £100 to be of good behaviour for his part in the hunt for the Sabinis in Maiden Lane. The gang's information was sadly awry that night because they broke up a tailor's shop in the belief it was a Sabini-owned club. 1925 was something of a vintage year for Benneyworth. He was back in court on 1 September for throwing a typewriter through the window of a barber's shop in Waterloo. For that he forfeited his £100 and, undeterred, with three others he broke up the Union Club in Frith Street on 27 September. As was often the case witnesses were far too afraid to identify him and he walked free.

The police, asked for their comments, were dismissive, saying that the fight at the corner of Middlesex Street had been a minor incident and the fight in Shaftesbury Avenue was a total invention. They accepted the Maiden Lane incident and that Monkey Bennyworth had been involved which, since he had appeared in court, he clearly had. As for the Hampstead Heath fight, there was no evidence that race gangs were involved. And as for allegations that Flying Squad officers were standing by watching some of the incidents, this was totally incorrect. Indeed, the newspapers should be ashamed of themselves for such irresponsible reporting. However, in the

House of Commons, the Home Secretary, William Joynson-Hicks, vowed to stamp out the race gangs.

In the same year Darby Sabini lost another battle when, following a series of unfavourable articles, he sued D. C. Thomson & Co., the proprietors of the offending publication, *Topical Times*, for libel. On the day of the action Sabini failed to appear and costs of £775 were awarded against him. He did not pay and bankruptcy proceedings were commenced.

In 1927, the so-called Battle of Ham Yard off Piccadilly took place with factions led by Wal Macdonald of the Elephant Boys and Harry Sabini, which resulted in Sabini being cut across the cheek. After that things died down possibly because another leading Elephant Boy, Bert McDonald, left for the United States along with the Sabinis' old rival Billy Kimber.

After that Sabini – tired perhaps of trying to keep the peace between the Jewish elements in his gang and the followers of old man Alf White, a survivor from the pre-war Titanics – rather drew in his horns. He retired to the calmer shores of Brighton leaving behind him Harryboy as the de facto leader of the clan. In October 1929, Darby was fined £5 for assaulting bookmaker David Isaacs. After an incident at Hove Greyhound Stadium, he had attacked him first in the Ship Hotel and then in a billiard saloon. When Isaacs was asked why he had not brought witnesses he replied, "How can I get witnesses against a man like this, when everyone goes in fear of their life of him?"

Things flared up again when, so the prosecution alleged, on 25 January 1930 another old villain and opponent of the family, Jack "Dodger" Mullins, along with half a dozen others, went looking for Sabini men in Soho and found Angelo Costognetti in the Argus Club in Greek Street. Costognetti was unmercifully beaten and thrown on the fire while a woman, Edith Milburn, who tried to protect him, was also given a seeing to. On 5 May, Mullins and the Steadman brothers, Charles and George, were acquitted. Mullins had a long history of rivalry with the Sabinis. On 2 July 1926 he had received four years and his friend Timmy Hayes nine at the Old Bailey after being found guilty of blackmail and assault. Mullins said he could prove the case had been got up by the Sabinis and "some of the Yiddisher people" in order to get him and Hayes out of the way.

A fight on 6 February 1930 in the Admiral Duncan, Old Compton Street, may have had its origins at Sandown Park when a Sabini man, Baxter, demanded £10 from an Elephant Boy, Jim Macdonald. Macdonald knocked him down and as a result was a target for reprisals particularly when Baxter enlisted the support of the ex-boxer George Sewell, who liked to be known as the "Cobblestone Kid" and was the father of the well-known character actor, also called George Sewell. In turn Billy Kimber asked the Phillips brothers, John and Arthur, to help Macdonald. Working on the principle that blessed is he who gets his blow in first the brothers and four other men attacked Sewell in the Old Compton Street public house, cutting his throat with a piece of broken glass. For their pains they received long sentences. Sewell temporarily retired to be with Darby Sabini in Brighton.

In June the next year the Elephant Boys went on a rampage breaking up Cypriot and Greek cafés in Rathbone Place and extending their activities down into Windmill Street and the café of Zacharias Panagi. This was not something that the Sabinis could treat lightly and reprisals were swift.

And just as swiftly as they had arisen so did the street fights die away. It was not until the middle of the 1930s, by which time the Sabinis had expanded their territory into greyhound racing, that they again came under serious threat. This time it was from Alf White, whose family, including his son Harry, and friends had been getting stronger over the years and were now set to challenge their former allies.

Frank Fraser, who as a boy carried a bucket for the Sabinis at the racecourses, may not have thought too much of Harry

White's ability on the cobbles but there is no doubt White undertook his fair share of pre-war protection.

In January 1931 Harry White could be found along with the Russian-born Eddie Fleischer, or Fletcher, in a fight outside the Phoenix Club in Little Denmark Street. Casimir Raczynski, who wrestled as Carl Reginski, and a Sabini man called Fred Roche had been attacked as they left the club, and White and Fleischer were accused of malicious wounding. The matter, as did so many of these affairs, blew over. When the case came up for committal, Roche said he had made a mistake while still suffering from the effects of the attack. Now he was sure that, whoever hit him, it was neither White nor Fleischer. The one independent witness, Thomas Jeacock, who had identified the pair, was pleased to tell the court that Roche assured him he had made a mistake. In such ways were things sorted out. Running parallel with that case was one concerning Raczynski's brother, Nicholas, manager of the Phoenix, who was accused of taking an iron bar to a customer and a waitress. Again the witnesses failed to come up to scratch. Indeed, they failed to come to court.

The mid-1930s saw a fresh outbreak of Sabini activity. On both occasions it was the formidable Bert Marsh who was involved. In different ways they were each a triumph. On 6 March 1936 he led a raid on Croydon airport from which gold bars and sovereigns were shipped to Brussels and Paris by Imperial Airways. The boxes were placed in a safe room, a duplicate key for which had been made and, amazingly, only one man, Francis Johnson, remained at the airport overnight. At 4.15 a.m., while he was on the tarmac supervising the landing of a German airliner, the gold was taken.

A cab which had been hired in King's Cross and loaded with the boxes was driven to Harringay where wrappers and seals from the gold were found in the room of Cecil Swanland. Four men were charged but the only one convicted was Swanland who had already served long sentences of penal servitude. He claimed the boxes were empty when they arrived but no one believed him. None of the bullion was ever traced but, shortly after, a Sabini bookmaker took to betting in the Silver Ring at the London tracks under the name Nick Gold.

Later that year, on 1 September, Marsh, along with another Sabini man, Bert Wilkins, was charged with the murder of Massimo Monte Colombo, stabbed to death in a dispute over who would control betting pitches at the Wandsworth greyhound track. There was clearly money around because Marsh and Wilkins were defended by eight barristers including three silks led by the enormously fashionable Norman Birkett KC. The money was said to have been put up by "Racing men" and "the pretty young Mrs Marsh, mother of eight" who had drawn her savings and pawned her jewellery. While on remand Marsh and Wilkins had "saved" a warder "who might have been killed", said the judge, from an attack by another prisoner. Convicted only of manslaughter Marsh, who had a number of convictions for assault, drew a very lenient twelve-month sentence and Wilkins was given three months less.

In between the Marsh triumphs came the so-called Battle of Lewes Racecourse on 8 June 1936. It followed an incident at Liverpool Street Station in London when a member of the Whites had his throat cut. Now up to thirty men went to the course specifically to deal with two Sabinis. They did not find them and instead set on bookmaker Arthur Solomons, who twenty years earlier had been acquitted of the attempted murder of Billy Kimber, and Solomons's clerk, Mark Fraser. The Flying Squad had been tipped off and, led by Inspector Ted Greeno, arrests followed. At Lewes Assizes the men, who had been defended privately by the extremely expensive J. D. Cassels KC, drew up to five years.

1937 saw two serious outbreaks of violence, in the second of which Michael Macausland, now an Elephant Boy, was killed – "Murdered," said relatives at the inquest. The killing of Macausland in July followed an affray in Soho the previous February in which his brother had been involved. Now he died after a beating near his home in King's Cross. Two White men, Eddie Raimo and Jock Wyatt, were later discharged at the Old Bailey. They would both go on to be key men in the history of London crime, with Raimo maintaining his allegiance to White and Wyatt turning his undoubted talents to safe-breaking, for which he received twelve years in 1950.

It was after this that an accommodation was reached. The Sabinis would have the West End and the Whites would control the King's Cross area. They became known as the King's Cross Gang and Alf White would hold court in the Bell Public House or Hennekeys in the Pentonville Road, exercising strict discipline among his followers. "No bad language was allowed," recalled John Vaughan, a former police officer who had served in King's Cross. "First time you were warned. The next time – out." It had been the same with Darby Sabini: women were to be treated properly and Italian youths could not drink before they were twenty.

Immediately after the declaration of war against Italy there was rioting in Soho. On 9 June 1940 the police raided the Italian Club in Charing Cross Road, Greeks fought Italians and restaurant windows were smashed.

In a pre-emptive strike by the authorities, Darby Sabini was arrested as an enemy alien at Hove Greyhound Stadium on the night of 6 July. Now he and his brothers, along with Bert Marsh, were interned.

The consensus of opinion is that they were interned not so much for their Italian connections – few of them spoke the language to any degree and some had children serving in the armed forces – but to break up the gang and, indeed, as a reprisal for the Croydon bullion raid.

Harryboy (alias Harry Handley, Henry Handley and a few other names), who was partial to highly polished, spring-sided boots, was arrested eight days after his brother, which left the

Whites very much in control of things. Aligned with them now were the Yiddishers.

By November, Darby Sabini had still not appeared before a tribunal to determine whether the reasons for his detention were justifiable. Now, he was described as being in semi-retirement and was believed to be a man of considerable means.

The police report leading to Harryboy's arrest described him as:

> one of the leading lights of a gang of bullies known as the Sabini gang who under the cover of various rackets have by their blackmailing methods levied toll on bookmakers ... He is a dangerous man of the most violent temperament and has a heavy following and strong command of a gang of bullies of Italian origin in London.

Harryboy appealed against his detention but this was delayed and so Harryboy, ill-advisedly as it transpired, applied for a writ of habeas corpus, by which an accused must be brought before a judge rather than face continued detention. He had already offered his home, worth some £15,000, as surety if he could be granted bail. In his affidavit in support of the application for leave to be granted, he said he had never been known as Harry Handley. However, the evidence of his arrest was that the police had gone to his house at 44 Highbury Park, Highbury New Barn, in north London on 20 June 1940 and asked his wife where Harry Handley was. The reply had been "upstairs". It was also successfully argued that he could be described as being of "hostile origin" even though he had an English mother and his father had died when he was a child. Harry was released from detention on 18 March 1941 but the authorities were none too pleased. He was promptly rearrested for perjury and on 8 July that year he received a sentence of nine months' imprisonment.

It was the questioning of Darby Sabini that threw some more light, and indeed shade, on his background and family. His real name, he said, was Frederick Sabini and he accepted he was also known as Frederick Handley. He was born in Clerkenwell in 1888. His mother was English and his father, who had been an asphalter, had come to England from Italy in 1850. He had only been abroad twice in his life, when he boxed in France. He had four children: Doris, an elocutionist; Ann, then aged nineteen, who was working in a forestry camp; Rene, aged thirteen, who had played in army concerts; and a son, aged seventeen, who wanted to go into the RAF. He himself had joined the East Surrey Regiment in 1908. He had wanted to join a defence regiment at the start of the war but had been refused on the grounds of his health. He was a printer's representative and was a life governor of some eighteen hospitals. It later turned out that a donation of £40 or more secured a life governorship in some of them. He accepted he was also known as Attavios.

Off he went to Brixton prison and while he was there his old adversary, Detective Inspector Ted Greeno, took the opportunity to blacken his character and those of some of his leading henchmen. Sabini was "A gangster and racketeer of the worst type. One who it is most likely enemy agents would chose as a person to create and lead violent internal action against this country." He was No. 6 on the list of those deemed most likely to assist the enemy. No. 2 was Augustus Cortesi and although the name of No. 1 is deleted from the police file it is likely it was his brother Enrico. In third spot came Harry Sabini and the list also included Pasquale Papa, Silvio Mazzaro, Alfred White, James Ford, Herbert Wilkins and, in twelfth spot, Edward Smith, known as Emmanuel, the financier of the Sabinis. Indeed, MI5 reported that there had been plotting between enemy agents and people such as Nos 3 to 12.

It was while in Brixton that Darby wrote a further explanatory letter: "My real name is Octavius Sabini not Frederick Sabini or Frederick Handley. I used the name of Fred Handley has [*sic*] my boxing name. Darby is my nickname. My friends call me Fred but I am not the same has [*sic*] Frederick Sabini my brother. Signed Octavius Sabini."

Whatever is correct, the developments left Soho wide open to Alf White. One of the Sabini men who remained outside the internment sweep was Antonio "Babe" Mancini. It was he who would lead what was left of the group to maintain Italian interests.

Before the Second World War protection had been something of an art form. A fight was started in a club and a certain amount of damage was done. Perhaps a foot went through the skin of the drum, tables were overturned, a few glasses were broken. The next day came a visit from a sympathetic representative of the Sabinis or others who would point out how disruptive such incidents were in frightening off punters and how they could be avoided by payment of a small weekly sum. By 1941, however, the rules of the game had changed. Now it was thought best to inflict the maximum amount of damage possible on a rival's premises. If the club closed for good, so much the better. There was one fewer competitor.

On 20 April 1941, "Fair Hair" Eddie Fletcher and Joseph Franks were involved in a fight with Bert Connelly, the doorman of the Palm Beach Bottle Party, a club in the basement of 37 Wardour Street, which also housed the Cosmo on the ground floor, the West End Bridge and Billiards Club on the first and was the haunt of prostitutes run by the Messina brothers. Fletcher was given a beating and banned from the club by the manager Joe Leon, whose real name was Niccolo Cariello.

Ten days later Fletcher returned and Sammy Ledderman, a Soho inhabitant of thirty years – he was a friend of Jack Spot and later gave evidence against the Kray twins – went into the Palm Beach to tell Mancini, the dinner-jacketed catering manager and doorman for the night, that "They're smashing up the [Bridge and Billiards] Club."

What had happened was that Fletcher and other members of the Yiddisher Gang, including Moishe Cohen, had been playing pool and cards in the club when in walked Sabini men Joseph Collette, Harry Capocci and Albert Dimes, the last then currently absent without leave from the Royal Air Force. Fighting broke out, started by Albert Dimes, said the witnesses who may not have been wholly impartial. The police thought that the intention was to destroy a rival club. The unfortunate Fletcher received another beating and was taken to Charing Cross Hospital, then a matter of minutes away. Patched up, he had then returned to Wardour Street once more, allegedly to retrieve his coat.

At first Mancini seems to have wanted to stay out of trouble but Joe Leon then asked him to go to the door of the Palm Beach and let no one in. He stood inside the door and then changed out of his evening clothes and went upstairs to see the damage.

As he was on the stairs he heard someone say, "There's Babe, let's knife him." Mancini thought the speaker was Fletcher. He sensed someone was behind him and went into the club followed by Fletcher, Harry "Little Hubby" or "Scarface" Distleman and another man.

It was then that fighting broke out yet again, with Albert Dimes being restrained by his elder brother, Victor. Distleman was stabbed. Few of the forty people in the club saw exactly what happened but the consensus of such witnesses who were prepared to speak up was that it was Mancini who stabbed him. In fact, Distleman had said to two companions, "I am terribly hurt. Babe's done it." It did not have the same evidential strength as a formal dying declaration but it certainly did not help Mancini.

Mancini had then chased after the unfortunate Fletcher and had almost severed his arm. When he was interviewed he told Detective Inspector Arthur Thorp, "I admit I stabbed Fletcher with a long dagger which I found on the floor of the club, but

I don't admit doing Distleman. Why should I do him? They threatened me as I came up the stairs and I got panicky." The next day, however, he said he had the dagger wrapped in a rag with him when he went up the stairs. Mancini had, in fact, known "Little Hubby" Distleman for something in the region of fifteen years.

Mancini was unlucky at his trial. The brief to the prosecution suggests that if he offered a plea to manslaughter, "Counsel will no doubt consider it, as the witnesses of the assault on Distleman are vague and shaky." It is not possible to say now whether any such plea was offered or whether the prosecutor did not accept it. It was argued that if self-defence was rejected a death in a gang-fight in such circumstances should only be manslaughter and indeed the judge, Mr Justice McNaughten, summed up to that effect. In fact, in a not dissimilar case three months earlier, this is exactly what had happened. The jury, however, after a retirement of a bare fifty-five minutes, convicted Mancini of murder – a decision with which the judge concurred – and an appeal met with no success at all. The judge had, if anything, been too favourable in his summing-up, said the Lord Chief Justice. A further appeal to the House of Lords also failed and Mancini became the first London gangster to be hanged since the First World War, when robber Joseph Jones met his end.

Following the Mancini trial Dimes, Collette and Capocci were again arraigned, this time before the Recorder of London, Sir Gerald Dodson. One by one the witnesses for the prosecution failed to identify them and the trial collapsed. Capocci was acquitted but Dimes and Collette were bound over with the sum of £5 to come up for judgement in the next three years. "You were probably expecting prison," said the Recorder, "and no doubt you deserve it." Dimes was handed over to the RAF, but he did not remain with them for very long.

According to his biography, *The Soho Don*, the fight allowed Billy Howard, another long-time Soho and south

London resident, then currently a deserter, to take control of 37 Wardour Street and provide the necessary protection for much of the war.

According to the newspapers, on 17 June 1943 Darby Sabini, who by then had been released from internment, was convicted of receiving £383 of wine and silver which had been stolen by soldiers from the Uckfield house of a retired Sussex magistrate. The jury had rejected his defence that he thought that he was buying goods from a hotel that was being sold. The Recorder, Gilbert Paull, passing sentence, told him in the time-honoured style that judges love to use to receivers, "It is men like you who lay temptation before soldiers. If there were none like you there would be no temptation to steal." Sabini, who was said to have no previous convictions, received three years' imprisonment. This presents a problem. It was "Fred Sabini" who had been convicted on this occasion and if, in fact, it was Darby, then the fingerprints that were taken on his arrest should have shown up on the police files as matching a man with previous convictions.

After the war Harry joined his brother in Brighton. Darby's son had joined the RAF and was killed in action. In the late 1940s he functioned as a small-time bookmaker with a pitch on the free course at Ascot, a danger to no one, and certainly not the up-and-coming Jack Spot and Billy Hill.

When Darby died in Hove in 1951 his family and friends were surprised that he apparently had so little money. Yet the man who had been his clerk, Jimmy Napoletano, was stopped leaving the country on his way to Italy with £36,000, a substantial sum for those days when £500 could buy a terraced house in some parts of London. Sabini's wife returned to live in Gray's Inn Road, Clerkenwell. Bert Marsh died, a rich man, on his way to see his model daughter when he had a heart attack and crashed his car in The Bishop's Avenue, Hampstead. Albert Dimes became a close friend of Billy Hill and a trusted friend of the Philadelphia Mafioso Angelo Bruno.

Darby Sabini lives on in fiction and film as Colleoni, the gang-leader in Graham Greene's *Brighton Rock* (1938). One of the key scenes in both the book and the 1947 film is the meeting between him and Pinky in a Brighton hotel. The slashing of Pinky at the race meeting is based on the Lewes battle of 1936.

15

Mimile Buisson and the Front Wheel Drive Gang

By the end of the 1930s the undoubted leader of the Paris underworld, known as *le milieu* or *la pègre*, was Émile Buisson. Small with very black hair and black eyes, he was born on 19 August 1902 and was known as "Mimile le Dingue" (Mimile the Mad). He and his brothers came from Paray-le-Monial in the Saône-et-Loire district of central France. Their father, addicted to absinthe and his daughters, was eventually sent to prison for having carnal knowledge of minors and died in an insane asylum, as did their mother.

The elder Buisson brother was Jean-Baptiste, known as Fatalitas, which was tattooed on his chest, and sometimes – if not to his face – as Screwball. He was called up in the First World War, deserted in 1917 after three years' service and was sent to the Battalion d'Afrique (known as the Bat d'Af), the notorious penal battalion in Algeria. On his release, he went to Paris where he set himself up as a pimp.

Émile began his criminal career on 14 November 1919 when he received fifteen days' imprisonment for theft in Lyon. Almost immediately on his release he was sentenced to twenty months, also to be served in the Bat d'Af. For a time he seems to have done well and for his courage in the fighting with the Rifian tribesmen of North Africa he was awarded the Croix de Guerre. If he made anything of his award on his discharge it was in recruiting a higher class of girl to prostitute herself for him. Crime and short sentences followed him and his brother remorselessly until, in February 1932, Jean-Baptiste received an eight-year sentence for armed robbery and Émile devoted himself to obtaining his brother's early release.

By October 1934 Jean-Baptiste was in the relatively lax prison at Mulhouse where he deliberately smashed his leg to get into the prison hospital. In a cast, he jumped from the window and, breaking his leg again, limped to his brother's waiting car with the help of Émile Courgibet.

Born in Paris, Courgibet had lived an interesting life. In November 1918 he had killed one of his girlfriends, whom he believed to be unfaithful, stabbing her in the heart. He had overstayed his sick leave on her account and was technically an army deserter. For this he received eight years in Guiana followed by ten years' *interdiction de sejour*, the French law that forbade a convicted criminal from residing in the city or town where he was sentenced. He escaped prison in 1922 and managed to stay at large for the next six years. Once returned to the penal colony, he escaped again and made his way back to Paris via Spain. In all he escaped six times.

The trio went to Switzerland and then via Genoa to China. At the time crime in Shanghai was in the hands of the so-called Green Gang, originally a secret society founded to restore the Ming dynasty but which over the years had turned to crime. At first the brothers worked as gun-runners for the gang before they bought a nightclub, using the proceeds to deal in prostitution and drugs. They returned to France after the body of a Chinese man, who was said to have cheated a Maltese friend of theirs, was found in the Whangpoo river.

On 27 December 1937 the Buisson brothers, together with a team including Courgibet and Abel Danos, known as "Mammoth" because of the size of his stomach, executed a well-planned bank robbery at Troyes. Then, on 6 April 1938 while stealing some 1.8 million francs, Émile earned his nickname. When clear of their pursuers he turned and began to shoot again. Legend has it that one of his companions, Charles Desgrandschamps, called, *"Mimile, viens vite! T'es dingue, quoi?"* (Mimile, hurry up! Are you mad?)

It was Desgrandschamps who informed on Émile Buisson to the police. When the police called on him they found his girlfriend, Yvonne Pandelet, had hidden some of the banknotes from the robbery in an umbrella.

Desgrandschamps, known as Big-Foot Charlie for his lack of agility, died while attempting to rob the Café des Gourmets in the rue Violet, not far from the Eiffel Tower in Paris, in July 1947. He was accidentally shot by one of his own men, Dubois, with a burst from a Sten gun. The gang took him to the Boucicaut Hospital where he died on the operating table having had the wit to give the police a false name.

Although the others in the Troyes raid were arrested, Courgibet escaped on the *Normandie* to New York. His was one the few success stories of the time. Under the name of Ferdinand Châtelain, he worked as a cabinet-maker. He later married an American girl and became an expert antique furniture restorer. He was arrested in 1952 and deported to France where he served a two-year sentence before returning to New York to continue in his business.

On 24 February 1941, in the first of what became known as the "Traction Avant" – Front Wheel Drive – robberies in which the gang's preferred method of transport was a Citroën 11, Émile Buisson shot two elderly bank messengers in cold blood as he robbed the Credit Lyonnais in rue Notre-Dame-des-Victoires, not far from the Louvre in Paris.

On 13 May 1943 he was sentenced to life imprisonment for the Troyes bank raid. At first he was held at Clairvaux prison but after attacking a guard in an unsuccessful escape attempt, he began to feign madness and was transferred to the Santé, near Montmartre, to await trial on a capital charge. He was held there until early 1947, by which time he had convinced the authorities that he was indeed mad and was sent to the criminal asylum at Villejuif.

On 3 September he escaped with the help of Jean-Baptiste, along with Roger Dekker and Henri Russac, who had bribed the guards. Escaping with him was the dapper Réné Girier, known as Réné la Canne or Réné the Stick. One of the major criminals of the 1940s, Girier first appeared before the courts at the age of fourteen when he forced the locked door of his father's bedroom and stole money. He progressed from this to leading a small band of multi-talented and faceted men. He played a good game of tennis while Jackie Cruel, his gunman, was a talented amateur painter; Arsène Goddard had received a secondary school education while Jean Debusigne, a car thief, held an arts degree; another, Jose Arellano, had studied to be a teacher. The break-up of the gang and the arrest of Réné, naked in a hotel bedroom but with an automatic under the pillow, came after a gang fall-out. Two of the team had decided to join a rival organization and then shot each other in a café after a quarrel. One was dead but Girier was traced through the other.

Days later Buisson and three others held up the clientele of the Auberge d'Arbois near the Place de l'Étoile at the top of the Champs-Élysées. As they escaped he emptied a machine-gun at the police. That night they all celebrated in a Montmartre bar but days later Émile shot and killed Henri Russac whom he believed had taken a diamond ring and not put it in the kitty. When the police raided the Buisson hide out at 57 rue Bichat, near the Quai des Jemmapes on the Canal St Martin, out of the window went Émile leaving the police to arrest his brother and Dekker.

Buisson now put together a new team including a Breton tough guy called Francis Caillaud. On 10 May 1948 they robbed two workers who were carrying 70,000 francs drawn from a post office at Draveil in the southern suburbs of Paris. Hold-up followed hold-up: two jewellers and a garage at Boulogne-Billancourt; a payroll at Neuilly-Plaisance; and another robbery near Étampes. A Corsican who Buisson believed had doubled-crossed him was found shot in the head, with his tongue ripped out; Roger Gourmont, a bank manager, was shot in the stomach during a raid at Champigny-sur-Marne in 1949; on 17 February that year a cashier was shot in Versailles.

There are various stories of Buisson's final capture. One, by the detective Roger Borniche, is that the police learned that Buisson and his mistress Yvette were at an inn the Auberge de la Mère Odue at Claville for lunch on 10 June 1949. Pretending to be a doctor from Deauville, Borniche went into the kitchen, where Buisson was talking to the chef, and asked the patronne to make a telephone call for him "to his clinic". When Buisson turned his back, Borniche pinned him down while his wife Marylyse put the handcuffs on him.

The other version, put out to annoy the Gendarmerie, is that Buisson was captured by Commissaire Chevenier while he was lunching at Aux Trois Obus, a small restaurant near the Porte de Saint-Cloud Métro station. With some panache Buisson asked if the Commissaire would have a brandy with him before making the arrest. Criminals were always offered a glass of rum on the scaffold and Buisson remarked with some humour that the brandy he drank with Chevenier would be his "drink before the last".

From the time of Eugène François Vidocq, head of French national security service, the Sureté, in the nineteenth century, French detectives had rewarded prisoners who made confessions with food and wine, and Roger Borniche was no exception. He would supply Buisson with a bottle of wine every time he took him for questioning. Unfortunately, after his arrest Buissson lost his nerve and to Borniche's disgust he became a *casserole*, or grass and named, among others, François Marcantoni.

Word of this bad behaviour spread and, to defend the family honour, his brother "Fatalitas" Buisson shot Michel (or Jean)

Cardeur, known as Michel l'Avocat, in the Sirène bar just off the Grands Boulevards in Paris on Christmas Eve, 1950. Cardeur had been taunting Jean-Baptiste about his brother turning informer and also suggesting he was homosexual. Fatalitas was arrested in Juan-les-Pins on 3 April 1953 and sentenced to life imprisonment. He was released in 1969 and died in the early 1980s.

Émile Buisson was guillotined at the Santé prison at 6.05 on the morning of 28 February 1956 on one of the coldest mornings of the century. Like a number of other French criminals he had the legend "Cut along the dotted line" tattooed on his neck. He is said to have remarked to the executioner Monsieur de Paris, "I'm ready, Monsieur. You can go ahead. Society will be proud of you." He was buried in the cemetery at Thiais in the section reserved for the condemned.

Of the others in the Front Wheel Drive Gang, Abel Danos, who had begun life as a small-time gas-meter bandit, became a member of the French Gestapo and was thought to have executed between 100 and 200 Resistance workers in the Second World War. After the Liberation he was captured but escaped and worked on the black market, specializing in forged ration coupons. He is known to have taken part in a number of underworld killings and in October 1948 was involved in the shooting of police officers in Genoa, Italy, during a robbery. He killed two more police officers in Menton on his return to France and was then caught in a police trap in December. When not working, this cold-blooded killer lived a life of domesticity in Le Lavandou, then a small fishing village in the south of France, with a wife and two children whom he adored. While awaiting his trial he shed some six stone in weight. It was three years before it was decided he should die for his war crimes and he faced a firing squad at Fort Monte-Valérien on 14 March 1952. It is said he died with some dignity, accepting a glass of rum with a steady hand and refusing a blindfold.

One of the more extraordinary stories of that period of French gangsterdom linked Pierre Loutrel, known as Pierrot le Fou, and Joseph Brahim Attia, known as Jo le Moko. A Tunisian whose father may have been killed in the First World War – other accounts have him dying in poverty in a Paris hospital in 1933 – le Moko had met and formed a deep friendship with Loutrel while serving in the Bat d'Af. They were released at the beginning of the war with Loutrel accepting an offer by Inspector Bony to join the French Gestapo in the rue Lauriston where, working with other members of the Milieu, including Danos and Pierre Giblaise, he is said to have shot some eighty Resistance workers.

Le Moko, who initially also worked for the French Gestapo, had then joined the Resistance. He was captured in 1943, tortured and then sentenced to death. Reprieved, thanks to Loutrel and Abel Danos, who convinced the head of the French Gestapo, Henri Lafont, to hand him over to the Germans, he was sent to the Mauthausen concentration camp. There he earned the respect of all nationalities, risking death by stealing food. The punishment for capture in this enterprise was slow strangulation. When the Allies marched through northern France, le Moko went on the March of Death in which the camp guards forced the surviving prisoners to walk ninety miles to keep them away from the liberating armies. Again he gained the respect of his fellows, dragging and carrying other weaker men to prevent them being shot and thrown into ditches.

By the end of the war Loutrel had also changed sides, becoming Captain de Normande and working for the FFI (French Forces of the Interior) in Toulouse. Surprised in a bar by an old acquaintance, Degatz, who said *"Tiens, c'est Pierrot de la carlingue!"* (Well, if it isn't Pete from the Gestapo!), he shot him dead claiming that he had done so to protect the honour of the Resistance. The police allowed him provisional liberty while they completed their inquiries and Loutrel went off to Marseilles and Paris where he is credited with the albeit brief kidnap of the actress Martine Carol, to whom he sent roses the next day as an apology.

Now, on the business front, he teamed up with Marcel Rouart, known as "Pepito le Gitan", and together they carried out a series of enterprising and daring raids along the Mediterranean coast. On 22 July 1946 they stole over £77,000 from the Nice post office, at the time a record amount for a French hold-up. They then turned their attention to Paris and held up the cashier's van on the Quai de la Rapée, taking £40,000 from the Métro, as well as armed robberies on the Avenue Parmentier and the Quai de Bercy. As for le Moko, the police and press became convinced he was the third member and in command of the gang.

In September 1956 the police received word that the three were staying at the Hôtel des Marroniers at Champigny-sur-Marne. In the ensuing battles in which the police shot dead Benôit Prost, a retired bookmaker from Montmartre who owned the hotel, and the gang killed one and injured a number of officers, all fled. It is accepted that le Moko was present but took no part in the shooting and escaped separately in the general carnage. This was the end of the Traction Avant Gang.

On 6 November, Loutrel and le Gitan robbed a Paris jeweller in the rue Boissère off the Avenue Kléber in the fashionable sixteenth arrondissement. There are conflicting stories whether the jeweller, M. Serafin, managed to turn the gun around and shoot Loutrel or whether he accidentally shot himself damaging his femoral artery. There is no doubt, however, that le Gitan killed Serafin. Now Loutrel feared that if he was taken to hospital his body would be used for dissection and he begged le Gitan to get help from le Moko.

Le Moko met up with them on a piece of waste ground at Ivry and then brought Loutrel back to the house of a friend, Henri Courtois, who lived near the Porte d'Orléans. He then hired an ambulance to take him to Mantes, not far from Versailles, where he could hole up and possibly recover.

Le Moko sentimentally described his friend's death in Derick Goodman's *Villainy Unlimited*:

> The pain was too much for him and Pete began to chew on a little golden figure of the Holy Virgin that hung on a chain round his neck.
>
> "Take it out of my mouth when I go. In a few moments I will be with Her in eternity. And with God. I know he is Great and filled with forgiveness. He will pardon me where my fellow-men would not."
>
> ... I held him tightly right to the end – like I learned the hard way in the penal battalions of the Legion under the blazing African sun.

Now le Moko had the problem of disposing of Loutrel's body. He solved it with the assistance of Courtois rowing across the Seine and burying it on an island in midstream. Le Moko made Courtois promise he would not reveal the circumstances of Loutrel's death and he kept the promise for three years, during which time Loutrel was reported as committing a series of daring robberies and escapes across France. Le Moko was arrested in Marseilles in July 1947 and during his questioning repeatedly told the police that Loutrel had fled to South America.

In due course le Moko was charged with nine robberies and sent first to Aix, where he was able to bribe a warder to bring in prostitutes, and, after an abortive escape attempt, to the Baumettes prison in Marseilles. Meanwhile, Courtois had opened his mouth in one bar too many and, once the body of Loutrel had been exhumed, a charge of illegally detaining a corpse was added to the accusations against le Moko. He was acquitted of the robberies but received a sentence of seven years for this last offence, serving his time in the Fresnes prison near Paris. He was released in December 1953 and opened a bar, the Gavroche, in Montmartre.

Then in 1956 he was rearrested while gun-running in the Free Zone in Tangiers. He decided to confess to a double murder at Montfort-l'Aumaury near Paris and was promptly extradited and charged. It must have been galling for the police, who had, after all, been chasing the dead Loutrel for years, to discover that le Moko had deceived them once more. He was able to prove that he was not in France at the time of the murders and once more he was released to return to his bar. Under the laws of the Free Zone in Tangiers he could not be extradited and so escaped the gun-running charge. Le Moko was also thought to have acted for the French Secret Service both in the kidnapping of the revolutionary Moroccan Mehdi Ben Barka and that of Colonel Antoine Argoud, a supporter of French Algerians.

In 1969 a small-time thief Christian Jubin broke into le Moko's bar, killed the barmaid and her boyfriend, and attacked le Moko's daughter. Fortunately for Jubin the police arrested him before le Moko found him. In an escape attempt Jubin later took the investigating judge, who was interrogating him, as a hostage but he was soon recaptured. He died, still in prison, of throat cancer in 1990. Le Moko, who had been awarded the Legion d'Honneur after the Second World War, died on 22 June 1972.

Another Traction Avant gang-member, François Marcantoni, became a partner in a Paris bar co-owned by Antoine "Toto" Rossi, brother of the immensely popular singer Tino Rossi. He also became a friend of Alain Delon and Jean-Paul Belmondo, and was implicated in the death in October 1968 of Delon's bodyguard, Stefan Markovic, whose body was found in a rubbish dump in the Paris suburb of Élancourt. Markovic had written a letter saying that in the event of his death Delon and Marcantoni would be to blame. The subsequent scandal threatened the world of French politics, and touched upon

President Georges Pompidou and his wife. Delon, who denied any involvement, was never charged and Marcantoni was finally found not guilty in 1976. He later said, "Only three of us know the truth, Delon, me and God and God isn't an informer." He died in August 2010.

16

Billy Hill, "Boss of Britain's Underworld"

Billy Hill, a villain's villain if ever there was one, who in turn was Jack Spot's friend, partner, rival and nemesis, was born in 1911 in Seven Dials, near Leicester Square then one of the rougher parts of the West End of London. John Capstick, who later became a Detective Chief Superintendent and was said rather romantically to have placed a red rose on the grave of the early gang-leader Darby Sabini, joined the police in 1925. After his training he was posted to Bow Street and on his second night he was allowed to go out on the beat alone. He was patrolling Monmouth Street when he was lured to the now very fashionable Neal's Yard where he was given a good beating and kicking by the locals. When he limped back to the station he did not receive much sympathy. On being told where the incident had happened, the station sergeant nodded saying, "I thought so. That's where they break all you young coppers in."

While growing up, Hill wanted for little. One of some twenty-one children, his family had a fine criminal pedigree. His mother was a receiver and his sisters and brothers were thieves, the star of whom was Maggie, one of the best shoplifters of her generation and known as "Baby Face, the Queen of the Forty Elephants". She took the name partly from the shape she assumed by the time she had packed her bloomers and coats with stolen merchandise and partly from the Forty Thieves team of shoplifters of which she was at one time the leader. She married the celebrated Birmingham thief and general villain Reuben "Brummy" Sparkes. Capstick described Maggie as:

> Utterly fearless, she knew every trick in the book and she could put away three fur coats and a bolt of cloth in the time it took any of her team-mates to snitch a pair of cami-knickers. A stout, handsome woman, she liked to work with a slim young woman not much more than half her age, and a highly efficient pair they were. I hate to think how much money they made on their regular trips to the Midlands.

The Forty Thieves was a very long standing gang of mainly women shoplifters who had been in operation since at least the beginning of the twentieth century. Membership was highly prized and carefully controlled. If not a case of waiting for dead women's shoes it was very much a case of "once in, never out" until retirement. Defection was punished. At the time Hill was growing up, the undoubted leader was Alice Diamond, a regular visitor to the Hill household. Another visitor was the celebrated American criminal, Eddie Guerin, who, at the turn of the century, had escaped from Devil's Island.

By the time he was sixteen, Hill was a fully fledged burglar working with his sister, Dolly. He worked for a greengrocer and, in their innocence, customers would tell him not to deliver their orders until such and such a time because they would be out. Dolly had a telephone and Hill would phone her so she and her husband could burgle their homes safely. Hill was also carrying out burglaries on his own.

The early part of his career came to an end in 1927 when he and a man he named as Albert Smart were robbing a flat in Golders Green. Smart used the lavatory and then foolishly pulled the chain. The noise was heard; a neighbour telephoned the police and the pair were arrested a few streets away. On 5 January 1929, as Herbert Williams, Hill was sent from the Inner London Sessions to borstal for three years. In his memoirs, compiled with the considerable help of his Boswell, the journalist Duncan Webb, Hill wrote of life in the Portland Borstal near Weymouth and where the inmates pounded stones, morning and afternoon, to fill a bucket with ground powder.

The stone pounding came after his attempted escape with another boy, Lawrence Edward Harding, on 18 September 1929. Because of the geographical location at the end of a spit successful escapes from Portland were rare and their attempt was hopeless for the start. They were dressed in the regulation grey shorts and shirts, a certain giveaway if they were seen. They had to find some clothes and at about three in the afternoon they were ransacking the house of a Commander Basil Bowen when they were heard by his maid, Mary Matthews. When she poked her head into the kitchen where Hill was hiding behind the door he hit her with a pastry-covered rolling pin, cutting her head and stunning her.

Harding, who was now over twenty-one and had already received twelve strokes of the birch, was sentenced to twelve months hard labour on top of his sentence and twelve strokes of the cat-o'nine-tails to go with it. Hill was given a more modest nine months along with twelve strokes of the birch.

On Hill's release it was his sister Maggie who helped him. She was serving another sentence in Holloway but she had left some money for him and with it he bought some first-class burglar's tools. Hill did not, however, last long on the outside. He completed two successful burglaries and on the seventh day he was arrested in Maida Vale and charged with being a suspected person. On 19 September 1931 he received twenty-one days' imprisonment at Marylebone Police Court, just long enough for the authorities to revoke his borstal licence, and he was sent back to Portland. He had only a short time to serve and, by his account, he already had the nucleus of a team around him which loosely formed the Camden Town

Gang. As was often the case, borstal had in no way improved the inmate's conduct and on 14 February 1932 at Clerkenwell Police Court he received three months for loitering with intent.

In contrast to Jack Spot, Hill was a good paymaster. Importantly, at that stage he did not take more than his share of a job: "If we were five-handed on a job I split the wages five ways. I did not take two shares for myself and divide the remainder between the other four."

By 1933 Hill was taking £70 a week, something he thought was good money, which indeed it was. That was when he came a cropper while burgling a doctor's house in Bromley. He was disturbed and as he ran down a railway track to make his escape, he stumbled and fell, badly burning himself. This time, on 11 January 1934, he was given three years' penal servitude from West Kent Quarter Sessions.

It was on his release that Hill took lessons in smash-and-grab from the great thief, Charlie "Ruby" Sparks – no relation to Reuben Sparkes. Sparks had been involved in smash-and-grab raids as far back as the mid-1920s and had been fortunate to avoid a charge of murder when a woman died after being knocked down following the first ever smash-and-grab raid in New Street, Birmingham. Now, in 1934, Hill set about improving the technique. He was so successful that by the early months of 1935 the newspapers were reporting major thefts on an almost daily basis. Questions were being asked in the House of Commons and, as a counter measure, the Flying Squad was expanded. Hill began to look for alternative employment.

And that alternative was safe-breaking. He may never have been the top man in this field but he certainly ranked in the first half dozen. Generally, because of their experience with explosives in the mining industry, safe-breakers came from the northeast of England, Scotland and Wales, but Hill was soon in demand. He claimed to have lost count of the number of safes he blew and he also was hired on the continent. This line of work came to an end in October 1936 at the County of London Sessions when he received twenty-one months for shop-breaking followed smartly by a concurrent four years at Middlesex Quarter Sessions for a similar offence. And that ended Hill's pre-war criminal career.

The Second World War provided the greatest single opportunity for organized crime in Britain and, led in London by Billy Hill, criminals now took advantage of it. One significant thing was the expansion of their markets. Just as middle-class Americans would not have thought of consorting with criminals until Prohibition, the war narrowed the class boundaries. With dozens of prohibitive Emergency Orders being made in Parliament there were opportunities beyond the criminals' wildest dreams. Now middle-class women were prepared to deal with black-marketeers to obtain extra food, clothes, cigarettes and petrol coupons. Government offices were raided for ration books. The German bombing of cities provided a great opportunity for looting and, dressed as air raid precaution (ARP) wardens, thieves were often inadvertently assisted by members of the public to clear stock from damaged shops. The blackout and consequent ban on car lights helped the getaway drivers enormously. Seeing the opportunities available, people who would not normally commit crime helped themselves. In 1943 thefts from railways stations exceeded £1 million (£40 million in today's terms) and in the next year the figure almost doubled. A new generation of criminals was born.

Ever the organizer, Hill set about the situation with unmatched enthusiasm. Writing of the black market he would recall, "It was the most fantastic side of civil life in war time. Make no mistake. It cost Britain millions of pounds. I did not merely make use of the black market. I fed it."

And one way in which he fed it was through the theft of bedsheets from a services depot in the southwest of England. Lorry load after lorry load was taken. He estimates that thousands of sheets were stolen each week and sold at £1 a pair. He also raided a warehouse full of fur coats which were sold at £6 each. Whisky went for £500 a barrel, the same price as a barrel of sausage skins. He was, he said, clearing around £300 to £400 a week, a fantastic sum for the time.

It is a wonder he had any time for his other career. Once again he became the master of the smash-and-grab raid. The police were convinced that Hill was behind, if not an active participant in, most of those early raids. On 1 February 1940 Ciro's Pearls in London's Bond Street lost almost its entire stock. The next month Hill was arrested after a mid-morning raid on Carrington's, the jewellers in Regent Street. At about 10 a.m. on 20 March a small maroon car was driven over the pavement into the shop doorway, blocking access. A second, bigger, black car pulled up and the driver smashed the window with a carjack. Some £6,000 worth of rings, which in today's terms would be estimated at around £250,000, was stolen. Hill was placed on an identification parade but not picked out.

He was arrested again after a car mounted the pavement in Wardour Street on 21 May. At first passers-by thought the car had been out of control but a man in the passenger seat stood up and, leaning out of the sunroof, robbed the shop through the broken display window. Another robbery took place at Phillips in New Bond Street when jewellery worth £11,000 was taken. This time the second car, which had been stolen, had the engaging new number plate MUG 999. Hill survived another identification parade.

His luck ran out on 26 June 1940 when he and two long-standing friends, Harry Bryan, nominally an Islington bookmaker, and "Square Georgie" Ball, were arrested in a failed robbery on Hemmings & Co. in Conduit Street. Bryan had previously been convicted in the celebrated 1936 Clerkenwell bullion robbery when £2,000 worth of gold ingots was stolen in a snatch from a lorry. This time a policeman, PC Higgs, threw his truncheon through the windscreen and, with the crowd's assistance, Bryan and Ball were arrested. Hill fled down Bond Street into Bruton Street but by now the crowd and two more policemen were after him. He managed to get on to a roof and tried the old trick of saying to a policeman who climbed after him, "He's in there", but in almost pantomime tradition the crowd shouted, "That's him." Bryan and Ball drew three years apiece but Hill managed to negotiate a charge of conspiracy that carried a maximum of two years.

A one-month sentence at Marylebone for being a suspected person followed Hill's release and then, in the terms of the trade, it all came on top when he was given information about a potential armed robbery. On 15 July 1942 a postmaster in Islington was to be the target during the lunch hour. Teddy Hughes went with Hill, and Jock Wyatt acted as lookout. The robbery went well until a lorry driver rammed their getaway car. Hughes and Hill were caught in the car and Wyatt, instead of sauntering away, tried to run and was also arrested.

In those days it was possible to exchange part of a sentence for strokes of the cat-o'nine-tails and Hill and the others asked Sir Gerald Dodson, the Recorder of London, if this could be done. It would have been a question of all three of them accepting twelve stokes but unfortunately Hughes had a weak heart and it was not thought that he could stand the punishment. Consequently Wyatt and Hill received four years and Hughes a year less.

Hill claimed that, with the war almost over and himself now out of prison, he had been within a hair's breadth of a £7 million robbery of savings, insurance and postage stamps. The post office van left Harrow and drove to High Wycombe where the stamps were collected. Then it was driven to a side street while the men went into a café for lunch with only one remaining outside to guard the van. Hill regarded the robbery as no more difficult that shelling peas for his team of four. He thought that the whole swoop on the van would take no more than ninety seconds. However, it was a question of careless mouths cost jobs. The police had heard of the plans and the route was switched. Hill was still prepared to go ahead but, when he learned that Superintendent Robert Lee, "one of the smartest bogies in the business", was "sniffing around", the job was abandoned. Hill would later deceitfully claim that he then, "packed up active crime soon after that, and carved my way to the top of the underworld in London to settle down to a quiet career running my clubs and spielers". Spielers were illegal drinking and gambling clubs.

Shortly after the war he was charged over a warehouse breaking. He maintained he was innocent and, given his full and frank admissions relating to his other escapades, he was possibly telling the truth. He decided to do a runner and leave England for good.

He discussed this with his wife, Aggie, who wanted him to take her with him on the basis that she might be able to stop further foolishness on his part. Hill felt the need to complete one last quick and profitable job to prepare for the future. On the east coast an RAF officer was selling gash parachutes as surplus parachute silk to a south London villain. Hill, dressed as a police officer, and friends tailed the villain's lorry and stopped it. The south Londoners ran away and Hill took the lorry. Hill netted over £9,000 from the night's work.

A diplomat friend obtained Hill a passage on a ship and he went to South Africa via Lisbon, but Aggie was left behind. Within a week he was in Johannesburg where he saw that a familiar East End face, Bobby Ramsay, a tricky little fighter who looked like a pocket edition of Freddie Mills but who had no real punch, was due to box there. Hill soon made himself busy. At the time the king of the city's underworld was Arnold Neville, a seventeen-stone ex-wrestler who controlled the gambling with his partner, Sammy Abnit. They fell out and Abnit approached Hill with a view to opening another club.

Neville caught wind of Hill's plans to open the Club Millionaire as a gambling school and said that if the club opened on the following Sunday he would break it up. Hill regarded this meeting as effectively a showdown for control of Johannesburg. According to Hill's memoirs he had been given a revolver by a reporter who disliked Neville and now he carried it with him. Hill also had a large hunting knife that he gave to Bobby Ramsay, who was on the door.

Neville also owned the Stork Room, and Hill had a spy placed in it to warn him when Neville and his team were on their way. On the opening night of the Club Millionaire on 12 May 1947, Neville and his team of eight appeared there about 1.30 in the morning.

Two days later there was an account of the ensuing entertainment in the Rand *Daily Mail*: "Mr Arnold Neville the former wrestler of Highland Road, Kensington was given nearly one hundred stitches in the Johannesburg General Hospital early yesterday morning after being attacked outside a city night-club. His assailants slashed his head and buttocks with razors and his condition is serious."

Hill had been stopped from shooting Neville by Bobby Ramsay who knocked his arm in the air. The supporters fled and Hill, firing his revolver, caught up with Neville and scalped him with the hunting knife he had taken back from Ramsay.

After the fight Hill had driven in a hired car through the night to Durban. The driver was sent back with the car to Johannesburg where he was promptly arrested and, when told that Neville had died, promptly gave Hill up. Hill had booked into the Waverley Hotel under an assumed name but it was only twenty-four hours before the police were at his door.

Given bail of £75 he knew that it was only a matter of time before an application for his extradition came through and he pre-empted it by skipping his bail and taking a flight to Egypt. He stayed in Cairo and made his way back to England and the East End where Jack Spot arranged for him to hide out with the Upton Park Mob.

At the South African trial Ramsay, the remaining British representative, said he had merely been playing cards and had not known there was any plan to defend the club. He received three months.

Back in England Hill did yet another last job, this time in Manchester with Sammy Josephs and Teddy Machin, netting some £9,000. He served three years in Wandsworth and it was then that he repeated a well-known prison stunt when he saved a screw from an attack by a seemingly out-of-control, south London hardman, Jack Rosa. The day after receiving a flogging for an offence, Rosa attacked an officer with a knife in the workshop. Hill intervened and was roundly condemned by prisoners, who were in the know, who chorused that he was a bastard for saving the screw's life. Rosa apologized for the attack, claiming that it was the effect of the cat-o'-nine-tails that had sent him berserk. He escaped punishment and was said to have been paid £5,000 for his troubles. For his bravery, Hill had his sentence reduced by six months. On his release in 1949 he was met at the prison gates by a jovial and cigar-smoking Jack Spot.

Once released it was back to the gaming tables and Hill leased the New Cabinet Club from Eva Holder, who in 1950 was convicted of defrauding Peter Haig Thomas. A former Cambridge rowing coach who had married into the aristocracy, Thomas, at the age of sixty-eight, had fallen in love with this temptress some thirty years his junior, who relieved him of £35,000. She received two years' imprisonment. After taking over the club, it was onwards and upwards for Hill.

1950 and 1951 were peaceful and highly profitable years for both Spot and Hill. The latter wrote:

> Visitors and strangers must have found the West End a
> rather dull place with no running gang-fights and feuds . . .
> The truth was that we cleared all the cheap racketeers out.
> There was no longer any blacking of club owners and

restaurant keepers. In fact so peaceful did it all become that there was no gravy left for the small timers.

So far as prostitution and the Messina brothers were concerned, on the face of it neither Hill nor Spot were interested. Under the surface, however, the Messinas paid a form of tax to them.

"Hill reigned almost with the blessing of the police," said a solicitor's managing clerk from the period. "He was a very likeable bloke, always paid his bills. If you overlooked his reputation you'd never have dreamed who he was. Whilst he was in control there was a peaceful scene. He kept discipline." Others believe the peaceful reign was simply because Spot and Hill paid off the police. "All top men, they work with the law to a certain degree," recalled one northern hardman. An even less charitable view comes from one of Hill's former friends. "He kept control with the razor. People were paid a pound a stitch, so if you put twenty stitches in a man you got a score. You used to look in the evening papers next day to see how much you'd earned," said the noted safe-breaker, Eddie Chapman.

The first months of 1952 were not good ones for the forces of law and order or for the insurers of the General Post Office. A post office van was ambushed in Bruce Grove Road, Tottenham, in February and later mail vans were stolen, along with registered letters, in Marylebone and the West End. On 18 May came the theft of £11,000 in notes from sacks on the Brighton to London train.

Then, three days later, came the first really successful, major post-war robbery. The Eastcastle Street Great Mailbag Robbery was undoubtedly a Billy Hill production, devised, arranged and orchestrated by him. A post-office worker who had been steadily losing in one of Hill's spielers came to his notice and was approached for useful information. It was supplied in return for the cancellation of his gaming debts and Hill went to work.

The robbery was carried out with immaculate precision. A mail van was kept under observation and followed every night for months on its journey from Paddington Station to the City. Rehearsals took place in the suburbs under the pretext of shooting a film. Cars were stolen specifically for the raid. On the night of the robbery, once the van left Paddington a call was made to the West End flat where Hill had lodged his men. Four men climbed into a stolen green Vanguard, and another four into a stolen Riley.

Because of roadworks near Oxford Street there was a diversion and as the van turned into Eastcastle Street one of the cars blocked the driver's path. Six men then attacked the three post-office workers and looted the vehicle. They drove off in the van, leaving two of the three workers unconscious on the pavement. The cash was transferred into boxes on a fruit lorry. Eighteen out of thirty-one bags were taken. At first it was thought that £44,000 in old notes had been stolen but the full damage became known later in the week. The total was in the region of £287,000. The police claimed the thieves left the remaining bags because they were interrupted but according to Hill they were left because there was not any more room in the lorry.

There were bolt-cutters manufactured by a Sheffield firm and a trench coat with the mark "ZD 662 C19" left at the site of the robbery. Three buttons from the coat were missing but these clues led nowhere. In time it became apparent that these were simply false ones planted to divert the police.

This was the era of the new robber. The liability of the General Post Office was only £5 for each of ninety packets but rewards totalling £25,000 were put up by the insurance companies. Despite intense police activity for over a year, headed by Superintendent Bob Lee, then second-in-command of the Flying Squad, there were no charges.

Hill, just like Spot after his 1948 Heathrow Airport robbery (detailed in the following chapter), found that the police took reprisals. They might not have been able to pin the Eastcastle

Street robbery on him but they were able to raid his spielers on an almost nightly basis. Eventually he handed them over to others. He was now also having domestic troubles. His wife Aggie was on his back, trying to persuade him that with the money from the robbery he could actually become legitimate. He maintained that he owed a loyalty to the men with whom he had worked over the years. However, with some of his earnings he invested in a legitimate toy business.

The previous year Hill had become emotionally involved with "Gypsy" Phyllis May Blanche Riley whose early career had been somewhat chequered and who was then working behind the bar in one of his clubs. She had, by some accounts, run away from home in east London and had joined the Upton Park gypsies from where she had taken her soubriquet. She had also been on the game, minded by a Maltese pimp known as Tulip who took her from Hyde Park to Mayfair, where she was then run by a pimp known as Belgian Johnny. In turn he passed her to Johnny Belan with whom she remained until Hill fell for her charms and fiery temperament. The enforcer "Mad" Frank Fraser remembered her: "She was a cracker, really good looking and real fire." One of Spot's friends, Gerry Parker, describes her as, "Not pretty but a good-looking woman with jet black hair and high cheekbones. She had a mouth on her but she was a fine-looking woman."

Domestically, there were, however, problems with Gypsy. Now Queen of the Underworld she was unhappy to be reminded of her past. When in September 1953 she was approached by Tulip she persuaded Frederick "Slip" Sullivan to have him thrown out of a club known as French Henry's. In turn, Tulip was protected by the tearaway and all-time loser Tommy Smithson. Sullivan took a bad beating at his hands – Hill says his throat was cut – and reprisals were required to maintain the status quo.

When it came to it, Tommy Smithson, in his own chequered and largely unsuccessful career, suffered at just about everyone's hands. Smithson, an ex-fairground fighter with a penchant for silk shirts and underwear, a man of immense courage and little stability or ability, was known as Mr Loser. Born in Liverpool in 1920 and brought to the East End two years later, he served in the Merchant Navy until his discharge in the 1950s. Back in Shoreditch he now found things had changed. Maltese immigrants had assumed control of clubs and cafés, and Smithson decided to set up his own protection racket devoted to these Maltese businessmen as well as working a spinner with club-owner Tony Mella around the dog tracks.

Now after cutting Sullivan, Smithson went into hiding, only to be given up by the Maltese he had been protecting. Told there was a peace offer on the table Smithson was asked – ordered is perhaps a better word – to attend a meeting at the Black Cat cigarette factory in Camden Town. He took with him the Paddington Club owner Dave Barry and at least one gun, a Luger. Arrayed against him were Hill, Spot, Slip Sullivan's brother Sonny and Moishe "Blueball" Goldstein. Spot explained to Smithson that they were simply there to talk and he handed over the gun. Just as Spot was putting the gun away, Hill suddenly slashed the unprepared Smithson. The slashes on his face were in the form of the sides of the letter V down each cheek meeting at his chin; it was a Hill trademark.

Smithson was also slashed on the arms, legs, chest and other parts of his face. He was then thrown over a wall into Regent's Park and it was left to Spot to send Moishe to call an ambulance and drive Hill back to his flat. It could have been a hanging matter.

Fortunately for everyone Smithson did not die. Somehow he survived and forty-seven stitches were put in his face. Nor did he talk to the police. His reward for honouring the code of silence was a party, the soubriquet "Scarface" and £1,000 with which he bought a share in a drinking club in Old Compton Street. According to some accounts it was Spot who paid the compensation. The slashing by Hill of Smithson was, in effect, the last joint enterprise of the now two rival bosses of London's underworld.

Billy Hill's last serious court appearance, at least in the dock, came in February 1954. The year before Hill had fallen out with his former friend, Freddie Andrews, whom he had known since childhood. According to Hill, Andrews thought he should have climbed a great deal higher up the criminal tree and resented the fact that he had not. He began drinking heavily and calling at Hill's club, challenging him. In December 1953 Andrews answered a knock on his front door and was slashed. He believed Hill was his attacker and, in a fit of uncharacteristic underground behaviour, went to the police.

By the time Hill's trial came before Sir Gerald Dodson at the Central Criminal Court the deal had been done. Andrews had been paid and given assurances about any help he might need in the future. Now he failed to recognize Hill as his attacker. It was not a gesture that appealed to the Recorder who was obliged to order Hill's release.

Hill was now casting about for something new. He had enjoyed his trip to Africa the previous year and now came the opportunity to combine business with pleasure. As Hill had discovered during his holidays there, Tangier was, at the time, a free city governed by an international commission under licence from the Sultan of Morocco. It was also a home from home for smugglers. Cigarette smuggling was then, as it is now, capable of providing enormous revenue. There was a great demand in France for what were known as "Les Blondes", made with light-coloured American tobacco. The export of cigarettes from Tangier was then perfectly legal as was the transfer of the cargo to another vessel provided it was done outside territorial limits. It was the second boat that ran the gauntlet of customs patrols as it tried to land its cargo without interception. There was also the danger of pirates.

Billy Hill bought a boat called the *Fourth Lady*, renamed it the *Flamingo* and, sailing under a Costa Rican flag, put together a crew who would know how to deal with potential invaders.

The first Captain was Michael Henderson who had worked for George Dawson, the cockney financier later imprisoned for fraud. The crew itself was a motley one made up largely of underworld friends of Hill who obviously felt that he owed something to the unreliable Freddie Andrews. When Georgie Ball asked if Andrews could be brought along Hill unwisely agreed and his former friend was placed in charge of the engines. "He's quiet. The type you'd rather have on your side than not," wrote Eddie Chapman of Ball sometime later. There were no such encomiums for Andrews. There was also Hill's old friend Franny Daniels, a successful escapee from the 1948 London Airport robbery as well as another old friend, Patsy Murphy. Another on the team was the former boxer George Walker, the brother of the talented heavyweight Billy. When his own boxing career was over he began to work for Hill and from time to time acted as his minder.

Hill also engaged Eddie Chapman. After the war he had worked on the fringes of legality in both Tangier and West Africa. He was fluent in French and German and could turn his hand to more or less anything. Chapman's version is that he purchased a share in the boat for £2,000 from Hill, who seems to have had the best of the deal. He paid only £2,900 for the boat.

Chapman and Hill flew to Tangier where the *Flamingo* was at anchor. Henderson had now been replaced by Bill Beamish, a friend of Eddie Chapman who knew when to keep his mouth shut and was a fine sailor. When his mouth was open he too had the advantage of speaking a number of languages.

Unlike many former prisoners Billy Hill retained an affection for prison food. He was not averse to porridge and Eddie Chapman thought that if he had the opportunity he would eat bully beef – which in the 1930s and 1940s was served in prisons on a Sunday – every day of his life. Accordingly the

Flamingo was stocked with four sacks of potatoes and 156 tins of corned beef.

There was no question of Jack Spot being invited and he was well out of the trip. Just about everything that could go wrong eventually did so. Chapman says that he and Hill stayed at a small and inconspicuous hotel but their arrival had been already noted by the police and they were promptly hauled downtown to be interviewed by the police.

Nor did their appearance in Tangier go unremarked by the locals. There were rumours that they were there to rob a bank or burn the ships of the other contrabandoliers. There was also the story they had been hired to kill. There were visits to bars and brothels by some of the crew; there were fights and offers of work. Chapman established a company, Anglo-American Fidelity, which would guarantee employees would not abscond with the takings of the insured: "This to me was a splendid idea. Who better than us to investigate thefts? It seemed too, like a legalised protection racket which, after all, is what insurance companies really are!" Then there was an offer to kill a man's brother for which Chapman took a deposit of $1,500. It was the usual scam with the brother paying him £500 not to be murdered. There was at least one successful smuggling run.

While in London, Hill had been approached with the offer of a truly hare-brained scheme. It was nothing less than the effective kidnap of the Sultan of Morocco, who was then in detention in Madagascar. The aim was to return him to his supporters and so force the French to restore him to his throne. Hill thought that a spot of smuggling would mask the true intention behind the voyage. This was where Chapman would be so useful. With his charm and command of French he would persuade the Sultan and his sons that freedom lay aboard the *Flamingo* from where he would be taken to a seaplane and then flown back home.

Now, in Tangier, negotiations were satisfactorily concluded. A down payment of £3,000 was made against a fee of

£100,000 for successful completion and an arrangement was made to take on two Arab men to be part of the crew. The final arrangements were to be concluded in Barcelona where the boat could draw arms and provisions. The rendezvous never took place because of a fight in the brothel quarter of Tangier. The Queen and the Duke of Edinburgh were due to visit Gibraltar and there were anti-British cries from the Tangier residents. A Spaniard was knocked about and the reprisal came in the form of an attack on the *Flamingo*. This was repelled but it was followed by another trip to the Sûreté when Chapman and the others were given their sailing orders.

They sailed first for Ceuta and then disappeared. Indications had been given they were making for Beirut. "*La Motovedetto Fantasma*" – Ghost Ship – said the Italian papers enthusiastically when the boat appeared in Savona near Genoa, and soon there was a *Sunday Chronicle* reporter in tow. By now Hill, Chapman and the others also had their own detectives following them quite openly. Hill thought it was both because they were suspected of gold-running and that some of them were suspected of involvement in the Eastcastle Street robbery. Now they were ordered out of Savona but before the boat was allowed to sail Beamish, as captain, was fined a modest 25 shillings because 400 cigarettes had disappeared from packages sealed by customs officials.

By the end of the trip the enmity between Hill and Freddie Andrews had resurfaced and it became clear that Hill had poorly disguised intentions to deal with him. "Often when I was alone, working and doing some repairs with Arthur [Freddie Andrews] I looked at him and tried to picture what he would look like with his throat cut," wrote Chapman. The safe-breaker was no longer into this sort of aggravation and it was arranged that he should stay in Corsica and so avoid the forthcoming troubles. However, once on shore he was again ordered by the authorities to leave. It was then arranged he would rejoin the boat in Barcelona for the run to rescue the Sultan but by then the voyage had ended.

The *Flamingo* had put into the civil port at Toulon, allegedly to shelter from bad weather, and never left. Her arrival had not been auspicious. Initially, she had sailed into the naval port and had promptly been escorted out. In the early hours of 22 July the boat caught fire and, according to Bill Beamish, who was badly burned, the fire was deliberate. He claimed that three people had set the engine room on fire and had thrown him on to the flames, saying he knew too much. He survived to tell the tale. The police put an armed guard on deck and halted repairs.

Eddie Chapman says the culprit was Andrews who, when drunk, had set fire to the vessel by sprinkling petrol over the engine and then, after climbing the ladder, he had tossed down a lighted match setting the engine-room alight. He had been seen and challenged by Beamish, whom he threw into the flames. He then claimed that it was Beamish who had set fire to the boat. Freddie Andrews promptly went missing and it was thought he might have again fallen foul of his old underworld connections.

Now Hill decided the boat was jinxed and, while sunning himself in Nice, he prematurely announced his retirement to the faithful Duncan Webb: "I've made my pile so I'm quitting." Aged forty-three he was now sitting peacefully in the sun in the south of France, spouting to the ever-faithful journalist. The spielers were bringing in a good sum each week, everybody was behaving themselves. If there was any trouble he would be told in his daily telephone call and would catch the next plane back to deal with things but as far as he was concerned he was retired. Within a matter of weeks, however, he would pull off his last great coup.

This, his second major triumph, was another robbery. On 21 September 1954 his team robbed a bullion lorry in Lincoln's Inn Fields, London, clearing £45,000. It was another meticulously planned job and is an interesting example of Hill's methods both in planning the robbery and ensuring he was never charged.

At 4.30 p.m. on the day of the robbery a man and a woman sat in a black Austin outside Rothschild's bank watching Reginald Crane load two white boxes into a lorry owned by his employers, Higgs Transport. Each box contained around a hundredweight of gold bullion. Crane was then joined by John Levy as his escort and the lorry was driven to Jockey's Fields, a narrow mews-type street off Theobald's Road. Twenty minutes later the bullion was unloaded and placed in the freight room of the airline KLM, which had offices there. Just before 6 p.m. another Higgs Transport vehicle, driven by James Kent, was backed into the road to collect the load. The moment it stopped outside the KLM offices, the black Austin parked diagonally across the road, blocking the lorry's exit to Theobald's Road. The driver locked the car and walked to a nearby public lavatory, leaving by another exit. As the bullion was being transferred a small blue lorry began to back down the road, crashing into Kent's lorry. As it did so a man leaned out and snatched the bullion and the blue van accelerated away. The whole operation took less than a minute.

A man's felt hat, a transparent wrapping and a mop head were found in the Austin along with two sets of fingerprints that could not be matched to police records. The next day the van in which the gold had been taken was found in Ormond Place, a quarter of a mile away. In it were a green tweed coat, a light trilby with a dark band and a blue scarf with white spots. These were disregarded because they were thought to be false clues left by the robbers.

Once again Hill's old adversary Chief Superintendent Robert Lee took part in the inquiry, this time rather by accident. In promotional terms he had rather paid for his failure to deal with the Eastcastle Street job and had been transferred to No. 3 District which covered Holborn. Now it was a question of rounding up the usual suspects. Most of those involved with the airport robbery had now been released and there were also, of course, the suspects from the successful Eastcastle Street robbery who were still at large. Within forty-eight hours there had been police raids on five houses in north London and another twenty-seven on homes in south and east London. Fifty arrests were made and five men were held for identification.

Alibis were completely in place. Two of the men had fortunately reported a lost dog to a police station at the moment of the robbery. Another had genuinely been in a Soho drinking club at the time. Two suspects were stripped and hoovered to try to find gold particles. It was not a success. Now came tips that the gold was to leave the country from Southampton in a private yacht. It was not. Then came another tip that it would be smuggled out of the Surrey docks in east London. It was not. A raid was now organized on a Hill's toy warehouse on the Whitechapel Road.

On the morning of the raid of his premises Hill was followed by a plainclothes police officer. Hill lost the tail at Aldgate tube station by leaping out of a train when the doors began to close, leaving the officer stranded. He telephoned his warehouse and received no reply although his staff should have been there. He telephoned again and, when a man answered, asked to speak to the senior officer. The receiver was replaced. Hill took a taxi to his solicitor and made a statement saying he believed his warehouse was being raided and that nothing would be found there. Meanwhile the police were having a fine time examining some 50,000 dolls that called out "Mama" when they were turned upside down and Teddy Bears that went "A-a-h".

Hill then arrived at the warehouse with his solicitor. Some wood shavings had been found in an upstairs room and Hill was asked where they had come from. He replied that he had never seen them before. He was then shown a carpet on which the police suggested there was an imprint of the boxes of bullion. Hill said that he could not see any marks and wanted the carpet and the wood photographed. A photographer was found and the photographs were taken but Hill was still not satisfied. He wanted them photographed all over again and reluctantly the police acceded. Now Hill placed a ten-shilling note on the carpet and asked for it to be photographed so that the numbers showed on the print. He said he did not want to leave the chance that, euphemistically speaking, the photographs might be mixed up with others back at Scotland Yard. The note was then handed to his solicitor.

Now he was asked for his alibi and he produced the perfect response. He knew exactly where he had been. It was at the offices of the *People*, where he had seen the old and respected journalist Hannen Swaffer. He had been there for hours. And who else was there? None other than Duncan Webb. That, so far as Hill was concerned, was the end of the case.

In April 1955 Reginald Crane, the driver of the first Higgs Transport lorry, pleaded guilty to conspiracy to steal and receiving, along with another man, Albert Beech, who had, at one time, worked for KLM. Crane had been paid £1,000 to allow the robbery to take place. Beech had received £200 of the money. It appears the men had been approached in a public house where they had been heard talking about their jobs. The gold was never recovered. Webb, no doubt on very good authority, believed that it had been smelted on the night of the robbery and buried in a garden north of London. No more arrests were made.

Webb, again theorizing, wrote that the robbery idea had come from the crash of a KLM flight on 5 September 1954 when a plane had gone down on the mud flats of the River Shannon, killing twenty-eight passengers. Hill had learned that the flight had also been carrying diamonds and he sent men to find out where the jewels were with instructions to follow their path when they were recovered by the airline. The trail led back to London. "Mr X has a lot of men working for him all over the world. As the genius behind some of the biggest crimes in Britain this century, he needs to have," Webb gushed.

It is difficult to pinpoint the exact time of Hill's abdication as the Boss of Britain's Underworld. More, it was a gradual erosion of his power coupled with an increasing lack of interest. Domestically Hill took up with Diana, allegedly an African princess, by whom he had a son, Justin. Another version of the story is that Justin's father was another old-time villain, Johnny Dobbs, but there is no doubt Hill adored the boy. He could not, however, bring himself wholly to give up Gypsy, and Diana, who had a history of mental problems, killed herself. Hill ended his days being looked after at his flat in Bayswater by an old borstal friend, Percy Horne. A heavy smoker, he died on 31 December 1983. After Hill's death Gypsy brought up the boy, shielding him both from the press and the underworld.

Reg Kray thought Hill was the best of London's underworld leaders: "As a prelude to this story of my friend Billy Hill, I like to think that in some ways I have come close to emulating him; to be honest, I acknowledge that he stands alone and there will never be another Billy Hill."

17

Jack Spot

Jack Comer, born Jacob Comacho, was far better known as Jack
Spot, either (he said) because he was always on hand if you were
in a spot of bother or (probably more likely, if more prosaically)
because of a mole on his face. He built his whole career on
a story that, incredibly, no one bothered to check for half a
century. He had, he said, led a Jewish contingent that broke up
a march led by the fascist Sir Oswald Mosley through the East
End of London on 4 October 1936. Using a club made out of a
hollowed-out chair leg then filled with aluminium, he had felled
Mosley's bodyguard, the all-in wrestler King Curtis, known as
Roughneck. For this he had been manhandled by the police
and sent to prison for six months. It was all lies. There was no
march. Mosley and his men remained on one side of a cordon
as the police battled the anti-fascist element. When told to do so,
Mosley's men obediently trotted off towards the Strand. Spot
was never arrested and therefore there was no jail sentence.
Nevertheless he made his reputation out of the incident. He
billed himself as a champion of the Jews, someone who would
protect them. Such protection may have been provided, but it
cost small shopkeepers and stallholders a weekly fee.

Jack Spot's parents, Alexander and Rifka, were Polish Jews
who had met and married in the East End. Spot, born on
12 April 1913, was the youngest of four children. There
were two older brothers, Piza and Irving, and a sister,

Rebecca. Times were hard for the immigrant Jewish and Irish communities in the early days of the twentieth century, and Myrdle Street, Whitechapel, where the family lived, was never the best address in the East End. "It was dirt poor. You didn't earn enough to pay the six shillings a week rent," said Gerry Parker, one of Spot's henchmen.

After he left school for a time Spot ran a typical fairground scam called "Take a Pick" at the major race meetings. The mug punters paid 6d to pull a straw with a winning number from a cup. If they were extremely fortunate they won a cheap prize while Spot cleared between £30 and £40 a day. Later the enterprise was extended to Petticoat Lane where Take a Pick earned him another £50 a morning. He was also an active bookmaker on the free courses. On a bad day he welshed, leaving before paying out on the last race.

As a youth he drew two small convictions for loitering with intent to steal from motor cars in 1933, and in 1935 he was bound over for house-breaking. His one real conviction was in April 1939 when he received six months for an assault on one-time friend Ishkey Simmons at the Somerset Social Club in the City of London – Simmons had refused to pay his weekly protection money. It was while Spot was serving his sentence that he came to the notice of the one-eared – it had been bitten off in a fight – Arthur Skurry from West Ham and earned this very hard man's approval. Over the years Spot forged an alliance with the Upton Park gypsies who generally "protected" small market stallholders. Fighters they may have been but they were not smart and as the war ended the Upton Park Mob, with luminaries such as Skurry, Teddy Machin, Porky Bennett and Jackie Reynolds, effectively became Spot's boys.

Unlike many gang-leaders Spot had actually served in the war. Annoyed he was not given a commission, Spot raged on about how demeaning and wasteful it was for a man of his ability to be obliged, for three years, to shine his boots and buttons, to suffer from a sergeant's temper and to take orders from "pasty-faced little runts with officer's pips". Fight followed fight and he gained a reputation as a troublemaker. Eventually, following a short time with the marines, he was sent to see a psychiatrist who recommended him for a medical discharge in 1943. He returned to the East End to find his parents dead and his brothers and sisters scattered. One brother was, in fact, serving in the RAF.

It is now impossible to trace the accuracy of most of Spot's stories but, according to him, he gravitated to the West End where in November 1943 he became involved in a fight with a man known as "Edgware Sam" – in all Spot's stories the men are called Manchester Mike, Bristol Bert and so forth – in the grandly named Piccadilly Club, in reality a spieler in the Edgware Road. Spot's henchman, Gerry Parker, was told that the quarrel was over the serious matter of who should be served their tea and sandwich first. Other accounts suggest there was anti-Semitic bullying of the barman over not putting enough sugar in Edgware Sam's tea, which certainly makes for a more heroic account. Spot intervened and, after knocking Edgware Sam down, hit him with the metal teapot. Sam ran out of the club, some said to get a gun.

Whether Spot believed this or thought that Sam had gone to the police, he feared a prison sentence and, advised by his friend and mentor, the London club-owner and receiver Abe Kosky, fled to the north of England, a land where the black market and organized crime were rampant. Goods were being stolen from the ships at Hull docks and the cash had to be spent somewhere.

Where illegal gaming and drinking clubs are established, protection is sure to follow. According to Spot he helped a club-owner, Jack Marks, known as Milky, of the Regal Gaming Club in Brunswick Street, Chapeltown, Leeds, to clear out a Polish protection racketeer from his club. He became the owner's bodyguard and, as a reward, was given a pitch at the local greyhound track. Next, he dealt severely with an ex-coalman who seemed to believe he had a no-loss betting account, expecting payment when he won and his losses to be erased. Spot swiftly disabused him. He also dealt with Liverpool Jack, said to be the leader of the toughest gang in Leeds, and apparently another formidable man, London Alf, who was in the north at the time. Whether these men existed or were merely imaginary fodder for the good stories he later told to the Sunday newspapers is a moot point. Spot certainly did spend some time in Leeds but local recollection of what happened differs from his own.

Whichever version is correct, from then on Spot's future in Leeds was assured. He undertook to protect members of the local Jewish business community against anti-Semitism and he brokered a partnership between a leading northern bookie and Abe Kosky. Spot found the north an exciting place.

He also worked as what he described as a "troubleshooter" for various other northern clubs until he heard Edgware Sam had been jailed for fraud. Perhaps fraud is too grand a word. It seems to have been for working the "tweedle", a con trick that involves taking a ring into a jeweller's for valuation and then declining to sell it. At the last moment the grifter changes his or her mind and offers the ring once more. This time, however, the ring appraised by the jeweller has been switched and he is now offered a fake in the hope he will not bother to examine it a second time. In any event Spot returned to London, pleaded self-defence to the Edgware Sam assault charge and was acquitted.

Now he was in great demand in the major northern cities. Gerry Parker recalls:

In Manchester the old bookmaker Gus Demmy wanted a pitch and he couldn't get one. The man who was running them wouldn't talk to him. Jack called a meeting with him in the Midland Hotel and asked why his "cousin" couldn't have a pitch. Everyone was Jack's "cousin". Jack gave him a dig – and remember a lot of big men can't punch their weight but Jack was well over six foot and 17 stone and he could. After that Gus got his pitch and Jack was made.

He had trouble in getting a pitch for himself at Doncaster races, having to stand up to another racecourse bully, and later claimed he assisted officials in the north to allocate pitches in a fairer way. It was something he maintained stood him in good stead when there were troubles at Ascot shortly after the war.

He was also well regarded in Birmingham and he moved, as required, between the major cities. Spot was certainly back in London by the end of 1944 when, with the German bombing over, things gradually returned to normal and with normality came the opportunities beloved by any criminal. In his book *Jack Spot, The Man of a Thousand Cuts*, echoing Billy Hill's earlier memoirs, he claimed modestly that:

> I was the first man to realize that criminals could be organized, each crook becoming a small part of a master plan in which every cog and spindle operated perfectly.
>
> I became the planner and master mind.
>
> I became the Boss of the Underworld!

It was this sort of attitude which would eventually lead to his downfall but for the moment things went accordingly and, by the end of the war, Spot was doing very well for himself. He claimed he had met with the American gangster Sam Clynes, said to be a former member of Murder Inc., and received a good deal of advice from the great man. The advice included how to treat members of his team if they went to prison. Clynes suggested a weekly pension of £20 for wives at a time when a policeman's wage was between £9 and £11. Unfortunately, too often Spot failed to pay and in turn paid the penalty for it. After Clynes's death, he claimed, he paid for a funeral service and a headstone.

One problem with this story is that it is another almost total fabrication. The name Clynes is probably an amalgamation of James Hynes and Harry Kleintz. Hynes was certainly an American and, it was claimed, he was shot when the gangster "Little Augie" Orgen was killed. Later, together with Kleintz, he came to England where, following a robbery on a jeweller's they both received five years on 28 June 1928 at Newcastle Assizes. Further long sentences followed and Hynes died in Parkhurst on 12 April 1943. Spot can never have met him. But why should that get in the way of a good story?

What was much more accurate was that Spot was running Botolph's, a gaming club masquerading as the Aldgate Fruit Exchange in the daytime, on behalf of Abe Kosky, now a black-market millionaire, and running it extremely profitably.

During the daytime clerks in white collars and bowler hats arrived at their desks. At 5 p.m. they put on their hats and coats and left, and the transformation began. The desks were shifted into an anteroom, the blinds were pulled down and soft lights were switched on. By seven o'clock the place had been turned into what Spot described as, "the biggest gambling club London had ever known". Play continued until seven o'clock the next morning. "We never had an argument much less a fight," claimed Spot. This was not surprising because, apart from Spot, on the door was the fearsome Arthur Skurry who, despite fearing "he would look like a poof", had been persuaded to exchange his cap and choker for a suit. The fact that he had half an ear bitten off only enhanced his status.

If there was a big winner Spot would arrange for him to be seen home by little Hymie Rosen, Moishe "Blueball" Goldstein – so-named because of the colour of one of his testicles – or George Wood. Quite apart from the pretence of masquerading as the Aldgate Fruit Exchange the real reason Spot's club stayed open and untouched were the huge sums being paid weekly in bribes to the police.

By now Spot's then friend Billy Hill was out of prison and it was time to oust the Whites who had taken over from the Sabinis in the West End and on the racecourses. First Spot dealt with Eddie Raimo who had beaten up a Jewish bookmaker at Yarmouth Races. Then another White man, Johnny Warren, mocked Spot over the fact that he was drinking lemonade in a Soho public house. Spot followed him to the lavatory and knocked him about. "Bump. Down in the piss he went," he recalled.

Later he met up with Machin, George Wood and Hymie Rosen and they went to Al Burnett's Stork Club in Sackville Street where Harry White and, said Spot, seven of his men were drinking. Spot knocked White down and in the ensuing fight Billy Goller had his throat badly cut. In the days when the death penalty was in force, Spot had forgotten his own maxim, "You must never cut below the line here, cause, if you do, you cut the jugular – and the hangman is waiting." Spot was rushed down to Southend and hidden away in Benny Swan's B52 Club at the end of the airport runway while Goller was given the last rights. Amazingly he survived but it was not until he recovered and was paid off that Spot returned to London. When he did he went to see Harry White and said he now wanted 30 per cent of his racecourse takings.

In their respective autobiographies both Hill and Spot give graphic accounts of the autumn 1947 battle in which the Whites are chased out of town, with one man roasted on a fire. Naturally each man plays a more heroic part in his version of the story, with a triumphant Spot supposedly telling his men, "Get rid of the ironmongery." As a result Sten guns, grenades, revolvers and ammunition were dumped in the Thames, far from the prying eyes of Scotland Yard.

On 28 July 1948 the job that was to have been the first major post-war robbery took place at Heathrow Airport – then still called Heath Row, but also known as Thief Row due to the number of thefts that took place there. The robbers included the cream of the Upton Park Mob: the Wood brothers, Teddy Hughes, Franny Daniels and Teddy Machin. So, not necessarily correctly, Spot has been given the credit for planning the robbery. It was probably planned by the unsung Abe Kosky at Botolph's.

Sammy Josephs, a thief with whom Spot had worked previously, had discovered that cargoes were kept overnight on a fairly regular basis and the target was to be the bonded warehouse, which contained nearly £250,000 worth of goods including diamonds and was due to receive £1 million in gold the next day. The job had been meticulously laid out with inside help, with the gang maintaining a twenty-four-hour watch on Heath Row over a two-month period. Dummy parcels were sent from Ireland and Franny Daniels, who as an authorized driver was allowed in the customs sheds, checked they had arrived. Then a warehouseman approached Donald Fish, chief security officer of BOAC, to report he had been offered £500 to dope the warehouse staff. The Flying Squad was called in.

The plan had been to drug the guards at the warehouse and at first the raid seemed to go according to plan. The worker carrying tea was intercepted, and a barbiturate was dropped in the drink. But at the last minute the guards had been switched and replaced by members of the Flying Squad. The tea was put on one side and the three "guards" lay on the floor, seemingly drugged. The members of the gang entered, hit one of the detectives with an iron bar to ensure he was unconscious and then took the keys from his pocket. At that moment other members of the Flying Squad attacked the robbers. Five escaped. Teddy Machin fell into a ditch, was knocked unconscious and as a result was overlooked in the search for the robbers. Franny Daniels held on to the underside of a van and, instead of being dropped off at the first set of traffic lights as he hoped, was carried to Harlesden Police Station, from where he made his way home. Scorched by the exhaust, he carried the burn on his shoulder for the rest of his life. The great burglar, Billy Benstead, also escaped. The next day a patched-up collection of the remainder limped into the dock.

In due course, Sir Gerald Dodson, the Recorder of London, had a field day:

> All of you men set your minds and hands to this enterprise. You were, of course, playing for high stakes. You made sure of your position by being ready for any situation with weapons of all kinds. This is the gravity of the offence. A raid on this scale profoundly shocks society. You went prepared for violence and you got it. You got the worst of it and you can hardly complain.

Teddy Hughes received twelve years' penal servitude. Jimmy Wood went down for nine, George Wallis, who was really George Wood, picked up eight. As for Spot the police could never prove that he was the organizer but his interests were disrupted and, under pressure, his gambling club in St Botolph's Row was closed.

However, things were going well for Spot on the racecourses themselves. After the war, things may have been changing on racecourses – women were seen smoking in the enclosures at Ascot and, worse, placing bets, something thought to be likely to lose them their badges the next year – but welshing by bookmakers was still rife. They would turn up with barely enough money to pay out on the first race and would be quite prepared to scarper. According to Spot it was he who solved the problem at the request of the Chief Steward, the Duke of Norfolk. Modestly he would tell the story that he had been recommended by the northern racecourse inspectors he had helped at Doncaster – or sometimes he claimed it was a senior police officer who had put his name forward.

Spot helpfully explained that organization was needed. The Free Side of a course had to be enclosed and a set number of pitches drawn up. These would only be allocated to bookmakers with a bank account with enough money to guarantee settlement. Altruistically, Spot would take it upon himself to make sure the allocations were fair and just.

Whoever tells the story there is little doubt that Spot ousted Jimmy Wooder and his Islington mob from Ascot in a pitched battle on the course. Spot claimed that when the opposition was routed there was a frightened little man who was about to be evicted from his pitch. "Let him stay," said Spot generously. The man was the once great Darby Sabini. Later Spot would receive unstinted praise for his work. "You've made racing a pleasure, Jack. We no longer go in terror of our lives," he was told by small-time bookmakers. If they paid the great man enough that is.

For some years, life in the London underworld was peaceful. Spot had no real interest in theft or the rackets as such, just protection, and he left things to Hill who in four years pulled off two spectacular robberies. But then they began to drift apart. For a start their wives, who physically resembled each other, did not get on. The object of Spot's affections, Rita Molloy, came from a poor Dublin family. Her father died when she was seven and at thirteen she was wrapping soap in a factory earning 11s, 6d a week. She had then become a cinema usherette. On any showing she was outstandingly beautiful even after, at the age of nineteen, while driving to a football match, her head was badly gashed in a car crash at Bray. She received £200 damages: "The biggest sum I had ever handled until I met Jack . . . I went to Liverpool where most of my relatives live. I wanted to see the world I had read about in glossy magazines."

That world included Haydock Park races where she met Spot on one of his protective visits north. And it was off to the then notorious Adelphi Hotel in Liverpool where, it was said, more women fell than horses at Becher's Brook. In 1948 they moved into Hyde Park Mansions in Cabbell Street, London, where they lived for the next nine years. The relationship was something of a trial for her devout Catholic mother. Here was her daughter associating with a Jew. For once it was something with which Spot had to learn to live. He and Rita married on 8 July 1954 at Marylebone Register office. They later had two daughters, Rachelle and Margaret.

Billy Hill had ditched his earlier common-law wife, Aggie, for the fiery and foul-mouthed "Gypsy" Phyllis Riley whom Rita regarded as a cut below her. A holiday together in the south of France was decidedly not a success. Hill (in the *People*) and Spot (*Sunday Chronicle*) vied with each other for newspaper coverage, with Hill garnering far more than Spot. Most serious of all, the Italians led by the old Sabini men, Bert Marsh and Albert Dimes, wanted to reclaim the bookmakers' pitches that they saw as their rightful possession.

Spot was now on the slide. The Jockey Club was helping the big credit bookmakers prepare for the legalization of off-course betting and the smaller bookmakers and their protectors were being squeezed. Now members of Spot's team were starting to go their own ways or into Hill's arms. He was also losing his reputation. The word was out in the underworld that he was a grass. "We'd had his sheet pulled from the Yard," said the daredevil safe-breaker, Eddie Chapman, who had been released from prison during the war for work in German territory, "and there it was for all to see." Spot was facing isolation. Even worse, this one-time hardman was becoming something of a figure of fun. Domesticity with Rita suited him. Now he was being openly mocked that when the baby cried he had to go home to look after it. To paraphrase the song, "Big Bad John became Sweet Jackie now".

In March 1953 Spot was arrested for possessing an offensive weapon under the Prevention of Crime Act, which had just come into force. He had received a telephone call that someone had a "nice fur coat for sale – very cheap".

Spot would recall:

Me, like a mug, I go and meet him. He gives me the fur coat and I paid him and walked away. Then out of a car come four detectives. One of them was known as Careless – he couldn't care less is right. And I'm taken to the station. They bring a knuckleduster round and they say "You're charged with carrying an offensive weapon". It was all the work of that cunt Sparks who was the right-hand man of another bastard – Greeno – biggest thieves the world's ever known.

Curiously the receiving charge relating to the coat was dropped and as for the offensive weapon there was no percentage in those days in alleging it had been planted. That was a quick route to a conviction and imprisonment for defaming gallant officers.

So Spot said he was a commission agent in Camden Road. Often he had £300 or £400 on him and, as he had a feeling people were getting to know this, he bought a weapon in a store in Holborn about two weeks before his arrest. The explanation was accepted and he was perhaps lucky to be fined only £20. And the name of his partner in the betting office? None other than the old-time villain Alf White whom he had ousted all those years ago. There may have more than a hint of sadism in Spot's behaviour. He obviously needed an explanation for the weapon and, reminding him just who was the master, he used his old enemy just as he did White's son, Harry, when he forced him to give evidence on his behalf at a later trial.

Spot was convinced the whole thing had been a set-up and he believed Herbert Sparks, head of the Flying Squad and the right-hand man to Ted Greeno, had been acting for Billy Hill. He was certainly right to regard the policemen with suspicion. The very dubious Greeno had, on the surface, a glorious career. Sparks's own was, by the end, in ruins.

On 21 October 1954 Spot committed a serious blunder, forgetting the cardinal rule which then prevailed that however tiresome a journalist might be he should not be touched. The journalist on the *People*, Duncan Webb, was writing Billy Hill's autobiography in serial form at the time and was at a hotel in Kingston-on-Thames when he received a message to telephone a man, Nadel. He did so and found it was Spot who said he had to see him right away about the series.

At 10.30 that night Webb met him on the steps of the Dominion, then a cinema, in Tottenham Court Road. Spot greeted him by saying, "Come on, it's bad." He took him into an alleyway where he knocked him down. Webb's wrist broke when he fell.

Spot's private version was slightly different and in some respects it bears scrutiny. He claimed the meeting had been in the Horseshoe pub, Tottenham Court Road. Webb had told him that Spot was no longer the Guv'nor and that Hill had taken over. Then he had made the dangerous remark, "How did Hitler miss you?" "So I took him round the back of the Dominion and we had a nice talk and I gave him a right hook which I shouldn't have done."

Spot was initially charged with grievous bodily harm. He may have lost much of his power in the West End but he still had some contacts and Webb was straightened with £600. The blow which knocked him down had, on reflection, not been with a knuckleduster but had been more of a push. On 18 November 1954 at Clerkenwell Magistrates Court, Spot now pleaded guilty to a charge of actual bodily harm and was fined £50 with 20 guineas costs.

The next year Spot feared trouble at the Epsom meeting in spring. He thought the legendary hardman and Hill henchman Frank Fraser was going to be there and he recruited the Kray twins, Ron and Reggie, as muscle. He need not have bothered. Fraser was in Broadmoor mental hospital at the time so the twins merely lounged about and collected their wages. Spot had a run in with Bert Marsh who wanted a return of the pitches at the August meeting that year. But the real trouble came on 11 August. Spot was in his drinking club, the Galahad in Charlotte Street, when he was told that Albert Dimes wanted to see him. They met near Old Compton Street and, seeing Spot had a knife, Dimes ran away. Now Spot made a serious tactical blunder. Instead of letting Dimes go and so lose face among the watching Italians, he chased after him. Dimes turned and they struggled for the knife. The fight moved into a fruit shop on the corner of Frith Street where they fought almost literally to the death until, ironically, the Jewish fruiterer, Bertha Hyams, broke up the fight by banging Spot over the head with a brass weighing pan. Spot staggered to a barber's shop usually used by Dimes where he collapsed. Dimes was picked up by Bert Marsh and driven to the Charing Cross Hospital. Spot went to the Middlesex hospital. Their injuries were horrific. Spot had been stabbed over the left eye and in the cheek, neck and ear. He had four wounds in his arm and two in his chest, one of which penetrated a lung. Dimes needed twenty stitches in his forehead. He also had a wound in his thigh and a stab in his stomach had just failed to penetrate the abdominal cavity. Both were charged with affray and grievous bodily harm.

The subsequent trial was a fiasco. First the judge refused separate trials, and then he agreed that the affray charge should be withdrawn. He invited the jury to acquit Dimes on the grounds he had been acting in self-defence. The jury refused. He then decided separate trials were the order of the day, with Spot to go first. An eighty-eight-year-old vicar, Basil Andrews, who seemingly happened to be passing, and Christopher Glinski, a Polish war hero who was also in the area at the time, both said Dimes, the taller, fairer man, was the attacker. Spot was found not guilty. No evidence was offered against Dimes and the incident became known as "The Fight That Never Was".

The police were not pleased and repercussions were swift. Inquiries were made into the backgrounds of both Glinski and the parson and, soon, Rita and two of Spot's long-time henchmen, Moishe Goldstein and Bernard Schack, went into the dock charged with conspiracy to pervert the course of justice. The parson was now repentant. He had been tempted and had fallen. His evidence had been false. The trio were found guilty. Rita was fined £50, Goldstein received two years and Schack a year less. In a later trial Glinski was found not guilty of perjury and later awarded £250 damages for libel against various newspapers.

Spot would have been well advised to leave London but in yet another dreadful miscalculation he decided to have both Dimes and Billy Hill, whom he believed was behind his troubles, shot by the up-and-coming Joey Cannon from the Notting Hill family. Instead, Frank Fraser took the gun away from Cannon and explained the facts of life to him. Now it was Hill's turn to begin reprisals.

On 2 May 1956, as Spot and Rita were returning to their flat in Hyde Park Mansions they were set upon by a team led by Frank Fraser. Spot was dreadfully beaten with a shillelagh, a type of club that he had given Hill in happier times, and also was badly slashed. He could not identify his attackers but Rita could and, a trifle unsportingly, proceeded to do so just this. Fraser and fellow henchman Bobby Warren received a seven-year sentence; others were given two years less.

There was one more reprisal. This time Billy Hill arranged for Tommy Falco to be slashed outside the Astor Club off Berkeley Square and to say Spot had been his attacker. It was a failure. Spot was acquitted after the Glasgow hardman Victor "Scarface" Russo said he had been approached by Dimes and offered £500 to allow himself to be slashed.

It was not, however, the end of Spot's troubles. The journalist Webb may have been straightened so far as the assault case was concerned but £600 was not enough and he brought a civil action for damages. He claimed that he had been working on a book and, since his wrist had been broken, he had been obliged to hire a typist to help him. He was awarded £732, a tidy little sum for the time which would have enabled him to buy a property if he had received the money, which he never did.

There were not, however, many more happy moments to come for Spot. Now, pursued by Webb, it was bankruptcy time. It is incredible that Spot really made no attempt to pay his debt to Webb. It was almost as if it was, to make a pun, a blind spot. One of his men thought, "Spot couldn't have cared less about being made bankrupt. He thought it was a joke. It wasn't as if he was the chairman of ICI." It did, however, have certain disadvantages, such as the forfeiture of the lease of his flat in Hyde Park Mansions.

One argument regarding the bankruptcy is that it shows that Spot's fortunes had slumped to such a depth that he was unable to raise the money to pay Webb. Perceived wisdom is that the acquittal in the Falco slashing case saw the end of his business interests in both the West End and the East End. It may be that this was something put about by Hill and the Italians but, on this occasion, perceived wisdom was wrong. Spot may not have been the force he had been but he still had a considerable number of interests. For a start there was the 41 Club on the corner of Dean Street and Greek Street, the home for some current and up-and-coming Soho faces, and the protection of hot-dog stalls in the West End. Then there was the Jewish connection in Petticoat Lane. Mickey Bailey, an East End face, recalled that even after the trials: "They couldn't give him money quick enough. It was all, 'Where's Spotty?' Spot would sit and someone would write figures in the book. It was all one-pound notes and half quids. It was protection."

In Spot's bankruptcy examination he agreed that in December 1954 he had received £3,200 for articles in the *Sunday Chronicle*, and he now accepted that the details he gave in the pieces were exaggerated. In one of them he said he had twenty suits at £40 each, but now claimed that he was confused because of the beating. He and Rita were evicted from Hyde Park Mansions on 19 July 1957. Rita half-jokingly offered to let a reporter have her silver mink stole for £300.

On 4 September 1957 Spot went to Canada on the *Colombia*, travelling tourist class. He was seen off in Liverpool by Rita and the story was that he was going to see his sick brother in Winnipeg. After Spot sailed, Rita went back to Dublin. It was a quick visit for both because he arrived back in England on 15 September. Information had been sent by Scotland Yard to the Canadian authorities. Even before the boat docked Canadian immigration had announced there would be a full inquiry the moment he landed. Spot claimed to be an agent for a fruit and clothing firm in London but a deportation order against him followed shortly. The suggestion was that he had been planning to open a chain of illegal betting shops.

In January 1958 Spot applied for his discharge from bankruptcy, which Duncan Webb, no doubt egged on by Hill, opposed, saying that the defence to his original action had been vexatious and he had not received a penny. The discharge was granted but suspended for six months.

After the hearing Rita spoke to the newspapers telling them that she thought better days lay ahead: "It has been two and a half years of hell, fighting for, and sticking to my husband who, though he was no saint in the past, is and has been a good man to me and our children and has now left his past life behind."

She went on to say how they had been thwarted at every hand's turn. He had tried to set up a greengrocery stall on a poor pitch in Churton Street, Westminster, with his brother but his application for a licence had been turned down. She claimed that, through the "evil men who run the underworld", Spot had been unable to get work even as a lorry driver or chauffeur. Now friends had offered to set them up in a coffee-bar or restaurant. She had been working as a waitress for the past three months trying to learn the business: "We won't make a fortune, but maybe we'll find peace of mind . . . Seven years of marriage to my man have made me grow up quickly." Incredibly she was still only twenty-eight. When it came to it there was no restaurant and no coffee-bar. Spot was finally discharged in June 1958 and he and Rita opened the Highball Club in Lancaster Gate. In the meantime he had his portrait painted by Robert Thomas, a Bristol-born artist, with a view to it being exhibited at the *Summer Exhibition* at the Royal Academy that year. Sadly it was rejected.

There is a tendency to think that crime in London is based in the Soho, the West End, the East End and in south London, and that it stops at Marble Arch. This is principally because it has never been chronicled. There has long been a thriving west London crime scene with more than its share of families, feuds, drinking clubs, spielers, protection and organized prostitution. So when Spot and Rita decided to open the Highball, they were not only avoiding the stigma attached to them in Soho, they were going where the money was. Spot proudly showed reporters around the club, which sported a sign of a tasteful cherry on a stick in a glass surrounded by other dancing cherries on sticks. Inside it was furnished with reproduction Louis XV furniture and a jukebox.

"We've not had any trouble here," he said hubristically, "and we aren't looking for it. We just want a peaceful club among our friends. We're limiting membership to our friends."

There was a chain on the front door to keep out unwelcome visitors. Well, it was supposed to keep out unwelcome visitors and it did its work until August when two men came into the club and hit a visiting seaman, Peter Edwards, over the head. They then ran to a parked van where a third man handed them crowbars and they rushed back into the club and started to break it up.

Ominously, in early August 1958 Billy Hill denied the report that he was to take over the Stables Club in nearby Lancaster Mews: "Don't make me laugh. A club near Spot's place? Don't believe a word of it." Hill was right. It was not a safe area and there was worse to come for Spot. Around 1.30 a.m. on 13 August the club was set alight. Spot was still newsworthy enough for the *Daily Express* to print in their 4.30 a.m. "stop press" edition that the police were investigating the matter. The next day Spot was the front-page headline, "Jack Spot: Fire Bug Raid", in the *Daily Mirror*. Admittedly it was the quiet season and he shared top billing with "Too Busy For Love", which told of the singer Connie Francis and a hitherto unknown Anne Bielby who had won a series of beauty contests. The police had no doubt it was arson. Furniture had been piled in the centre of the room and petrol was suspected as an accelerant. The job had been offered around the underworld but just who was actually behind the arson attack has long been a matter of speculation. Later Reg Kray would claim personal responsibility but it is likely that he was acting for Hill.

By now, Spot had learned his lesson: "I know who is responsible but I never complained to the police." Later he was interviewed in one of the last issues of the dying pictorial weekly magazine, *Illustrated*. He was pleased with his efforts at striking blows against fascism. There was, he thought, a lot less anti-Semitism about than had been the case pre-war. He was perhaps even more pleased that the magazine's library had 352 cuttings about him compared with the more modest 262 about the Lord Chief Justice, Lord Goddard, and the comparatively derisory 173 for Sophia Loren. He was a trifle disappointed about the rejection of his portrait: "What a pity, It would have been better than being hung in Pentonville." He was now completely reformed. His favourite drink of champagne and whisky had been replaced by non-alcoholic drink. He wished he had listened to Rita when she told him to get out of Soho. She had just been voted as one of the three most beautiful women in the world by the Union of Post Office Workers. The other two were Queen Soraya of Iran and Drusilla Demetriades, a Cypriot whose fiancé had been killed by terrorists. That day Rita was too ill to be interviewed properly but when asked whether Spot, if left alone by his enemies, could make good she replied, "Yes he could and soon." Apparently, within the fortnight he would open the Silver Slipper in Bayswater, a new club being financed by a big firm. He never did.

For the moment Spot went with Rita to Ireland where he worked for a bookmaker and this left a vacancy among the Jewish community in the East End, which was partially filled by the hardman Harry Abrahams. Later, Spot returned to the East End, living in Romford Street next to the street where he was born. Sometime after their return from Ireland Rita left her husband for a period, living with another man in the Earl's Court area. It was not a success. He started beating her and she returned to Spot.

On 6 February 1962 Spot was in the dock for the last time in his life. He had been working at J. Lyons at Cadby Hall in west London and had been dealing in meat stolen from the firm, selling it to local restaurants. He was fortunate. The matter was treated on the basis that the meat was for his own use rather than for resale and he was fined £12 for the thirty shillings worth of meat. He told Seymour Collins, the stipendiary magistrate at West London Court, "I'm sorry this has happened. I lost my job because of it. I have to look for another." He had given his name as John Colmore and his address as Romford Street, Whitechapel. He omitted to mention a furniture shop in the Gloucester Road in which he had an interest. Spot was not long out of a job but it is ironic that, as a man who spent so much time championing the Jewish cause, he more or less ended his working career in Thomas Wall's bacon-packing factory near Isleworth station.

Rita died at the age of sixty on 10 September 1988 at the Charing Cross Hospital. She had been suffering from cancer for some time. Jack Spot aka Colmore, Comer, Comar,

Comor, Comacho and other names, died on 12 March 1995 at Nazareth House, Isleworth. The causes of his death were certified as a cerebrovascular accident and immobility. He left no will. As he had wished, some of his ashes were later scattered in Israel.

18

The Painters and Dockers War

How many people died or disappeared during and after the struggle for the control of the Federated Ship Painters and Dockers Union (always known as the Painters and Dockers) in Melbourne, Australia, during the 1970s depends on who is telling the tale – there were certainly two dozen deaths, including one woman, but possibly up to forty. And how many were shot but survived is impossible to calculate. Of course, not all the deaths related to the battle for control; some were over the division of spoils from robberies, some over women, some over that expensive word, "respect"; one child was an innocent bystander. But deaths they all were.

After the Second World War the leadership of the Melbourne branch of the union became increasingly corrupt. Those in control were the ones who benefited most from the wholesale theft of cargos, the blackmailing of owners so their ships could leave port, "ghosting" (the practice of requiring owners to pay for more men than were actually employed), tax fraud, starting price bookmaking, standover (extorting money or valuables, usually from other criminals), prostitution and sly-grogging (selling liquor without a licence); there was also the "Lemon Tree", the allocation of work in return for kickbacks. The proceeds were divvied up between union council members and their cronies. For those in power or close to it the union was a gravy train. In 1957 Lou Wright, regarded as sub-normal at the time of his trial for the murder of a friend in 1938, admitted to walking around with £100 in his pocket. By the time of his death in 1980 he had acquired a small fortune of nearly $300,000 (all dollar figures in this chapter are in Australian currency). One year he had under-declared his taxable income by $67,000. This was at a time when the average weekly wage of a docker was the equivalent of between $100 and $120.

Part of the problem was the composition of the membership. Working as a ship's painter and docker was filthy work, carried out often in freezing and insanitary conditions, and it was certainly not for the faint-hearted. It did, however, provide employment for those released from Melbourne's Pentridge prison who could not find work elsewhere and so the prison and the union became a revolving door. On the other hand neither ex-policemen nor nightwatchmen were welcome. The punishing work aside, there were fringe benefits. One of the bonuses offered by the union was that false identities were readily available to its members. As a result criminals could easily stay in work while on the run, and false claims for unemployment benefits and multiple claims for workers' compensation could be made. All but two of the Victoria branch senior members in the early 1970s had at some time or another used aliases. One of its secretaries, Jack "Puttynose" Nicholls, used at least four. The New South Wales branch was just as keen on name-changing. On 3 February 1975, at a meeting of the branch executive committee forty-three members, of whom twenty-two adopted Italian-style aliases, changed their names. Another benefit of membership was that it could be used to defeat a consorting charge that had been introduced with the aim of stopping criminals mixing with each other. Union men found by the police hanging around in public houses with other criminals could rely on the defence that they were waiting to be picked up for work.

By the late 1960s it was estimated that seventy of the top hundred criminals in Victoria had links with the union and in 1970 serious trouble erupted after the secretary, Jimmy Donegan, died of liver disease. At the time of his death he was awaiting trial on a charge of receiving part of the proceeds of a $580,000 robbery of a Mayne Nickless van in Sydney. After his death a bitter struggle broke out for control of the union. On one side, on the so-called Blue Ticket for the December 1971 election, was Pat Shannon, a man with thinning hair, a bulbous nose, a schoolteacher wife and three daughters. He had once run a pub in Adelaide and was appointed caretaker secretary after the death of Donegan. Now he sought re-election and wanted his friends Arthur Morris as President, Fred Persson for Vice President and the banana-nosed Doug Sproule, who had a conviction for wounding a policeman with intent to murder, in the all-important if quaintly named position of Vigilance Officer.

On the White Ticket was Billy Longley, who had joined the union in 1967 and was later convicted of receiving in the Mayne Nickless case. Known as "The Texan" either because he carried a Colt .45 or after the character of the same name in a television Western series, Longley had already been acquitted of the shooting murder of his first wife, Patricia, and then, after a retrial in 1961, of her manslaughter. He had also been acquitted of a charge of shooting with intent to murder in May 1959 and again after a fight in the Rose and Crown in Port Melbourne ten years later.

Longley did not oppose Shannon for secretary, but he wanted to be president alongside his own men in the other important positions: Burt Aspel as Vice President and James Frederick Bazley, known as "Machine Gun" because of his rapid speech, as the Vigilance Officer. On paper Bazley's early career did not really suggest he was suitable for the job. In 1947 he was convicted of carrying an unregistered pistol while working as a bouncer at an illegal baccarat game in Lonsdale Street. Just before Christmas 1964 he was convicted of a robbery of $2,970 from a bank in Collingwood. He escaped from prison twice and was finally released in 1969. Later he would be convicted of the murders of anti-drug campaigner Donald McKay and Douglas and Isobel Wilson, two couriers for the Mr Asia drug syndicate. However, given the union's penchant for violence perhaps he really was suitable.

Now began a decade of violence. On 26 March 1971 docker Thomas Connellan survived after he was shot in the back as he was walking home past Preston Girls High School. The violence intensified during the election campaign that year when, at the end of November, Robert Crotty, a Longley supporter, was involved in a fight behind a South Melbourne hotel. As he went to shake hands afterwards he was hit with a brick and then kicked and beaten. He was left with brain damage until his death seven years later. Witnesses told the police he had fallen over and hurt himself but the name of docker and standover man Les Kane was touted as his actual killer.

Retribution was swift. One of Crotty's supposed attackers, Alfred "The Ferret" Nelson, disappeared from his Collingwood home three days before the election. Rather like the body of US Teamster Jimmy Hoffa, there has been great speculation over the Ferret's final resting place. At first his body was thought to have been left in his car in the Yarra River off No. 21 South Wharf. Certainly the car was there but when it was pulled out there was no Ferret inside. Another suggestion was that he was buried under tons of freshly poured concrete being used to construct a ramp on the docks. A third on offer was that his body had been burned in an incinerator some sixty yards from the union's offices in Lorimer Street, which runs alongside the Yarra. Other suggestions have included his disposal in the bilge tank of a Hong Kong freighter and that he was dumped at sea. It is always possible that his death was not as a result of the union dispute; he was thought to have fallen out with a major Melbourne criminal, Joey Turner. Nelson was supposed to have been minding Turner's $60,000 share of the proceeds of the

MSS security company robbery in which the thieves, posing as detectives, had locked up the staff and disappeared with the takings. On the other hand his disappearance coincided with that of another Longley supporter, Alfred "Darky" Brown.

On 10 December 1971, the day of the ballot, Longley arrived early at the union offices where the dockers were lined up at the trestle tables to vote. He had his men outside the Williamstown docks helping their supporters vote inside – one story is that Bazley had a gun in one hand and, appropriately enough for a prospective Vigilance Officer, a foot on the ballot box.

According to Longley's evidence at the Costigan Royal Commission into the union's affairs a decade later, it was then that the opposition White Ticket forces, including Charlie Wootton, Danny Corsetti (who later received seven years for his part in the MSS robbery), Bobby Dix (who had been fortunate enough to be acquitted of the murder of a soldier at the Army barracks at Camp Pell in 1947) and Doug Sproule, arrived in five cars. A gun battle broke out and Longley and his supporters were driven from the docks.

That was when the ballot boxes disappeared only to reappear stuffed with White Ticket votes. The rest of the morning was punctuated by gunfire and concluded with the resignation, said to have been at gunpoint, of the protesting returning officer Pat Cullen.

What was amazing was that the union members operated in a complete vacuum. There was no report of the battle in the next day's papers and it was not until 16 December that even a mention was made of the shootings. Much more space was devoted to a youth gang known as the Devil's Raiders from Williamstown that had been creating havoc in North Altona.

Longley may have lost but it was certainly not the end of things. The next day Doug Sproule's car was found burned out. Asked how this could have happened he suggested it might have self-combusted. Taken away by the police for forensic examination, the vehicle was found to be riddled with fifty bullet holes.

The day after the election another Longley supporter, Desmond Bernard Costello, who at the time was living in Preston under the name of Studd, was kidnapped. Again this may not have been strictly union rivalry. Ten years previously Costello had been acquitted of the murder of the crippled Melbourne standover man, Osmond "Hoppy" Kelly in Fitzroy. Costello was also thought to have been yet another receiver of the proceeds of the Mayne Nickless raid as well as being one of the abductors of Nelson. His body was found on 14 December 1971 dumped in a ditch at Clifton Hill by the site of the new Eastern Freeway. One arm was shattered and part of a hand had been blown away, suggesting he had been trying to protect his face. In a version of the underworld slogan "we only catch and kill our own", Terrence Gordon, the Federal Secretary of the Union, told the press, "I know managing directors who have got shot, wharfies who have got shot. What is happening within the Union is the Union's own affair and will be settled inside the Union." In time the statement would be thrown back in the face of the union by its critics.

That month Ian Revel Carroll, known as "Fingers" and who would later go on Chuck Bennett's Great Bookie Robbery, was arrested on two charges of carrying an unlicensed pistol. Fined $150 he denied he had been a bodyguard for a union official.

Over the next fifteen months there were numerous incidents of gunfire between the rival groups including, on 20 December 1971, Laurence Richard Chamings, whose brother had been killed the previous year in a quarrel over bail money, being wounded in the shoulder. He survived, for the time being. Jim Bazley also survived a shooting in May 1972 when he was hit in the thigh and shoulder as he stood outside his North Carlton home, and again in the September when he was hit in the head and hand while sitting in his car. Longley's second wife and daughter also survived when, on 25 January 1972, the day after the results were published announcing the success of Shannon's team, a bomb was thrown at their home. After that Longley left for New South Wales to attend his trial for his part in the Mayne Nickless receiving case, leaving behind his friend Linus "The Pom" Driscoll to sit guard on his house and family.

On 13 March 1972 the car and home in Longmore Street, South Melbourne, of docker and later brothel-keeper Joey Hamilton were shotgunned. The house had been mistaken for that of next-door neighbour Charlie Wootton, who had been one of Longley's White Ticket supporters. On the same day, Hamilton survived after being shot in the groin outside his sister's home. In May, the shooters finally got the right target when Wootton's house and car were hit. Two years later he was shot in the shoulder.

On 26 September 1972 Francis Bayliss, suspected of stealing the ballot box, was found with four sticks of gelignite as well as a sawn-off shotgun. Questioned, he said he needed them for his own protection. "You're not silly. You know what's going on," he told the police.

Then shortly after 4 a.m. on 15 December Brian Sulley was shot twice in the head as he walked away from the union offices in Lorimer Street. He survived to tell the police that he had heard two shots but had not seen who fired them.

There was great excitement when on 22 December 1972 a body was found in a field at Tarneit, near Werribee. At first it was thought it might be that of the Ferret, but on further inspection the body was far too big. In fact, it belonged to another Painter and Docker, the street-fighter and standover man, John Lewis Morrison, who was extensively tattooed and known as "The Face" because of scarring from adolescent pimples. His body was so badly decomposed it was not possible to give an accurate time of death but he had disappeared some six months earlier. Again, it may not have been union troubles that led to his death by shotgun. He had been having problems in Sydney following a moderately successful robbery there. His widow Gladys later married the top-class criminal, English-born Stuart Perry. Some years later Perry was believed to have been thrown out of a plane in Asia after $1 million belonging to a drug syndicate went missing.

Then, in May 1972, it was Pat Shannon who, pointing out that dockers were not flower-arrangers, tempted fate when he unfortunately added, "Remember, no stray bullet or bomb has harmed a non-Union member." It was less than a year before one did. A little after 6.30 p.m. on 21 April 1973, Yugoslavian-born hospital cleaner Zlatko Kolovrat went to the Moonee Valley Hotel on the corner of Rose and Brunswick Streets with his young sons, Nicolas and Peter. That evening they bought Coca-Colas and were sitting with their father and a Polish man just inside in the main bar. It was then that a man chasing Laurence Chamings shot him dead as he tried to reach the safety of the outside lavatories. A stray shot hit Nicolas Kolovrat between his eyes.

Naturally, no one was able to identify the killer but now, with the death of a young boy, the police were able to lean more heavily on the underworld than was often the case and eventually the name they came up with was that of Sydney standover man Barry "The Bear" Kable. Kable had an unfortunate childhood in which he saw his father Roy axe his mother to death in the backyard of their Newtown home in April 1944. From then it was all downhill and when, in March 1956, he was sentenced to three years for robbing a taxi driver, Judge Curlewis had said he was sorry he could not have him whipped.

One possibility was that Chamings had threatened to shoot Kable following an argument during a card game at a Melbourne Sunday beer party. There was also a suggestion that one Brendon McMahon had quarrelled with Chamings, who thought he had been cheated over the proceeds from a house-breaking. McMahon had escaped from Pentridge and was still on the run by the time Kable went on trial in October 1974. At least now Kable could provide the name of the man who might have attacked Chamings. The prosecution's evidence was not strong, with much of it coming from Kable's supposed confession to a prison snitch, never a species liked by juries. Kable made an impassioned statement from the dock and called as an alibi witness, Jill Frances Cayeux, who had known him for twenty years and was sure she had been drinking with him in Richmond that night. Kable was duly acquitted in less than fifty minutes. Cayeux was later sentenced to a minimum of three years for perjury.

Kable returned to New South Wales where at the end of February 1975 he was attacked by three unidentified men, tied to a chair and beaten with axe handles. Although he suffered considerable brain damage, he survived. At the end of his life he was living on the streets of Darlinghurst.

Meanwhile, still to come was an even more important killing in the history of the dockers and it was one which would directly lead to the disintegration of the union. On 17 October 1973 it was a mild, pleasant evening when Pat Shannon died in the Druids Hotel, on the corner of Park and Moray Streets, Port Melbourne. The Druids was not a hotel Shannon often used, but after drinking in the early evening with John Patrick Joseph Loughnan at O'Connor's Centenary Hotel, known as Murphy's, they moved three-quarters of a mile up the road to the Druids where, at around 9.15, they met up with Noella Jansen, Loughnan's partner, and Joan Hoskings, whose husband was in hospital. According to Loughnan, at about 9.50, "I heard crackers going off. All of a sudden Pat said, 'You cunt' and fell off the chair. He died before the ambulance arrived." In fact, Shannon was shot three times and it was the first bullet through the heart which killed him.

Over the years there have been continuing suggestions that Shannon was set up. At first the police were convinced that he had been lured to his death by a mystery call and possibly shot by a hired interstate killer. One lawyer of the time supported part of that theory: "Shannon was inveigled into a position sitting with people in a semicircle. Whichever way he faced he faced a door." Within a matter of hours of Shannon's death his long-time rival Billy Longley disappeared.

Unlike most cases involving dockers, this time the police had some help. Again within hours of the killing the father of docker wannabe and police-dobber Gary Harding received an anonymous telephone call: "The Dockies are out to shoot your son. Find him and hide him." He left a note out for his boy, warning him, and, panic stricken, he made a call to say he wished to see his police contact, Detective Sergeant Murray Burgess, urgently.

It turned out Burgess had a little diamond mine in his hands. A terrified Harding spilled his version of the evening – that he had pointed out Shannon to a Kevin Taylor and that when Shannon was shot he and his mate Alfie Connell were in Park Street a hundred yards away. It was Billy Longley who had ordered the killing and Taylor who had done the shooting. All he had done was throw the gun away into the water at No. 2 South Wharf.

At first Taylor denied knowing anything about Shannon's death, saying he had been with his girlfriend Karen and Alfie Connell's wife, Diane. But shown the gun, now retrieved from the docks, he changed his story. He said Longley, who had been in Ararat prison with him, had told him Shannon had tried to rape his wife. He had offered $6,000 for Taylor to shoot him.

On 26 March 1974, Shannon's inquest took place and in a blaze of publicity and newsprint the coroner committed Taylor, Connell, Harding and the still absent Longley to stand trial. When the trial itself began on 5 August the prosecution hedged its bets as to the motive. Longley had promised $6,000 to Taylor because either Shannon was giving his wife a hard time or it was the settling of old union scores.

Unusually all three defendants went into the box. First was Kevin Taylor who promptly changed his story. He hadn't killed Shannon as he had told the police. That night he had been at the Druids as a favour to Longley who had looked after him in Ararat prison. He had thought he was simply to wave the gun about and eject a few cartridges as a warning to Shannon. But as they walked to the hotel together he chickened out. Longley took the gun from him, went in, came out a couple of minutes later and told him to get rid of the gun but to keep the silencer. He had heard some women screaming but no shots.

Why had he changed his story? That was Longley again. He had threatened he would kill Taylor and his girlfriend if he went to the police. As a story it wasn't all that bad. And if he had got some support from Gary Harding he might have been all right. Unfortunately for him he didn't. Harding had his own agenda. There was no suggestion from him that Longley was the killer.

Cut-throat defences only benefit the prosecution. Taylor and Harding received the death penalty duly commuted to life imprisonment. Connell was found guilty only of manslaughter and was sentenced to four years with a minimum of two to be served.

Now, in a high-profile surrender with the press pre-warned, Billy Longley gave himself up. Thoughts of bail turned into pipe-dreams and he was sent to Pentridge, where Harding and Taylor were beginning their sentences, to await his trial.

Shortly after 2 p.m. on Saturday, 13 September 1975, when he returned from the visitors' room, Gary Harding was stabbed to death in his cell in A Division with a sharpened table knife. The knife was found in the lavatory in his cell. Suspicion fell immediately on Taylor who had been with him moments before and after his killing. For his part Taylor immediately spoke to a warder to say he had found the unfortunate Harding and that he had nothing to do with his death. It was a position from which he never resiled.

Longley's trial began on 10 November, two months after Harding's death. Trials can be very boring things for both the jury and the spectators, an endless trawl through masses of documents, but when Taylor came to give evidence without Harding to contradict him, things picked up both for Longley and the public gallery. Now Taylor had a third and final version. And, best of all, it provided cover for Longley. It was he, Taylor, who had done the killing. Longley was in no way involved. Certainly $6,000 had been on offer but from Harding on behalf of a man called "Puttynose" (Jack Nicholls) rather than Longley. In fact, the villain of the whole piece was the dead Harding who had told him Longley was due to be killed himself.

Longley did not give evidence but instead made a short statement, saying he knew who had planned to kill Pat Shannon but "they would kill me if I named them". That was the reason he could not "give evidence from the witness box and be subject to cross-examination". Any suggestion Pat Shannon had been having an affair with his wife was ridiculous. He had merely given Taylor a lift to the Druids and had then gone on to see a friend. He had not seen Harding at all that night. The gun that had been used was his but, he said, he had given it to Taylor a few weeks before to go rabbiting.

With Longley confident of an acquittal, on 19 November the jury retired for six and a half hours before returning a verdict of guilty. He was sentenced to imprisonment for his natural life. The publicity surrounding the inquest had no doubt gone against him as had his absence. Would he have done better to have stood his ground from the start? From a trial point of view he might but whether he would have survived is another matter.

In February 1976 Longley appealed against his conviction, claiming there was no evidence on which he could be found guilty. He lost by a two to one majority. The Chief Justice and Justice Lush thought there was sufficient evidence but, in a dissenting verdict, Justice Anderson said he would have allowed the appeal.

Over the years there were stories that Longley would bid for a retrial. In March 1980 he gave the *Age* newspaper a seven-page pamphlet arguing his innocence. In February the next year his new solicitors were reported to be sifting through fresh evidence that Longley claimed would clear him, but nothing came of it. Principally, his evidence was based on Taylor saying that he was not involved but the Court of Appeal had disposed of that evidence years earlier.

Why, in the first place, did Harding turn on Longley? As always there are various theories on offer. Once Harding had received the threats he may have run scared and tried to cut himself a deal for immunity or at worst a shortish prison sentence for manslaughter. After all, he was not the actual killer. Inexperience and possibly fear told on him. The unwritten general rule is that the first dobber gets the benefit, but not in his case. One of the questions that remain unanswered is: how did the dockers know quite so soon that Harding was involved?

Did Longley organize the killing of Shannon? To this day he continues to deny any involvement. His friend, the former detective Skull Murphy, is by no means convinced that he did: "I have certain reservations that the person who went to jail was the right bloke . . . but I didn't lose any sleep over it."

The Melbourne robber and enforcer Chopper Read, a great champion of Longley, does not believe he would have used idiots like Taylor and Harding when Ray "Chuck" Bennett, Linus "The Pom" Driscoll, who was a member of the Sydney Toecutters Gang, and, modestly, himself were all on hand. All were known, tried and trusted hardmen. Why would Longley use two clowns like Harding and Taylor on a spur of the moment job? He has a point. A key platform of the Crown's case was indeed that it was Longley's own gun that was used by Taylor but his lawyer, John Walker, thought only a fool would have allowed his own gun to be used. If, however, Longley did use Harding and Taylor and his own gun, it was an amazing miscalculation for which he paid dearly.

Read has an interesting and by no means wholly impossible version of events. He claims that, three weeks before Shannon was shot, Jack Twist, who had been a major figure both on the docks and in Melbourne crime generally in the 1950s, met Lou Wright, who was now a leading light behind the scenes in the union. They talked in a Port Melbourne hotel and Twist said that the union war had to stop, and that both Shannon and Longley must go. Others discount this saying that by the 1970s Twist was a spent force and was banished from Melbourne, but in 1982 Royal Commissioner Frank Costigan thought that Twist was one of a triumvirate – Puttynose Nicholls and Doug Sproule were the others – still in control of the union. Additionally Lou Wright, known as "The Godfather" and described by journalist Tom Prior as "particularly formidable", has been vastly underrated. There is also little doubt that people knew the killing of Shannon was coming: on the evening he was shot, Bobby Dix, one of his minders, did not appear. How on earth did Longley know Shannon was going be drinking in what was not one of his regular hangouts?

Not that speculation did Longley any good. For him, in April 1976, it was off back to Pentridge from where, in time, he would continue the chain of events that broke the union.

So who had killed the unfortunate Harding? Taylor was dobbed in by two prison snitches, Peter Grant and Tibor Bariska, both doing life for murder. If the police thought the evidence of the grasses was sufficient for a conviction they were wrong. For one reason or another, both snitches backtracked in quick time. Taylor was not even committed for trial.

It was the dockers who ruled the other prisoners at Pentridge. At any one time there would be a number of them serving sentences and they banded together. Unsurprisingly Longley was not popular with the majority of dockers then in Pentridge. Hardman he may have been but there was no way he was going to survive without help. And help came in the form of "Chopper" Read who, to get a respite from H Division, had Kevin Taylor slice off a good part of his ears. He had been before the classification board to ask for a transfer into the mainstream of the jail and had been refused. He was not satisfied and asked Taylor to oblige him. This at least got him in the prison hospital for a period.

It was another docker, John "Piggy" Palmer, who was later acquitted of the Car-O-Tel motel murder in St Kilda in 1984 and was then serving a sentence for rape, who sparked a five-year struggle that became known as the Overcoat War, because of the coats the prisoners wore to conceal weapons even in the height of summer. In it Read headed a team against a crew led by a career criminal connected to the dockers. In theory it blew up over a question of who had eaten the sausages that were to be served as a Christmas treat in 1975.

All this was merely an excuse. The dockers wanted Longley. One night acid was poured on his blankets as he slept but Read was determined to protect him. What Longley really wanted was a new trial and it was after Read had been badly stabbed in the war that he began to talk to a British journalist, David Richards, who wrote for the *Bulletin* and who had cut his teeth as a crime reporter in Melbourne. Richards persuaded senior Victorian officers to allow him to go undercover with Skull Murphy to see what senior members of the union were up to. And he found all sorts of things including the standover scheme, ghosting and tax fraud. He also discovered that a brother and sister were forced to allow a starting-price bookmaker to operate at the Station Hotel, Port Melbourne, and when the pair did not cooperate, there was a shotgun attack on the hotel.

Richards's findings, coupled with what Longley had to say, would be the catalyst that would ultimately bring about the deeply controversial and much criticized Royal Commission which opened on 1 October 1980, headed by barrister Francis

Xavier Costigan. And the star of the Costigan Commission was undoubtedly Longley, as indeed he had always intended. Longley's enemy, Jack "Puttynose" Nicholls, did not survive the Commission. Shortly before he was due to give evidence on subpoena, on 16 June 1981, he was found shot through the head in his car on the Hume Highway some 170 miles from Melbourne. On the day of his death he had been drinking heavily with friends in Albury. He left a note:

> To my members and executive, I tried very hard but the rotten Fraser government did not want me to survive. Do not think I have taken the easy way out but the rotten system has cut my life short. I had big ideas for advancement but these were chopped short. Farewell Comrades, Jack Nicholls XX

The coronial inquest returned a verdict of suicide but there were many, including Doug Meagher, counsel for the Commission, who thought Nicholls had been given either an ultimatum or some help.

Over the months the Costigan inquiry expanded to an extensive examination of how often illiterate union members had been used in tax-evasion schemes costing millions, drug-dealing, laundering and the Nugan Hand Bank collapse. In his report Costigan wrote:

> I became satisfied that the union, at least in Victoria, Newcastle, Queensland and South Australia (if not in Sydney as well), was an organized criminal group following criminal pursuits. At least in Victoria those in charge of the union recruit exclusively those who have serious criminal convictions. The union gives active assistance to those criminals, be it in the selection of criminal activity, or in harbouring and protecting the criminals from the consequences of their crimes.

It all led to the establishment of the National Crime Authority, but it did not lead to a new trial for Longley. However, it did get him out of Pentridge to the less harsh conditions of Ararat prison. In all he served thirteen years and on his release he joined the now retired Skull Murphy, setting up as business mediators.

As for the Painters and Dockers Union, dissatisfied members began to drift to other unions following the Costigan Commission's report. Then the Hawke government passed legislation that unions with fewer than 1,000 members should be deregistered and the registration of the Federated Ship Painters and Dockers Union was cancelled on 1 December 1993.

19

The Great Bookie Robbery

Some criminals have allure, some have talent, some have the ability to pay great attention to detail. Melbourne's Ray "Chuck" Bennett had all of those things. Like Bruce Reynolds, the leader of Britain's Great Train Robbery, he had the brains to organize and the charisma to lead a team. He was regarded by his peers as not only a top gang tactician but also as "one of the Australian underworld's foremost bank robbers".

Bennett, once a member of the so-called Kangaroo Gang – in reality a series of close-knit gangs who shoplifted in Europe almost with impunity in the 1960s and 1970s – was serving a sentence in Parkhurst, a high security prison on the Isle of Wight off the south coast of England, when he devised the Great Bookie Robbery of April 1976 in Melbourne.

Built in 1880, the Victoria Club at 141 Queen Street in the city's central business district was where Victorian bookmakers would meet to settle up on the first day after a weekend's racing. In 1975, towards the end of his sentence, Bennett obtained a period of home leave and, amazing as it may seem, returned to Australia on a false passport to case the premises before returning to complete his sentence.

Although security at the Victoria Club was incredibly lax for the amount of money floating around – some moonlighting detectives would look in to see things were all right and they invariably were – over the years a number of individuals and teams had looked at it and decided it was too much like hard work. They included highly talented robber James "The Jockey" Smith and the Sino-Australian Leslie Woon, whose career in both Melbourne and Sydney ran for over twenty years. It was Woon who had devised the Mayne Nickless armoured van robbery in March 1970. The *Victoria Police Gazette* described Woon as "not afraid to dirty his hands when planning a job. He doesn't mix with the criminal element; using different names for his flat, car and telephone". If Woon turned it down it must have been far too much like hard work.

Having completed his sentence, Bennett, who had acted as a minder for Billy Longley in Melbourne's waterfront union war of the early 1970s, put together a team and took them out of Melbourne for a period of training away from their wives and girlfriends. His second-in-command was another nominal Painter and Docker Ian Revel "Fingers" Carroll. Other members included Norman Leung Lee, who ran a dim-sum restaurant, Bennett's cousin Vinnie Mikkelsen, Anthony Paul McNamara and Dennis William "Greedy" Smith, who was always thought to have been the team's driver although he denied it to his death. Although they had all worked together before, neither of the leading standover brothers Les and Brian Kane was part of Bennett's team. Particularly Brian was thought to be unwilling to accept the discipline required. They were said not to have minded their omission but it must have grated. Another who missed out was Bennett's great mate the armed robber Brian O'Callaghan but that was because he was in Sydney's Long Bay prison at the time. Bennett is said to have given him $100,000 (all dollar figures in this chapter are in Australian currency) from the takings.

When Bennett was satisfied the team was ready, and after a weekend dress rehearsal when the club was empty, he chose the Wednesday after the three-day Easter weekend's racing when over a hundred bookmakers met to settle up at the club.

The money was delivered by armoured car at midday on 21 April 1976 and within minutes at least six men armed with machine-guns burst into the settling room, tackled the armed guards and ordered the bookmakers to lie on the floor. The team cut open the metal cash boxes filled with over a hundred calico bags of untraceable notes. Just how much money was taken has never been established. Certainly between $1.5 million and possibly $15 million are the parameters. The raid was over by 12.15 p.m. and most of the robbers were gone into the next-door office block and then into traffic in Queen Street. A reward of $70,000 was promptly offered. Curiously, this was one day when the moonlighting detectives were not performing their unofficial duty.

The immediate problem Bennett faced was disposing of the money. In 1998 Phillip Dunn QC, who had represented Norman Leung Lee, said his client had told him that for a month the money never left the premises. The robbers had rented offices upstairs from the Victoria Club and it was removed at their leisure over the next four to five weeks. "When you think about it, that's very smart, verging on genius almost," he said.

Far too many robberies have been solved because immediately after the robbery the participants and their relatives have gone round spending money like drunken sailors. Abstinence requires communal discipline. Laundering requires care and on this occasion the racetrack, one of the traditional avenues, was hardly open to them. The Great Train Robbers in Britain had been caught because they splashed out on cars in an endeavour to launder the money instead of changing it through a trusted solicitor. When blackmailer Peter Macari took $500,000 from Qantas airlines he bought a flat and fast cars that he could not possibly justify. Bennett was far too astute a leader to allow that to happen. Little by little some money went into property. Some went to Manila with Greedy Smith, who opened the Aussie Bar which was advertised on a hoarding at the North Melbourne rules football ground in Arden Street. The profits from the bar went into the purchase of brothels and bars throughout Asia as well as racehorses and to pay off up to fifty corrupt police officers in Manila. Some more money went to Canada. But there was a nasty scare when, on a visit to a solicitor, Bennett's mother collapsed. When the paramedics were called, they found some $90,000 in cash in her clothes. Amazingly no questions seem to have been asked.

It was not until 1977 that Norman Leung Lee was arrested and charged with the robbery. He was one who had been spending and had bought $60,000 of dim-sum equipment. He was also trying to launder money through a solicitor's trust account. On 19 August he took another $60,000 in a plastic bag to a solicitor saying he wanted to invest it on behalf of a friend. The police found out and for a moment the bubble seemed to have burst. But with Lee remaining as staunch as Bennett had expected, the committing magistrate ruled that there was no evidence to link the unmarked money to the robbery and refused to send Lee for trial. He was the only one of the team ever charged and his acquittal really spelled the end for the investigating squad.

But, just as there were few, if any, continuing success stories among Britain's Great Train Robbers so, over the years, the Great Bookie Robbers met more than their fair share of bad luck. Most of them, in fact, died early and often violent deaths. First there was the danger of other gangs including the Sydney-based Toecutters, named because of their tendency to snip off pieces of their victim to persuade them to share the proceeds, wanting a slice. It spoke enormously well of the regard in which Bennett was held that they decided to leave him personally alone. Others were not so lucky. A man named O'Callaghan was kidnapped and, although he could be heard protesting as he was dragged away that he was not the right O'Callaghan, he was never seen again. Another story that floated around after the robbery was that the discarded Les and Brian Kane might want to help themselves. There was speculation that Bennett would therefore make a pre-emptive strike against them. He was seen as not averse to removing his enemies before they had the chance to remove him. But, when it came to it, their quarrel seems to have been personal rather than business.

It was in the winter of 1978 that Les Kane first thought he was going to be seen to by Bennett, or at least that was when he told his second wife, Judi, of his fears. Apart from the standover business he had a good income from the Geelong docks, picking up several pay packets a week in different names. Brian, also a nominal docker, was a debt collector and enforcer. Few were brave enough to resist his invitations to pay up.

Just as standover man John "Nano the Magician" Regan could make people disappear in Sydney so could Chuck Bennett in Victoria. His technique was simple. He would knock on people's doors and say, "Come with me." And one of those who went with him was a friend of the Kanes, a young man with a deformed arm known as Wingy who had been going out with a girl fancied by a friend of Bennett. After the disappearance Brian Kane took up the matter with Bennett at a fund-raiser at the old Richmond Tigers Australian rules football player Francis Burke's pub in Richmond, but for the moment things remained calm.

The next incident was a fight between Brian Kane and Bennett's cousin, Vinnie Mikkelsen. Offered a drink by Kane in the Royal Oak in Church Street, Richmond, Mikkelsen replied, somewhat unnecessarily, "I don't drink with old men." Kane had been a Golden Gloves fighter but he was now forty; Mikkelsen was the younger but with less ability. Out on the pavement the fight ran for a good twenty minutes until Mikkelsen bit off part of Kane's ear. A spectator picked it up, packed it in ice from the bar and after the fight ended sent it with Kane to the hospital. It could not be reattached and from then on Brian Kane grew his hair long. It was thought that Bennett had set up his cousin to provoke a fight.

In August 1978 Les Kane, Judi and their two young children rented an apartment at Mountain Highway, Wantirna, fifteen miles out of the city. On 19 October three men were waiting in the house when the family returned around 9.15 p.m. from visiting relations. Judi Kane thought it was odd that their pet dachshund was sitting on the chair but Les told her the dog had learned to jump up. Inside Judi and the children were bundled into a bedroom while Kane was shot in the bathroom of the house. Judi Kane heard his body being dumped in the boot of his pink Ford Futura and the men driving off. What was so odd was that the three men, two of whom Judi had known for years, did not attempt to mask up. One was Chuck Bennett and the second was Vinnie Mikkelsen. The third was Laurie Prendergast, a friend of freelance Melbourne hitman Chris "Mr Rent-a-Kill" Flannery.

Kane's body was never found and the whisper was that it was quite possible that he became dim-sum in Norman Lee's restaurant. But there were sure to be reprisals and at the end of November Mikkelsen's house was burned down.

In the meantime Brian Kane went against all the known rules of gangland conduct and decided that Judi Kane should go to the police. His reasoning appears to have been that they would do the walking for him. They would find Bennett and he would kill him once they had done. The others could wait. It did not work out quite as easily.

On 1 December 1978 that year Prendergast was arrested and in the evening Judi Kane picked him out on an identity parade. Bennett and Mikkelsen were arrested later, Bennett for an armed robbery in Yarraville unconnected with the Victoria Club. Despite an incident when an attempt was made to force her car off the road, and a fierce battering from some of Victoria's top barristers when the trial started in September 1979, Judi Kane stuck to her guns, identifying all three men. But there were problems for the prosecution.

"What was obvious was that the Crown case had very serious issues," said one lawyer who watched the trial, "and the defence challenged every bit of it." There was no doubt that Kane was a wife-beater. Judi Kane had needed plastic surgery on two occasions after his ministrations and it was suggested at the trial that she had either killed her husband herself or, more probably, had arranged for his disappearance.

Then there was the lack of forensic evidence. According to Judi Kane her husband had been machine-gunned, yet there was no chipped paint and no cracked mirror in the bathroom, let alone a bullet hole in the wall where he was shot. Surely not every bullet had hit Kane. The only evidence that her husband had been alive on the day he was meant to have been killed was from Judi. Many thought that while Kane was certainly missing it hadn't happened quite in the way the jury was being told. Some thought he might have been killed up to a week earlier. All the defendants called alibis and, something unusual in a major Australian criminal trial, Bennett actually gave evidence. Norman Lee came to court to say Bennett had spent the evening with his family. Prendergast had a brother Billy Lewis who closely resembled him and there were suggestions Judi Kane could have seen Lewis.

In 1970s, before DNA testing, juries liked "no body" cases even less than they do today. Some Australian states still had not come round even to prosecuting when no body could be found. Kane had not been gone all that long. Given his lifestyle there was always the chance he could still be in hiding. Part of the defence case was based on the evidence of two people who claimed that they had seen Les Kane after the alleged shooting and abduction. On 21 September, after a retirement of only two-and-a-half hours, the jury returned verdicts of not guilty.

Brian Kane could never accept the death of his brother or the verdict. "There wasn't going to be a life for Brian after Les's death, ever," says a family friend. "He just wanted Chuck's head on a platter." Once, seeing lawyer Phil Dunn having coffee with Melbourne's leading criminal of the time, Graham "The Munster" Kinniburgh, outside a café in Lygon Street, he attacked him, calling him a dog and demanding to know how he could have acted for Mikkelsen. It was only the intervention of Kinniburgh, saying "he was only doing his job", that prevented a serious incident.

After the acquittals Prendergast went straight into hiding and Mikkelsen flew out of Melbourne the next day. Norman Lee went to Singapore. From then on until his death Chuck Bennett was in Pentridge prison, awaiting trial for armed robbery, although he declined to go into segregation. He knew reprisals were likely and was said to have taken out fresh life insurance. His thirteen-year-old son was sent out of the country.

While there had been strict security at the Kane murder trial there was none on 12 November 1979 when Bennett was taken to Court 10 on the first floor of the old Melbourne Magistrates Court on La Trobe Street to answer the robbery charges. Bennett was waiting without handcuffs and with an unarmed guard outside the courtroom. Also on the landing was a man wearing a dark suit – some witnesses thought brown, some thought blue– and apparently carrying a small briefcase, sitting on a bench at the head of the stairs and making no effort to hide himself away. The man shot Bennett three times in the chest with a .38. Bennett staggered down the stairs and out of the courthouse into a courtyard where he collapsed. Taken to St Vincent's Hospital, he died within the hour.

The gunman escaped, after threatening Bennett's escorting officer and a federal policeman, possibly via the rear stairway leading to the court's car park. From there it was easy enough to go into any of the surrounding streets. Other accounts, however, have him walking down the front stairs of the court building and into a waiting car.

Unsurprisingly the underworld buzzed with rumours, one of which was that Brian Kane and his brother Raymond had imported an interstate hitman for a fee of $50,000. The name of Toecutter Linus "The Pom" Driscoll was the one on most police officers' lips. This was unlikely since he was also thought to have modified the machine-guns Les Kane's killers had used. Another rumour was that two police officers, one of them Sergeant Brian "Skull" Murphy, had given the gunman the money to kill Bennett. Another theory was that the killer was contract hitman Chris Flannery, possibly with an assist from a police officer. This was certainly suggested by the press but even given his tendency to go where the money was, this was unlikely as Flannery was aligned to Prendergast. At the inquest the coroner found that there was no evidence whatsoever to suggest that Murphy and another officer were implicated in the murder. Many years later Murphy was asked "if a Brian had killed Bennett". He replied, "Yes, but it wasn't this one."

Both Raymond and Brian Kane made statements that they were not involved. Raymond gave Frank "Mr Frank" Galbally, the lawyer of choice for the discerning Melbourne criminal, the names of the people he had been with, adding that he would make himself available for interview. Brian Kane's statement was shorter and more combative: "I do not believe there can be any evidence whatsoever connecting me with this killing. Therefore I will say nothing further about this matter as there is no way in which I can assist the police."

Nearly forty years on it is now generally accepted that Bennett's killer was Brian Kane. After Bennett's acquittal Brian Kane had become more and more secretive, calling friends and family at odd hours, arriving in the dead of night, never giving his name over the telephone. In fact, Kane had been getting into the courthouse night after night at around midnight, pacing out the distances. His escape route also became clear. He was taken straight to suburban Essendon and put on a light plane to Adelaide where he boarded a commercial flight to Perth. And there he stayed for the next three months. Kinniburgh acted as a messenger telling the family how things were going. Eventually Kane was told he was no longer hot – at least as far as the police were concerned – and he returned from the west coast.

The day after Bennett's death, his old mate Brian O'Callaghan, still serving a thirteen-year sentence for armed robbery, escaped from a van taking him to work at the Long Bay prison bakery. With O'Callaghan temporarily on the loose and possibly making his way to Melbourne, the press and police predicted immediate trouble and possibly an all-out gang war, but, for the time being, that did not materialize. Callaghan evaded capture for two years until he was dobbed in and caught in a house in Carlton, Melbourne, but he does not seem to have busied himself on his former mate's behalf.

Within the month, however, John Mervyn Kingdom, a friend of the Kanes, walked into St Vincent's Hospital in Melbourne with three bullets in his groin and stomach. He told the police he had been walking in the North Fitzroy area when he "felt a pain" but naturally had neither heard nor seen anything. One theory was that he had been kidnapped and shot as a reprisal for Bennett's death. Things quietened down for the next few months but then there were further reprisals. But not at first from the Bennett side.

Around 6.45 on the morning of 15 July 1981, Norman McLeod, Mikkelsen's brother-in-law, walked across the lawn and got into a Mazda parked outside his home in Coolaroo when he was shot three times through the side window by two men, armed with shotguns, who ran away down a branch of the Moonee Ponds Creek. McLeod had been killed by mistake: he had borrowed Mikkelsen's car. No charges were ever brought.

Brian Kane spent 26 November 1982 with an old friend, Sandra Walsh. In the evening they went to the Quarry Hotel in Lygon Street, not far from the city centre, for a few drinks. About an hour later, around 9.30, Sandra went to the lavatory and Kane was at the table when two men came in. One of them, tall and thin and wearing a black balaclava, walked over and shot him in the face, knocking his teeth out. Kane died the next day.

If the police hoped to get any help from Sandra they were wrong. "He was shot and that's all I'm saying," was all she would say at first. Later, she made a statement in which she said she had driven him in her Jaguar to the Quarry Hotel. But even that was a mistake, she told the coroner eleven months later. She had been confused. Earlier in the day she had lent her car to a Trevor Russell who had dropped the Jaguar off there during the evening.

And in criminal circles, amongst those who should have known better, the names of Vinnie Mikkelsen and the appropriately named armed robber Russell "Mad Dog" Cox (who was still at large after his successful escape from the supposedly escape-proof Katingal prison in New South Wales) were being barked. Neither man was ever charged. Much later, when the case was reopened in 2009, the name Greedy Smith came into the frame.

As for the other members of the Great Bookie Robbery gang, over the years those suspected of being on the Victoria Club job were arrested for other jobs, served long sentences and died young. Anthony McNamara died in Collingwood in 1990. He had become a drug addict and it was suspected that he had been given a hot shot.

After Brian Kane's death, Norman Leung Lee eventually returned to Victoria to take part in a series of bank robberies. On 28 July 1992, after a robbery at the Ansett Air Terminal, Lee failed to close the doors of the getaway van and fell out. Chasing after the van he was shot and killed by the Police Special Operations Group. A post mortem showed he had a heart condition and the chase after the van might itself have been fatal. Another who was shot by the police in the Ansett raid was Stephen Barci, who received a ten-year minimum sentence, as did the driver Steven Asling. At least Barci had some fleeting pleasure during his time in jail. On 4 March 1998, six years into his sentence, he managed to have a twenty-nine-year-old woman smuggled into Dhurringile minimum security prison dressed in prison uniform. She was there for over six hours before dogs searching for drugs found her under a blanket.

Bennett's sergeant-at-arms, Ian Carroll, following in the master's footsteps, became one of the great planners of armed robberies including an attack on a bullion van in Tooborac, Victoria, in spring 1981. He would leave nothing to chance and team members were supplied not only with weapons but also a medical kit in case of injury. On 3 March 1983 he was killed by "Mad Dog" Cox, born Melville Peter Schnitzerling, who was the former lover of Melbourne's Queen of the Underworld, "The Matriarch" Kath Pettingill. Carroll was killed in an argument in his own backyard in a supposedly safe house in Mount Martha on Mornington Peninsula. Searching the house the police found what they described as a "huge number" of weapons including machine-guns and uniforms from a security firm, some hidden in a false ceiling. The house had also been used as a hideaway by a number of criminals including Cox and the former South Australian police officer, Colin Creed.

After the shooting Cox fled with his green-eyed, dark-haired, vegetarian girlfriend, Helen Eva Deane, who was Chuck Bennett's sister-in-law. For the next five years they led the police on a merry dance, with the *Sydney Morning Herald* quoting a police spokesman saying of Deane, "She's a crook, but obviously she's doing something right. Like Cox she's no fool. She hasn't even been sighted for five years." Cox was not caught until he was trapped in a failed robbery in the smart Melbourne suburb of Doncaster in July 1988. He was later tried for the Carroll murder and acquitted after the magistrate said he could not decide who had fired the first shot. He and Creed were named as part of a gang that had pulled off nine armed robberies in Victoria and New South Wales, netting them in excess of $1.3 million. Cox was finally released in December 2004 and went to Queensland.

If Greedy, sometimes "Fatty", Smith was indeed part of the Great Bookie Robbery as opposed to merely laundering the proceeds, he partially survived the robbers' curse, living until August 2010 when he died following a heart attack at the age of sixty-five. In his later life he had sold drugs from his Rolls-Royce. On the downside he had suffered from diabetes and melanoma, and part of his leg was amputated. The remainder of his leg had the emblem of North Melbourne AFL club, of which he was a keen supporter, embossed on it. In his career he had acquired over fifty convictions and in February 2002 he received three years on a series of drug charges. He died still denying that he had been a driver in the Bookie Robbery and the getaway driver in the killing of Brian Kane. Chuck Bennett's mate, Brian O'Callaghan, regarded as one of the great robbers of his era, died in October 2010 at the age of sixty-two. He had been a drug addict for some years.

In 2009 the police said they were within reaching distance of the men who had shot Brian Kane but no arrests have ever been made.

20

Jimmy "The Gent" Burke and the Lufthansa Robbery

Just over a year after Melbourne's Great Bookie Robbery, what was then the biggest hold-up in American crime history took place in the early hours of 8 December 1978. Six or seven masked men cleared US$5.8 million from the Lufthansa warehouse at John F. Kennedy International Airport, New York. There may have been immediate celebrations among the gang-members but by the end of the story the bodies of the participants and their friends would be piled far higher than those of their Melbourne counterparts.

The planner of the robbery was James "Jimmy the Gent" Burke, an Irish American associate of Paul Vario's crew, who were members of New York's Lucchese family. Burke acquired his nickname both because of the quality of his suits and his habit of giving hijacked lorry drivers $50 bills to get them home. His long-time friend and fellow crew member Henry Hill, who is a pivotal figure in Nicholas Pileggi's book, *Wiseguy*, thought he had a dangerous temper:

> If there was just the littlest amount of trouble, he'd be all over you in a second. He'd grab a guy's tie and slam his chin into the table before the guy knew he was in a war. If the guy was lucky, Jimmy would let him live ... Jimmy had a reputation for being wild. He'd whack you. There was no question – Jimmy would plant you just as fast as

shake your hand. At dinner he could be the nicest guy in
the world, but then he could blow you away for dessert.

Over the years his victims included his wife's former boyfriend,
whose body was found in pieces in his car on the day of Burke's
marriage, and a young man who refused to pay his own mother
the $5,000 he owed her. Burke paid the money to her in the
morning and killed the man in the evening. Other victims
included the usual informants and potential witnesses against
him, including a long-time, close friend who had turned him
over in a cigarette hijack as well as William "Billy Batts" Devino,
a man with connections to the Gambino family, killed in June
1970. It was suggested he had offended Burke's friend, Tommy
DeSimone, whose grandfather Rosario and father Frank had
been successive bosses of the Los Angeles Crime Family.
DeSimone's sister had been Burke's long-term mistress. The
more likely reason is that while Devino was doing time on a
narcotics rap, Burke had taken over his loan-sharking business
and did not want to hand it back. DeSimone and Burke beat
him almost to death in the Suite nightclub in Jamaica, Queens,
New York. After they put him in the boot of the car they were
involved in a minor traffic accident and realized Devino was
still alive. They then drove him to DeSimone's mother's house
where they collected a knife and stabbed him to death in a
forest in Connecticut. There are a number of versions of what
happened to the body – buried under a dog kennel, in the
basement of Robert's Lounge, a wiseguy hang-out near the
airport on Leffert's Boulevard, South Ozone Park, or in a car
crusher. Take your pick.

Born on 5 July 1931 Burke was brought up in the Manhattan
Foundling Home and over the first thirteen years of his life was
constantly moved from foster home to foster home where he
was alternately loved and abused. He was happy in one home
at least and throughout his life would give these substitute
parents a handsome sum in cash each month. In 1944 his

then foster-father turned to slap him while driving and was killed when he lost control and crashed. Burke's foster-mother blamed him and abused him before he ran away. From there it was a short step to delinquency and the Mount Loretto jail for young offenders on Staten Island.

His defining moment came in September 1949 when, aged eighteen, he was caught passing cheques on behalf of Lucchese associate Dominick Cerami. He remained staunch and when he was sent to Auburn prison to begin his five-year sentence he was welcomed as a hero for his behaviour. At the age of twenty-five he was so highly regarded that his services were wanted by both the Lucchese and the Colombo families. By 1970 he had become a big-time lorry hijacker. He also owned Robert's Lounge, where the mixed clientele included cargo handlers, thieves and undercover cops.

One way or another almost all well-planned robberies require inside information. On 7 April 1967, Henry Hill and Thomas DeSimone pulled the Air France robbery. Hill had heard from Robert "Frenchy" McMahon that the airline was handling a shipment of $480,000. The main problem was a guard with a key to the safe. This was solved by getting the guard drunk and taking him to a motel where a prostitute was waiting. When the guard took off his pants, they took the key to copy it and replaced it without his knowledge. At 11.40 p.m. on a Saturday, Hill and DeSimone drove to the Air France cargo parking lot in a rented car with false plates and left with the money. As a tribute to the mob chiefs who considered Kennedy Airport their turf, Hill and DeSimone gave $60,000 to Sebastian "Buster" Aloi, the fifty-seven-year-old *capo* for the Colombo crime family, and another $60,000 to their own *capo*, Paul Vario.

The Lufthansa robbery was no exception to the "inside help" rule. This time the man on the inside was cargo agent supervisor Louis Werner. Werner was $20,000 in debt to bookmaker and hair salon owner Martin "Marty" Krugman, who ran bookmaking out of Robert's Lounge. Now the slate would be wiped clean if Werner gave up the required information. He was, after all, trying to support an estranged wife, a mistress, a loan-shark, four children and a $300 a day gambling habit on a $15,000 annual salary. Werner gave detailed information of the layout of the cargo terminal even down to advising where the robbers should park.

Just like Chuck Bennett in Melbourne, Burke, who had just come out from a stretch over another cargo theft, selected his men for the Lufthansa robbery with care. Those thought to have been on the raid were his son, Frank James, named after the nineteenth-century outlaw, DeSimone, Angelo Sepe of the Lucchese family, loan-sharker and trafficker Louis "Fat Louis" Cafora and Joe Civitello Sr, along with Gambino family member Paolo LiCastri. Burke put them through rehearsal after rehearsal until he was satisfied with their performances.

Just before 3.15 a.m. on 11 December 1978 Lufthansa cargo agent Kerry Whalen saw a black Ford Econoline van parking near a loading platform for the vaults. When he walked toward the loading bay to investigate, he was struck over the head with a .45 pistol. Whalen saw a series of armed men running into the cargo terminal. Another man took his wallet and told him that they now knew where his family was and that they had men ready to visit them. Whalen nodded to indicate that he would cooperate with the robbers.

Senior agent Rolf Rebmann heard a noise by the loading ramp and when he also went to investigate, the masked men handcuffed him. They then used a one-of-a-kind key they had been given by Werner and walked through a maze of corridors to where two other employees would be. Once they had been rounded up, two gunmen ventured downstairs to look for unexpected visitors. The other men marched the employees to a lunch room, where the remaining employees were on their 3 a.m. break.

The gunmen burst into the lunch room brandishing their firearms and showed the bloodied Whalen as an indication of their intentions if anyone got out of line. They knew each employee by name and forced them on to the ground. The robbers knew that Rudi Eirich was the only guard that night that had the right combination to open the double-door vault and forced John Murray, the terminal's senior cargo agent, to call Eirich on the intercom pretending that there was a problem with a load from Frankfurt and asking him to meet him in the cafeteria. When Eirich approached the lunch room he was taken at gunpoint down two flights of stairs to the double-door vault.

Eirich later reported that the robbers were well informed and knew all about the safety systems in the vault, including the double-door system. One door had to be shut before the second was opened to avoid activating the alarm to the Port Authority of New York and New Jersey, which maintained a police force at the airport. Once inside, the gang ordered Eirich to lie on the ground and began sifting through invoices and freight manifests to determine which parcels they wanted.

Around forty parcels were removed. Eirich was then made to lock the inner door before unlocking the outer door. Two of the gunmen were assigned to load the parcels into the van while the others tied up the unfortunate man. The men left at 4.16 a.m. telling the employees there would be trouble if they called the Port Authority before 4.30 a.m.

The raid had taken just four minutes over the hour but there was one potentially disastrous mistake. The African-American gofer Parnell Stephen "Stacks" Edwards, who was not on the heist itself, was scheduled to take the truck used in the raid to New Jersey to be compacted. Instead, he abandoned it full of ski masks, footprints and fingerprints in Canarsie about a mile and a half down the road from the airport. Luckily for the raiders, it turned out that, in those pre-DNA days, the prints were not forensically usable. With major heists the police know there are a limited number of operators who can execute such an operation and suspicion fell first on the crew of John Gotti but then quickly on Burke's crew if for no other reason than the proximity of their hangout, Robert's Lounge, to the airport.

However, within a matter of weeks, people associated with the raid began to die or disappear. No great effort was made to hide the murders and it was thought that Burke was making examples of those he feared might talk. And, of course, dead people did not require their share of the proceeds. Unsurprisingly, the first to go was Stacks Edwards, killed by Tommy DeSimone. His body was found under the covers of his bed in his apartment in Ozone Park, Queens. He had been shot six times in the head and chest.

The next was the bookie Marty Krugman. He had been demanding his $500,000 share. The incentive to dispose of him was irresistible and he was killed on 6 January 1979 at a bar on Rockaway Boulevard. He had received only $50,000, $40,000 of which he had given to Louis Werner.

Tommy DeSimone disappeared on 14 January 1979. It was thought he had been killed as part of the aftermath of the heist but it is more likely that he was murdered by the Gambino crime family as a reprisal for the death of Billy Batts. His body was never found. Three days later it was the turn of Richard Eaton who had worked as a courier and frontman for Burke. His hog-tied frozen body was found trussed up in a trailer in Brooklyn. It was thought he had taken $250,000 from Burke in a cocaine scam and that he had also skimmed some of the money he had been laundering from the heist. Before his death he had been tortured.

Tommy DeSimone's girlfriend, twenty-seven-year-old Long Island beautician Theresa Ferrara, was killed on 10 February that year. She received a telephone call to meet someone in a diner and disappeared after telling her niece she had the chance to make $10,000. Her dismembered body, which was only identified through X-rays, was found on 18 May when it was washed ashore near Toms River, New Jersey. She was suspected of having helped Eaton and his friend,

Florida-based club-owner Tom Monteleone, skim some of the takings. In March Monteleone disappeared.

What must never happen after a major robbery is for the participants to demonstrate new-found wealth. Brooklyn parking-lot owner Louis Cafora had once been Jimmy Burke's cellmate during his time in prison and now he was contracted by Burke to launder some of the money from the heist through his collection of legitimate lots. Unfortunately Cafora not only told his wife Joanna about gang business, including the heist, but within a matter of days he bought her a custom pink Cadillac Fleetwood. To compound this error, he drove the car to a gang meeting near the JFK Air Cargo Center where FBI officers were still investigating the heist. Neither his body nor that of his wife was ever found.

By May 1979 the FBI were looking at Werner as a major suspect. He had been under suspicion not only because he frequented Robert's Lounge but because he had bought himself a new camper van shortly after the robbery. At first he told the FBI the money had come from a winning betting streak but they continued to press him. In fact, he had only met one member of Burke's team who was still alive, the Air France cargo night supervisor, Joseph "Joe Buddha" Manri. If Werner were to cut himself any decent sort of deal he would have to give up Manri who had been involved in the earlier job and who, he hoped, would in turn give up other names. Manri and his fellow Air France supervisor, Robert "Frenchy" McMahon had been approached by the FBI with a view to entering the witness protection programme but unwisely they were holding out. This particular problem was easily solved by Burke. The bodies of both men were found in a Buick Riviera parked in Brooklyn on 16 May. Both had been shot in the back of the head; it was thought they had been hit by Paolo LiCastri for a fee of $50,000. In turn, on 13 June the naked body of LiCastri was found on a burning rubbish dump. He had been shot.

On 18 February 1979 Werner was arrested at a bowling tournament. The courts moved more speedily in those days and on 16 May 1979 he was found guilty of the plan to rob Lufthansa and received sixteen and a half years. He died in Oklahoma in 2007.

In the end Burke was betrayed by his long-time friend, Henry Hill, who was himself facing serious drug charges and who believed he was next in line to be killed. In 1982 Hill gave evidence against Burke when Burke was convicted for his part in a point-shaving scam involving members of the Boston College basketball team. Three years later it was Hill's crucial evidence that convicted Burke of the murder of Richard Eaton. Hill told the court when he had asked about Eaton, Burke had replied, "Don't worry about him any more, I whacked the fucking swindler out."

On 19 February 1985 Burke was sentenced to life imprisonment. He died on 13 April 1996 at the age of sixty-four in the Wende Correctional Facility near Buffalo, New York. He had been suffering from stomach cancer. All told, some thirteen people connected in one way or another to the robbery died. Paul Vario, who was said to have been a major beneficiary from the theft, was never charged but later received a six-year sentence for extortion at the airport. He died in May 1988 at the federal prison in Fort Worth. Burke's son, Frank James, was never convicted of his suspected part in the Lufthansa robbery. On 18 May 1987 he was found shot dead on Liberty Avenue, Brooklyn. He was twenty-seven. In 1992 Burke's daughter Catherine married Anthony Indelicato of the Bonnano family.

Perhaps surprisingly Hill has survived outside the witness protection programme, from which he was expelled for criminal offences. At one time he ran a restaurant called Wiseguys in West Haven, Connecticut.

21

Bertie Smalls and the Wembley Mob

Small-time pimp and big-time bank robber Derek Creighton "Bertie" Smalls died on 31 January 2008, aged seventy-two, an alcoholic who was by then effectively out of the criminal scene. This was something of a surprise because, at the beginning of the 1970s, members of the London underworld had taken out a contract on him reputed to be then worth between £50,000 and £100,000.

Long retired he may have been but nevertheless Smalls did receive obituaries in the national papers. He was entitled to them. He was a man whose activities effectively changed banking practice. In the 1960s wages were normally paid in cash every Friday and banks had no grilles separating cashiers from customers. It was a system of which Smalls and his colleagues took full advantage.

He was also the first of the modern supergrasses. However, he was only continuing a fashion started in the early eighteenth century when, on Christmas Eve 1705, John Smith, known as "Half-hanged Smith", survived an attempt to execute him. He dangled for fifteen minutes before the crowd demanded that he was cut down. He is said to have rewarded the authorities by naming over 350 pickpockets and house-breakers. His lucky escape did not deter him. He continued his criminal career until he was transported to Virginia in 1727.

Born in north London, Smalls was a stocky man who wore a Zapata moustache and, going prematurely bald, carefully arranged his remaining strands to cover the bare patch. When he chose to use it, he had considerable charm, and early in his criminal career he ran a small string of prostitutes. There was, says a detective who knew him, no sense of coercion: "It was more as if they were doing him a favour."

By no means a fastidious man – another detective said of the sheets on his bed, "They're grey. The sort you can't buy in the shops" – Smalls's fellow bank robber, John McVicar, told sociologist Laurie Taylor that Smalls liked sex with women who were menstruating.

What Smalls did have was a good sense of humour. A series of interlocking lanes, which provided a good escape route for bank robbers, ran off the high street in Wood Green, north London. After one robbery a young woman pushing her baby in a pram was terrified when four masked men carrying guns pushed past her. Just when she thought she was out of danger, along panted the overweight, unmasked and sweating Smalls. As she pressed against the fence he stopped and remarked, "Effing awful way to make a living, in'it, girl?" and lumbered on.

Smalls also had a streak of decency or at least good manners and it was this that finally did for him. When he knocked over a woman in the street after a raid on Ralli Brothers merchant bank in Hatton Garden, which netted £296,000, he stopped and bent down to help her up. Later she identified him from a police photograph.

In the 1960s and 1970s, in the days before security cameras and CCTV, bank robberies were the most profitable and quickest way of separating money from its rightful owners. One major robber of the time recalled:

How did we look out the banks? On a Monday Georgie and I would drive round looking for a bank with a side turning. This was in the days before bandit glass – it was us made them put it in. One of us would go in and change a note to see what drawers there were and then on a Friday we'd go in mob handed with pick-axe handles. Security vans were often picked by chance. You'd see them collecting and see them again the next week. You'd watch them doing pick-ups and use your judgement about how much each pick-up was worth and just what the van was carrying.

Teams were often arranged on an ad hoc basis rather as might be expected for a pick-up game of football on a Sunday morning in the park.

One of the labour exchanges for robbery work was the Log Cabin club in Wardour Street, London. It was full of robbers, cut-throats and buyers. We used to go direct to the club and say to people, "You fancy going to work tomorrow?" It could have been a pawn shop, it could have been a post office.

In complete contrast there were the meticulous operations run by Bertie Smalls with a small group of experienced and thoroughly reliable men including the getaway driver Danny Allpress, also known as Teale, son of a well-regarded London villain. Allpress, who had aspirations to be a motor-racing driver and who, it was said, could turn a car on a sixpence, sold used motors in Warren Street. He and Smalls worked together over the years. Bryan Turner, who had been invalided out of the RAF with a head injury before becoming a house-breaker, was also on Smalls's team. He laundered his money through a cash-and-carry in Kilburn and ran a Greek card game called kalooki, which resembles rummy, at one of north London's many afternoon drinking clubs. Turner's friend was Bruce Brown, captain of Ashford Manor Golf Club, who had served three years for office-breaking and was a golfing partner of DCI Dick Saxby, head of the divisional Criminal Investigation Department at Wembley. Another regular was the country squire Philip Morris, born in Hanwell, who with his criminal earnings had bought a sixty-acre farm at Troon, near Camborne in Cornwall, where he was regarded as a soft touch for local charities. Morris was later convicted of manslaughter when a milkman, Francis Kidwell, was shot dead in a £148,000 Securicor robbery in Ewell in January 1974. He was sentenced to seventeen years.

With the arrival of the motorways it was now easier to undertake robberies outside a normal working area. Often a local team would put up the job and it would be carried out by others.

The modus operandi of all bank robbers of the time when wages were paid in cash on a Friday was that raids were conducted during opening hours. Balaclavas were worn, sometimes with a mask underneath, and a ladder was used to get over any security grilles if they did not reach the ceiling. Those that did would be smashed with a sledgehammer. A shot would be fired in the ceiling to concentrate the attention of staff and customers alike. Because of his weight and general unfitness, Smalls would stand on guard just inside the door of the bank.

The first of Smalls's raids was on the National Provincial Bank in Brighton, which netted £72,000. Then followed the Ralli Brothers robbery in March 1969. There was one more that year; three in 1970; four in 1971; and ten in the gang's last year of operations.

In September 1970 two of Smalls's regulars, Bobby King and Donald Barrett, along with Smalls's wife Diane were arrested over the robbery of Lloyds Bank in Bournemouth. Of Smalls there was no sign. Barrett made a confession naming names but would not give evidence against King or Diane. The case collapsed with the disappearance of Smalls's au pair who, it had been hoped, would be a crucial witness for the prosecution. Diane Smalls and King were acquitted but Barrett received twelve years from Mr Justice Lawton at Winchester

Crown Court. His other reward was a postcard from Spain, sent to him in jail, which read, "Wish you were here." For a time it was thought that Smalls had the au pair killed but after the case he produced her at a solicitor's office where she was given a severe dressing-down by the police.

Smalls, who had by now acquired a conviction for possessing a firearm, was now well in police sights as leader of what became known as the Wembley Mob, but so far there was no evidence against him.

By 1972, the Wembley Mob was one of the most prolific teams in London and the Home Counties. Shortly before the raid on the Barclays Bank in Ilford, which ultimately proved his downfall, Smalls earned £10,000 (about £200,000 in today's money) for his part in a robbery on a savings bank in Brighton.

The Ilford robbery carried all the trademarks of the gang's meticulous methods. Through an informant, they learnt that the bank received large deposits consisting of the takings of a Tesco supermarket and that when these large amounts arrived, the security van was preceded by a red Mini presumed to be sent to inform the manager. This enabled the robbers to pick the appropriate day to secure the largest amount of cash.

After recruiting two employees of the security van company, Smalls sent one of the robbers into the bank dressed as a City worker, complete with pinstripe suit and an umbrella, to write a cheque to distract staff when the van approached. The raid went smoothly with the corrupt security guards handing over the money and the robbers escaping in seconds.

Within five days, most of the gang had fled abroad to lie low. Smalls travelled by ferry from Newhaven to Dieppe in France before taking a train to Paris and then flying to Torremolinos, the Spanish resort whose popularity with Britain's fugitives was already beginning to earn the Costa del Sol region the nickname of Costa del Crime.

Ironically, it was the efforts of another informant, who gave
police the names of every member of the Wembley Mob, that
led to Smalls's arrest.

Three days before Christmas 1972, Detective Inspector Vic
Wilding went to see Smalls, who was back in the country, at
his home in Selsdon. Only the au pair – the same girl who
had vanished two years earlier – was there and she told him
that Smalls and Diane were going to spend Christmas near
Northampton. She pointed the house out to them and at 5. 30
a.m. DCI Brewster of the Regional Crime Squad knocked on
the door. Smalls opened the door in his underpants and the
police charged in, knocking Brewster over in the rush. Later
Smalls said he had opened the door to let in the cat, which had
a trick of scratching to gain admission. "You let the rats in, not
the cat," said Diane sourly.

Peter Donnelly, the clerk in the firm of solicitors which
represented Smalls, remembered:

> He was nicked for the Wembley bank. He was shipped
> from Northampton to Wembley, and it was there several
> weeks later they produce statements of his interview. I
> thumb through them and there's a reference to Smalls
> saying you give me outers and I'll give you names. I went
> to see him. "Did you say it?" He's hedgy. "I've got to
> have guarantees." I go to see Marshall or Wilding, I forget
> which, and ask if it was a serious proposition. Yes, but we
> don't believe he'll do it. If he does what will you give us?
> They start thinking it's possible and I tell him go and sit
> tight, keep your trap shut. At this stage no one else had
> been nicked.

Donnelly went to see Smalls in Brixton prison and told him that
he had to put his cards on the table. He had to give up details
of the robberies and the teams. Smalls was reluctant to go into
details but eventually a skeleton of the jobs was drawn up.

I arranged a meeting with Wilding and Marshall at Wembley with my boss Peter Steggles. They've got a clip board with a list of names and robberies I could see upside down. I say "Everything on there you can have plus XYZ additional robberies." That seemed to take them off guard. From then we had the advantage. They were reluctant and thought it would be difficult to have anything in writing. Nothing in writing – no deal. Then general talk. They say they'll take instructions.

Steggles and Donnelly told the officers that they would draft heads of agreement of their conditions. Their main concerns were that there had to be the immunity from prosecution for Smalls and Diane, and that there had to be security. Steggles and Donnelly also insisted any deal had to be agreed with the Director of Public Prosecutions. There were two meetings before a letter was drafted, which was the final document.

On the third day Jim Marshall had gone on holiday and was away for the actual statement which was odd bearing in mind he was in control. Bertie had given so much detail they were then starting to look for corroboration and they heaved in the au pair from the Bournemouth job; got a statement from her as to various robbers including Bertie descending on a flop when they played around with one of the sawn-offs and mistakenly it was fired into the floorboards. They managed to identify the address, took the carpet up and the damage was still there with the pellets.

Then they needed Diane and she was never happy with this. I met her on Brixton Hill and said if you don't do it the deal won't be accepted because we didn't know whether they'd say the evidence was sufficient. I said "do it or it may not go through". Very reluctantly she made the

statement but then at court she refused to take the oath.
She stood by him but the relationship was over anyway.

An out-of-court deal was arranged that the local magistrates
would technically give Smalls bail but that he would be
remanded into police custody. He was then taken to a hotel by
Wembley Stadium and was put in a suite where David Cassidy
had stayed the week before. Smalls and the police would sit for
twelve hours a day during which time he would reminisce. As
the days went by, Smalls was moved to new addresses, always
guarded by shifts of police officers and policewoman. The
only time Donnelly could see him was at an arranged point
which he would be told about half an hour in advance. Peter
Donnelly recalls: "I'm sure there was a contract out. Publicly it
was said to be £100,000 but I heard from Bertie's friend, the
safe breaker Jackie O'Connell, that it was only £50,000."

There was always the chance that when it came to it Smalls
would lose his nerve and not go through with his evidence
even at the stage of committal proceedings:

> One of the final conditions was that if the statement wasn't
> used and Bertie Smalls would not be a witness then his
> statement would remain on police files but not used against
> him at a trial. But there was such a level of corruption at
> that time that sooner or later it would have got out and
> he'd have been dead.

But what many saw as the turning point came when Danny
Allpress, at one time Smalls's closest friend, called out from
the dock, "Well, Bertie, who's been having Slack Alice while
you're away?" The others in the dock began to laugh and
Smalls pulled himself together and told his tale. Jack Slipper,
one of the officers in the case, believed the taunt was crucial
in making Smalls betray his fellow criminals. Donnelly is not
quite so sure:

I don't think the Slack Alice remark enamoured them to him. His attitude was with hindsight most of them when pulled in tried to do exactly the same and he got in first. From that point of view he felt justified. Before then he was on remand for possession of a firearm. He got out but he was skint and one of them was meant to have given Diane money to look after her but they didn't. I think that annoyed him as well.

Smalls went through with things both at the committal proceedings and again at the Old Bailey. When he completed his evidence there the defendants sang Vera Lynn's "We'll Meet Again". It did not appeal to the trial judge.

The scale and importance of Smalls's betrayal earned him special treatment. An agreement was drawn up with Sir Norman Skelhorn, the Director of Public Prosecutions (DPP), granting Smalls complete immunity.

It was the first – and only – time that a self-confessed criminal has been allowed to escape all punishment in return for turning Queen's Evidence. When the convicted men appealed to the Court of Appeal, Mr Justice Lawton was up in arms that such a deal could have been sanctioned by the DPP. But when the appeals came before the House of Lords it was Lord Justice Lawton's turn to be criticized. Bargains between the DPP and criminals were nothing to do with the courts, said their lordships sternly. In the wake of the agreement, the law lords ruled it had been an "unholy deal" and required that all future supergrasses should serve a prison sentence, albeit one that was significantly reduced. It was later agreed that in ordinary circumstances a supergrass would have a five-year tariff.

In the year after the arrest of Smalls's team, the number of robberies in the area of London where the Wembley Mob had been most active fell from sixty-five to twenty-six. Although the case opened the flood gates for a succession of supergrasses – the next being Bernie O'Mahoney, who gave up his own team – the rash of bank robberies continued until the late 1980s when, with a number of shoot-outs with the police and a corresponding number of deaths among their ranks, career criminals abandoned the high ideals of not involving themselves in the drug trade and began financing such deals as a quicker, easier and much safer way of earning a living.

In fact, the defendants didn't meet Smalls again out of court. Despite predictions in the underworld that he would soon be dealt with – the price on his head was said to be up to £1 million – amazingly Smalls never encountered much trouble. He declined the offers of Scotland Yard to go into a witness protection scheme or to be given plastic surgery and a passage to Australia. There was a knife-fight in a car park in south London and for a time Smalls avoided pubs and clubs where friends of the imprisoned men congregated, but apart from that there was no real trouble. After a few years he returned to his old haunts.

He spent the rest of his life what is called "ducking and diving", dabbling in property and receiving his pension from the Yard. There was one more conviction for a minor assault on a police officer in the 1990s for which he was fined. It was arranged he would write his memoirs with Ted Lewis, author of the bestselling *Jack's Return Home*, which was made into the film *Get Carter*, but given the predilection of both of them for early morning vodka the project never got off the ground. However, in 1975 he sold his story to a national newspaper.

Of those who worked with him many disappeared into obscurity but the driver Danny Allpress, who had received twenty-one years reduced to eighteen on appeal, died while on bail, charged with using a digging machine to remove a cash dispenser from the wall of a bank. He had pancreatic cancer. More of a success from the penal reformer's point of view was Bobby King who took a degree while in prison and on his release went into social and charity work. King later saw Smalls in a north London street after his release from prison and said he had considered it a test of his reformed character that he was able to resist the urge to kill him. Smalls was possibly correct: he had got in first and, in the curious logic the underworld sometimes displays, the others accepted that they might have done the same thing.

Smalls also featured in a curious situation involving Jimmy Saunders, convicted of the February 1970 Barclays Bank Robbery in Ilford. The evidence against him was almost wholly a series of verbal admissions he is said to have made to Commander Bert Wickstead. Smalls, in his long statement, said that Saunders had not been on the raid and this presented a serious problem to the police. If they were to rely on him as a witness of truth against his co-robbers then he must be treated as one in Saunders's case as well. Saunders was released by the Court of Appeal, which, with some adroit reasoning, decided he must have confessed to Wickstead but that he had been drinking and was boasting when he did so. Saunders was awarded substantial compensation but in the 1980s was later convicted as a member of what was known as the Grandfather Gang, a team of middle-aged to elderly bank robbers, and received fifteen years.

Less of a success was Donald Barrett who had grassed on Smalls and King in Bournemouth. He received seventeen years reduced to twelve by the Court of Appeal but then in turn he became a supergrass, not once but twice. First in 1981 he received fourteen years, which the Court of Appeal halved. He served just under three and a half years and within a year he was at work again.

Then in 1985 a young boy found a remote-control device outside the home of David Croke, leader of a team of armed robbers of which Barrett was a member. He kept it for six months before he saw a *Crimewatch* programme. In it a security guard's wife and daughter were handcuffed and threatened. The guard agreed to have what he was told was a remote-controlled bomb attached to him as he drove the robbers to a depot where £500,000 was stolen. The boy persuaded his mother it was worth handing over the device to the police. Barrett was arrested on the way back from a £280,000 gold bullion heist in south London. He immediately rolled over again and this time, in May 1988, received sixteen years, a 25 per cent discount. Croke received twenty-one years. The amazing thing is that the team must have known Barrett was a grass twice, if not three times over, but still agreed to work with him yet again.

One team member who disappeared abroad just before Smalls started to sing was his long-term friend John Short, who had owned the Duke of York in Torremolinos where the gang used to go for rest and recuperation. He changed his name to McGrath and while in Canada, along with another friend, Roy Radovan, sold trotting horses for racing in and around Montreal. Unfortunately the horses either had a touch of the slows or, more seriously, did not match their pedigrees. The Montreal police received discreet inquiries from "businessmen" complaining about the horses. No, they did not want to press charges, merely to know the whereabouts of the vendors. Radovan's body was found in the Hudson River. Short returned to London where six months later he was arrested. In April 1978 he pleaded guilty to other robbery and firearms charges and received a total of twenty-one years.

From a criminal's point of view the great success story of the Wembley Mob was Mickey Green, who was named by Smalls as being with him on a post office raid in Portsmouth in July 1971. He fled before he could be arrested and later became one of the world's biggest cocaine dealers. He had homes in Ireland, where his properties were later confiscated; France, where he was sentenced to seventeen years in his absence; England; the United States, where he lived in a house once owned by Rod Stewart; and in Spain. By 2011, now aged nearly seventy, Green was thought to be worth around 85 million euros and to be living somewhere near Marbella. Some of his money is believed to have been buried in safes in the hills in the area. He has been on the run for over twenty years.

As for the police, the case was not all unalloyed joy. There was a bitter row over whose informer should benefit from the bank rewards. Chief Superintendent Dick Saxby, Bruce Brown's golfing partner, was accused of stealing £25,000 from Brown's safety deposit box. The subsequent police investigation cleared Saxby, who then retired from the force. Then Detective Constable Joan Angell, a member of the Regional Crime Squad, claimed that an informant of hers, "Mary Fraser", known as Maltese Mary, who ran the Kismet drinking club in London's Little Newport Street, had named Bruce Brown and Bryan Turner as two of the Wembley robbers. Now Angell claimed a reward for Maltese Mary. The paperwork for this claim then disappeared, and the police inquiry found that the reward totalling £2,175 had been paid to a "William Wise". The officers who had claimed the money on his behalf were Saxby and Detective Chief Inspector Vic Wilding. Both were eventually cleared of misconduct by another police investigation. Wilding left the Metropolitan Police to become a security officer for Barclays Bank.

Angell resigned in disgust and in 1976 Maltese Mary received an ex gratia £1,000 reward. Although she later said she was still going to campaign for her money, she never received it. She later returned to Malta and her club was taken over and run by Jerry Fallon, a former member of the Flying Squad.

22

The Kray Twins in Soho

The first sign that the Kray twins, Ronnie and Reggie, were moving into London's West End came in 1956 when they were involved in a drinking club, the Stragglers in Cambridge Circus near Leicester Square. The twins, along with their elder brother Charlie, had been born in the East End and were steadily moving upmarket. They had provided protection for Jack Spot who felt threatened by the Italians at the 1955 Epsom Spring race meeting and were now extending their fledgling empire of clubs and billiard saloons from Stoke Newington, Whitechapel and Aldgate. In retrospect the twins thought they had no time for Spot:

> It wasn't that we liked him. We despised him really. We just turned out with Spotty to show everyone that *we* was the up-and-coming firm and didn't give a fuck for anyone. Old Spotty understood. Whatever else he may have been he wasn't stupid. He knew quite well that though we were there in theory as his friends, we meant to end up taking over from him.

On paper at least, Reggie Kray was a great admirer of Billy Hill, looking on him as his mentor:

> When I was in my early twenties, the man I wanted to emulate most of all was the former gang boss of London's

underworld, Billy Hill. The prime reason for my admiration was, that apart from Billy being very physical and violent when necessary, he had a good, quick thinking brain and this trait appealed to me most of all.

Others say that in his declining years Hill was terrified of the pair.

The Stragglers was run by a docker, Billie Jones, but the clientele were prone to fighting among themselves, something that reduced the profits. Jones's friend, the ex-boxer Bobby Ramsey, who had taken the rap and served three months in South Africa after Billy Hill slashed the club-owner Arnold Neville, mentioned the problem to the twins. In a matter of days the club was running smoothly and profitably, and they were given a share. Ramsey remained a close friend of the twins, appearing for them on wrestling bills when they ran shows at the York Hall in Bethnal Green and other venues in the East End.

Soon the twins started to lean on the wealthy but still up-and-coming property developer and racketeer Peter Rachman. As a sideline of his property empire, Rachman built up a chain of gambling clubs and in 1956 opened El Condor nightclub on Wardour Street in Soho, under the management of another of his protégés, Raymond Nash of the Lebanese gangster family. For a time El Condor became the in-place. Princess Margaret was seen there and the regulars included both the Duke of Kent and the rogue peer Lord Tony Moynihan, who recalled Rachman as a father figure.

Quite how the twins actually met Rachman is not clear but one story is that a fight in the Latin Quarter nightclub in Wardour Street, where Rachman was holding a party, led to him giving Ronnie Kray a lift back to his home in Valence Road. It also led to an agreement to pay £5,000 to avoid trouble in Notting Hill, where Rachman was leaning on recalcitrant tenants.

Rachman caving in to the twins so quickly is difficult to understand. The people who worked for him included three of the most uncompromising men in the business. The senior of them was the retired heavyweight wrestling champion, Bert Assirati, who had links to the old Italian families. Once, when stabbed in the arm, he had arrested his attacker with the knife still in him. The second was another wrestler, the joker Peter Rann, who practised his falls on the concrete in Hyde Park. He would wind up the third of Rachman's henchmen, the half-mad and completely out-of-control Norbert "Fred" Rondel who, although German, had wrestled as the Polish Eagle. On one occasion, arriving late for a judo class, Rondel apologized and told his sensei he had just killed a man in Tottenham Court Road for staring at him. He had knocked the man's head off and it had rolled across the pavement. Further enquiries showed he had attacked a tailor's dummy. Rondel later went on to legal fame in a case which reached the House of Lords, trying unsuccessfully to sue his barrister for negligence when he was convicted of cutting off a man's ear. He maintained he had merely bitten it off: "To defend myself I got one in a headlock . . . and he tried to get hold of my private parts, so I tore his hand in half . . . Anyway so when his head slipped out, I tried to pull his head back but his ear came off in my teeth you see."

Both Assirati and Rondel were, at one time or another, on the door of Rachman's club La Discotheque in Wardour Street. But guns do more damage than fists and teeth. In March 1963 after Assirati was told to make himself scarce one evening, the relief doorman, ex-Guardsman Dennis John Raine, was shot in the leg. He had refused entry to two men earlier in the evening.

It was in La Discotheque, so another story goes, that Mandy Rice-Davies was not quick enough serving a drink to Ronnie Kray one evening. He grabbed her wrist and she, not knowing who he was, slapped him. It was a slap which cost Rachman a further £5,000 to avoid the otherwise inevitable trouble.

The twins were also apparently leaning on the painter Francis Bacon. One Soho figure of the time recalls:

> Francis Bacon was tucked up by the Krays. He went into Wheeler's one day with a black eye and two of their men came up to the table and said "You're here. Don't forget. We told you." The man with him said, "What's this about?" One of them said, "You his wife?" and the man did the pair of them. The waiters loved it.

On their behalf Jack "The Hat" McVitie, the one-time Kray man later killed by Reggie, cut a man's throat in a club upstairs from the Log Cabin in Wardour Street. One habitué of the Log Cabin recalls:

> It was up a flight of stairs and in a sort of hut on a flat roof. The Krays either wanted it or wanted money from it but the Scotsman who ran it wasn't having it. I thought it was rather appropriate when I heard he got stabbed in the throat by Reggie.

The club which caused the most trouble for the twins at the time was the Hideaway in Gerrard Street. The club's history had been chequered. At one time in the early 1960s, when it was the Bon Soir, it had been owned by "Mad" Frank Fraser, Albert Dimes and the owner of a nearby fashionable French restaurant. Dimes lost heart and Joe Wilkins, nephew of Bert Wilkins, the old Sabini man, took his interest and also lost money. Fraser recalls:

> I don't know why but the club never did well; it was a nice little place with a band and a cabaret and we had a licence to drink until 3 a.m. but it never took off. We realized that the only way you were going to make a profit was on the insurance.

Thanks to Wilkins, the club duly went up in smoke and it was Leopold Harris, the fire-raiser from the 1930s, now working as an insurance assessor, who ensured Fraser and the others had a good pay day. In 1933 in what was then the longest trial at the Old Bailey – thirty-three days – Leopold Harris received fourteen years for arson. He had been financing a number of agents who were set up in business with highly combustible stock. Fraser's story is not as fanciful as it sounds. Whilst he was in prison Harris was still advising insurance companies from his cell. He was released in 1940.

On 16 December 1964 the premises were reopened as the Hideaway by Huw Cargill McCowan, the homosexual Scots baronet. The Krays had already demanded 20 per cent of the takings and threatened to take 50 per cent. In return the premises would be trouble free, but their kind offer had been rejected by the feisty McCowan. They booked a table for ten on the opening night and failed to appear and two days later a fight involving their friend, the writer "Mad" Teddy Smith, broke out in the premises. After the fight McCowan settled on 20 per cent but also went to the police.

On 10 January 1965 the Krays were arrested and charged with demanding money with menaces. Leonard "Nipper" Read, who was investigating the Krays, pinned his hopes not on the evidence of McCowan but on that of the club's manager, Sidney Vaughan, who had initially backed up McCowan's version of events. He was wrong to do so. Vaughan made a statement to a local vicar that he was being paid £40 a week to support McCowan and that the whole thing was a cook-up. At the committal proceedings he was a hostile witness.

The twins were represented by the extremely clever and extremely dubious solicitor's clerk, Manny Fryde, who at one time may or may not have qualified to practise in South Africa. The first trial was aborted after Fryde said he had seen a juror speak to a policeman, something the juror denied. The second ended in a disagreement. By the time of the third trial

McCowan's background had been investigated by a private detective. He had alleged blackmail in three previous cases and had been in a mental hospital. The jury acquitted after a retirement of only ten minutes. Within hours the Krays "bought" the Hideaway, renaming it the El Morocco and throwing a lavish party there on the same night. Now the Krays effectively had a licence to roam both the West End and the East End.

By the mid-1960s the Krays were taking money off a number of Soho clubs owned by the strip-club proprietor Bernie Silver, who had the Gigi and the New Life in Frith Street and the New Mill in Macclesfield Street off Shaftesbury Avenue. They also had part of the protection money obtained by others from the Astor, the Colony, the Bagatelle off Regent Street and the Starlight off Oxford Street.

Apart from isolated acts – a man who they believed was going to poison them had his jaw broken in a club in Old Compton Street – the Krays kept their more psychotic behaviour out of Soho. True, once Ronnie went to shoot Frankie Fraser in Isow's restaurant in Brewer Street but Fraser never appeared that evening. That restaurant's doorman, Nosher Powell, had to take extreme care when he walked the streets at night after he had barred the twins for not wearing ties.

It was a call to their Stoke Newington club, the Regency, which was feared more than a West End encounter. The late Mickey Bailey, himself a former East End hardman, thought:

A summons from the Twins wasn't to be ignored. Invariably one of the firm would come round. When they come they'd say, "Ronnie, or the Twins, want to see you tomorrow morning. Get over between ten and twelve." The meeting was always at their house, The Regency or Pelliccci's which was a café in Bethnal Green Road. There was two Pelliccis, Nevio and Terry and invariably it would be in Terry's. If it was at their mother's or Pellicci's you knew you didn't have a problem but if it was at the Regency it could be one. This was where they held their court.

It was on behalf of Bernie Silver that the pair engaged in their most bizarre enterprise. They agreed to arrange the killing of the Maltese club owner George Caruana with whom Silver and other club-owners had fallen out. Whether Silver actually knew that Caruana was to be killed rather than beaten up is doubtful. In any event the fee was £1,000 and there were other rewards such as the prestige which would accrue, particularly as the twins were then in negotiations with members of the Mafia over stolen bonds.

The assassin was to be a Scot, Paul Elvey, who was arrested after a tip-off as he boarded a plane to London from Glasgow. In the days before scanners and body-searches, Elvey had managed to take three dozen sticks of dynamite through the airport in his luggage. The dynamite was to be placed in Caruana's car to explode when the ignition was turned on. He had also been given a crossbow and told to practise until he was proficient. He would then be told the name of his victim. He was also to kill another man, this time at the Old Bailey, by jabbing him in the leg with a poisoned needle protruding from a suitcase, made especially by the former speedway rider Francis "Split" Waterman. Again, in those days there was little if any security thought to be necessary at the Old Bailey. Jurors, counsel, defendants, police, friends and witnesses all mixed happily in the one tearoom in the basement.

When it came to it, Kenneth Barraclough, the stipendiary magistrate who heard the committal proceedings, found the allegations of conspiracy to murder Caruana too confusing and indeed improbable for him to rule that there was a case to answer. But by then the damage was done. Witnesses had begun to come forward in the cases of the murders of George Cornell, shot to death by Ronnie in the Blind Beggar public house in London's Mile End Road over an insult in a West End nightclub, and Jack "The Hat" McVitie, stabbed to death by Reggie in a basement flat in Stoke Newington after he had turned the twins over in a contract and had boasted about it. In 1969 the twins were sentenced to life imprisonment for their deaths.

By this time Rachman was dead, aged forty-two, following a heart attack on 29 November 1962. Two years earlier he had married his long-standing girlfriend Audrey O'Donnell but he continued his relationship with Mandy Rice-Davies and a number of other women including the nightclub hostess Christine Keeler. After his death little money from his reputed fortune was found. Shortly afterwards, in the wake of the Profumo scandal when the Tory politician John Profumo was found to be having an affair with Keeler at the same time as she was sleeping with Ivanov, the Russian attaché, a furore broke out over Rachman's treatment of his tenants and the word Rachmanism was coined by Ben Parkin, the Labour MP for North Paddington.

As for his henchmen, Assirati retired to Brighton and Peter Rann went to Blackpool. Norbert Rondel continued his life as a club-owner in Soho, serving more prison sentences over his persecution of the former Rachman protégé, Serge Papinski, to whom he had taken a dislike. Rondel was also alleged to have set up the robbery which led to the Spaghetti House siege in Knightsbridge in 1976. He was acquitted after allegations of jury-nobbling. He died in 2009. Mandy Rice-Davies later married an Israeli businessman and opened a series of successful nightclubs. She is said to have described her life as "one slow descent into respectability".

23

The Dixie Mafia

Every self-respecting gang-leader needs not only a doctor on hand but also a lawyer. The Ship Painters and Dockers Union members and indeed most other criminals of the era in Melbourne, Australia, in the 1970s had Frank "Mr Frank" Galbraith; in England the Kray twins had Manny Fryde, said to have once been a South African solicitor; Jack Spot had Bernie Perkoff; and the Great Train Robbers had Ellis Lincoln and George Stanley. For their defence every decent gangster in Glasgow looked to Joe Beltrami when they were in trouble and the less decent to James Latta, who additionally gave pre-crime advice and went to prison for attempting to pervert the course of justice. Some defence lawyers such as Beltrami kept their clients at arm's length; others have aligned themselves too closely with their clients. In New York, Dutch Schultz had Richard "Dixie" Davis and down in Dixie itself, in Biloxi, was the firm of Halat and Sherry, whose fortunes were entwined with the Dixie Mafia.

The Dixie Mafia, known also as the Southern Mafia and somewhat derisively as the Corn Bread Mafia, is rather like the definition of an elephant – difficult to describe but readily recognizable when seen. Membership has been much on the "ol' boy" basis with no requirement of racial or family ties. The Dixie Mafia, said to have been named by the lawman Rex Armistead, was first noted in the late 1960s as an amorphous bunch of loosely associated criminals who traced their history back to Prohibition, which in the case of Mississippi was 1909. Prominent among them for a time was the Stateline Mob, which existed from 1940 to 1970. What was also required for them to flourish were understaffed and ill-equipped police departments, preferably with officers who could easily be corrupted. In the report of the Texas Organized Crime Prevention Council for 1978 it was estimated there were around 220 members of the Dixie Mafia involved in robbery, burglary, narcotics, auto and other thefts and murder-for-hire contracts. The organization was confirmed as having no formal structure but with members in New Mexico, Texas, Oklahoma, Louisiana, Arkansas, Mississippi, Alabama, Georgia, Tennessee, Florida and, possibly, Arizona.

Its informality was in complete contrast to "The Company" operating out of Albuquerque, which was working just as a profitable big business should. It dealt in sinsemilla, the highly potent form of marijuana. There was a board of directors, a personnel department, plant medical officers and manicurists. Manual workers received $1,750 a week together with two ounces of marijuana to stop petty theft. The lighting bill for the spring of 1989, to ensure that the plants grew healthily, was a solid $6,800. Run by brothers Gordon and David Wohlert, The Company had started in a small way, buying thirteen cuttings from a Washington state dealer for $27,000. And from little seedlings acres grew. In 1990 thirty members, including the brothers, pleaded guilty after being caught in a Drug Enforcement Agency sweep known as Operation Green Merchant. David Wohlert, who spent eleven years in custody, was pardoned in November 2010.

All that was required of a Dixie Mafia member was an ability to make money from extortion, prostitution, gambling, bribery and drugs coupled with a willingness to dispose of anyone who turned informer before the case came to court. It may not have had the same tight structure of the Italian Mafia but it could be just as, if not more, deadly. It was said that in a ten-year period from 1968 the Dixie Mafia disposed of 156 people and there was not a well between West Texas and Mississippi that did not have a body in it. That may have been a low estimate.

Something of a throwback to the days of prohibition, the Dixie Mafia's spiritual capital may have been Hot Springs, Arkansas, known as "Bubbles". It was one of the so-called safe cities for criminals. In the 1930s, Richard Galatas ran the White Front Cigar Store there and acted as a liaison between criminals and the police chief, Dutch Akers. However, the Dixie Mafia's de facto home was the gulf town of Biloxi, Mississippi, often regarded as a wide-open town and dubbed Byzantium-by-the-Sea; it was home to dozens of strip and gambling joints. A causal effect on crime in the area had been when the government used the former Biloxi Country Club as a training ground for half a million servicemen during the Second World War. With a service base came gambling, liquor violations, prostitution and loan-sharking. Illegal gambling flourished openly and unchecked with, in the 1960s and 1970s, sex joints opening up under the benevolent eye of the sheriff, Eddie McDonald. The whole atmosphere provided a spawning ground for basic organized criminal enterprises. From time to time the police made inroads and in 1967 they had actually managed to get Harry Bennett, a Biloxi gambler who had an interest in a juice joint called Deano's Lounge, to turn state's evidence. Unfortunately he was shot dead on a parking lot, the first of twenty-five murders over the next four years that could be traced to the Dixie Mafia. Harold Diddlemeyer served eight years for conspiracy over Bennett's death and died in prison but in a recent book Mike Gillich claims Kirksey Nix was the actual killer, something Nix has denied.

The scope of operations has run the gamut of old-fashioned crime rather than white-collar crime with members travelling the Southern circuit and recruiting others to undertake specialist out-of-town, or state, jobs. For instance, a robber could be recruited in Louisiana to deal with a bank in Texas; a Texas contract killer might be recruited to operate in Georgia.

Because of its informal structure a number of men could be said to have headed the Dixie Mafia simultaneously. One who certainly was at the top of the tree was Biloxi's Mike "Mr Mike" Gillich, of Croatian descent, who at his peak owned a string of motels, strip-cum-nightclubs and backroom gambling joints. If, at that time, there was an unofficial head of the Dixie Mafia, then it must have been Gillich, a child of the Depression. Whatever may be said about him he was a great worker, far removed from the pearl homburg wearers of the Mafia. He had been a waiter and bartender when he met the professional gambler W. E. "Eater Bill" Sanford, a man with underworld contacts throughout the South. In the early 1960s Gillich set up his first club offering striptease and gambling. From then on his political and police contacts and hard work ensured the success of a string of clubs on Biloxi's Strip. Known as a man who kept his word and kept his mouth closed, he became the financier for the Dixie Mafia.

In February 1992 a long-time member was quoted by Jeff Kunerth in the *Orlando Sentinel Tribune* as saying: "What makes them dangerous is that they don't think, they just act. If anybody had done any thinking, they wouldn't kill no damn judge. When you kill a judge, that means you'll kill anything. They don't draw a line, everything is fair game."

The good ol' boys had long been quite capable of taking on the judiciary. When, in January 1980, Georgia Superior Court judge George A. Horkan had sentenced four gang-members to eight to twelve years for possession of cocaine, a contract, happily unfulfilled, was taken out on his life.

For a while the Dixie Mafia was thought to be dead, but recognition that it was only sleeping came with the death of another judge, Vincent Sherry. He and his wife, Margaret, were shot and killed in their home in Biloxi on 14 September 1987. They had not been seen for some days and their bodies were found when Sherry's law partner, Peter Halat, went to their house. The investigations into their death uncovered an amazing web of intrigue both in Biloxi and in the state penitentiary at Angola, Louisiana.

The Sherrys had three children including daughter Lynne. Additionally they had adopted Eric, the son of Margaret's brother. Margaret Sherry was a relentless and public campaigner against crime and vice in Biloxi; Vincent made his living from it. He represented members of the Dixie Mafia, entertaining them at his home, and he was happy to drink in their clubs and go out on fishing trips when he and others were provided with prostitutes.

George Phillips, the United States Attorney for the Southern District of Mississippi, recalled: "I used to say we didn't have organized crime in Mississippi, and I was wrong. The Dixie Mafia has been very efficient and pretty deadly over the years."

The story of the killing of the Sherrys began with the imprisonment of Kirksey McCord Nix Jr for the robbery and murder on Easter Sunday 1971 of Frank Corso, a wealthy grocer in New Orleans's French Quarter. Nix Jr was the son of a lawyer who had made his way up from being the janitor in the Oklahoma House of Representatives to being elected to the House. His mother, Patricia, also a lawyer, married oilman B. B. Kerr after divorcing Nix Sr.

Unfortunately Nix Sr, despite his rank, wealth and position as an appellate judge, had friends among the Dixie Mafia, notably Biloxi's Mike Gillich. When Nix Jr was sent to the Keesler Air Force Base, his father told him to get in touch with the stripclub owner. There, after he had finished his service, he dealt in drugs, rolled punters looking for sex, pimped and ran the badger game.

In December 1965 Nix Jr was charged in Fort Smith with carrying illegal weapons. He was found not guilty but two years later he was a suspect in the killing of gambler Harry Bennett, who was thought to be about to give evidence against

Dixie Mafia members. Who did the actual killing was never proved but it led to two dozen more killings in six states over the next four years.

Another of the Dixie leaders of the time was Jack Hathcock, who ran what appeared to be an ordinary restaurant and dancehall, the Forty-Five Grill near Phoenix City just inside the Mississippi state line. In fact, the restaurant, opened in 1950, was a gambling whorehouse with a reputation for violence towards any punters who complained about crooked games and was a focal point for organized crime including, of course, bootlegging. On 22 May 1964, Hathcock was killed by Carl Douglas "Towhead" White at the Shamrock Motel 100 miles east of Memphis on the Tennessee–Mississippi border. Hathcock's wife Louise claimed she had shot him in self-defence when he was giving her a bad beating. It was actually administered some minutes earlier by White, who was her lover. Charges were dropped.

On 1 February 1966, the legendary reforming, if corrupt, Tennessee sheriff and former professional wrestler, Buford Pusser, killed Louise Hathcock after she opened fire on him when he went to arrest her for robbery at the motel. In turn, White ambushed Pusser on 12 August 1967, severely injuring him and killing his wife, Pauline, as they drove near the Methodist Church, New Hope. Pusser had been lured into the trap after reports of a disturbance near the church. He named four people responsible – Towhead White, Carmine Gagliardi, George McGann and Gary McDaniel – with Kirksey McCord Nix Jr as the contractor of his wife's killers.

Nix was never charged but the others died in relatively short order and legend has it that Pusser was responsible for their deaths. At the very least, on 4 April 1969 White was killed by Berry "Junior" Smith who ran the Old Hickory Grill in Guys, Tennessee, and was one of Pusser's informants. Smith successfully claimed he had killed White in self-defence, but there have been suggestions that Pusser contracted a hitman to deal with his long-time enemy.

Gagliardi's bullet-ridden body was said by some to have been found floating in Boston Harbour but, in fact, he died from a drug overdose while serving a sentence at MCI-Walpole in January 1975, having been convicted of the murder of Joe Lanza whose still-warm body was found in Gagliardi's car.

In 1970 both McDaniel and McGann were shot to death in Texas. Again there were suggestions that Pusser had been responsible but in McGann's case, Ronnie Weeden was convicted of the shooting after McGann intervened in a domestic dispute. Hitman McGann was regarded as responsible for the deaths of Dixie Mafia figures Doris Grooms and George Fuqua, who had been thought to be skimming from the organization. On 21 August 1974 Pusser died near his hometown of Adamsville in a car crash.

Nix Jr's downfall was the Easter Sunday 1971 attack on Corso's home in Lakefront, New Orleans, one of a series of robberies he carried out with Peter Mule who had acted as enforcer for the Carlos Marcello family and John Fulford from Florida. James Knight, who turned prosecution witness, was the driver of the getaway Mustang. Corso was reputed to keep a quantity of cash and possibly drugs at his home. The door was broken with a hydraulic jack but Corso's wife Marion was still up, painting Easter eggs for the children. Hearing the noise she put on the light in the back porch and saw Nix and two others. In the ensuing gunfight, over thirty shots were fired and Corso was killed. Nix was badly wounded, shot in the stomach. Clearly Nix could not be taken to a New Orleans hospital so his then wife, Sandra Rutherford Nix, contacted a friend and he was flown back to Dallas. Unfortunately he was too badly injured to be patched up by a friendly doctor and was taken to hospital. As a matter of course, the authorities reported the gunshot wounds to the police. Nix's 9 mm automatic was found at the Corso house with a bullet jammed in the chamber.

In a display of family solidarity Judge Nix resigned from the bench to defend his son, as did his mother, Patricia Kerr. The case was bitterly contested with allegations that the identification by Mrs Corso had been fabricated by the police. The bullet in Nix's stomach was explained as the result of an attack by a now dead Mafia hitman who had been refused a loan by Nix. The girlfriend of the dead hitman was pressed into service as a corroborating witness.

There was also the difficulty of the flight to Dallas. If Nix had been an innocent victim why did he not go to the nearest hospital? In the absence of Sandra, now killed in a car accident, the hitman's girlfriend supplied the answer that on no occasion should the police ever be involved in such matters. In March 1972 Nix and his two associates were found guilty but the jury voted against the death penalty and they received life "at hard labour". The sentence meant that they could never be paroled. If appeals failed – and they did at both state and federal level – Nix could only receive a governor's pardon. In a way it was the making of Nix's criminal career. Initially he was in Leavenworth serving a five-year sentence and when that was completed he was sent to Angola. He was fortunate in that, in a change of administration in Louisiana, Edwin Washington Edwards was returned to office as the state's governor in 1984. Edwards had been known for his liberal grant of the pardon to criminals who could pay for it. During the previous four years Republican David Treen had put a halt to the system. Now Edwards revived it, naming Howard Marsellus as chairman of the state pardon board. One of the first to benefit was Mitch Schwarz, a career criminal with close links to both New Orleans's boss, Carlos Marcello, and the Dixie Mafia.

Once Schwarz was pardoned it was clear that a pardon for Nix was now possible but it would cost him serious money to get to Edwards. Now he set about making it. From inside Angola, Nix began an elaborate scam on homosexuals by setting up what appeared to be a gay dating agency. With the help of his girlfriend, Sheri LaRa Sharpe, daughter of a Fort Smith brothel-owner, whom he had known since 1965, he conned around a million dollars from lonely men. Aiding and abetting them were Nix's new wife Kellye Dawn, whom he purported to marry in prison, and the law offices of Halat and Sherry.

The scheme was a variation on a theme. There have been many similar scams designed to separate the lonely and lustful from their money. One of the most outrageous was in the 1970s when Ron Reed arrived in Toledo, Ohio, where he went to a fortune-teller, Carolyn Matusak, who had the answer to life's woes for him – her beautiful friend, Kyle Stratton, was due to inherit a substantial fortune. Unfortunately she was on a dialysis machine after a car accident; worse there was a lawyer in the background keeping all visitors from his client's hospital bed. So began a platonic friendship with Ron writing, exchanging photographs and the pair making clandestine telephone calls. When Ron learned that the lawyer was withholding money for operations he took out loans to pay for them. This carried on for years until, when he bought a new car for himself, Carolyn accused him of thinking more of himself than Kyle who, but for her illness, would be his wife. Ron confided in a friend who advised him to go to the police. Sadly the fictitious Kyle had not even been faithful to Ron. She had been in correspondence with at least another twenty men all of whom had been sending her gifts and money.

Nix's variation involved placing an advertisement for a "summer lover" in a local paper and, when it was answered, writing back explaining that the lover, Eddie, was in some serious if temporary difficulties. Could Eddie call collect and explain things? A picture of a handsome young stud was enclosed. The call came through from a rehabilitation programme for first offenders. The victim would speak to a correctional officer who explained that the lover was a decent boy at heart. Eventually the victim would put up the air fare.

Then followed a series of disasters for Eddie, all of which, to keep him out of prison and to get him nearer the victim, required more and more money to be sent. The writer James Dickie, on whose novel the film *Deliverance* was based, lost $17,000 in this way. What was amazing was that all the parts – Eddie, the correctional officer, policemen, social workers, anxious fathers and so on – were played by Nix. And, with variations and refinements, it was successfully repeated time and again. The proceeds of these scams went into an account at Halat and Sherry. Apart from purchasing privileges in Angola, the bulk of the money was to be used to try to obtain parole. Other money was invested in a house on the Gulf Coast, a Trans-Am which Kellye Dawn was allowed to drive, and allowances for both her and Sheri LaRa. Nix would later state that his expenses to buy privileges in prison were $12,000 a month. As for complaints by the victims, the police were not all that interested in the misfortunes of elderly chicken-hawkers. Even had they been, the complicated telephone system in Angola would almost certainly have thwarted their efforts to find out which of the prisoners had been operating the con. It was estimated that over $1 million had been scammed from victims in a four-year period.

In 1985 a federal grand jury indicted Governor Edwards and his brother Marion for racketeering but, if anything, this only increased the number of pardons on offer. Edwards was going to need money to pay for his defence. Then came another blow. Carlos Marcello, Mitch Schwarz's associate, was indicted and now Nix realized there was going to be no pardon for him. He wanted his money back from his lawyers. The problem was that $100,000 was missing from the Halat and Sherry account. Halat went to see Nix and told him that it was Sherry who had siphoned off the money.

The bodies of Sherry and his wife were found at their home at 203 Hickory Circle by Pete Halat and a firm's associate, Chuck Leger, at around 11 a.m. on 16 September 1987. There was no question of murder-suicide nor of robbery. Sherry's still-full wallet was found on his body and his wife's purse, containing slightly under $50 and her credit cards, was intact. Nothing of value was missing from inside the home and there were no signs of theft or a break-in. It was clearly a planned murder.

In addition to shell casings in the room, small pieces of foam were also found scattered around the area from which the shots had been fired. The foam had come from a silencer attached to the barrel of the gun. It was, however, apparent that the killer or killers knew the Sherrys and their movements. The Sherrys had been about to leave for Baton Rouge and were not going to be missed for a day or so.

The problem facing investigators was that, in effect, there were no clues or, for that matter, viable suspects. Halat, as Sherry's law partner, was considered but exonerated. Sherry had suffered from high blood pressure and so had been ruled out of an insurance policy. Halat and the firm would suffer by his death rather than gain from it. Generally lawyers, provided they stay at arm's length from their clients, are not murder targets. Another suggestion was that Margaret Sherry was about to expose a major corruption scandal in Biloxi. She had consistently threatened to run for mayor and, if successful, to shut down the Strip which, for all practical purposes, meant Mike Gillich. If the intended victim had been Margaret Sherry then a possible suspect was Mayor Blessey who stood to lose most from her clean up of vice. The Sherrys' daughter, Lynne Sposito, was told, "Seventy-five per cent of Biloxi thinks Mayor Blessey did it, darlin'. The other twenty-five per cent are related to him." But there was no evidence against him either.

One other line of inquiry was the adopted son Eric, who did not know of his adoption. He seemed indifferent towards his parents' death, which worked against him. He remained high on whatever list of suspects the police had, particularly as there were reports that he had been seen in the Biloxi area on the night of their death. At the Sherrys' funeral Halat announced that, as a tribute to Margaret and her work, he would now run for mayor.

It was Lynne who continued the fight to trace her parents' killer. At one time, when she persuaded the Biloxi Police Department to go to Angola to interview Nix, it seemed as though she might have some success. But although Nix had a suspiciously detailed knowledge of the layout of the Sherry house nothing came of it. The investigation was wound down and the FBI would not take it up. She then hired a private investigator, ex-state trooper Rex Armistead, one time Director of the Organized Crime Strike Force in New Orleans.

It was the killer Bobby Joe Fabian, serving life, who finally provided a lead. In 1970 Fabian had kidnapped and killed George Lee Lennox, the millionaire breeder of Tennessee Walking Horses, which have a particular gait. Lennox was stabbed in his legs with a screwdriver and then shot. The next year Fabian sent the screwdriver as a Christmas present to Lennox's family. In 1970 he robbed two women of jewellery and guns, one of which was used two weeks later in a Louisiana shooting. While on the run Fabian kidnapped two Louisiana officers, Wendell Lewis and Bill Curry, who stopped him for a routine traffic offence, later shooting them both in the legs. For this he received life sentences.

Fabian had been another involved in the gay scam but had fallen out with Nix, whom he believed was taking too many chances. These included the nominal employment of Sheri LaRa whom Halat had "married" to Nix in a telephone ceremony. Halat had also taken her on as a paralegal so she could have unsupervised visits with him.

Now Fabian, rightly, became convinced that Nix had a contract out on him and he went to the police. He was moved to another prison, literally just before another Dixie Mafia man was found in the prison yard with a knife.

Throughout Armistead's investigation, the name of Peter Halat, now Mayor of Biloxi, was in the frame. In the autumn of 1990, Kellye Dawn, who was now seeking to annul her marriage to Nix, pleaded guilty to one count of felony theft in exchange for agreeing to become a witness. She had been indicted on fifteen counts by a grand jury in 1989.

In a nine-month period until the day after the Sherry murders, 345 phone calls were made between Halat's law office and Angola prison but because of the complicated circuit board it was impossible to trace who had made the outgoing calls from the prison.

When on 21 May 1991 the indictment of the grand jury in the killing of the Sherrys was finally handed down, Halat's name was not included. He called an immediate press conference describing this as his vindication and complaining about unfair media treatment. The defendants included Nix Jr, the one-legged John Elbert Ransom, who was already serving a manslaughter sentence and who was said to have been the hitman at a fee of $35,000, and Mike Gillich.

On 11 November 1991 Nix, Ransom and Gillich were convicted of a rolled-up conspiracy indictment that included both the scam and the contract to kill. They received consecutive sentences totalling fifteen years in each case. Once again Halat said that he had been vindicated and threatened to sue WLBT, an NBC affiliate television station in Jackson, Mississippi, for airing a report that said he was involved. It was never actually made clear during the case by the prosecution why Sherry and his wife had been shot.

Gillich finally saw the light at the end of the tunnel and turned state's witness giving evidence against Halat and the actual hitman, a fairground worker Thomas Holcomb, a long-standing partner of "Little" Henry Cook Salisbury who was alleged to have killed a man in an Oklahoman bar for stomping on his Stetson. In 1969 Salisbury had been sentenced to thirteen years for armed robbery and argued, ingeniously if unsuccessfully, he had been prejudiced because, as a white man there had been no negroes on the jury.

In October 1996 Halat was charged with ten counts of racketeering including murder, all connected to the death of the Sherrys. Also charged with conspiracy to murder were Sheri LaRa Sharpe, Nix Jr and Holcomb.

Gillich would tell the jury that he and Halat had discussed killing Sherry and that they had agreed to split the cost. Potential hitmen were John Ransom and Robert Hallal but eventually they settled on Thomas Holcomb at a fee of $20,000. The money was paid over by Glen Paul Cook who went to prison for witness intimidation in the trial. Aged sixty-six he was released on parole after sixteen years. He lasted only two days on the outside before being arrested for domestic violence.

A year later Halat was convicted. The defence case had lasted barely an hour. Nix and Holcomb received life, Halat was given eighteen years and Sheri LaRa five.

Gillich served nine years and after his release he married a former stripper, Frances, whose first husband had been Henry Salisbury. Sheri LaRa Sharpe was released in June 2002 and John Ransom in November the following year. Holcomb, still serving his sentence, died in prison in Beaumont, Texas, in April 2005.

In 2005 an appeal by Halat against his sentence was dismissed on the grounds that, in exchange for an undertaking by the prosecution not to appeal against his sentence imposed below the guideline range, he had agreed he also would give up his right of appeal. He is due for release in 2013. Nix Jr remains in prison.

In January 2007 the five-member Lousiana Pardon Board unanimously refused an application by Bobby Joe Fabian, which was supported by Lynne Sposito, to have his life sentence commuted to thirty-six years, the amount of time served. In 2009 Fabian said, "Kirksey was trying to make a

move on me. Things were rocking back then. You play anybody
short, and that's the last time you play them short. I'm glad I
did something right before I go, but I sure wish some other
people would do the right thing."

Because of the loose structure of the Dixie Mafia there can still
be concurrent kings. In 1983 another king, Charleston club-
owner Paul Mazzell, a father of seven, was convicted along
with Eddie Merriman of the murder of hustler Ricky Lee
Seagraves. The twenty-nine-year-old had been attacked at the
Majik Market convenience store in Ladson near Charleston
on 30 October 1978, pistol-whipped and dragged to a waiting
truck. His offence had been robbing one of Mazzell's drug
dealers.

Seagraves's body was found in a shallow grave on 31
July 1981 after a tip-off by Danny Hogg, one time Golden
Gloves boxer, a bouncer and enforcer for the Dixie Mafia,
then serving time on an unrelated charge. Hogg told the
authorities he had abducted the man on Mazzell's orders.
Mazzell had then killed and buried him. The trial was
conducted with refuted allegations that the prosecution
was brought for political advancement. The foreman of the
jury was the uncle of a State Law Enforcement Division
agent who had worked on the case. Hogg, who had failed
a lie detector test when asked if he had killed Seagraves,
was given immunity, and defence witnesses who had heard
him brag how he had killed the man were not permitted to
give evidence. In particular Hogg's wife Lisa claimed her
husband had come home wearing bloody clothes, which he
had burned in a friend's fireplace. The trial judge allegedly
gave improper instructions to the jury, unchallenged by the
defence. The summing-up had, it was argued, not allowed
the jury to return a verdict of accessory after Seagraves's
death, something which Mazzell admitted and which would
have carried a maximum of fifteen years.

Merriman died in prison but Mazzell, still maintaining his innocence, was turned down for parole on five occasions. He suffered three heart attacks and was released in November 2005. He died six years later aged eighty-two. In April 2008 Hogg was killed when he was hit by a passing box-truck when he was placing a broken-down truck on a wrecker on Interstate 26 near the town of St George.

Mazzell's name also came up in the trial of professional poker player and burglar Clifford Henry Bowen who had been convicted, entirely on identification evidence, of the triple murder of Ray Peters, Lawrence Evans and Marvin Nowlin. The trio had been shotgunned as they sat around a poolside table at the Guest House Inn Motel in Oklahoma City on 6 July 1980. Ray Peters, who was a working partner of Seagraves, was thought to have ripped off Mazzell in a deal involving prescription medication. Bowen's convictions were eventually quashed on 24 June 1986 when it transpired that a police officer, Lee Crowe, who resembled Bowen, had a good reason to kill Peters. Another suspect was a former police officer turned drug-dealer Harold Dean Behrens. He was not retried and died ten years later.

The Dixie Mafia, if it still exists today, has been marginalized to the brink of extinction. Legalized gambling, run by huge out-of-state gaming and entertainment corporations, ruined the monopoly it had in the days when gambling was confined to the Biloxi Strip. Members of Mike Gillich's family nonetheless profited handsomely when they sold their properties to these out-of-state companies.

Many think the "real" Dixie Mafia existed only in the 1960s and 1970s and that its activity in the 1980s somehow does not count. Drug-dealer, pimp and contract killer Bobby Young was convicted of the 1984 killing of John "Big Red" Panzavecchia over a drug deal gone wrong. Young shot him four times in the head and dumped his body in a canal in Broward County, Florida. As a souvenir he took Panzavecchia's Rolex and was wearing it in 1987 when he was arrested over the shooting of Craig Marshall – who survived – in a dispute over a custom-made sailboat. Between the death and his arrest, for a reputed fee of $60,000 Young had also killed, so he admitted, the powerboat racing millionaire Don Aronow, close friend of the then Vice President George Bush Sr. Aronow was ambushed in his white Mercedes outside his offices at 188th Street by a killer in a Lincoln. In 1995 Young pleaded guilty to second-degree murder and received a nineteen-year sentence. He was not required to name those who had contracted him. He died in prison in March 2009. His co-defendant, Ben Kramer, champion powerboat racer, the owner of Apache Powerboats and drug lord, pleaded no contest over the murder and received nineteen years to go with a life sentence for marijuana smuggling. In 2010 he appealed, claiming that he had not been told that Young had named Colombian drug interests as his employers and not Kramer. The appeal was dismissed but Young still has a number of supporters who think that the Colombian connection might be correct.

Back in February 1972 a meeting was hosted in the city courtroom at Biloxi by the newly elected District Attorney Albert Necaise. Present were the mayor, the police chief, the Harrison County prosecutor and the owners of thirteen stripclubs in Biloxi and Harrison County. Also present was the sheriff of Harrison County, thirty-eight-year-old Howard Leroy Hobbs, who had worked his way up from dispatcher to chief of the Gulfport Police Department.

Elected the previous year, Hobbs, described as a handsome, strong-jawed, steely-eyed man of integrity, was regarded as a great white hope to drive vice from the city. At the meeting it was agreed that the clubs would clean up their acts. There would be no prostitution, no B-drinking – when girls solicit punters for high-priced drinks which do not contain liquor – no passion pits, no nudity and no gambling. The arrangement lasted less than a month and so began Hobbs's twelve-year reign of corruption. He was said to have a fatal weakness for a good-looking woman and anyone with money. In time he became a close associate of Carlos Marcello as well as Dixie Mafia figures Jim Blackwell and D. J. Venus III.

By 1978 an FBI report on Hobbs listed some of his sins as frequenting prostitutes, openly associating with Henry Cook Salisbury and other Dixie Mafia figures, engaging in large-scale gambling, using the sheriff's department's helicopter to ferry high-rollers to games and hiring his cousin Louis Feranda as Biloxi's jailer – although a court had banned Feranda from holding a position in law enforcement. But Hobbs was a popular man with the voters and was twice returned to office. Admittedly in 1982 he had taken some steps to deal with the opposition. He was alleged to have been in a plot to kill an opponent who was thinking of running against him – $50,000 had been on offer to kill Gulfport's Chief of Police, Larkin Smith. The next year came disaster. Hobbs was caught waiting for an airdrop of cocaine in an FBI sting.

That year his name surfaced in the trial of James Edward Creamer for the murder of Dewey D'Angelo, one-time owner of Biloxi's Red Carpet Club who, when that closed, ran the Gringo Room. Creamer told the jury he had been instructed to leave the body in Hobbs's jurisdiction so that any investigation into the striptease club-owner's death could be controlled. Another witness, Phillip Cryer, who had helped out in the D'Angelo murder, told the jury how Hobbs was taking $150 a week from striptease club-owners. Despite all this and being under indictment when he ran for a third time for office, Hobbs polled 20 per cent of the votes. Creamer was sentenced to life imprisonment for the D'Angelo murder. Hobbs's friends, Jim Blackwell and D. J. Venus III, also pleaded guilty to conspiracy to murder D'Angelo and were sentenced to twenty years' imprisonment in a deal which allowed them to avoid capital murder charges.

In December 1993, a twenty-eight-count federal indictment was handed down against Hobbs who in May the next year pleaded guilty to racketeering and was sentenced to twenty years' imprisonment with the judge, William H. Barbour, telling him, "You sold your soul to the devil." He served nearly twelve years and died at his home in March 2008. He was seventy-three. The year before his death he had again campaigned for the position of sheriff. "I wasn't as pure as the driven snow," Hobbs told Biloxi's *Sun Herald*. "But I wasn't Saddam Hussein, either."

In 2001 former Louisiana Governor Edwin Edwards received a ten-year sentence on racketeering charges. In 2009 he was refused a pardon by George W. Bush but was released to a halfway house in January 2011. By now the eighty-three-year-old had a new fiancée, thirty-two-year-old Trina Grimes Scott, who had befriended him in prison.

Most recently there have been allegations that the Dixie Mafia, which now requires members to have a day job and so provide an explanation of wealth, is linked to the Outlaw Motorcycle Gang (OMCG) and is still involved in drug distribution and contract killings.

24

The Cocaine War

The first Colombian cocaine-dealer of any note to flourish in the United States was the former pickpocket and prostitute Griselda Blanco de Trujillo, born in 1943. Born in Cali she was brought to Washington, DC, at the age of three. The daughter of a prostitute and turned out on to the streets herself at the age of eleven, she was regarded as totally unprincipled. One story of her early career is that, barely into her teens, she kidnapped another teenager from the barrio. She began dealing in drugs in Washington and later moved her operation from Jackson Heights to Miami.

The bisexual Blanco, known as Muñeca (doll in Spanish) because of her doll-like looks when she was young and before she took to sampling her own drugs, was also known as the Black Widow because of the numerous deaths of her many boyfriends and husbands. She claimed that she shot her second husband, Alberto Bravo, in the mouth when he annoyed her and she was reputed to have killed another. By her first husband she had three sons, Dixon Trujillo Blanco, Uber Esnyder Trujillo Blanco and Osvaldo "Chiqui' Trujillo. A fourth boy, Michael Corleone Blanco, was named after the youngest son in *The Godfather* and became a successful record producer in Miami.

By the mid-1970s, unusually for a woman at the time, she was running her own gang called Los Pistoleros, full membership of which required the candidate to kill an enemy and bring back a finger or ear as proof. It was the Pistoleros who were said to have invented the art of killing from the back of a high-speed motorcycle. One member's speciality was to tape shut the eyes and mouth of victims, drain their blood in the bath and pack the bodies into TV packing cartons. In 1974 Blanco was indicted over possession of 150 kilos of cocaine. She fled to Colombia but returned to operate in Miami seemingly unmolested by the authorities for the next decade. By 1979 she was the best-known cocaine smuggler in the United States. At one time she had an interest in a Colombian factory that manufactured girdles and bras with compartments to hide the drug.

On 11 July 1979 she instigated what would prove to be a turning point in her career, the Dade County Shopping Mall Massacre in the Dadeland mall, Miami. The machine-gunning of two victims and the subsequent shooting up of the car park as the killers fled was the culmination of a war that had been active since the previous November and that had resulted in the death of twenty-four Latin drug-smugglers. Two hitmen got out of a white Ford van advertising party supplies. Armed with automatic weapons they went to a Crown liquor store where Blanco had arranged to meet two drug competitors. Her hitmen shot the two targets, but unfortunately they then chased two liquor-store employees, who had been witnesses, through the mall, pushing aside shrieking little, old blue-haired ladies and spraying bullets. The two witnesses were wounded but survived and the hitmen escaped in a Mercedes. When the police examined the abandoned van they found it was made of reinforced steel. Bulletproof vents came down and abutted against the rear of the door, and six-inch gun ports were drilled in the sides and back of the van. There were machine-guns, two M1 rifles, shotguns, automatic pistols and thousands of rounds of ammunition.

The Dadeland massacre happened, it would appear, either because of the theft of four kilos of cocaine or because Blanco, then in Colombia, did not wish to pay for it, which amounts to the same thing. The Byzantine thinking behind the Colombian drug killings, in which whole families are eliminated, can be illustrated by this shoot-out.

As far as can be pieced together, earlier Herman Jiminez Panesso, who was wanted by the police in New York and was regarded as No. 1 or No. 2 in the Colombian ring running drugs to Miami, had been hit in the face; Jaime Suescan had then strangled Jiminez's fifty-year-old maid who had witnessed the assault. Suescan was then murdered and the Dadeland killings were believed to have been in retaliation for his death. Suescun's immediate boss was Carlos Panello Ramirez who feared that Jiminez would kill him as well and he determined to get the first hit in. Meanwhile, Blanco owed Jiminez money – debts in these circumstances generally die with the creditor – and the girlfriend of Paco Sepulveda, a Blanco man, had been sleeping with Jiminez. It was convenient, therefore, for a number of people that Jiminez should be eliminated.

Whatever the truth, it was the beginning of what were known as the Cocaine Wars.

By the early 1980s Blanco's main gunman was Jorge Ayala, known as Riverita after a character in a Colombian cartoon, who had lead an interesting career. Born in Cali and one of the few literate gunmen of the period, from the age of twelve he was brought up in Chicago where he actually graduated from high school. He became a talented car thief, stealing cars to order for the Chicago chop shops. He also had a sideline in bringing immigrants over from Mexico in batches of five to ten at a price of $1,000 a head. His career really took off around Christmas 1979 when he stole a car which turned out to belong to drug-dealer Fernando Builles and contained $400,000 worth of cocaine. The story goes that Ayala fronted the man and asked for $400 to return the haul. Builles gave him $1,000 and offered him and his friend, Carlos Nossa, $5,000 to drive a truck to Miami. He stayed there working as a small-time enforcer and guard of drug stashes. In 1981 he and Carlos decided to leave Builles and sent their wives back to Chicago to avoid reprisals.

Blanco acquired Ayala in an interesting way. In April 1981 he, Nossa and three other members of his crew were in the Jacaranda nightclub in Miami, when Nossa was warned to get out as a hit was due on a nearby table. Not realizing it was a Blanco hit, Nossa tipped off the potential victims. Realizing they were in serious trouble two nights later the pair met with Blanco promising they would do the hit themselves for nothing. Now Ayala began to work for Blanco and her current common-law husband Dario Sepulveda in their struggle for control of drugs in Miami. Chief among numerous enemies was the short, fat Papo Mejia whose man, Hermanos Granados, had been the subject of the intended nightclub hit.

On Blanco's instructions Ayala kidnapped Granados from the car park of a Ramada hotel, tied him up, locked him in a cupboard and left him to be collected by Blanco's men. In turn, some days later they presented him with a gift. When Ayala opened his present, in the box was Granados. He had been shot, his throat cut and body drained of blood and folded so his bones would fit inside. Within a week Papo Mejia's father was shot and killed in the Midway shopping mall.

Next in line was Marta Gomez, Mejia's mother-in-law. She was kidnapped when she went to Miami's Mercy hospital where Mejia's wife had just had a baby. She was interrogated by Blanco but refused to say where her son-in-law might be, so she was shot in the head and dumped in the canal that ran along the side of Pembroke Pines Road, east of the Everglades. Amazingly, she survived.

Now paid between $20,000 and $50,000 a hit to be shared with his crew, with a similar amount of money as a bonus, Ayala was looked on lovingly by Blanco. Even if the hit failed he was still paid. In June 1981 he received $30,000 after two attempts to kill the Gonzalez brothers failed. One brother survived because Ayala's MAC-11 jammed and when a bomb was planted at the other Gonzalez's home no one was in. She also wanted Ayala to be her next husband or at least lover, something about which Dario Sepulvada was in no position to argue. It was a privilege Ayala declined, later saying, "I told her 'Griselda, I'll kill for you, but that's where I draw the line, because everyone who fucks you ends up dead.'"

Another enemy went down in the following month; however, this time it was not a Mejia man. A funeral notice for rival Oscar Piedrahita's infant son was posted after the child died following a swimming-pool accident. Ayala received $50,000 for shooting Piedrahita in the driveway of his home at Miami Lakes before horrified mourners. And now killing followed killing, including Carlos Nossa because Blanco thought he was turning against her. At least Ayala was not required to do the hit.

On 7 February 1982 Blanco sent Jorge Ayala to kill drug-dealer Jesus Castro who, in an appalling show of disrespect, had kicked one of her sons up the backside. Ayala shot at and missed him as he drove along South Dixie Highway and 168th Street. Instead, he hit his son Johnny who was coming up to his third birthday, killing him outright. The distraught Castro placed the boy's body in ice, tucked three red roses into his red and blue tracksuit and left him behind a Miami mosque. When Ayala reported what had happened, Blanco is said at first to have been annoyed at the botched job but later really rather pleased because of the acute distress it had caused Castro.

When drug-dealers Alfredo and Grizel Lorenzo were late settling their account of $250,000 over the purchase of five kilos of cocaine, on 17 May that year she sent Ayala, Miguel Perez and Carlos Venegas to kill them as an example to others. They found them watching television with their two young daughters. They shot Alfredo where he was and Grizel was chased around the house before she was killed. The elder girl finally managed to telephone her grandmother to come

to them. Later she identified Ayala and Cuban Miguel Perez
who had come to work for Blanco in the previous January. He
was, it was said, a man who would kill his mother for a dollar.
Two months later Ayala returned to Cali where he recruited
his brother Alonso, then a mounted policeman.

Unsurprisingly, by then Mejia had teamed up with two
other dealers to eliminate Blanco, offering $300,000 for her
death. As a result one of them, Edgar Antonio Restropo, was
shot while watching a soccer game at Miami Lakes Drive. The
unlucky mother-in-law of Mejia also went down, this time
permanently. In late August 1982 Mejia was found to be in Las
Palmas in the hills outside Medellin, Colombia. Ayala, along
with Blanco's son Osvaldo, followed him to a bar, threw a
grenade at him and shot him in the leg. Mejia fled and although
Ayala toured the hospitals he could not locate him. Then it
was learned he would be coming through Miami airport and
Miguel Perez was offered $100,000 to stab him to death with
a bayonet. Ayala warned him it was simply foolhardy but on 15
September 1982 Perez went ahead, stabbing Mejia in the chest
as he was met by a little girl in the arrivals area. Again Mejia
survived but Perez was chased and caught. Losing his nerve
Ayala took $80,000 of Blanco's money and fled to Chicago.

It was eighteen months before Ayala heard from her again.
She telephoned him, all sins forgiven and forgotten, offering
him $300,000 if he would return to Miami to dispose of a new
trade rival. But now Miami was getting too hot for Blanco. She
owed $1.8 million to her friend, another female drug-dealer
called Marta Saldarriaga Ochoa and, rather than pay her, had
her killed. The woman's body was found wrapped in a plastic
sheet in a canal in Kendall, Dadeland. Blanco was fortunate. In
an effort to stop the escalation in violence Saldarriaga's father
claimed he alone had the right to vengeance and he declined
to exercise it.

Over the years, many rumours and legends about Griselda
Blanco emerged: she had bought Eva Peron's diamonds and

the Queen of England's tea set; she killed strippers and topless dancers for fun, and once shot a pregnant woman in the stomach; her lover bought her an emerald and gold encrusted MAC-10 as a Christmas present; she had frequent lesbian and bisexual orgies.

The Saldarriaga killing, however, was the end for Blanco in Miami and she moved to California to join her oldest three sons. Osvaldo in particular lived the good life. His Beverly Hills house was rented for $16,000 a month. Every morning a florist would come to spread a blanket of fresh flowers on his pool. In the driveway were a Rolls-Royce, two Aston Martins and a Porsche. He had paid $184,910 for the cars in cash before his twentieth birthday. As for brother Uber, the story goes that he was running around with a Wasp girl in Miami. Her father did not approve of her seeing "a spick": the girl dumped Uber; Uber told Griselda; Griselda had the father shot by her gunman, Jamie Bravo.

Eventually Blanco became addicted to the drugs she had been taking over a twenty-year period, and under her supervision her largely illiterate sons took over most of the trafficking. She switched her base of operations to Irvine, California, where she lived with her youngest son, Michael Corleone Blanco. On 20 February 1985 she was arrested in Irvine on narcotics trafficking charges, reputedly reading the Bible when the police arrived, and in June 1985 she was sentenced to ten years in New York. Now aged fifty and her looks mostly gone, she was serving her sentence in Dublin federal prison near Oakland, California, when she began a correspondence with a twenty-five-year-old minor drug-dealer, Charles Cosby. Soon Cosby began visiting the jail where, it seems, inmates were allowed to wear what they liked and to roam freely. Soon the penis was mightier than the pen and the pair began to consummate their relationship on the stage of the prison theatre. Later Cosby engagingly described his seduction of the woman twenty-five years his senior:

> She hadn't been with a man in six or seven years [until] this young, suave black nigga swept her off her muthafuckin' feet. My thoughts in the back of my head was, "If I come at the bitch in a real way, maybe one day she'll bless a nigga." I ain't come out like, "Well, bitch, I want the hook-up, that's all." I finessed the bitch.

As he hoped, their post-coital talk turned to drugs and Cosby claimed that during 1993 she arranged for him to receive between twenty-five and thirty-five kilos of cocaine supplied by her sons back in Colombia. She wanted him to split the profits from the sale with Michael Corleone. There were persistent rumours she might be extradited to Florida and now their conversation also turned to escape. The first plan involved a helicopter. There had been a number of successful helicopter escapes from American prisons dating back to December 1985 when an alleged murderer, James Rodney Leonard, and two armed robbers were freed by Joyce Mattox. She had hijacked the pilot and had them transported from the Perry Correctional Institution at Pelzer, South Carolina, to a getaway car parked five miles away.

Blanco's next plan was to have John F. Kennedy Jr kidnapped and held hostage against her own release. Fortunately for him Cosby declined to take part and instead told the FBI. She was transferred to Miami where she received a further twenty-five years.

Her three oldest boys, Dixon, Uber and Osvaldo, drew ten years apiece and ended in federal prison in Lewisburg where they met Rayful Edmund III. Edmund, who had set himself the target of being the most powerful drug baron in Washington, DC, was making his money out of importing cocaine for conversion to crack. He bought from the dealer Mario Villabona, one of the first to expand the Cali cartel's horizons from Miami and into the ghettoes of the cities around the United States. Edmund had his comeuppance when a van containing 500 kilos of cocaine stamped with the Cali mark of the scorpion was stopped by a highway patrol officer. Edmund was devoted to his mother, Constance "Bootsie" Perry, who had worked as a pill peddler on the streets and who had been arrested with him and his sisters in 1989. He had pleaded guilty in a forlorn attempt to get their sentences capped.

He met the Blanco brothers in 1990 and the men quickly formed an alliance brokering deals from prison. In 1992 the brothers were paroled and deported to Colombia. Edmund continued working with them, buying 1,000 kilos between January and October 1992.

The prison distribution organization was simple. Edmund III would call someone in Washington from Lewisburg, who would patch him through via a conference call to Osvaldo, then in Medellin, Colombia. Osvaldo would arrange a shipment of drugs into the United States. A courier would go from Washington to Miami to pick up the drugs, which would be brought back to Washington to be sold on the streets there.

According to an indictment lodged in Pennsylvania, two of Edmund's middlemen were Michael A. Jackson and James Marshall "Jim-Jim" Corbin Jr. The pair defaulted on a deal in the middle of the year and failed to account for it to Osvaldo, but Edmund was able to negotiate their safety. This was hardly necessary. Osvaldo Blanco was killed in a Colombian nightclub within a few months. The other two elder sons are also reputed to have been killed.

Then, in 1995, Edmund helped government agents set up a sting that ensnared his own girlfriend and five others. He hoped that this time his cooperation would actually reduce his mother's prison sentence. What greater love . . .

The month before Griselda Blanco's arrest Ayala and another friend, Fernando Garcia, had been refused change for a $20 bill by a bank clerk in Chicago and, pulling out guns, they stole $3,000. It was an inept action because they were filmed on the bank's security cameras. Eighteen months later

Ayala was arrested on a weapons charge in Florida. The police in Chicago were informed and in turn they informed Metro-Dade Homicide that Ayala might be the man they were looking for.

His first case was not a success so far as the authorities were concerned. His brother Alonso had pleaded guilty to the murder of a drug-dealer but when Ayala went on trial he was found not guilty.

Still facing the death penalty Ayala was finally turned by the authorities. Now he would give evidence against Griselda Blanco in exchange for the state not asking for the death penalty against him in the murders he had undertaken for her. He would receive twenty-five years without parole. It was thought she could face the death penalty but it was likely she would plea bargain for a non-capital sentence.

This was when the troubles began. The authorities certainly had a major weapon in their hands but they had overlooked Ayala's undoubted charm, particularly over the telephone. Some people, particularly those who work in boiler-room scams selling fake shares, can operate better over the telephone than in real life. Ayala may not have been able to sell shares but he could sell himself as a sex object. This was curious because, despite an operation to lower his voice, he retained a high-pitched whine. Perhaps this is not so curious: after all, he had met his wife Marisol by telephone in 1994 and although this cannot have been down the line he had impregnated her during a jailhouse visit.

It is always desirable for the prosecution to keep their witnesses sweet and Ayala was moved to a state-county jail facility where things were much freer and easier. Once in the facility he became a frequent caller to the Major Crimes Unit and the Miami-Dade State Attorney's office. The calls, which were more or less on a daily basis, often lasted hours at a time and were made "collect" and recorded on the office telephone bills.

Questions were raised and several secretary cum witness coordinators admitted they had received personal calls from Ayala but none admitted having telephone sex. They had, they claimed, received no supervision or guidance on how they should deal with these calls.

At the other end of the line Ayala, who defined telephone sex as involving masturbation, said the calls had sometimes involved sex and sometimes not. The calls had developed into personal relationships and since Ayala was happy to spread his favours, by February 1998 the women in the office were no longer speaking to each other. They gave a number of reasons – telephone sex, although naturally this had involved the other girls and not themselves, jealousy and long-standing dislike.

Ayala agreed he had discussed opening an escort agency with one of the girls, Raquel Navarro, and sent her a number of $50 money orders to be used to buy lunches. One Christmas he had sent her $150. He lent her $2,000 to buy jet-skis and his son from an earlier relationship took some of the money to her house. He had also talked to another of the girls about getting her a firearm. That woman wanted it to kill a third woman, Sherry Rossbach, who got her husband to drop a Thanksgiving turkey to Ayala in the jail. One of the other girls had discussed the size of Ayaya's penis and finally admitted she had had telephone sex. Why didn't she, Rossbach, flirt with Ayala? Rossbach thought that was beneath her. Suspensions all round followed and the veteran prosecutor Michael Band was called on to conduct a full investigation. That also ended in tears. Rossbach promptly claimed he had touched her breasts after a long period of sexual harassment. Band, vehemently denying the allegations, resigned "for the good of the department". Two girls who agreed they had forged Raquel Navarro's signature on some subpoenas were sacked, as was Raquel herself. Rossbach came out best; she was reinstated.

In February 1997 Miguel Perez was convicted of the killing of Edgar Antonio Restropo. He had run an alibi defence that he had been at home quietly reading the Bible before he played a game of dominoes with his pregnant wife. He had already been sentenced to fifteen years for the stabbing of Mejia. He was released in March 2008.

Actually it was Griselda Blanco who came out best of all. On 1 October 1998 she was allowed to plead "no contest" to three counts: the second-degree murders of Alfredo and Grizel Lorenzo and the attempted murder of Chucho Castro. She was sentenced to twenty years on each to run concurrently. The Dade County Shopping Mall Massacre charges were dropped. She had already had one heart attack in prison and it was hoped that she would not live long. Contrary to expectations she survived. Of course, twenty years did not actually mean twenty years and, released in June 2004, she was deported to Colombia. She was last reported as being seen at Bogota airport in 2007.

Despite all this, in the drug hierarchy Blanco is now regarded as no more than a middle-level trafficker, a floater who moved on the edges of the industry. But, there again, as late as 1976 the Colombian equivalent of the FBI still regarded Pablo Escobar as little more than a mule.

25

The Birth of the Prison Gang

Status in the outside criminal world is no guarantee of an easy ride in prison. Indeed, there is always the danger that, as the gunfighters of the Wild West had found, some young upstart is always willing to try to make his reputation at their expense. One early example was Mickey Cohen (1913–76), the Californian gang-leader, who did badly inside almost from the start. Within the first couple of years of his sentence in Atlanta he had been attacked and severely beaten. So, as prison life has become more violent, groups have banded together initially to provide self-protection societies. They have rarely ended as such.

It is generally accepted that prison gangs originated in 1957 with the banding together of Mexican youths led by Luis "Huerto Buff" Flores at the Deuel Vocational Institute in Tracy, California. Although their aim was initially self-preservation, according to a prison report they soon began to control homosexual prostitution, gambling and the distribution of drugs in the prison. However, the old-time mobster Jimmy Fratianno suggested that the Mexican Mafia, known as "La Eme", the Spanish word for the letter M, one of the most powerful of prison gangs, had been formed in Folsom by a one-legged Irish American, Joe "Pegleg" Morgan, a fluent Spanish speaker who gathered a dozen Mexicans around him. True or not, Morgan, who was born in San Pedro in 1929, had an interesting career. He went to prison in 1946 after beating his girlfriend's husband to death and burying the body. While on remand he switched papers with another man who was awaiting a transfer to a forestry camp and disappeared. Recaptured, he was sentenced to nine years in San Quentin. He was then its youngest inmate. In 1955 he led an eleven-man jailbreak and fled to Utah. In 1976 he was sentenced to a two- to ten-year sentence for drug-trafficking. He died in the Californian State Prison in Corcoran. He had been suffering from liver cancer.

From such acorns do oak trees grow. Membership spread as prisoners were transferred across the state. Recruiting members into a prison gang is simple. If the new prisoner, or fish, wishes to survive he must band together with a group. Even a small group sentenced together will not be strong enough to protect its members. It will be absorbed into one of the major gangs where the rank the street member had on the outside is abandoned and he starts again on the ground floor.

Once released, the prison gang-member returns to the street-gang with an enhanced reputation. Indeed, many young gang-members see imprisonment as a desirable goal. Young members on the street can be used by prisoners to deliver messages and drugs, and also carry out contracts on behalf of the inmates. In return when, rather than if, they receive a prison sentence they will be received into the protection of a prison gang.

There is little doubt that by 1984 Eme had grown into one of the four most powerful prison gangs. It was not long before it and other gangs began to operate outside prison and by 1986 Eme had teamed up with Chinese interests to distribute heroin throughout the United States.

That year the members began to deal in heroin on the streets as well as in prison and by 1988 Eme was thought to have around 600 members and had organized itself on the structure of its role model, La Cosa Nostra. Members who were recruited had been leaders of street-gangs who, in prison, had shown their loyalty – or fear – by killing another inmate. Membership became "In by blood, out by blood", allowing only those who had killed or assaulted a prison officer or another prisoner to join, and a policy that his own blood had to be spilled again before he would be allowed to leave the gang. Members who adopted the Christian religion, disobeyed orders or practised a homosexual way of life were targets for killing.

Any hope the authorities may have had that prisoners were not still controlling gangs on the outside was dispelled in 1995 when the reputed godfather of the Mexican Mafia, Benjamin "Topo" Peters, appeared in court again. In 1980 he had been sentenced to life imprisonment for killing a man in a dance hall. Now Peters and his senior lieutenant, Reuben "Tupi" Hernandez, were charged with conspiracy to murder rivals who stood in the way of the gang's alleged efforts to control the streets of southern California. By now they were involved in a power struggle for control of the organization.

The allegations against Peters, Hernandez and their reputed enforcer, Daniel "Black Dan" Barela and another nineteen suspected members including boxer Raymond Ronald Mendez, one-time sparring partner of welterweight champion Carlos Palomino, were that they controlled prostitution, gambling and drug-dealing in the prisons throughout California. They had, it was said, also been taxing street-gangs for protection. Those who resisted were beaten, kidnapped or killed. Messages had been passed by using false names to rent mailboxes. When a member of the Mexican Mafia made a call from the prison, the person on the other end would set up a conference call with a third party, a common practice amongst the leaders of prison gangs. Hernandez had already been convicted of a triple murder. In 1989 he had undertaken the contract killing for $10,000 of a drug-dealer who had run foul of the organization. After shooting the man point-blank in the head he then killed a young woman and her boyfriend who, by sheer misfortune, happened on the scene.

It was alleged that Benjamin Peters had helped to plot the March 1992 killing of Charles "Charlie Brown" Manriquez, who had assisted in the production of a film, *American Me*, about the Mexican Mafia. Ana Lizzaraga, a gang counsellor who worked on the production, was also killed in October that year because it was considered that the film was disrespectful to the gang. Another count was conspiracy to murder the director, Edward James Olmos. What had apparently upset the hierarchy was that the film features a hero loosely based on the co-founder of the Mexican Mafia, Rudolfo "Cheyenne" Cadena. In the film he is seen being sodomized in prison and, as is often the case, repeats the practice on a young woman after his release. The Mexican Mafia is particularly opposed to homosexuality and these scenes caused great outrage. In the film the hero is killed by his own men but, in life, Cadena was killed in 1972 by members of the Nuestra Familia. He was stabbed some seventy times with home-made knives fashioned out of toothbrushes before being thrown from a balcony. Yet another count in the indictment was that of conspiracy to murder a former member, Donald Garcia, for preaching Christianity while in prison.

The Mexican Mafia had, it was alleged, attempted to impose its control on the streets when, in the late summer of 1993, it sent out an edict that Hispanic gangs in southern California, particularly in Santa Ana and Anaheim, should settle their differences and stop the proliferation of drive-by shootings. It was made explicit that if factions did not comply with the request, members would face the wrath of those behind bars. What would be permitted, however, was the walk-up execution.

By the autumn of 1996 the pleas of guilty from the smaller fry in the case began to trickle in. Three men pleaded guilty on 4 October but thirteen members of Eme were still on trial by the spring of 1997. Their friends were not making things easy for the judge and prosecution. Despite a US marshal on permanent guard in the courtroom, someone managed to carve the "M" symbol on the judge's bench.

In the case *State v Mendez and others*, the lawyers for the defendants argued that, as in biker gang trials, individuals may have committed crimes but the group itself has not. Indeed, the defence claimed that Eme did not exist but, if it did, it was only as a vastly misunderstood social club. One lawyer, Morton Boren, acting for Jesse Moreno, categorized it as a "loose organization of friends and associates concerned about each other's welfare". He maintained that, in any event, his client was not part of "this benign outfit". Unfortunately for this line of argument, Mr Moreno, a huge shaven-headed man, was shown to the court to have a six-centimetre high tattoo saying MAFIOSO on his chest.

The end of the trial came on 30 May 1997 when ten members including Peters, Hernandez and Moreno were convicted and sentenced to life imprisonment. Whether it would end the violence in prison was another matter. Lighter fuel was still being poured on inmates followed by a lighted match tossed on to the soaked victim. Despite Hernandez being under strict security during the trial someone, who has remained unidentified, still managed to stab him twelve times.

The great rival to Eme has been another Mexican-American gang, primarily from the rural areas of Southern California, La Nuestra Familia (LNF). Formed in Soledad in the mid to late 1960s, about ten years after the Mexican Mafia, initially it sold protection to those under attack from Eme. But soon business expanded and it moved into the extortion rackets for itself. When it challenged the Mexican Mafia for control of heroin-trafficking inside the Californian prison system, LNF became the original gang's most bitter enemy. By 1972, the group was reorganized by Robert Rios "Babo" Sosa, known as "The General", a Puerto Rican from Santa Barbara who had a murder conviction overturned and was serving five years for robbery. In that year thirty prisoners died as a result of the war between the rivals. By 1975 LNF had grown beyond the prison walls with an outside regiment established in Fresno.

La Nuestra Familia has operated under a strict constitution with membership on a "once in, never out basis" similar to Eme, also calling for an oath that puts the gang's interests before any others. In 1980, Sosa was deposed – it was alleged he had been ordering needless murders. Two years later the membership was thought to be around the 800 mark. The command structure has a general with supreme power, and promotion is through the ranks of *soldados* to lieutenant. Captaincy is achieved by the number of hits undertaken by the member. LNF has been a leader in establishing contacts with the outside world, passing messages through magazines such as *Low Rider* and *Teen Angel* for wannabes to undertake contract killings.

As their oath states, an LNF member is an LNF member until death:

> If I lead, follow me.
> If I hesitate, push me.
> If they kill me, avenge me.
> If I am a traitor, kill me!

"They" were Eme and Sur 13, a smaller gang of Surenos, principally Mexicans from Southern California under the control of Eme.

Allied to LNF in its war with the Mexican Mafia has been the Black Guerilla Family, begun in 1966 in San Quentin as the Vanguards by George Jackson, a former member of the Black Panthers, who was shot and killed on 21 August 1971 trying to escape from the prison.

An influx of members came from the Black Liberation Army, which had undertaken the 1981 robbery in New York of a Brinks armoured truck in which a guard and two police officers were killed. Over the years it has been the most politically motivated of the prison gangs. From time to time the leadership, seeking cultural unity and the protection of black prisoners, has adopted an almost Maoist attitude. By the mid-1980s there was a clear division between the political faction of the Black Guerrillas and the recruits who had joined to share in the criminal profits. The organization has been controlled by a chairman or supreme commander supported by a central committee.

The Aryan Brotherhood, a white, Nazi-oriented gang formed in the mid to late 1960s in California's Folsom and San Quentin prisons, grew out of the Diamond Tooth Gang who glued bits of broken glass to their teeth. When they smiled, the sunlight glittered off their teeth, making it look as if they had diamonds in their mouths. Later they changed their name to the Bluebirds before becoming the Aryan Brotherhood. By the mid-1970s membership was estimated between 250 and 500. Today membership is thought to be in the region of 30,000 in and out of prison.

At first, the Aryan Brotherhood functioned more or less on democratic lines with every member having a vote – a simple majority to prevail – as to which snitch or defector should be killed or merely disciplined. But with rapid growth such altruistic nonsense withered and died. Within a few years, the Brotherhood had members in all of California's prisons and many of the federal prisons in the United States. Just as the pigs did in George Orwell's *Animal Farm*, so older members realized that it was time for reconstruction.

In approximately 1982, inmates in the California 26 faction met and formed a twelve-man California Council – since reduced to six men – to govern the faction's affairs. The members of the Council then formed a three-man California Commission, which functioned as what has been described as a blasphemous Father, Son and Holy Spirit of violence, murder and death. Commissioners made the big, strategic decisions for the Brotherhood. Under them were the councils, which had five to seven members and which ran the day-to-day operations of the gang.

These three Commissioners were the shot-callers, the Terrible Triumvirate of the Aryan Brotherhood. They decided who would live and who would die and, as the Brotherhood climbed over the prison walls and into the outside world, who would run drugs, who would rob banks, who would extort money. Their power would be absolute. The long arm of the Aryan Brotherhood reached anywhere and everywhere.

The Californian Commissioners were Barry Byron Mills, aka "The Baron", Tyler Davis Bingham and Thomas "Terrible Tom" Silverstein. On 22 October 1983 two guards were stabbed to death in separate incidents by Brotherhood members in the penitentiary at Marion, Illinois. The first came in the morning, when Silverstein was being escorted from the shower to his cell. He stopped next to the cell of Randy Gometz, another member. Two of the guards with him were not close enough and he reached his handcuffed hands into the cell. The third officer, who was closer to him, heard the click of the handcuffs being released and saw Gometz raise his shirt showing a homemade knife protruding from his waistband. It had been made from the iron leg of a bed. Silverstein grabbed it and attacked one of the guards, Clutts, stabbing him twenty-nine times. There was no question of an escape. While pacing the corridor after the killing, Silverstein explained that, "This is no cop thing. This is a personal thing between me and Clutts. The man disrespected me and I had to get him for it." He then went calmly back to his cell. Later he claimed that Clutts had been setting up some Cuban prisoners to kill him. After the murder he was moved to a special cell in Atlanta, Georgia, but was freed by a gang of Cubans during a riot there in 1987. He was recaptured – traded in by the Cubans – and moved to Leavenworth.

Heavily but not exclusively biker-orientated, the Brotherhood developed branches in state prisons in California, Arizona,

Wisconsin and Idaho as well as throughout the federal prison system. In the early 1980s there were incorrect rumours that it was in decline. Instead, it has gone on to be one of the most violent of all the gangs, with activities ranging from extortion and protection to contract killing both inside and outside the prison system. Prior to a riot in the prison at Santa Fe it had no real control of the drug market, preferring to use its power to disrupt. From then on it captured a small amount of the drug market, remitting its share of the profits to the Mexican Mafia.

In April 1972, one hour after La Nuestra Familia member Fred Castillo had been transferred to the Chino Institute, he had been stabbed to death by the Brotherhood's Fred Mendrin and Donald Hale on behalf of the Mexican Mafia. The following December they were sentenced to life imprisonment. It is thought that the murder marked an alliance between the Aryan Brotherhood and the Mexican Mafia. There has also been a loose alliance with the followers of Charles Manson, with some of the women calling themselves Aryan Sisters, but the Brotherhood's pact with the Mexican Mafia in their combined wars against both La Nuestra Familia and the Black Guerrillas, for control of the drug trade, has been of greater importance. Despite this, in 1987 there was an attempt by the Aryan Brotherhood to form an alliance with the Black Guerrillas to kill prison guards, but this was short lived.

In July 1996, when the late New York mobster John Gotti, the "Dapper Don", wanted retribution against a fellow inmate who had attacked him in the federal penitentiary in Marion – the prison once considered the nation's toughest – he knew to whom he should talk. He went straight to the two inmates running the Marion chapter of the Brotherhood and told them he wanted the man killed. They assigned the job to a member and told two other men to let the gang's Federal Commission know about the pending hit.

They got the message out of Marion, and the oral memo moved slowly west until September 1997, when it reached the Administrative Maximum Facility in Florence, Colorado, which was now the deepest, most heavily guarded, most closely watched hole in the Federal Bureau of Prisons system.

Better known as Supermax, the so-called ADX (derived from "Administrative Maximum") is the prototype for the nation's super-maximum-security prisons, designed and managed to isolate the country's worst criminals. It is now the Brotherhood's home office, with at least two senior gang-leaders incarcerated there.

A 110-page federal indictment filed in October 2002 in Los Angeles alleged ADX inmates Mills and Bingham had been able to continue running the gang from inside prisons for nearly a quarter of a century. During that time thirty-two murders were ordered, sixteen of them successful, although Gotti's contract was not. It also alleged that Mills and Bingham had smuggled out a message in invisible ink aimed at started a race war in a Pennsylvania prison. According to the indictment Mills and Bingham also helped the Brotherhood develop many criminal enterprises outside prisons, across the country.

In the subsequent trial at Santa Ana, Brotherhood members apparently saw themselves in a different light, citing as their inspiration thinkers from Nietzsche to Machiavelli. One witness said there was a formal oath that began, "Integrity, loyalty and silence comprise the principal ethics of honor." It was in fact a shorter version of the creed that had surfaced first in 1975 in a report to the Senate Subcommittee on Civil Disorder. It may not quite scan but the sentiment is clear:

> An Aryan brother is without a care,
> He walks where the weak and heartless won't dare,
> And if by chance he should stumble and lose control
> His brothers will be there, to help reach his goal,
> For a worthy brother, no need is too great,
> He need not but ask, fulfillment's his fate.

> For an Aryan brother, death holds no fear,
> Vengeance will be his, through his brothers still here,
> For the brotherhood mean just what it implies,
> A brother's a brother, till that brother dies
> And if he is loyal, and never lost faith
> In each brother's heart, will always be a place.
> So a brother am I, and always will be,
> Even after my life is taken from me,
> I'll lie down content, knowing I stood,
> Head held high, walking proud in the brotherhood.

As usual the defence argued that its clients had only banded together to protect themselves in the violent and racially divided prison system. They also contended that the government witnesses were perjurers whose testimony was bought with cash or promises of parole.

In July 2006 Mills, Bingham, Christopher Gibson and Edgar "The Snail" Hevle were convicted of racketeering and conspiring to murder black inmates in several prisons. The prosecution wanted death sentences for Mills and Bingham, something it believed would itself kill the Brotherhood. The jury, however, was deadlocked over their penalty. The four were all sentenced to life without parole and they went back to ADX.

A year before the indictments were unsealed one of the more dreadful deaths indirectly caused by the Brotherhood was that of Diane Alexis Whipple, a former member of the US women's lacrosse team. On 26 January 2001 she was attacked over a twelve-minute period and killed on the sixth floor of an apartment block by two pure-bred Presa Canarios, which tore out her throat. The dogs, Bane and Hera, were being looked after by two lawyers, Marjorie Knoller and her husband Robert Noel, on behalf of Paul "Cornfed" Schneider, whom they had encountered while legal aid lawyers and had "adopted" as their son. Schneider and Dale Bretches were running a dog-fighting ring from Pelican Bay State Prison. Knoller had taken them for a walk on her own when they encountered Whipple in the hallway. The lawyers' convictions for manslaughter were based on the claim that they knew the dogs were aggressive towards other people and did not take sufficient precautions with the large and dangerous animals. Whether they had actually trained the dogs to attack and fight remained unclear. In August 2010 the San Francisco Appeal Court upheld Knoller's conviction and affirmed her sentence of fifteen years to life. Noel had received a two-year sentence. Both were disbarred. Whipple's civil partner successfully sued for $1.5 million, which she donated to charity.

By then, on 4 September 2003, the dogs' owner, Schneider, had pleaded guilty to conspiracy, racketeering and smuggling as well as to the death of Sonoma County Sheriff's Deputy Frank Trejo. He been shot and killed in a robbery by other Brotherhood members, one of whom, Robert Scully, had been released the day before from Pelican Bay. Schneider was again sentenced to life in prison. This was his third life sentence. The hearing had been secretly rescheduled to protect him from the Brotherhood, who were seriously displeased with him.

Less known among prison gangs is the Texas Syndicate, another Mexican-American gang. It was founded in California in 1974, originally with an all-Texan membership, and established a command structure not dissimilar to those of the other prison gangs. Once released from California the members returned home and were soon rearrested and imprisoned in Texas. Again, at first, the motives were self-preservation but with members becoming increasingly violent they soon expanded to become the biggest single and dominant gang in the Texas prison system. By the early 1980s they were thought to be trying to link with the Aryan Brotherhood.

The Texas authorities had believed that the Aryan Brotherhood, the Mexican Mafia and the Texas Syndicate did not provide any threat to security and discipline in the prison system. They were sadly disabused when, in 1984, a power struggle broke out that resulted in fifty-two gang murders in prisons over the next two years.

Over the years there have been other self-help groups based on nationality, such as the MS 13 or Mara Salvatrucha, again a Californian gang, this one made up of Salvadoran refugees. As the heavily tattooed members were deported they recruited others in Central America until in 2009 it was thought that the gang had a total of around 30,000 members with up to 10,000 in the United States. Because of the gang's excessive violence members were being recruited by the Mexican Sinaloa drug cartel in its long power struggle with Los Zetas.

In 1985 the groups were joined by potentially the most powerful of gangs, the Consolidated Crip Organization (CCO). Until then the membership of prison gangs was generally in the low to middle hundreds each but with the birth of the CCO came the potential to call on up to 50,000 members. It was not surprising that within two years the great rival of the Crips, now called for prison purposes the United Blood Nation – and also referred to as the Bloods or the Red Rags – should enter the market. Curiously, possibly because of internecine struggles over leadership, neither gang has lived up to its potential as an overwhelming force in prison indiscipline and criminality. By now there were a number of lesser and splinter gangs such as the Sindicato Nuevo Mexico, aligned to the Mexican Mafia and which recruited younger members than the senior organization. There is also a small but vicious Burgue Clique also known as Los Carnales, most of whose members have killed police officers and acted as a "hit" group for the Mexican Mafia on La Nuestra Familia members. Another group, the Juaritos, originating in Mexico but principally from Albuquerque, is a strong and violent street-gang whose members have kept their rank and identities in prison. The Juaritos, operating on both sides of the wall, are involved not only in trafficking drugs but also in the smuggling of illegal immigrants. In 1990 it was estimated that there were fifteen prison gangs operating on a local or federal level. This may well have been an underestimate. Other gangs surviving in the prison system in New Mexico alone included the Roswell Group, the South Side San Jose, the White Group, Happy Homes and Los Padillas.

By the early 1990s there had been over 700 prison gang murders, 1977 being a vintage year with some ninety-six killings.

However, by the mid-1990s the prison authorities were confident that the prison gang was almost a thing of the past and, if not, the gangs were confined to one or two correctional areas such as the dreaded Pelican Bay and Corcoran. They were being over optimistic. Indeed, in January 1996 in Z Mod, a Douglas County juvenile jail, such were the hostilities between imprisoned Crips and Bloods that officials said that if the fighting did not quieten down, then instead of being with their homeboy gang, members would be obliged to share cells with their enemies.

In August 1996 there was a series of fights in the Californian prisons, all of which appear to have matched southern Latinos against Afro-Americans. Pelican Bay held the first of the contests on 20 August followed by a similar disturbance at Tehachapi just over a month later. On 27 September the half-hour disturbance at the Californian State Prison, Sacramento, known as the New Folsom, resulted in ten inmates in hospital and one killed by staff gunfire. In the ensuing search fifty-six weapons were found. Initial reports suggested that the Latinos had made an unprovoked attack and fighting immediately spread to ten areas on the yard, spilling into the medical centre and the industries complex. Reports suggested that while the staff were opening fire, the Latinos crawled along the ground to stab their rivals who, if they stood up, were then at risk from the guards.

Meanwhile, there were further problems for the authorities who had apparently neglected to observe the rise of branches of the Crips and Bloods in prisons in Florida. The new umbrella gangs, Folk Nation (with tattoos of pitchforks and six-pointed stars) and People Nation (with tattoos of five-pointed crowns, a top hat and cane), had, according to reports, colonized prisons in thirty-one states. There were reports they were increasing their membership not only among the inmates but also among the prison staff. In 1994 240 separate prison gangs, including Jacksonville's Westside Mafia, were identified in Florida which, two years later, was estimated to have no fewer than another twenty gangs in prisons throughout the state.

By the twenty-first century, the mobile telephone had become another curse of the prison authorities. In 2020 8,600 mobile telephones had been seized from prisoners including one from Charles Manson. One guard was said to have made $150,000 smuggling them into prison.

A regime of isolation seemed to the authorities to be the only option to stamp on prison gangs but like so many other penal policies it does not seem to have worked. In 2011 the *Los Angeles Times* reported that overall there were 1,056 prisoners in isolation in Pelican Bay; all but twenty-six because of gangland affiliations. If an inmate killed a guard the maximum time in isolation was set at five years but overall 300 men had been in isolation for a decade and seventy-eight for more than twenty years. If a man in isolation named other gang-members and provided details of their alleged activities they could be moved to a special yard but their safety, and that of their families on the outside, could not be guaranteed.

26

The Scottish Godfather

For nearly half a century after the Second World War, the King of the Glasgow (and therefore Scottish) Underworld was Arthur Thompson, described by Joe Beltrami, his one-time lawyer, as:

> an impressive-looking figure – about five feet ten inches tall and weighing about ten stones. He was well built, in a not-so-obvious way – his suits were well cut and sober, his ties and shirts conservative. Distinguished looking, his face displayed marks of by-gone conflicts. He had more acquittals than most.

Thompson was born in September 1931. His parents lived in a tenement in Glasgow's North Side and were eventually rehoused in Blackhill. His brothers became pub barmen and bouncers but Thompson had his sights set higher. He wanted to own the pub. In the meantime he worked as a debt collector and enforcer for the then King of the Glasgow Underworld, Morris Mendel, bookmaker, loan-shark and brothel-owner. There were also signs that Chinese interests were opening brothels in part of the Gorbals and they had to be dissuaded. As a result of one fight Thompson was sentenced to eighteen months.

On his release he slowly built a reputation as a hardman dealing with such men as the Gorbals street-baron Teddy

Martin, described as having a ferocious temper and Italian looks that drove women wild. He and Martin had an uneasy relationship. On the upside, in 1954 Thompson engineered Martin's escape from Peterhead prison in Aberdeenshire.

While Paddy Meehan, a noted safe-blower who had learned his trade from Glasgow's legendary Johnny Ramensky, was collecting Martin in what was the first successful escape from the jail, Thompson set up a diversion. He arranged for prison clothing to be smuggled out of Glasgow's Barlinnie prison and had it marked with Martin's Peterhead number. Once Martin was out and drinking in a local hotel, Thompson rang the police in an anonymous call telling them that Martin was hiding in a loft in Blackhill. The police found the clothing there and presumed Martin must already be in Glasgow. Roadblocks were removed in Aberdeenshire and it was safe for Martin to travel south.

Thompson's efforts to acquire the necessary capital to build his own empire received a blow the next year when he and Meehan blew a series of safes at the Commercial Bank in Beauly, near Inverness.

The raid was not a success. There was little in the six safes and the pair took only just over £400. On the way back to Glasgow they stopped for petrol and the garage-owner took the registration number of their Humber Snipe because "it was not the sort of car one usually associates with such men". Worse, Thompson had dropped his house key in the road outside the bank. Meehan received six years and Thompson half that.

Six years later his relationship with Teddy Martin went sour and on 25 March 1961 Thompson shot him. Principally because they had learned to handle explosives in the mines, Scottish safe-breakers were in great demand in London and the south and Thompson, Meehan and Martin were offered the chance to take part in a raid said to be worth £1 million on the Westminster Bank at the junction of City Road and Old Street. Meehan and Martin had been down for a reconnoitre. Now

Thompson was expected to put up his share of the expenses and he offered Martin a £100 note, then rare currency, in a public house. Martin took umbrage, claiming that Thompson was trying to set him up. The £100 note could have come from a robbery and its serial number traced if Martin had tried to cash it.

A week before the robbery was due to take place Thompson shot Martin in Meehan's flat. Martin was lucky. Meehan's wife Betty was in the next room and came rushing in. According to the Bushido code of honour – practised by the Japanese samurai – under which Thompson operated when it suited him, Martin, bleeding heavily, could not now be touched again. The standard practice would have been to dump Martin elsewhere and leave him to die. Instead, Meehan called an ambulance and Martin was taken to hospital in a coma. Quite properly, when he revived he could not say who had attacked him other than it was a man in a mask, about six-foot-two and with a cockney accent. No charges were brought but it was clear Thompson had effectively disqualified himself from the London bank job and new talent had to be found.

In fact, Thompson was well out of it. On 23 April 1961, Martin, now fully recovered, was caught in flagrante when an office worker heard the safe being blown. Meehan stayed in London looking for another job. He took one put up by his London contact, Billy, at the Edmonton branch of the Co-operative Bank and was standing over the safe when the police walked in. He received eight years and Billy five. He always maintained he had been grassed by the woman with whom he had been staying.

Safely back in Glasgow, Thompson, well taught by Mendel, began to expand his interests. He would keep his eye out for profitable businesses – sawmills, garages, corner shops, and pubs – and would offer to buy a share. The arrangement was usually reasonably satisfactory to both parties. The owner received a fair price for half the business, a wage and a share of the profits. He also had readymade protection.

By 1966 Thompson was, however, in the middle of a twenty-five-year war with the powerful Welsh family from Blackhill. First, Patrick Welsh and his main man James Goldie died when Thompson bumped their van off the road with his Jaguar and they crashed first into a wall and then a lamppost. Despite eyewitness evidence from two off-duty police officers, Thompson was acquitted after the original charge of murder was reduced to unjustifiable homicide after claims that he had not been the driver. There was an almost immediate reprisal. The following August, Thompson and his mother-in-law, Maggie Johnstone, climbed into his MG, parked outside his house in Provanmill Road. As he started the car there was an explosion and Johnstone was killed. The bomb which killed her had been placed under the passenger seat because it was thought that Thompson had a chauffeur. Three of the Welshes were acquitted.

In July 1967 Thompson's wife Rita led a raid on the Welsh family's home and went to prison for three years for the invasion in which Patrick Welsh's wife was stabbed in the chest. The police, if not exactly frightened of Thompson, were careful. One senior officer sent his family away during the prosecution for the deaths of Welsh and Goldie and another emigrated immediately after the case.

Just how friendly he was with the London teams depends on who is telling the story. Certainly when the robber Robert "Andy" Anderson got over the wall during the Ronnie Biggs escape and turned up on the doorstep of Atlantic Machines in London's West End, run by Eddie Richardson and Frank Fraser, the latter was able to turn to Thompson for help. Within forty-eight hours Thompson met Fraser and Anderson in Edinburgh and hid Anderson for months until he developed itchy feet and was sent to Bobby McDermott, the then king of Manchester.

As for the Krays there is the story that when Thompson heard they wished to see him he walked into their Regency Club in Islington, produced a shotgun, and said, "You'll no' forget me now." On the other hand police files at the National Archives show that he was regarded as a close friend and that he had possibly killed George Cornell in the Blind Beggar on their behalf.

In 1968, on remand awaiting trial for a warehouse burglary, he was called into the prison governor's office and introduced to MI5 officers who showed him his file, which included details of his involvement with Protestant loyalists in Northern Ireland. His biographer Reg McKay says Thompson was now blackmailed into becoming an informer if he did not wish his file to fall into the hands of the IRA, something that would have meant certain death. He served two years of the four-year sentence, passing on information while inside and later from the streets.

The party line is that Thompson was never at home with drug-dealing but he was sucked into it through his son, Arthur Jr – known in the press as the "Fat Boy" and by the Glasgow underworld as "Arty" and sometimes "Arty-Farty" because of his habit of breaking wind – and some of his London contacts. In 1985 the Fat Boy, who ran what was known as the Barlanark Gang, went down for eleven years on heroin-dealing charges while maintaining he had been framed by the Glasgow villain "Blind" Jonah McKenzie. For a time the Fat Boy was able to get his cut of profits while inside but he had never been overly popular. By 1991 it was thought the gang was making in the region of £200,000 a week but then it fractured and his cut dried up. He was released on a parole plan that year and came out of prison vowing to kill the five men who, he said, had ripped off his earnings.

On weekend home leave he returned to the heavily fortified family home, known as the Ponderosa after the ranch in the television Western *Bonanza*, and on 18 August arranged to have dinner with his sister at an Italian restaurant in Glasgow. At the last minute he went to the Café India, a smart Indian restaurant, with his mother and his common-law wife, Catherine. Shortly before he arrived a man, said to be Paul Ferris, a former collector for Arthur Sr but who was now estranged from the family, had approached the manager, asked if there was a Thompson there and insisted on searching through the 200 or so customers before he was satisfied there was not.

After his meal the Fat Boy walked back to the fortress, had a word with his father and walked to a nearby property to see whether his brother Billy was taping a film on his video-recorder. He rang the bell and a woman who answered the door saw the Fat Boy staggering away. He had been shot. One bullet had grazed his cheek, one fractured two ribs but the third had hit his heart. His last words were, "I've been shot, hen." The family did not wait for an ambulance. He was put in a car and driven to hospital where he was pronounced dead on arrival.

The police and Arthur Thompson Sr had various theories about the killers. To the police it must have smelled like an inside job. Who knew at which restaurant Arthur Jr would be? Would outsiders really linger outside the well-protected home awaiting his return? Could a message have been sent to them from the time he left the restaurant?

The Fat Boy's funeral was graced by lawyers, MPs and entertainers, but the real *coup de théâtre* was provided by Arthur Thompson. On the way to the cemetery the cortège passed a car in which were the bodies of Joe "Bananas" Hanlon and Robert Glover, two of the men Thompson suspected of killing his son. Both had been shot in the head with a .22 pistol and a second bullet had been fired into their anuses. "What a stroke and what a send off for the boy," said Frankie Fraser approvingly. Overall Hanlon had not led a lucky life. A car he had once owned had been blown up; an ice-cream van from which he sold heroin had been torched; and he had been shot twice, once in the penis.

Naturally, there was a police swoop on Fortress Thompson but it came to nothing. Arrested, questioned and released, the family returned to what had become a compound kitted out with surveillance cameras and floodlighting.

That left the third suspect, Paul Ferris. He was duly arrested and charged and in 1992 went on trial. The thread running through the prosecution's case was that Ferris, Hanlon and Glover had all been involved. Much of the evidence against Ferris came from a fellow-prisoner and supergrass, Geordie Dennis Woodman, who told the jury Ferris had confessed to him. Woodman was not an ideal witness. He, his wife and her brother had been involved in a particularly nasty kidnapping of a farmer in Dumfriesshire in an effort to make him draw money from various bank accounts.

How had Ferris made the confession? According to Woodman by shouting through the bars to him in the next cell where he had been put after escape tools had been found in a previous one. They had been planted, he said. Cross-examined by Donald Findlay QC, the flamboyant director of Glasgow Rangers Football Club, Woodman told the tragic story of the death of his children in a road accident. It was something for which the court and jury naturally had sympathy for several days until Findlay revealed that the children were alive and well, and living in England. Indeed, Woodman had sent them a Christmas card from prison after their "death". Most of his evidence could be matched, word for word, from reports of the death of the Fat Boy found in the Scottish editions of the *Sun* newspaper. As the days went on Woodman's evidence became more and more wild including an allegation that Ferris's solicitor had tried to bribe him. By the end of his two weeks in the witness box he was completely discredited. The other evidence did not seem much more reliable, but a former girlfriend of Robert Glover told the jury that after the killing of the Fat Boy, Glover had come to the caravan where she was living with another man and sat for some hours – in the man's absence – telling her of his and Ferris's involvement.

Nevertheless, Ferris – "clever, articulate and passionate" said one trial-watcher who added that "the most convincing accused are either those who are innocent or are those who are guilty but who know the police have manufactured the evidence against them" – had some problems to face. For a start he had been in the wrong city at the wrong time.

He came from a spectacularly criminal family. As a child he had been bullied by the Welsh family and after serving a number of short sentences worked for Thompson collecting debts. He had, however, moved to London to "repot" himself, as one lawyer described it. But, on the day of the killing he had flown to Glasgow to buy clothes for his child. He had heard of the shooting and had swiftly absented himself, hiring a car and driving back to London. His defence was that the third man had, in fact, been Jonah McKenzie, partially blinded by Hanlon in May 1991 as a reprisal for the attack on the man's ice-cream van. McKenzie, a staunch Thompson man who had picked up seven years when the Fat Boy had received eleven, denied the allegation.

It was also part of the defence to show that Hanlon and Glover were innocent and a substantial number of witnesses came forward to provide, if not a complete alibi, at least a partial one. The trial lasted fifty-four days and cost £4 million.

At the end Ferris was acquitted of the Fat Boy's murder and also of supplying drugs, the knee-capping of another Barlanark gang-member, Willie Gillen, and the attempted murder of Arthur Thompson, whom he was said to have tried to run down in 1992 outside the Ponderosa, now heavily barricaded with steel doors. Thompson gave evidence for the prosecution against Ferris, something which showed how far he had fallen from the criminal pantheon.

The *Daily Record* announced there was a £30,000 contract on his life. Ferris went to Manchester where he was fined for a small drugs offence and in early 1997 he was arrested in London and charged with dealing in arms, alleged by the prosecution to be on their way to be designer accessories for the black Manchester drug gangs. He received ten years, reduced on appeal to seven. While in prison he wrote *The Ferris Conspiracy* with journalist Reg McKay. After his release he went into the security business and with McKay wrote a number of further books.

In the ensuing troubles his family did not escape unscathed. Willie Ferris, his father, required 100 stitches after being beaten with a hammer and a baseball bat. His car, bought on a disability pension, had its tyres slashed and was later set on fire.

On his release, Woodman was given a new identity, but hitmen traced him to the south of England, where he and his girlfriend survived a gun and knife attack.

Towards the end of his life Thompson began seriously to lose his grip and in times of stress gave way to what an associate called "wet farts", something of which the great man was deeply ashamed. He had committed the cardinal sin of abandoning members of his team when they went to prison and with this his popularity and safety waned. In November 1989 he was shot while washing his car in front of a lock-up garage. He booked himself into the private Nuffield Alpine Clinic where he told the doctor he had injured himself when a drill bit sheared off. The same year his daughter, Margaret, died of a heroin overdose. It was put about she had choked to death after a drinking bout but her dealer boyfriend, Gerry "Cyclops" Carbin fled to Spain and did not return until after Thompson's death. In turn he died the next year from necrosis.

Thompson died in March 1993 following a heart attack. He was sixty-two. His funeral cortège was suitably spectacular. Frank Fraser flew up from London to attend, bringing with him a wreath made up of 200 roses in the form of a heart. The funeral itself was not without its moments. Someone had planted a fake bomb in the grave and this had to be removed before the burial could take place.

But that was not quite the end of the Thompson story. His youngest child, Billy, despite lacking the acumen of his father and elder brother, set out to restore the family pride and position. Early in his career he had served two sentences, one of eighteen months for carrying a harpoon gun, telling the court on both occasions that he was in fear of his life. He survived a stabbing in 2000 and then in 2001 Robert Morrison and Christopher Irvine were found not guilty of the attempted murder of Billy, who was now a heroin addict. They were, however, found guilty of assault and sentenced to eight and five years respectively. A neurosurgeon gave evidence that Thompson's skull was like a shattered eggshell. At the time of the trial he could only respond to the simplest commands.

His condition was not expected to improve but gradually it did, so much so that by 2006 he was well enough to stand trial for the mugging of an old age pensioner. He was acquitted following a non-proven verdict. In July 2008 it was at Thompson's house that fellow drug addict John Morrison Jr died following an overdose. He had been released that morning from prison.

27

Brink's-Mat and After

In 1983 there were two spectacular robberies in London. The first, over the Easter bank holiday, was when a team led by John Knight carried out what came to be called the Great Bank Note Raid: £7 million was removed from the Security Express headquarters in Curtain Road, Shoreditch, east London, when six masked bandits burst in about 10.30 a.m. One guard had petrol poured over him and was threatened that, if he did not give them the combination for the safe, he would become a human torch.

As with the Great Train Robbery twenty years earlier, it was a job that had been on offer for some years and had taken a considerable time in the planning. The Security Express building had been known as Fort Knox and was thought to be a virtually impregnable fortress. The underwriters put up the then staggering sum of £500,000 as a reward, but it was police work that paid off. One of the men involved had been under observation for some time and, when he was being questioned about another major robbery, he told the police he had stored money from the Security Express robbery at his home. This led to the arrest of Alan Opiola, who was later given three years and three months with a recommendation he serve this in police custody. He became a principal witness against the Knight family.

Ronnie Knight, once married to the actress Barbara Windsor, herself the former girlfriend of Charlie Kray, was not charged at the time but on 10 June 1985 John and James Knight, Ronnie's brothers, and Billy Hickson were three of five men jailed for the robbery. John Knight received twenty-two years and James eight for handling stolen monies. Hickson received six.

With his new wife, Ronnie Knight went to live in Spain, one of the so-called Famous Five wanted men unwilling to return to Britain. It was reduced to four with the conviction of Frederick Foreman, a long-time friend of the Kray twins, who in 1990 received a nine-year sentence for handling part of the Security Express money. On 2 May 1994 Knight, in some disgrace on the Costa because his high profile, eventually returned to Britain courtesy of the *Sun* newspaper, which, it was said, had paid his family up to £185,000 for his story. He was charged with robbery and dishonest handling. For months gossip circulated in the underworld that Knight was going to tell all in return for a deal, and what a story that might have been. In the end, however, he remained staunch and received five years for dishonestly handling part of the proceeds. The remaining three of the most wanted British men in Spain were Ronald Everett, once also a close friend of the Krays, John James Mason, who was acquitted of conspiracy in the £8 million robbery of the Bank of America in 1976, and Clifford Saxe, one-time landlord of the Fox pub in Kingsland Road, Hackney, where the Security Express robbery is said to have been planned. Saxe died in 2002 while awaiting extradition, and then there were two.

Within six months the Security Express robbery had paled into insignificance. On 26 November 1983 at 6.40 a.m. the biggest ever robbery took place when £26 million in gold was lifted from the Brink's-Mat warehouse on the Heathrow trading estate. Its ramifications would run for nearly two decades. Again, the guards were threatened – one with castration, others had petrol poured over them, yet another was coshed for not producing keys with sufficient speed. The gang drove off with 6,400 bars of gold waiting to be sent to the Middle and Far East. It was clearly a job executed with help from the inside. The premises had been opened with a key and the gang knew the guards' names as well as the workings of the vaults and locks.

It was only a matter of days before the police latched on to the last guard to arrive that morning – Tony Black – who had missed the robbery because he was ten minutes late for work. Black confessed. His sister was living with Brian Robinson, one of a number of villains over the years to be known as "The Colonel". Black identified two more of the team: Tony White and Michael McAvoy.

In December 1984 Robinson and McAvoy received twenty-five years each. White was acquitted. Later, there was said to be £50,000 on offer to free McAvoy and Robinson. Black, who had given evidence for the Crown, was handed a six-year sentence. "Never again will your life be safe. You will be segregated at all times and you and your family will forever be fugitives from those you so stupidly and wickedly helped," said the judge, the late Mr Justice David Tudor Price.

There was still the problem for McAvoy of how to protect his share of the loot. A very large amount of gold was missing and in the way of things this could attract a great number of high-quality predators. It was essential for him to have, on the outside, people whom he could trust to help him. Two such people were Brian Perry, who ran a mini-cab agency, and John "Little Legs" Lloyd, who lived with a woman called Jeannie Savage. In turn, they recruited Kenneth Noye, a man with a prodigious work ethic from a respectable background but who had drifted into crime, beginning with receiving stolen cars. By the time of the robbery he had a haulage company as well as a long criminal record involving assault, theft and receiving as well as firearms offences. One attraction was that he had legitimate haulage and building businesses to cover his activities. Unfortunately, he was also, at the time, the subject of a completely unconnected Customs and Excise surveillance operation.

One step further down the line came John Palmer, then in his thirties, who had set up a small bullion-dealing firm, Scadlynn, on the outskirts of Bristol. His co-director, apparently in day-to-day charge, was Garth Chappell. By 1984 Palmer was effectively out of the business and running a chain of jewellery shops in the southwest and Wales. The gold stolen from Brink's-Mat had been in marked ingots of extremely high quality. It could not be offered to legitimate dealers and instead it was Noye's intention to launder the gold through Scadlynn. First, it was essential to remove the serial numbers from the bars. To this end he employed Palmer, who had his own smelter.

It is not difficult to mix and then separate one metal from another and in essence the scheme worked as follows. The recast gold, now without its serial numbers, was transported to Scadlynn, mixed with copper and silver and, as apparent scrap, it was sent to the Assay Office for weighing and taxing. Now thoroughly respectable, it could be sold to bullion dealers who would reverse the process and clean out the impurities.

Before this, however, they needed to provide the appropriate paperwork for the Assay Office and therefore to purchase legitimate gold bars. On 22 May 1984 Noye went to Jersey with £50,000 in notes as a deposit and discussed with the Charterhouse Japhet Bank the initial purchase of eleven one-kilo bars. On 30 May he paid for the bars and deposited them in a safe deposit box in a Bristol branch of the Trustee Savings Bank. The price was around £100,000. Uneasy about the deal, Charterhouse informed the police.

Now Noye was in a position to move eleven bars a week to be resmelted at Scadlynn. Better still, he could provide legitimate paperwork to cover the transactions. He would sell at the going scrap rate plus VAT. As was often the case with smelting frauds, there was a separate scam on the VAT, which was not declared and which Scadlynn was allowed to keep. The money from the sale itself was deposited in the Scadlynn bank account at the local Bedminster branch of Barclays, whose manager must have thought all his Sundays had come at once. In time it was withdrawn in cash and by the end of the year £10 million had been transferred to Noye, Perry and Lloyd.

Noye moved his share to the Bank of Ireland in Croydon. Jeannie Savage and McAvoy's girlfriend, Kathy Meacock, used the same branch, alternating deposits with the others. The bank did not think to report the transfer of such large sums. Perry now, and rather confusingly, recruited Gordon John Parry, whose father had been involved with Frank Fraser in the 1940s, who was dealing in the property boom of the time. Earlier Parry Jr had served three years for a drugs charge, against which he had been defended by Michael Relton, a Westminster-educated solicitor who had a practice near Horseferry Road Magistrates Court. £793,000 from Scadlynn was laundered by Relton and Parry through the Bank of Ireland in Balham to Douglas in the Isle of Man where there was another branch. In all £1.5 million went through the Balham branch.

The surveillance operation on Kenneth Noye ended in disaster. An undercover police officer, John Fordham, clad in a balaclava helmet, was stabbed to death in the grounds of Noye's home at West Kingsdown in Kent. Noye, charged with the murder of Fordham, gave evidence that: "I just froze with horror. All I saw when I flashed my torch on this masked man was just the two eye holes and the mask. I thought that was my lot. I thought I was going to be a dead man." He stabbed Fordham eleven times.

In November 1985, he and Brian Reader, who was with Noye at the time, were acquitted of the murder. However, in July of 1986 both were convicted of handling the Brink's-Mat gold, along with Garth Chappell. Reader received nine years and Noye, whose defence was that he was a gold smuggler and VAT fraudster as opposed to being a thief and receiver, ended up with fourteen. There were still plenty of figures in the underworld who believed that his defence was correct. No Brink's-Mat gold was ever found on his premises and, although £100,000 of gold was discovered, tests showed this could not have been from the Brink's-Mat robbery. Garth Chappell received ten years.

The convictions of Noye and Reader were the greatest successes the police had on the Scadlynn side of the operation. The next year, John Palmer, who had been invited to leave Spain, was put on trial at the Old Bailey, charged that he conspired with Noye and Reader dishonestly to handle the gold. He was acquitted and went to live off the proceeds of his timeshare business in Tenerife.

Nor was there any greater success in the case of John Fleming, who was also alleged to have been involved in cleaning up the proceeds from the Brink's-Mat robbery. He was deported from Florida in 1986 and, in March of the next year, with evidence given against him by a new supergrass, lawyer Patrick Diamond, charged with dishonestly handling nearly £500,000. At the committal proceedings at Horseferry Road Magistrates Court, he was found to have no case to answer. Fleming told reporters, "I feel a great relief. It has been a bad year," before he went to Spain where he was involved in a car accident and again deported.

As for McAvoy and Robinson, they were awaiting the hearing of their appeals when Fordham was killed and realized that, without a substantial sweetener, any slim chance they had of getting a few years off their twenty-five-year sentence had evaporated with his death. They put up a deal to Deputy Assistant Commissioner Brian Worth. If they gave back half their share of the bullion then perhaps a good word could be put in at the Court of Appeal. The proposition foundered when they learned their friends on the outside holding the funds would put up perhaps a million or two, but nothing like the amount required for any possible reduction. McAvoy, in particular, was annoyed. He wrote from Leicester prison in November 1986 that he was considering informing. He was not going to be "fucked for my money and still do the sentence". But when it came to it he was not prepared to grass.

The Brink's-Mat laundering trials continued into the 1990s. By their end several of those convicted early on in the proceedings, such as solicitor Michael Relton who had received twelve years, had been released. It was thought, at one time, that he too might give evidence for the Crown but, perhaps wisely, he declined the opportunity.

By 1993 Noye was in Latchmere House in Richmond, Surrey, once a remand centre for boys but now a resettlement centre for villains coming to the end of their sentences. The regime was fairly relaxed with the men allowed out to work during the day and given extensive weekend leave. During this time, it was believed that Noye had been involved in a plan to import cocaine from the United States as well as laundering dirty money. Unfortunately it appears that a detective may have tipped off one of Noye's partners in the operation, as a result of which a shipment of drugs was cancelled. It is said that Noye paid a modest £500 to the police officer for the information.

It was not the first time that Noye had been involved in allegations of bribery since his imprisonment. In 1988 he was said to have offered £1 million to a senior officer who, in turn, was cleared of any misconduct.

In the end it was through the civil courts that Brink's-Mat saw a return on its losses. The proceeds had been shrewdly invested by Michael Relton and others. Many of the fifty-seven defendants in the civil proceedings settled the claims and so preserved some of their assets. Two of them who fought on were Tony White, acquitted of the robbery, and his wife. With the lesser standard of proof required in a civil case, Brink's-Mat was in a strong position. Now it relied on White's background, his propensity for violent crime and his association with two convicted Brink's-Mat robbers to show that in all probability he was involved in the robbery itself. There was also the question of alleged admissions made by him to the police when he was interviewed. There was a further problem for the Whites. Tony White had been released from prison on licence on 8 April 1983 following a twelve-year sentence for conspiracy to rob. Since then, until the robbery, he had been in receipt of unemployment benefit, raising the question as to how he was funding his lifestyle.

He was clearly associated with some of the other suspects. On the night of the Brink's-Mat robbery the Whites had been to a club, the Studio, in New Cross Road, London, which was run by Gordon Parry. Also, there had been a further twist to the negotiations carried out by McAvoy to return some of the millions in exchange for a reduction in his sentence: Tony White had been asked by McAvoy to act as go-between and he had met two senior police officers at the National Theatre in London on 25 March 1986. Nothing came of the meeting but this good turn rebounded on White. Brink's-Mat said that this was corroboration that he had direct personal knowledge of the robbery. In the meeting it was said that White admitted he knew the gold had been converted into cash. Worse, Brian Perry – convicted of conspiracy to handle stolen goods – had also been present at the meeting, apparently at White's own request. This, it was said, showed that White was the trusted helper of a robber and an associate of a launderer and that the money that he handled was his and/or McAvoy's share of the takings.

There is no doubt that, after the robbery, the Whites had been successful investors in the property market. In March 1985 he had purchased a property in Brockley Road, south London, for £33,000 and sold it two years later for more than double. In May of 1985 he purchased another property in Beckenham, Kent, for £146,000 and again doubled his money, as he did with a third property also bought in May 1985. In the March of that year he had paid £800,000 into bank accounts in Dublin. When he was arrested in October 1989 in Spain for a currency offence he was carrying approximately £125,000 in cash. All this came about, said Brink's-Mat, because of his involvement in the robbery.

In the end, it was the verbal admissions in the interviews on 6 December 1983 that did for the Whites. Goodbye £26 million, for that, plus a little change, was the amount the proceeding judgement decreed that Tony White should pay Brink's-Mat. Mrs White was ordered to pay just over £1 million.

Most of the others involved in the Brink's-Mat case also failed to retain all their gains. In January 1993 Mick McAvoy was ordered to make an interim payment of over £27 million, as was Colonel Robinson. Kathleen, McAvoy's second wife who had married him in the gymnasium of Leicester prison, was given an eighteen-month suspended sentence for dishonestly handling £300,000 of the money. She had been living in Bickley, Kent, with her Rottweilers – called Brinks and Mat. Tony Black, the security guard, also had an order for £27 million made against him. He was living in the witness protection programme with, it was said, a £1 million contract on his head. John Fleming, who had been discharged by Norma Negus, the stipendiary magistrate at Horseferry Road, had an order for over £11 million made against him in Florida in October 1992. Gordon Parry, who received nine years for laundering part of the money at a retrial, had an interim order of £12 million made against him. Brian Perry, who at the time of his trial was being minded by the legendary, if now ageing, "Mad" Frank Fraser, was ordered to repay £5 million. Michael Relton was ordered to hand over £12 million and the documents relating to the property companies through which money had been laundered. Patrick Diamond received nine months for dishonestly handling part of the proceeds and, in 1992, a Florida court gave judgement against him for over $9 million. The orders and settlements did not, however, stop some of the players from continuing to lead handsome lifestyles. After his release Relton, for example, could be found in fashionable London restaurants.

Nor were Tony White's troubles over by any means. After his acquittal on the Brink's-Mat robbery he had also been acquitted at Croydon Crown Court on a charge of involvement in a very substantial drug-importation conspiracy. Then, in Bristol in 1996, when faced with three separate indictments all involving drugs, he pleaded guilty to two charges and was remanded in custody for sentence. The other charge remained on the file.

The investigation had begun in April 1994 when a number of the defendants had been seen and photographed with Belgian Louis Dobles outside London's Tate Gallery. In January 1995, when the *Frugal*, a catamaran chartered by Dobles, landed at Pevensey there were about a hundred police and customs officers waiting on the beach. No drugs were found on board and Dobles was also missing. The beach was searched and ten plastic-wrapped bales containing 309 kilos of cocaine were retrieved along with a wet suit, mobile telephone and petrol cans. Later, a pick-up truck was found, containing four passports, each in a different name but sharing a photograph of Dobles, who escaped back to Belgium.

It was not until 14 July 1997 that White was sentenced for his involvement in the shipment of cocaine worth £3 million found in the false floor of a Volkswagen camper van coming through Dover. He received eleven and a half years and old-time bank robber George Caccavale, who had arranged the arrival of the *Frugal*, collected eighteen years along with Terence Reeves. The boat's skipper, Robin Sergeant, picked up the same. Another old friend was John Short, the old running mate of 1960s robber and supergrass Bertie Smalls, who received nine and a half years for his part in the camper-van smuggling. White picked up an eight-year concurrent sentence for his part in the smuggling of cannabis in a lorry coming into the country through Portsmouth.

On 16 November 2001 Brian Perry was shot as he walked away from his car to his south London office. Two men were charged but acquitted when the prosecution case collapsed in March 2006.

His death was followed on 14 May 2003 by that of sixty-three-year-old George Francis who was shot and killed as he arrived in his green Rover 75 at his Bermondsey office from where he ran a courier service "Signed, Sealed and Delivered". Francis, who had been questioned over the Brink's-Mat robbery but never charged, stepped out of his car and the gunman shot him four times in the head and chest at point-blank range.

Francis had led a colourful life. Long suspected in the underworld of being a grass, he had been a relatively small-time thief and enforcer until, in late 1979, he took up with a number of armed robbers who were moving in to the very much more lucrative and very much less dangerous territory of drug-trafficking. "Silly" Lennie Watkins, also known as "Teddy Bear", proprietor of Edward Bear Motors, Fareham, hatched the plot when he was serving a sentence in Maidstone for a supermarket snatch. Blocks of high-grade cannabis embossed with the Rolls-Royce symbol were smuggled from Pakistan in shoe containers, which produced millions for the gang. Four runs produced a street value of £10 million but, unfortunately, the team did not conceal their new-found wealth. In particular, Watkins took to lighting cigars with £20 notes.

A joint police and customs operation was mounted and on the fifth run officers watched as a container was fitted with a false bottom and loaded with sanitary-ware for a trip to Karachi. On its return, driven by Watkins, it was filled with shoes and £2.5 million of cannabis in the false bottom of the container. It arrived at Harwich and for some days meandered around the Suffolk countryside before the shoes were dropped off in Saffron Walden. The officers also saw a bag of guns being handed to Watkins.

The lorry was then driven to the Commercial Road on the borders of London's East End and the City, where the officers realized there had been a "show out" and their cover had been blown. Watkins also knew he had been watched and parked his lorry, leaving two sawn-off shotguns inside, to use a telephone box to ask for further instructions from his team. He was told to stay near the box until an orange van arrived, which would guide him to a "slaughter" or safe house.

As he waited by a bus stop he was approached by customs officer Peter Bennett and Detective Sergeant John Harvey. Watkins, who had a Lady Beretta in his parka jacket, fired at both men, hitting Bennett in the stomach. A seventy-six-year-old pensioner came to the men's aid and began beating Watkins with his walking stick as other officers arrived.

At his trial for the murder of Bennett at Winchester Crown Court, Watkins's story was that he thought a rival gang was trying to hijack his lorry and he had fired in self-defence. He did not do well in the witness box, telling prosecuting counsel, "I am not going to answer any more questions from made-up notebooks and rubbish from your firm, from the trickery department who pull more strokes than an Oxford blue." He received life with a minimum of twenty-five years and told the judge he hoped he would die of cancer. A number of other luminaries, including Freddie Foreman, were also on trial over the drugs. Foreman received two years after pleading guilty.

The Kray twins' friend and armourer Duke Osbourne died before he was arrested. His body was found on a playing field on Hackney Marshes. It was said he died of natural causes but another view is that it was from a drug overdose and that his body had been kept in a deep-freeze before being deposited on the football pitch. George Francis was acquitted after a retrial amid suggestions that witnesses had been got at.

Within a month an effort to free Watkins failed when a ladder was found propped against the wall of Winchester prison wall, with a lorry parked nearby. Watkins later committed suicide in prison.

As for Francis, in 1975 he was shot at point-blank range in the shoulder in the Henry VIII pub he owned near Hever Castle in Kent, in what was said to be a reprisal for his failure to pay for the nobbling of the jury. His survival came because he turned his head at the last moment.

Immediately after Francis's eventual murder in 2003, Harold "Big H" Richardson, who had been due to meet Francis that morning, became a prime suspect. The prosecution alleged he owed Francis £70,000 and had been slow in paying him. It turned out that Terry Conaghan had carried out the murder with John O'Flynn for a fee of £30,000 allegedly paid by Richardson. Conaghan had dropped his glasses while trying to move a CCTV camera in the yard and he was traced through DNA. Richardson was found not guilty. While sentencing Conaghan and Flynn the judge said, "Quite what the motive was of the person or persons who hired you was far from clear and I shall not speculate." The underworld believed that when he was killed Francis was still in possession of £5 million in gold.

Over the years Noye's name has been linked to a number of deaths although it is not suggested that he had either killed or instigated the killings. The first was Barbara Harold who received fatal injuries when she opened a parcel bomb. A friend of Noye's had quarrelled with her and her husband over a tax bill after he had bought their Spanish villa. The second was Alan "Taffy" Holmes, a former member of the Serious Crimes Squad who had worked on the Brink's-Mat case and who shot himself in the garden of his Croydon home. Holmes was under investigation by Scotland Yard's Complaints Division. The third was garage-owner and one-time saloon-racing champion Nick Whiting, who was abducted and stabbed nine times before his body was dumped on Rainham Marshes in 1990. The fourth, another ex-Scotland Yard officer, Sydney Wink, who had renumbered guns used in the Brink's-Mat robbery, shot himself in August 1994. Then there was millionaire builder Keith Hedley who was suspected of laundering some of the money and who was shot dead on his yacht in Corfu on 26 September 1996 as he chased three gunmen. Solly Nahome, a Hatton Garden jeweller connected to the north London Adams family, who was suspected of smelting down some of the gold, was shot outside his home in Golders Green in November 1998.

At about 11.15 p.m. on 19 May 1996 Noye was involved in what the prosecution described as a road rage killing when Stephen Cameron was stabbed to death on a slip road off the M25 at the Swanley Interchange while his fiancée, Daniella Cable, a girl with no connections to crime, watched helplessly. The prosecution's case was that when Cameron got the better of Noye in a fight, Noye went back to his car, collected a knife and stabbed Cameron to death. The fight was witnessed by an apparently respectable businessman, Alan Decabral. Later it was suggested in the underworld that the meeting had not been accidental and that Noye and Cameron knew each other.

Noye disappeared and there were sightings from all over the world – Portugal, the Canaries and Moscow were favourites. These stories were countered by persistent rumours in the underworld that he was dead. In fact, he had landed safely in northern Cyprus, which has no extradition treaty with the United Kingdom. This was just as well because his name cropped up at London's Southwark Crown Court when his friend John "Little Legs" Lloyd received five years for his abortive effort to break the bankcard system in Great Britain. Noye was said to have been a leading light in the failed scheme.

The prosecution's case was that Noye and Lloyd had set up a worldwide network of criminals to promote card fraud on a global scale. The scheme unravelled when they tried to recruit computer expert Martin Grant, who had previously been sentenced to sixteen years for trying to burn his wife and child to death. While he was being rehabilitated he was persuaded to take a job in a garage by Paul Kidd, another member of the team, and it was there that pressure was put on him. He contacted the prison chaplain and also a former policeman. Kidd received five years and it was said for a time that there was a £100,000 contract on Grant's life.

By 1988 Noye had tired of Cyprus and moved to Spain where he was traced and Daniella Cable flew out to identify him. She and the twenty-two-stone Alan Decabral gave evidence against him at the Old Bailey and he was sentenced to life imprisonment. The then Home Secretary David Blunkett set a minimum sixteen-year term before Noye would be eligible for parole.

After the trial it emerged that Decabral, far from being a respectable businessman who traded in vintage cars and motorbikes, was a long-standing associate of the Hell's Angels and that he had been involved in smuggling drink and tobacco and dealing in cocaine. Up to sixty guns had been found on his premises in the eighteen months prior to the trial. On 8 October 2000 Decabral was shot twice in the back of the head outside a Halfords store in the Ware retail park in Ashford, Kent. No charges have ever been brought.

When Noye appealed in 2001 the Court of Appeal would have none of it. There had been another seventeen witnesses on whose evidence the jury could rely. Decabral was just one piece in the jigsaw. Noye has continued his campaign, maintaining his innocence, and in October 2010 he was again given leave to appeal. It was rejected by the court on 22 March 2011 with Lord Judge saying, "Rather it was a gross over-reaction in the context of a fight with an unarmed man, almost certainly consequent on the fact that the appellant was losing it."

28

Martin Cahill, "The General"

Leading criminals often like to be recognized as military commanders. Over the years London has had its fair share of Colonels including Ronnie Kray and Brian Robinson. But in the 1990s Ireland had its own General in the form of tubby Martin Cahill, who arranged his hair Bobby Charlton-style to cover his baldness. Described as a cross between Bob Hoskins in *The Long Good Friday* and Del Boy in *Only Fools and Horses*, for a long time Cahill was referred to in the press as "The Man who denies he is The General". Although, of course, everyone knew he was.

Born in May 1949 on Dublin's North Side, as a result of slum clearances Cahill was sent to a Christian Brothers school in Crumlin in 1960. At the age of fifteen he was rejected by the Royal Navy and the next year was sent to an industrial school after two burglaries. On his release he went with his family, who had been evicted by the council over rent arrears, to Rathmines. He continued carrying out a series of burglaries and eventually received a four-year term. It was on his release from this sentence he began to attract the attention of the press when he refused to move after the council decided to demolish Hollyfield Buildings. Cahill lived in a tent on the site until he was persuaded to move by the Lord Mayor of Dublin who paid him a personal visit.

In 1983 he and his gang stole over £2.5 million from O'Connor's, the jewellers in Harold's Cross, on the outskirts of Dublin. The Gardai (the Irish national police force) had advance information about the robbery and on a number of occasions the premises had been staked out by them but no one appeared. Then on 26 July, with only twenty-five of the hundred-strong staff on the premises, the gang hid out in the boiler house. As each employee arrived they were locked in a lavatory and, when all had been accounted for, the manager was made to open the strong room. Thirty minutes later the gang had loaded their vans and left, setting off a smoke bomb as they did so. A reward of £25,000 was posted but not a single call was received. Insured for less than half the loss, the store went into administration four years later. There were suggestions that there had been an attempted drugs-for-jewellery swap but Cahill always maintained that, unlike many others, he had nothing to do with the drug trade.

After the raid the story grew that a man suspected of siphoning off some of the loot for himself was nailed to the floor. Cahill would later say that he had heard the story but could not deny or confirm it since he had not been there. Had it been true, he said, it was the work of some over-enthusiastic and undisciplined gang-members.

Three years later he was allegedly involved in the theft of the Beit art collection from Russborough House. By then he had moved into protection, leaning on hot-dog vendors and restaurants in Dublin's nightclub district.

The Beit collection had an unhappy career. Brought to Ireland by Sir Alfred Beit, a British MP who had retired to Co. Wicklow, it had already suffered when on 26 April 1974 four armed men, led by the British heiress Dr Rose Dugdale, tied up Beit and his wife and stole nineteen of their paintings including a Vermeer, a Goya, two Gainsboroughs and three Reubens. The Dugdale raid had been to hold the paintings hostage against the release of the Price sisters, Marian and Dolours, convicted in England of terrorist bombings on behalf of the Irish Republican Army (IRA). Eleven days later the paintings were recovered undamaged and Beit donated the collection to the state. It was kept at Russborough House, which opened to the public in 1976. Dugdale received nine years and in 1975 her husband, Eddie Gallagher, then kidnapped the Dutch industrialist Dr Tiede Herrema and held him hostage against her release. Gallagher received twenty years after Herrema was released unharmed.

This time, at 2.a.m. on 21 May 1986, the alarm went off but when Gardai officers arrived they were told by the staff that everything was all right. The loss of the paintings was not discovered until seven hours later. The stolen paintings included a Vermeer thought to be worth £5 million and a Goya. Seven less valuable paintings were found abandoned the next day. It was suggested that the gang had deliberately triggered off the alarm to lull the Gardai into a false sense of security. All but two of the paintings were later recovered in Britain, Belgium and Turkey.

Gardai officers also believed Cahill was involved in the December 1984 robbery of £90,000 from the Quinsmith branch in Rosemount Shopping Centre in Rathfarnham. Although he persistently denied any involvement, from then on he was closely monitored by the police. Not that it did them a great deal of good. By the end of the 1980s the blame for almost every major operation was laid at the General's door. His name was the first in the frame when over a hundred files were stolen from the offices of the Director of Public Prosecutions at St Stephen's Green, Dublin, in early September 1987. They included the highly embarrassing loss of the file of the socially well-connected Malcolm McArthur who in 1982, after he had run through his £80,000 inheritance, planned an armed robbery. The first step was to steal a car but when the owner, Bridie Gargan, surprised McArthur in Phoenix Park he hit her over the head with a hammer killing her. Another file concerned the death of Father Niall Molloy who died at the home of another businessman, Richard Flynn, in 1985. Flynn had been acquitted of the priest's manslaughter but his family was in the middle of an action for damages.

On the evening of 30 November 1988 members of Cahill's gang went too far, kidnapping Ann Gallagher, the postmistress at Kilmanagh, and her landlady. The next morning she was made to go to the post office and withdraw cash and stamps worth nearly £30,000. With her was another hostage, Myles Croft, who had a radio-controlled bomb strapped to his chest. After that a seventy-strong surveillance unit was set up specifically to monitor and harry the General, his henchmen and other target criminals.

In turn, the General and his gang did not make life easy for the police. Apart from threats to kill Detective Superintendent Ned Ryan, known as the Buffalo, whenever officers drove into housing estates they were rammed with stolen cars.

In the first weeks of 1988 a group of men had damaged Cahill's Nissan Bluebird. The Gardai accepted they were keeping the General under surveillance at the time but would not confirm if they had been in the area. Reprisals were swift. In the February the greens at a club where the Gardai officers played golf were dug up and twenty of their cars were damaged. Even when a loaded .45 Colt was found in a water tank at Cahill's home, the Director of Public Prosecutions would not prosecute on the grounds that it might have been planted by someone with a grudge.

The General's control of his gang was something of a benevolent dictatorship and members were free to work for themselves. The surveillance paid off in regards to these extracurricular activities. In February 1989 James "Shavo" Hogan was sentenced to eight years after being found in possession of firearms. Cahill was questioned but not charged. There was another setback for Cahill four months later when Eamonn Daly, son of a Crumlin schoolmaster and one of Cahill's most trusted lieutenants, went down for twelve years for an attempted robbery at Sandyford. He and another man wearing false beards and moustaches followed a Securicor employee into the Atlantic Homecare centre. In turn they were followed by plainclothes detectives and, when Daly pointed a gun at them, they jumped on him. Two other men escaped in the shoot-out. Daly was already on bail for a 1985 robbery at the Equity Bank in Grafton Street. Later Cahill's brother, Michael, pleaded guilty to receiving part of the Grafton Street proceeds.

For long periods officers almost literally camped out in Cahill's garden. For his part he maintained they should never be acknowledged or looked at and accordingly he had the glass in his car's wing-mirrors removed. On one occasion when the Gardai went to see him, Cahill would not let them in. One officer was attacked by a dog, which he shot. Then a girl with a pram left and almost immediately Cahill opened the door, saying not to worry about the dog, which was useless anyway. Later, the officers realized that the girl should have been stopped. On another occasion he offered the detectives £20 notes while his son stood by with a camera. Other times he would pull out a tape recorder and begin to dictate a complaint. Or he might pull down his trousers to show the police his Mickey Mouse underpants. In August 1991 Cahill was charged with dangerous driving, breach of the peace and obstruction. On his arrest he had apparently stripped off his clothes and done the same at the police station. A psychiatric report had been ordered but none was produced and he was released on £100 bail. When he emerged he had on a white nightshirt and a mask, with a model of a bird's nest strapped to his forehead. "One flew Under the Cuckoo's Nest" was handwritten on the front and back of the shirt. After asking reporters whether a bicycle was a boat and the street was the River Liffey, he rode off on the bike in triumph. The public loved it.

A non-smoker and non-drinker who liked racing pigeons, cakes and curries, Cahill lived in an agreeable *ménage à trois* with his wife Frances, her sister Tina and his children. But there was a deeply unpleasant side to him. He may have fed tea and biscuits to the women he held hostage and assured them they would not be harmed, but he did his level best to prevent a fourteen-year-old girl giving evidence against her father, one of Cahill's gang, who had raped and sodomized her. A bribe of £35,000 was offered and when that failed, her family was subjected to a series of threats. Despite this, she did go through with the case and her father received ten years. Cahill's motive apparently was that if the man went to prison, he would try to trade-off his sentence by turning rat. When it was discovered that Cahill had a large unmortgaged house and was told he would receive no more dole money, he shot the official who signed the letter in both legs.

The end of the General's command came at around 3.20 p.m. on 18 August 1994 when he was killed in an ambush at the junction of Oxford Road and Charleston Road in the Ranelagh area of Dublin, about half a mile from his home. Two men had lain in wait for him, one of them sitting on a black motorcycle posing as a council worker checking registration numbers. When Cahill slowed his black Renault 5, the other man ran towards him and fired a single shot, hitting him in the shoulder and head. With Cahill unable to control it, the car, still in gear, went slowly across the road and hit a pole. The gunman ran alongside, firing four more shots, and then escaped on the motorcycle.

After Cahill's death a statement claiming responsibility was issued by the Irish National Liberation Army (INLA) with whom he was known to have links. Within a matter of hours, however, the IRA telephoned a Dublin radio station to say that one of its members had carried out the execution. The INLA then issued a statement admitting its claim was false. No charges were ever brought. It is thought that he was killed either because he had helped loyalists stage an attack on a Dublin pub in which an IRA member was killed or that the IRA was simply fed up with his refusal to kow-tow to it.

In October 2007 Frances Cahill wrote a white-washing biography of her father in which she claimed that when the crucifixion of his associate after the O'Connor jewel robbery had taken place, Cahill had not done the nailing himself but, at the time, he had been merely questioning the man. Dr Jim Donovan, a state forensic expert, who had been injured on two separate occasions by Cahill booby-trap bombs, said, "Her father had no redeeming qualities. He was not in the normal grade of human being. He was extremely sadistic and devoid of humanity, he was a very evil man and also a very wealthy man."

29

Two Bandit Queens and a King

Dacoity, basically an equivalent of armed robbery, has been part of Indian rural life from time immemorial. The word comes from the Hindi *daka parna*, meaning to plunder. There can be house dacoits (home invaders), road dacoits and river dacoits. In law the term dacoity is used to describe an offence committed by five or more people, but before the Second World War it was invariably reported as being committed by large gangs varying in number between fifteen and thirty or more, armed with firearms that were described by Srikanta Ghosh in *The Indian Mafia* as "not just obsolete but prehistoric". Nevertheless these were sufficient to terrorize villagers. During the first half of the 1960s there were over 1,740 reported cases: "They have spread a nerve-shattering fear in the villages. The chopped noses, half-burnt faces, the brutally ravished female-folk, cold-bloodied countless murders, orphaned families, the fallow lands and the ruined and deserted villages all tell the tale of their atrocities."

The most celebrated dacoit of the last half century has been the bandit queen Phoolan Devi, the subject of countless books and articles and a well-regarded film. However, just how much of her story is true and how much is myth is another matter. In turn, a penniless villager, child bride, multiple rape victim and highwaywoman, she metamorphosed into a class warrior and folk heroine. For a time she was also a Member of Parliament for the Samajwadi Party.

The story goes that Phoolan Devi was born in 1964 in Gorha Ka Purwa, Uttar Pradesh, one of six children of a fisherman. From one of the lowest castes, at the age of eleven she was the victim of an arranged marriage, in exchange for a cow, to Putti Lal, a widower in his thirties, who beat and starved her. Apparently she left him and returned to the village where her father was locked in battle with his brother and nephew Maiyadin in a dispute over fifteen acres of land. Fighting her father's cause, she was framed by Maiyadin over a theft, imprisoned and continually raped by her jailers.

One version of her story is that on her release, Maiyadin arranged to have her kidnapped by the dacoit Babu Gujar, from a higher class sect, who naturally tortured her and repeatedly raped her until, in the middle of the sex act, he was killed by his deputy Vikram Mallah, who in turn became her lover. Now she was initiated into the craft of dacoity and became both a crack shot and his second-in-command. Robin Hood-like, she and her lover hijacked, kidnapped, looted and blew up trains, robbing the rich and high caste members of society and giving to the poor. She returned to her village where she killed her husband Putti Lal, stabbing him in front of the villagers.

When Sir and Lala Ram, who had been part of Gujar's gang, were released from a prison sentence they allegedly killed Mallah, kidnapped Phoolan Devi and gang-raped her. In this aspect of her life she seems to have suffered the same misfortune as Angélique, Sergeanne Golon's fictitious heroine of countless sexual assaults. She was also made to walk naked to the river to fetch water in front of a crowd of the jeering villagers of Behmai. But then, out of the bushes sprang a bandit from a neighbouring village who carried her away to begin another life of banditry.

Two years later, in 1981, she and her band were back in the village of Behmai to loot it when she recognized two of the men who had gang-raped her. Appalled that they had been sheltered by the village, she had its men from the Kshatriya (warrior) caste lined up and machine-gunned them. Twenty-two out of thirty died. Later she denied that she herself had taken part in the massacre. There followed a two-year hunt by the authorities after which she negotiated terms of surrender. None of her gang would be hanged; instead, they would receive a maximum of eight years. Her father's land would be returned and her brother was to be given a job in the civil service. Sensibly, her highly publicized surrender took place before a crowd of 10,000, including a number of foreign journalists, and before portraits of Mahatma Ghandi and the goddess Durga. Writer Khushwant Singh, quoted in the *New York Times*, thought her less than impressive: "I was told she was a beautiful woman but when I saw her photographs I was appalled though perhaps I should not have been. She was a gangster's moll servicing the whole gang. It was a tough life and it must have drained her."

Over the years her men, mainly from a higher caste than herself, were released but she remained in prison until she was pardoned in 1994. She had spent much of the time in the same cell as male members of her gang. That year she married Delhi businessman Umaid Singh, her sister's former husband. The film of her life appeared the following year and she sued over the claim she had been gang-raped, settling for £40,000. It was said, unkindly, that the money was the target rather than any feminist principles. As befitted a high-quality gangster, she gave interviews while wearing a tiger-skin sari and vivid red nail varnish.

In 1996 Devi stood for Parliament for the socialist Samajwadi Party and became a symbol of the Dalits or Untouchables. However, she failed to carry through her reform ticket for the oppressed and women's rights. She was defeated the next year amid suggestions she was abusing her position of power by, for example, having a train on which she was travelling make unscheduled stops so she could meet friends.

However, like so many other gang-leaders Devi put pen to paper once too often and her celebrity status spurred relatives of the village massacre to have charges against her revived. At the end of January 1998, the year she claimed she was nominated for the Nobel Peace prize, she disappeared after a court had refused her "anticipatory bail". The murder charges, however, were dropped and she was re-elected to Parliament in 1999, pleading that her failures should be forgiven and that she should be given a further chance by the voters.

On 25 July 2001, having left the Parliament building for the lunch recess, Devi was shot and killed under a neem tree at the front gate of her home. Sher Singh Rana, Dheeraj Rana and Rajbir were accused of the crime. Sher Singh Rana surrendered in Dehradun after calling a press conference. He confessed to the murder, saying he had been thinking about it for some time and that he was avenging the deaths of the twenty-two Kshatriyas at Behmai. On the morning of the killing he had driven Devi to the Parliament and then lain in wait before shooting her with a Webley & Scott handgun. He had then gone to the Delhi bus station and made his way to Haridwar and on to Rishikesh before arriving in Dehradun.

Sher Singh Rana, however, had a history of making false claims, saying on one occasion that he had been kidnapped during student elections. He escaped from Tihar jail in 2004, but was captured in April 2006 in Kolkata and sent to Rohini jail, Delhi. The same year, the Kshatriya Swabhimaan Andolan Samanvay Committee (KSASC), which had been a constant opponent of Devi, decided to honour Rana for "upholding the dignity of the Kshatriya community" and "drying the tears of the widows of Behmai". In 2011 it was announced the Indian tennis star Lander Paes would play the part of Sher Singh Rana in a forthcoming film. In the autumn of that year Rana was still awaiting trial.

Phoolan Devi was not India's only bandit queen in recent years although admittedly convent-educated Archana Sharma, born in November 1975, daughter of a retired major in the Indian Home Guard and one-time pop singer, operated in rather more illustrious circles.

Initially recruited by gangster Irfan Gogha, and not to be confused with either the physicist or the Bollywood actress of the same name, Archana Sharma was first introduced to the master criminal and former law graduate, Om Prakash "Babloo" Srivastava in Lucknow in early 1990. She then moved with Gogha to Dubai where she opened a fashion boutique and met Fazal-ur-Rehman.

Gogha was killed in Dubai in December 1999, either after allegedly falling foul of crime boss Dawood Ibrahim's brother, Anees, or having won a large sum of money in a club. His body was never found but his car was traced to a parking lot at Dubai airport. The man suspected of his killing fled to Pakistan.

Sharma has been suspected of heading a criminal enterprise that made over £6 million annually from kidnapping and extortion. Her technique was simple. She spotted rich potential victims, seduced them, drugged them, and had them abducted and ransomed. The money was paid through a Hawala transaction, commonly used when sending money between countries. In 1997 Lala Vyas, a hotelier, was ransomed for £700,000. Careless talk costs gangs, however, and while he was blindfolded he heard her speak of plots to kidnap another seven men in Delhi. A raid on her flat produced a cache of weapons as well as evidence to show she was behind the proposed Delhi kidnapping of hotel director Raju Punwani. This time the ransom was to be set at £900,000. She was arrested and absconded her bail. She collected £700,000 from an oil magnate and then on 22 May 1998 her gang kidnapped Sagar Ladkat in Mangalwar Peth. They had been tracking him for over a month. The petrol tycoon's family refused to pay up and his mutilated body was found on a building site in Kondhawa the next morning. At the end of 1998 her gang, allegedly paid with money from Dubai, killed a former government minister, Mirza Dilshad Beg, reputedly because he had links with another criminal organization.

Then in the December 1998 it was thought she had been cornered. Her mentor, Babloo Srivastava, in prison on forty-five charges of extortion, rioting and murder including that of a customs officer in 1993, had been advising her on a mobile telephone kept in a hollowed out bed-leg. He made hundreds of calls to her, which were then monitored, and she was traced to a bungalow in Jodhpur Park, a smart Kolkata suburb from where she was planning to abduct another hotel-owner. The plan, this time, was that she would drug him and, passing him off as a sick relative, take him to Kathmandu. On 14 December Srivastava gave the go-head but in a police trap four of the gang were killed in a gun battle. She escaped and was believed to have fled to Nepal. It is thought that since nothing has been heard of her for over a decade she may have been deemed to have outlived her usefulness and is dead.

Whether Charles Gurmuth Sobhraj, also known as Alain Gauthier and a dozen other aliases, ever headed a gang in the conventional sense of the word is open to discussion. Some would say he was a one-man crimewave but in fact he did have a number of helpers, both male and female. He could genuinely be described as a master criminal. Sobhraj was born the son of an Indian father and Vietnamese mother, Song, in Saigon in 1944. His father, a tailor, soon deserted the family and Sobhraj was brought up by Alphonse Darreau, a French lieutenant. One story is that Sobhraj was left behind with his natural father when his mother and Darreau, who was suffering from shell shock, left for France. His mother then sent for him. Another version of his story is that much against his will, Song took him with her.

In 1963 Sobhraj received a three-year sentence, which he served at Poissy prison near Paris. However, not only did he weather the harsh conditions of the jail, he managed to manipulate a prison official into granting him special favours such as being allowed to keep books in his cell. At around the same time he met and endeared himself to prison visitor, Felix d'Escogne, a wealthy if gullible young man.

On his release Sobhraj moved in with and continually sponged off d'Escogne, dividing his time between his benefactor's friends and the criminal underworld. As with so many criminals his was a double life. D'Escogne would take him to parties and Sobhraj would then give criminals the blueprints of flats he had visited in return for a down payment and a share of the proceeds. During this time, he met and began a relationship with Chantal Compagnon, daughter of a butcher – some accounts give her name as Hélène. On the night he proposed to her, Sobhraj was arrested for failing to stop while driving a stolen car. This time he was sent to prison for eight months, which he served in Rouen. After his release he and Chantal married.

He obtained a job from his brother-in-law, who ran a restaurant, and promptly stole $6,000 from him. Faced with more criminal proceedings Sobhraj took flight in d'Escogne's old car and headed for Asia with Chantal. He was sentenced to a year's imprisonment in France in his absence. In Greece, when he left behind a series of dud cheques and stole the money of an Englishman, he was sentenced to another year *in absentia*. He arrived in Bombay in 1970 where Chantal gave birth to a baby girl and on the face of it they mixed happily with the French ex-pat community. In the meantime, Sobhraj resumed his criminal lifestyle by running a car theft and smuggling operation, the profits from which were used to feed his long-standing gambling addiction.

In October 1971, Sobhraj was arrested and imprisoned after an unsuccessful robbery attempt on a jewellery store in Delhi's Hotel Ashoka. Along with a helper he had kept an American nightclub-dancer captive as they tried to tunnel through the floor of her room into the jeweller's beneath. They failed and instead ordered the unfortunate girl to summon the jeweller to bring samples to the room and promptly held him hostage as well. Sobhraj was arrested at the airport. The dancer was also arrested and spent some time in prison before she could prove her innocence.

Long before that, Sobhraj had escaped with Chantal's help by faking illness and then drugging his hospital guard, but they were both captured shortly afterwards. This time he borrowed money for bail from his father in Saigon and the couple fled to Kabul in Afghanistan where he was jailed for non-payment of a hotel bill. It was there that he began to lay the foundations of a serious criminal career. He hijacked a car, drugged the owner and put him in the boot.

He continued robbing tourists on the "hippie trail" only to be arrested once again. But once more Sobhraj escaped, in exactly the same way he had in India, feigning illness and drugging the hospital guard. This time he fled to Iran leaving his wife and daughter behind. A suitably chastened Chantal returned to her family in France. Other accounts have her falling in love with an American businessman and filing for divorce.

Sobhraj spent the next two years on the run, using up to ten stolen passports and touring Eastern Europe and the Middle East where he began to hone his technique. He would meet his victims in hotel bars in the major cities, and then drug and rob them. Joined in Istanbul by André, his younger half-brother, the pair cut a criminal swathe through Turkey and Greece. Both were eventually arrested in Athens. An identity-switch plan went wrong but Sobhraj escaped after pouring petrol from a shampoo bottle and setting fire to the prison van on the island of Aegina. Apparently André was left behind to serve an eighteen-year sentence.

It was in Kashmir and later Thailand where he improved on his drink-and-drug technique. Hippies were plentiful in both countries and they would be lured to Kanit House in Bangkok, where he had an apartment. Posing as an urbane gem-dealer, he duped them into going into partnership with him, reselling sapphires and amethysts that he would supply at a cut rate. Their problems were not in the jewellery, which was genuine enough, but that they never saw it. The catch lay not in the jewels but in the helpful tip he supplied to go with them. As an experienced traveller he was able to advise them on the most effective pills they must take against dysentery. They would rely on him to find the drugs and he kindly provided these pills – in fact, powerful sedatives. Once they were drugged, he would rob them. By the time he was traced to his flat in Bangkok in 1976 he was long gone, tipped off by a corrupt official. The police did, however, find the possessions of some twenty victims.

In Thailand, he met Marie-Andrée Leclerc from Lévis, Quebec, who was travelling with her then boyfriend and, seduced by the mysteries of the Orient and Sobhraj's blandishments, later returned from Canada to meet him again. Perhaps not wholly altruistically, she later wrote, "I swore to myself to try all means to make him love me but little by little I became his slave."

As a variation on a theme, Sobhraj gathered his helpmates in Thailand by getting them out of difficult situations, so they looked on him as their saviour rather than the cause of their problems. The modus operandi hardly varied. He would befriend tourists, very often French-speaking ones, and systematically poison them, telling them they had dysentery. Suggesting they hand over their passports and valuables for safekeeping, he would take them to his apartment where he would apparently nurse them, all the time giving them more weakening drugs. It was a time when the Bangkok police were not regarded as sympathetic to backpackers, particularly those who spoke little English, and as a result any complaints were likely to be ignored. Now he was also joined by a young Indian, Ajay Chowdhury, a fellow criminal who became his lieutenant.

It was in 1975 that Sobhraj and Chowdhury are alleged to have committed their first known murders. Sobhraj would later lay the murders at his lieutenant's door saying he knew nothing of them. Most of the victims had spent some time at Kanit House before their deaths and according to investigators had threatened to expose Sobhraj. The first victim was a young woman from Seattle, eighteen-year-old Teresa Knowlton, who had come to Bangkok on the way to enlightenment in a monastery in Kathmandu. She met Ajay Chowdhury at the Hotel Malaysia and went back to the apartment with him. Her body was found on 18 October.

Soon after a young American, Jennie Bolliver, was found drowned in a tidal pool on Pattaya beach wearing a flowered bikini. It was only months later that the autopsy and forensic evidence revealed the drowning to be murder. From a disturbed background she had broken up with a boyfriend and joined Sobhraj and Chowdhury.

The next victim was a young, nomadic, Sephardic Jew, Vitali Hakim, whose burned body was found on 28 November 1975 on the road to the Pattaya resort where Sobhraj and his clan were staying.

Dutch student Henk Bintanja, twenty-nine, and his fiancée Cornelia Hemker, twenty-five, were invited to Thailand after meeting Sobhraj in Hong Kong. Just as he had done with others, Sobhraj poisoned them. By the time he had nursed them back to what approximated health, they were in his palm.

The next visitor was Hakim's French girlfriend, Charmayne Carrou, coming to investigate her boyfriend's disappearance. Soon after, she was found drowned in circumstances similar to Jennie's death, and wearing a similar swimsuit. The deaths were eventually to become known as the "Bikini Killings".

It was off to Nepal where Connie Bronzich and her Canadian boyfriend Laurent Carrière were found dead, their bodies smouldering, just outside Kathmandu. Using their passports for his return to Thailand, Sobhraj then discovered that the French woman who lived in the flat downstairs at the Kanit House had begun to suspect him. She had found documents belonging to the murder victims and fled to Paris after notifying local authorities.

Sobhraj then went to Kolkata, where he is alleged to have murdered an Israeli scholar, Avoni Jacob, for his passport, which he used to move to Singapore with his Canadian mistress, Marie-Andrée Leclerc, and Chowdhury, and then to India and – rather boldly – back to Bangkok in March 1976. There they were briefly questioned by Thai policemen over the murders but, because authorities feared that the negative publicity accompanying a murder trial would harm the country's tourist trade, nothing came of the cursory investigation.

There was, however, one man who was still unhappy. Herman Knippenberg from the Dutch embassy was investigating the murder of the two Dutch backpackers, and suspected Sobhraj even though he did not know his real name. He started to build a case against him, partly with the help of Sobhraj's neighbour, and he obtained police permission to conduct his own search of Sobhraj's apartment. Admittedly, this was a full month after Sobhraj had left the country. There he found a great deal of evidence, including victims' documents and poison-laced medicines, but his findings still produced no sense of urgency in the authorities.

Sobhraj, Leclerc and Chowdhury's next stop was Malaysia, where Chowdhury was sent on a gem-stealing errand and disappeared after giving the jewels to Sobhraj. No trace of him has ever been found and it is widely believed, without any supporting evidence, that Sobhraj murdered his former accomplice before leaving with Leclerc to sell the jewels in Geneva.

Soon back in Asia, Sobhraj started rebuilding his clan, beginning in Bombay with two more lost women, Barbara Sheryl Smith and an Australian, Mary Ellen Eather. His next victim was Frenchman Jean-Luc Solomon, who died after being given a drug that was merely intended to incapacitate him during a robbery.

It all came apart in July 1976 in Agra where Sobhraj and the three women, including Leclerc, tricked a tour group of postgraduate French students into accepting them as guides. At the Bikram Hotel he conned them into taking his anti-dysentery medicine but this time he had miscalculated the dose. Instead of passing out in their rooms, the group began to drop like flies where they stood when the drugs started acting too quickly. Three of them quickly realized what was happening and jumped on Sobhraj, holding him until the police arrived. During interrogation, Smith and Eather quickly cracked and confessed everything. Sobhraj was charged with the murder of Solomon, and all four were sent to Tihar prison outside New Delhi while awaiting formal trial.

Conditions inside the notorious rat- and lice-infected prison were unbearable and both Smith and Eather attempted suicide during the two years before their trial. Sobhraj, however, had entered with precious gems concealed in his body and was experienced in bribing captors and living comfortably in jail.

Once the hearings began Sobhraj turned his trial into a show, hiring and firing lawyers on a whim, bringing in his recently paroled and still-loyal brother to help, and eventually going on a hunger strike. Mary Ellen Eather decided that her evidence had been obtained by the police by blackmail and denied she had seen Sobhraj give anyone drugs. The trial dragged on for eleven months before Judge Nath found Sobhraj guilty of the culpable homicide of Luc Solomon, not amounting to murder. He was sentenced to seven years, instead of the death penalty sought by the prosecution. Leclerc, who gave evidence against him, was found not guilty of the murder of Solomon but guilty of the drugging of the French students for which Sobhraj was sentenced to an additional five years. Sobhraj was also found not guilty of the murder of Avoni Jacob. In prison Leclerc developed ovarian cancer and was deported to Canada on humanitarian grounds. She was still claiming her innocence and was reportedly still loyal to Sobhraj when she died in April 1984.

Sobhraj's systematic bribery of prison guards at Tihar continued and he led a life of relative luxury inside the jail, with a television and decent if not gourmet food. Fellow prisoners also benefitted from his largesse. Revelling in his notoriety, he gave interviews to Western authors and journalists, such as *Oz* magazine's Richard Neville, who later became his biographer. He talked freely about the murders, while never actually admitting to them, claiming that his actions were in retaliation against Western imperialism in Asia.

Because a twenty-year Thai arrest warrant against him would still be valid on his expected release date, something that would result in his deportation and probable execution, he also needed to find a way to extend his sentence. In March 1986, in his tenth year in prison, he threw a big party for his prisoner and guard friends and, having drugged them with sleeping pills, simply walked out of the jail.

His plan was a total success, even though he was quickly tracked down and caught in Goa by Inspector Madhukar Zende of the Mumbai police. Just as he had hoped, his sentence was extended by ten years.

On 17 February 1997 he was finally released with most warrants expired, evidence lost and witnesses dispersed around the world. Without any country to which to deport him the Indian authorities returned him to France.

Back in Paris, Sobhraj hired a publicity agent and, charging $5,000 a time for interviews and photographs, led a perfectly comfortable lifestyle. There were television documentaries about him but negotiations for a film broke down. Now about the only country which remained interested in him was Nepal but instead of staying well away, possibly for the challenge and possibly for the notoriety, he gravitated towards it like filings to a magnet. In September 2003 he was recognized by a photographer in Kathmandu and two days later Sobhraj, now aged fifty-nine, was arrested in the Yak and Yeti Casino. He was charged with the murders of the North American backpackers Connie Bronzich and Laurent Carrière, whose charred and strangled bodies had been found outside Kathmandu nearly thirty years earlier. Sobhraj maintained he had never been in Nepal until shortly before he was arrested but it was alleged that, back in 1975, he had used a false Dutch passport in the name of Henk Bintanja to enter and leave the country. The burned and strangled bodies of Bintanja and his fiancée Cornelia Hemker had been found in a ditch outside Bangkok that year.

During his incarceration, the Nepalese police said they had foiled an alleged plan by Sobhraj to drug his guards and escape. A laptop computer, a wireless phone and a cellular phone were found in his cell along with an email in which he allegedly asked a female friend to help him arrange a dose of drugs for his guards, as well as transport to India and then on to France.

On 12 August 2004, Sobhraj was sentenced to life imprisonment on what he called the "fictitious evidence" of the Bronzich murder. His appeal to the Appellate Court was dismissed in August 2005. His Nepalese lawyer said there would be a further appeal to the Supreme Court and his French lawyer, Isabelle Coutant-Peyre, almost as high-profile as Sobhraj himself following her marriage to Carlos the Jackal, one of the most wanted terrorists of the 1970s, said she would file a complaint at the International Court of Justice and the United Nations Human Rights Commission in Geneva.

In 2008 Sobhraj claimed to have married twenty-year-old Nihita Biswas, his interpreter and the daughter of his lawyer, in a jailhouse ceremony. It was something the authorities denied, saying the family had merely been allowed into the jail for a short religious blessing.

On 30 July 2010, amid claims Sobhraj had been "denied justice", the Nepalese Supreme Court finally upheld the verdict of the twenty-year life term. The court also ordered the confiscation of all his properties. Sobhraj still had the Carrière case pending against him in the Bhaktapur district court. He was also being investigated over the murder of Annabella Tremont in January 1975.

There was, however, a new ray of sunshine in his life. In 2010 the United Nations ruled that Sobhraj's rights to a fair trial had been violated and asked the Nepal government to free him and give him compensation. As of November 2011, Sobhraj was still in prison.

30

The Triads in Soho

Rather as the origins of the Mafia in Sicily are said to have been to overthrow a repressive regime, it is generally accepted that the Triad organization began life in mainland China in the seventeenth century with an aim to overthrow the Manchu Qing dynasty and restore the Chinese Ming dynasty. From survivors of a monastic rebellion grew what Westerners call the Triads, derived from the emblem of a triangle representing earth, heaven and man. It was not until 1911 that the Qing dynasty was finally overthrown and by then the Triads had changed from being a semi-religious and political organization to a form of trade union and protection society at best, and a criminal organization at worst.

Secret societies were nothing new in Chinese history. At the end of the eighteenth century there had been the long-lasting White Lotus Society which, for a time, had liberated vast tracts of Szechuan, Hupeh and Shansi from the Manchu oppressors. After the Opium Wars the Cudgels carried out a guerrilla war for three years until, in 1850, their leader was captured and executed. From the 1860s the White Lotus Society was again active until the end of the century. A Triad branch of the society, the Fists of Righteous Harmony, whose members claimed they were impenetrable by bullets, gave its name to the Boxer Rebellion.

The major criminal Chinese presence in Limehouse and Soho in London before the First World War was that of the drug-dealer Chan Nan, known as Brilliant Chang, who had his drugs couriered from the East End to Soho, where he had a restaurant, until his conviction and deportation in 1924. He had long been under suspicion and as early as 1917 men arrested in Birmingham had correspondence on them that showed that Chang was the leading drug-dealer in the country. Police files show he was suspected of having agents in Paris, Brussels, Berlin and Antwerp as well as China.

His successor, Kwok Tai, who lived near Chang at 14 Limehouse Causeway, took over his empire while another Chinese dealer, Kwong Tai, lived at No. 12. Their friend Choy Loy (or Loi) also had a restaurant and was conducting his business from the Terminus Palace Hotel, Amsterdam. Loy had other restaurants in Hamburg and Rotterdam, and carried a certificate to say he was born in Hawaii and had acted as an interpreter in the United States. On 2 June 1921 he was sentenced to eighteen months hard labour after being convicted of unlawful wounding but was not recommended for deportation.

Other dealers of the period included Ah Kiu Tchai, alias Sei Sou, who was known to be a member of the Bo-On and "Three Finger" secret societies. These were said to be involved in smuggling drugs from – and guns to – the Far East for a syndicate operating from Yuet On & Co., a Chinese seaman's boarding house at 5 Wai San Lane, Hong Kong. Choy Loy was regarded as its chief European agent.

On 15 January 1924 Choy left Cherbourg, where he had been staying at the Hôtel Cambon, on the SS *Republic* for New York. An intercepted letter shows that he had earlier left New York because he was no longer safe from the rival Tong organization. He had clearly been in and out of the country, watched by the police.

On 8 May that year Choy was then in Margate where he was "surprising the postmaster of that town by sending frequent cablegrams in code". A Canadian drug-trafficker was staying at his London home and an internal memorandum warned off the local police from doing anything. On 8 November, on his return from another New York trip, Choy Loy was refused permission to land.

From then until the late 1950s there was no great presence of the Chinese in Soho. It is an East Ender, Francis McGovern, who spoke a little Cantonese, who is generally credited with giving the Chinese gamblers their start in the area. The story is that he won the Kaleidoscope, a café on the corner of Gerrard and Wardour Streets, in a poker game and allowed the Chinese to use the basement for gambling.

For a time the new arrivals were prey to homegrown talent. On 16 May 1963 John Henry Maguire received four years at the Old Bailey. Two months earlier he had been running a six-strong but short-lived protection racket demanding money from Chinese gambling dens in Gerrard Street and robbing waiters. In one case he had used a seventeen-year-old Irish girl to lure waiters into the back of a van. It was a time generally when Irish girls were being exploited by the denizens of Soho who were enticing them to England with prospects of working as waitresses and then turning them out on the streets.

For a time the Chinese themselves also employed English talent to protect them. One Soho doorman recalled:

I collected money from the Chinese. I was minding cash for them. I also worked minding a man who came here to gamble Sunday to Tuesday. I thought he owned a restaurant in Belgium. Then I heard he was a massive drug baron and had been nicked in Germany and got a sentence. Later it was reduced on appeal and when he came out he was shot dead and dropped in a canal in Holland.

Soon, however, Triad gangs – Wo Sing Wo; Wo On Lok, also known as the Sui Fong; 14K (formed in the 1950s and named after 14 Poh Wah Road, Kowloon); and San Yee On, each with a hard core of around ten members – were systematically working the six streets of Chinatown – Wardour, Gerrard, Macclesfield, Lisle, Newport and the southern side of Shaftesbury Avenue, demanding protection money from restaurant-owners and the gambling interests. As an indication of the amount of money involved, by 1990 14K were said to control a multimillion-pound racket of gaming and protection. In the 1990s they were joined by the Tai Huen Chai or the Big Circle.

Triad organizations require the euphemistically named "tea money" as a tribute, and the traditional chopping, using a fourteen-inch beef knife, is regarded as the ultimate sanction. If, for example, the restaurant-owner does not pay on the first approach, a negotiator is sent in. This meeting will be formal, with tea and perhaps a meal, in the private room of a hotel. However, before a chopping takes place a knife wrapped in a Chinese newspaper may be presented as a final warning. If the target remains intractable he may then be killed.

Apart from protection and straightforward blackmail, the Triads offer such services as loan-sharking. Also on offer are credit-card fraud, gambling, video-pirating and prostitution as well as smuggled cigarettes and, in the days before the mobile telephone, phone cards. In 2003 police were seizing 20,000 cigarettes a week. Cigarettes selling at £4 or £5 a sleeve in China were going for £45 in Newport Place. In the case of the Chinese-operated brothels in Soho and the remainder of the country, the women who staff them are usually Malay or Thai girls, brought into the country under the guise of being secretaries or tourists, who work a three-month stint before being returned home. For reasons of safety as well as loyalty, members of each Triad group will use their own brothel so, for example, 14K members will only go to a 14K-owned brothel.

If there was any doubt that there were serious crime figures in Soho's Chinese community, Triads or not, it was swiftly dispelled in February 1976. It was then that Kay Wong, a restaurant-owner from Basildon, was kicked to death in an illegal gambling club in a basement in Gerrard Street as he sat playing mah-jong. He suffered fourteen broken ribs as well as a ruptured spleen. The kicks were so savage that the toe of one of the attackers' shoes had split and later the police were able to trace a shop in Leeds where a new pair of shoes had been bought and to retrieve the old ones.

The attackers had wanted to know the address of Wong's son, Wong Pun Hai, whom they believed to be a member of the 14K gang and partly responsible for the murder in December 1975 of one of their relations in Holland. That murder had been because a dealer, Li Kwok Pun, had failed to make a heroin delivery. The 14K had displayed its displeasure by putting eight bullets into the man's chest.

There had been no problems with the Amsterdam police. The body, decomposing quietly in the dunes at Scheveningen, was not found until a fortnight after Kay Wong's killing. 1,500 guilders (then £300) had been left in Pun's pocket indicating to all who could read the message that it was not a robbery gone wrong. He may also have died because of his involvement in the murder of the so-called Godfather of Amsterdam, Fookie Lang, who was believed to be an informer who had cooperated with the Royal Hong Kong Police in one of their periodic and often unsuccessful blitzes on Triad crime. Lang had been shot dead outside his own restaurant on 3 March 1975. 14K had exacted their revenge and fled to London. In turn, they were now the hunted. Kay Wong was unfortunately in the wrong place at the wrong time. His attackers headed north to Leeds where they split up. Two returned to Amsterdam while one went to Wales. Duly retrieved they were charged with murder and appeared at the Old Bailey in November 1976. Convicted of manslaughter, they received terms ranging from five to fourteen years.

Some days after his father's death, Wong Pun Hai went to Vine Street police station with the dual purpose of claiming his father's body and clearing his own name of the death of Li

Kwok Pun. In turn he was arrested and put on trial for murder in Amsterdam with two others. All were acquitted. In the late 1970s he was running a fish and chip shop in the Midlands. In September 1984 he was alleged to have been involved in an attempt to extort £2,000 from a Soho waiter but was again acquitted.

Until recently the Wo Sing Wo were undoubtedly seen as the most powerful of the London Triad operations, a position they established in August 1977 with a ruthless attack on their then principal opponents, Sui Fong. It came in the Kam Tong restaurant in Queensway, then the most important London base of the Triads after Chinatown. Three customers were slashed with traditional swords and another who ran into the street was chased by a man carrying a meat cleaver. In those few seconds Wo Sing Wo established a control it has been reluctant to relinquish. Sui Fong was effectively banished to operations in west London.

On 11 January that year, with one of those splendid passages of hyperbole that judges love to use when they can see the next day's morning papers in their crystal balls, Old Bailey judge Michael Argyle had this to say to Roedean-educated Shing May Wong, when sentencing her for conspiracy to deal in drugs: "When your tiny shadow fell on Gerrard Street, metaphorically the whole street was darkened and you and your confederates walked through the valley of the shadow of death. When you drove to the West End of London it was to become spreaders of crime, disease, corruption and even death."

Argyle was rewarded. The *Daily Mail* dutifully reported, "At that her serenity was gone, she sobbed."

Shing May Wong's story is curious. The reason she gave for becoming involved in the drug world was to avenge her father, apparently a bullion dealer who had been kicked to death in Singapore by a gang of nine youths who lured him to a deserted spot when he was carrying 100 gold bars. Six of the youths were hanged but for May Wong that was not sufficient. She told the court she believed he had been murdered on Triad orders and so decided to infiltrate the group.

Abandoning her beauty salon and boutique business she became a bar hostess in Singapore. There she met Li Mah, the man who was to become her lover and who also received fourteen years' imprisonment. He, it was said, had fallen foul of the Triads when he owed them money and had agreed to work for them after his family was threatened. When he was sent to Britain to peddle drugs, May Wong left her husband and came with him. The third partner was a beauty consultant, Molly Yeow.

Their first consignment was to sell low-grade heroin and when they proved themselves they were issued with two pounds weight of good quality "smack", then worth £92,000 on the London streets at £15 a fix.

Over the next six months Wong and Li Mah brought in £500,000 and in two years her gang brought in £20 million. They were duly promoted, replacing a restaurateur Chin Keong Yong, known as Mervyn, who had become an addict himself and had started stealing from the Triads.

It was during a search of Molly Yeow's home in Montpellier Grove, Kentish Town, that the police discovered that May lived in St Mary's Avenue, Finchley. She was away in Singapore but she had left behind two little red books setting out in neat columns the names of retailers, stocks of heroin and the price paid for supplies. To lure her back the police gave out that Li Mah and Molly Yeow had been seriously injured in a car crash. May returned and was promptly arrested. Described by Argyle as "chief of staff", she received ten years.

As with most communities, the police have a problem in persuading victims to come to court. In 1985, when a Sheffield businessman, Chan Wai Chau, went to a traditional Chinese wedding in Gerrard Street, all went well until seven men arrived together. One walked up to Chan and kicked him, so identifying him as the target for the others. Three then stood guard while Chan was badly beaten and hit with meat cleavers. No one tried to intervene nor indeed could anyone remember seeing anything at all. For a time it was thought Chan would die and he told the police that both he and the other men were members of the Wo Sing Wo and had been involved in a quarrel over the rights to the lucrative Hong Kong soap-opera video market.

By the time the case came up for hearing in 1987, Chan, who had needed to have one of his legs and a thumb amputated, could remember nothing. Nor could he make any identification of his attackers. Nevertheless they were, perhaps surprisingly, convicted and received, just as surprisingly, modest sentences. By 1991 all but one of them were back on the streets of their home towns. The year after Chan's case another Chinese businessman involved in the video industry was attacked with cleavers in Shaftesbury Avenue. He had earlier brought a lawsuit against a man he alleged was pirating his videos.

For many years, however, there was a general disinclination to accept the existence of the Triad operation in London and the United Kingdom. In 1985 the House of Commons Select Committee said there was no significant Triad presence in Great Britain. Indeed, such activity as there was had so little significance "Triad" could possibly be dropped from the police vocabulary. Not everyone agreed. In 1980 the author Fenton Bresler had suggested there was a growing presence in Britain and in 1989 he said that every Chinese restaurant in London had at least one Triad gang-member on its staff.

By 1991, however, there had been a change in the official view. Detective Superintendent James Boocock admitted in an article in *Police Review*:

I was reluctant at first to accept that any Triad groups existed in London. I was anxious that any criminal elements that existed did not have their street credibility, and in consequence their ability to intimidate, enhanced by being labelled Triads, with all the fear that such a term generates.

Quite distinct from these street-gangs, however, there exists a number of very close-knit groups whose criminal empires are networked throughout the United Kingdom and beyond. They are shrewd, ruthless individuals who have no compunction in resorting to extreme violence in order to punish, intimidate or impose their will on vulnerable Chinese businessmen.

By June 1991 the situation in London had deteriorated substantially, with the intimidation of Chinese restaurant-owners rising to such an extent that the chairman of London's Chinatown Association called for the government to proscribe the different Triad gangs.

Then in 1992 the police must have thought they had a major breakthrough after Lam Ying-Kit had been shot in a Soho restaurant the previous year. Lam had made the mistake of coming from Hong Kong to try to take over a share of London's Triad crime from the regrouping Sui Fong. The benefits were the revenue from prostitution, loan-sharking, pirated videos and extortion. The dangers were many and the reprisals were swift. George Wai He Cheung, born in Leicester and known as Specky because of his poor eyesight, was nominated as the unlikely hitman. He had joined the Sui Fong after receiving help when he was on the losing side of a dispute with another Triad group.

The attempted execution went horribly wrong for both Lam and Cheung. After several failed attempts on Lam, in September 1991 Cheung went up behind the man and shot him. It was another botched effort. Although seriously injured Lam struggled with Cheung and forced him to drop the weapon. Cheung escaped to a waiting car but within a matter of hours was arrested in a round-up of known Triads. He quickly rolled over and was given a five-year sentence. Now the police had their first Chinese supergrass.

Probably Cheung was not an ideal choice as either gunman or grass. A complete outsider, he spoke better English than Cantonese. Suffering from bad acne he had a poor track record of attracting women; he could not get a job and his only friend seems to have been his dog, Rambo. All he craved was love and respect, he later told the jury at the Old Bailey.

Held in a special security unit and with a £100,000 contract said to be on his head, Cheung told the court of his initiation ceremony, how he became the bodyguard of a senior Triad figure, had slashed a man with a double-bladed knife and had been involved in extortion and drug-trafficking. The defence was simple. Cheung, in giving evidence, was trying to obtain a lighter sentence and out of spite following a row over a girl, he had also named one man, who had been a stuntman for the Hong Kong actor Jackie Chan. Everyone was acquitted. The police still had a long way to go in making a successful infiltration of the Soho triads.

It was feared that the Triad problem would get worse as 1997 approached and Hong Kong reverted to China. The Chinese Intelligence Unit based in the West End had no doubt that Triads resident in the United Kingdom were arranging for other gang-members to join them here.

The authorities were correct in fearing there might be an increasing problem. The so-called Snakeheads from mainland China arrived to challenge the long-established gangs. They included former soldiers from the People's Liberation Army and took up people-smuggling, kidnapping and torture with enthusiasm.

There were also signs of an increasing Vietnamese criminal presence in the area. In May 1999 three young Vietnamese were jailed for life following a random murder in Lisle Street. The victim had been asked, "Do you follow anyone?" meaning to which Triad group did he belong. The trio had already stabbed a man outside the Hippodrome in Leicester

Square.

Indeed the Hippodrome, which was promoting "Monday night is Chinese night", fell foul of the Triads when in 2002 warring gangs of the 14K and the Wo Sing Wo, with up to a hundred youths involved, fought each other. The promotion night was dropped later that year but there were objections to a renewal of the licence for the premises. After a series of conditions were agreed, including the use of security cameras to record the faces of club-goers, it was granted.

Approaching fifty at the time of her arrest, the diminutive Jing Ping Chen, known as "Sister Ping" – not to be confused with New York's equally sinister Sister Ping – is credited with having smuggled more than 200,000 men and women into Britain. Hers was a well-oiled machine with safe houses, cars, a dozen or more on the payroll and overheads of £35,000 a month. Set against this, it is thought one senior member of her organization earned £300,000 in two months. Her boyfriend, head of the 14K in Rotterdam, was there to provide muscle in the event of any difficulties.

Ping's empire unravelled after the deaths of fifty-eight Chinese whose bodies were found in an air-tight lorry in Dover during a heatwave in June 2000. In June 2003 she received three years in prison in Holland and was fined £8,000 but was cleared of any specific involvement in the Dover case.

Things were seen to be changing and the game became a great deal rougher when in April 2002 a small arsenal of guns, ammunition and fighting sticks was found at premises in Gerrard Street and Gerrard Place. The searches followed a fight between rival Triad gangs in a Soho bar the previous weekend.

Then on 3 June 2003 Chinese-born You Yi He, thought to be a member of the 14K, was shot and killed in the BRB bar in Gerrard Street. The gunman, wearing a red shirt and said to be of Chinese appearance with long hair, shot him from a distance of between ten and fifteen feet and then simply walked out of the bar. Various scenarios were written about the murder. One was that it was part of a battle for the control of Sister Ping's human-trafficking empire. It was generally believed Snakeheads were behind the killing.

The second theory was that it was over unpaid gambling debts owed by You Yi He or, perhaps more likely, it was that he who was owed money that had been illegally lent to gamblers in a Leicester Square casino favoured by Southeast Asian groups. His death had eliminated the necessity to repay the loan. One thing is clear, however: it was the first time a gun had been used successfully in a Chinese killing in Soho. Two years later it was thought that Triad money was still being laundered through the casino and that loan-sharking remained in place. The casino involved denied that this was happening.

An unusual recruit to the Triads was the seventeen-year-old Enfield grammar school boy Jerome Castrillo who in December 2008 received four years at the Old Bailey after being convicted of the manslaughter of drug-dealer Mick McGrath, who had been stealing drugs from a Triad gang. Castrillo had been recruited by older boys and initiated into the Wo Sing Wo on the promise of parties and girls. He had been asked to recite the three good rules – loyalty, honour and respect; and the three bad rules – gambling, drugs and women. McGrath, a one-time friend of the Great Train Robber Charlie Wilson, was hit with a vase while receiving a beating in his flat and died from his injuries. Three others were found guilty of McGrath's murder. Perhaps Castrillo's case is not as uncommon as at first seems. Triads have been recruiting schoolchildren throughout London since the mid-1990s.

In 1995 it was estimated there were around fifty Triad gangs operating and in 2011 that over 75 per cent of Soho's Chinese businesses still pay extortion money to the Triads.

31

The Zemours and Their Friends

Tradition has it that the first of the Zemour brothers (sometimes, but not on their tombstones, spelled with a double "M") to arrive in Paris was Roland, born in Setif, Algeria, in 1926, and that the others came over some years after his death. What is definite is that on 17 November 1947 Roland was shot in a Chicago-style killing in an argument over a prostitute by a rival pimp, Homère Filippi, son of the trainer of the great French middleweight boxer Marcel Cerdan, in rue Blondel off the boulevard de Sebastopol. Filippi was himself shot dead in Nice in 1963. However, an article in the 26 October 1948 issue of *Détéctive* placed his eighteen-year-old brother William (sometimes, including on his tombstone, Williams) as already being in the city. That year he was sent to the Fresnes prison, south of Paris, for living off immoral earnings.

The Zemours – the other brothers were Gilbert, Raymond and Edward – were Jewish Algerians. Driven out by the war with France, they had certainly turned up in Paris by 1955. They began their careers in a small way. There were confidence tricks, such as passing off Algerian wine as Bordeaux – father Raymond was a wine merchant – and cotton as silk as well as selling stolen goods. They also took advantage of the death struggle between the brothers of the Clan Atlan, for whom they initially worked, and the Perret family for the protection of businesses run by the Jewish Pieds-Noirs (Black Foots, the term given to Algerians of European descent) in Faubourg, Montmartre and Sentier. In fact, really all the Zemours had to do was sit back and wait and, of course, from time to time help things along the way a little. On 2 October 1965 Sion Atlan was killed at the Poussin Bleu, a café-restaurant in rue Geoffroy-Marie near the Grands Boulevards: on 21 December the next year his brother Réné was shot to death in the Au Bon Coin café in rue Choron near Métro Saint-Georges.

That disposed of the Clan Atlan but the Perrets did not last long afterwards. Led by their formidable mother Léo, who ran the bar-restaurant de Cornouailles in rue des Martyrs, a number of them were arrested for living off the immoral earnings of girls working in Les Halles, the Madeleine, Pigalle and the Bois de Boulogne. A search of the mother's apartment turned up a cache of machine-guns and disguises. Gilbert and Clément Perret went to prison for pimping and in the spring of 1967 their man Lucien Sans, known as "Bouboule", was machine-gunned at the Don Camillo bar in Saint Germain-des-Pres. A witness took the number of the killers' car, a Peugeot 404. It belonged to Gilbert Zemour who had earlier lent it to his mother. There was no suggestion, however, that Gilbert could possibly have been involved in the death of the last of a team many saw as his major rivals. After all he had been on his way to Toulouse at the time. The rest of the Perret team left Paris, heading first for the suburbs then Brest and later the Basque country where some of them joined the Grupos Antiterroristas de Liberación (GAL), the death squad which operated mainly in France to deal with ETA terrorists.

Until the end of the 1970s the Zemours did not have things all their own way. The Sicilians such as the Vellas and Gauthiers had been long established in Paris and were none too keen on the take-over of what they considered their rightful territory. It is also possible they suffered from their refusal to enter into drug-trafficking.

They put together their own gang with a collection of Jewish Pieds-Noirs and it was said that at their height the Zemours had an army of around 200. Certainly they needed a large staff for there was a considerable wastage of talent. There were over forty gang deaths between October 1965 and that of Gilbert Zemour in July 1983. In September 1976 alone it was estimated that the Pieds-Noirs had lost fourteen men and the Sicilians eight. Much of the spillage was over the long struggle for control of various private clubs that were the only legal venues for gambling in Paris.

Given that pimping and protection rackets are the passes to any grand criminal enterprise, from there the brothers were able to gain a foothold in other more profitable undertakings such as nightclubs and casinos. What they did was provide a service. A shop protected by them had nothing to fear from any other thugs. Nor did they extort more than the victim was able to pay.

Within a decade the Z Gang had taken a large slice of the Paris underworld. Not for nothing was père Raymond suspected of having set up a brothel chain from Brussels to Abidjan in the Côte d'Ivoire. Quite apart from the numerous prostitutes who worked for them in Paris and throughout Africa, the family had interests in the Eros centres – licensed brothels, without a madame, where the working girls rent small rooms for the day, or just a few hours – in most of the big German towns. They had nightclubs and casinos run by frontmen and the profits poured into their coffers. They had also invested heavily in property and the garment trade with contacts in Canada, Germany and Hong Kong. For a time they also had control of the Tiercé and racecourse rackets. Dapper Eddie Zemour carried at least £1,500 with him, had a large apartment near the Arc de Triomphe and changed his car twice a year. He was regarded as a prodigious womanizer.

What the Zemours apparently refused to do was to deal in drugs, something that detective Roger La Taillanter suggested was to their credit and, however bad the brothers were, showed they had a certain morality: "For them a man worthy of his name didn't exploit children." In the 1970s when the French Connection was in operation, the drug factories on the Côte d'Azur were at their height and police interference was at a minimum, the Zemours could have stepped in with everything to gain and little to fear but they did not.

Instead, Roger Bacry, a member of one of the suburban gangs, along with the Sicilian Jean-Claude Vella, known as "Petites Pattes" or "Little Paws", took over a number of Zemour members and went into the drug business buying from André Codemine, who had escaped from South America to Europe and had set up shop in Brussels. The venture was a failure and when Bacry petitioned to rejoin the Zemours they turned him down.

The beginning of the end of the Zemours came with the *affaire du Thélème*. In an attempt to end the bitter feuding with the Sicilians, on 28 February 1975 the Zemours were due to meet them in the Italians' headquarters in the Café Thélème on the rue Cardinal Lemoine. They were betrayed and the police raided the café, allegedly to intervene in the quarrel. However, only the Zemours were there. In the shoot-out between the police and the family, William was killed and Gilbert was shot in the back but survived. A Zemour cohort, Joseph Elbaz, was also killed by the newly formed anti-gang squad. Two North African lawyers who just happened to be there were also shot, but not fatally. The Zemour view was that the police had opened fire and that Inspector Jacques Chaix, who was undoubtedly hit in the shoulder, copped a bullet from his own men. In support of this, Gilbert Zemour pointed out that no charges had been laid against the surviving Zemour members. Unsurprisingly the view from the police corner was slightly different. The only reason no charges had been brought was because the guns thrown hurriedly on the floor by the Zemours could not be matched to any individuals.

William's funeral at the family grave at Bagneux was in the great tradition of gangland obsequies. His young widow Fabienne and the other women wailed as the hearse arrived, itself groaning under a mountain of wreaths. The coffin was solid mahogany with gilt handles. The mourners wore anything from mink and astrakhan collars to jeans and polo-neck sweaters. Photographers were threatened and ordered to hand over their film.

Following the café shoot-out, the first of the Sicilians' four leaders was killed. Jean-Claude Vella was found, forehead smashed, in the boot of a car parked in Avenue de Choisy on 14 September 1975. The Sicilians then lost two more chiefs and as backing the Zemours imported Israeli bodyguards. One of the Pieds-Noirs' most dependable killers was found with thirty-nine bullets in him in a side street.

After the battle at Thélème, Gilbert then reputedly turned quasi-respectable and went into the restaurant business in Brussels but he was still in close contact with members of the Milieu, the French underworld. Eddie managed to get into the United States and opened a restaurant, La Bonne Maison, in Miami although he was unable to obtain a liquor licence for it and it later went bankrupt.

Shortly before Christmas 1976 Gilbert Zemour issued proceedings against the Minister of the Interior over the death of William and also gave a lengthy interview to *L'Express*, a magazine which has followed the twisting footsteps of the Milieu over the years. Perhaps unwisely he also told *Paris Match* he would investigate William's murder himself.

L'Express questioned Gilbert Zemour closely about his family business and the deaths that were close to them. Naturally he had an answer for everything. For example, the gun found in the glove compartment of Gilbert's car the day after the shoot-out in the Café Thélème? No problem. It had been given by Yzi Spieghel, now dead, as a present to Gilbert's wife for her safety when she returned late at night to their home at Le Chesnay near Versailles. Indeed it was still in the wrapping paper.

Gilbert Zemour, who had once served a year for his involvement in prostitution, was also able and willing to give a rundown of his relationship with some of the underworld figures who had been killed over the previous few months. First, there was Raphael Dadoun, killed in the underground parking of his flat on 13 March 1973. Certainly Gilbert knew him but he wasn't a friend, nor had he been interested in Dadoun's affairs. In fact, the police knew full well that the dead man had had an interest in a bar in the rue Saint-Denis and had been killed in a quarrel over his share. For his part Gilbert would like to have all the girlie bars and hot pillow hotels shut down. The fact that they remained open was wholly a police affair.

And Pierre Nezmoz, shot while with friends in the Le Gentilly restaurant? Zemour had only seen him once in the Pariscope, a bar owned by Spieghel. So far as he knew it was something to do with the death of Dadoun.

Another body had been that of Marcel Barokhel, known as the Korean, killed on 11 October as he left his mother's home. Barokhel might be thought, as a North African, to be part of the Zemour set-up. Unfortunately Gilbert couldn't help *L'Express* much. Yes, he had met him on a "Hello-Goodbye" basis but he had no idea how the dead man lived his life nor had the police sought to question him.

And Roger Bacry, found dead at his mistress's home on 12 June 1974? Zemour did not like this one, describing him as a shit who had committed suicide too late to redeem his previous bad behaviour. What about Vella then? Of the rival gang-leader Gilbert Zemour had nothing but bad to say: "Good riddance. I saw him once with Gauthier in the hall of the Prince of Wales. They killed each other and the police know it."

As is not uncommon, commercial and showbusiness personalities were keen to hang around the Zemours, and Gilbert in particular made a speciality of cultivating them. Too close a connection did, of course, come with a high price and Le Taillanter believed a Swiss millionaire only escaped from

Gilbert's clutches after the gang-leader's death. Gilbert dined regularly in Brasserie Lipp and on one occasion he was placed next to Christian Bonnot, Minister of the Interior, who did not recognize him as his dining companion. The men chatted happily about the merits and faults of the police.

In September 1976, almost a year to the day after Vella's body had been found, the surviving Sicilian chief Marcel Gauthier was shot dead in Nice as he stepped ashore after a holiday in Corsica. Gilbert said, "That causes me great grief. The police know I had nothing to do with it."

On the Zemour side casualties included Robert Liwer, shot in the head while driving in the rue de Montevideo in the sixteenth arrondissement, and Yzi Spieghel, blasted on 17 October 1975 in the car park at his unfurnished flat: "You must ask M Leclerc [the police officer] about him. He put him forward as my front man." Michel Gharbu was removed in the rue de Vaugirard while Jean-Claude Atali was hit with thirty-nine machine-gun bullets in the eighteenth arrondissement.

In his interview with *L'Express* Gilbert Zemour was at pains to correct the false image put about by the police and press. His father had only lived in a small, three-room flat in Ormesson. William, contrary to popular belief, had never had a twenty-room villa at Le Chesnay. Instead, he had lived in what Gilbert described as a shack in rue Pierre l'Hermite and then for the last fourteen years in a four-roomed flat in the seventeenth arrondissement. Gilbert himself had lived in modest comfort in Le Chesnay in a five-roomed flat in the Palais Royale, which he leased for 2,800 francs a month paid for out of his salary as a furniture salesman, something he had become after being a wine representative.

"Cover-up," said the police to *L'Express*, although in private they doubtless said something much stronger. To give credit where it was due, however, they no longer thought that Gilbert had been involved in the shipment of 120 kilos of heroin seized on 13 May 1972 in Brussels.

The hardworking salesman Gilbert had somehow scrimped and saved his money because he was able to buy himself a flat in Miami and to set up a company, La Gipala Properties, in Canada. Where had the money come from? Apparently, he had inherited a goodly sum in Algeria and had further improved his finances with shrewd investments in France. The remaining Zemours were set for a period of relative calm and certainly prosperity. It ended in 1982.

On 15 January of that year, sixty-two-year-old Marcel Francisci, variously described as the owner of several Paris gambling houses and in 1971 as one of the five big fish who ran the French Connection from Marseilles, was shot dead with a Colt 11.43 mm, the classic French gangland weapon, while sitting in his white Jaguar in the underground car park of his flat in the rue de la Faisenderie in Paris's fashionable sixteenth arrondissement. In his pocket was a tape-recording of a conversation between two prominent lawyers with connections that reached to the top of President Mitterrand's administration.

He had received one shot in the stomach and one in the forehead, the traditional gangland coup. Small, round and balding he believed that in recent years he had escaped from the gangland wars. Previously, he certainly had some luck. When two Corsican gunmen went to bomb his home in Bougival outside Paris they blew themselves up instead.

At one time Francisci had tried to set up gambling at the Victoria Sporting Club in London, then run by a solicitor, the legendary entrepreneur Judah Binstock. He failed in this but his feud with fellow Corsican, Jean-Baptiste Andreani, left a trail of bodies in Paris and Nice.

Francisci had built up a political career as a local government leader of the Rassemblement pour la République (RPR) party in Corsica and was the mayor of his home town of Ciamacce. All went well until the pride of his empire in Paris, the Cercle Haussman casino, was shut down on the orders of Gaston

Defferre, Mayor of Marseilles, who was also the Socialist Minister for the Interior. Defferre accused high-ranking officials in the neo-Gaullist RPR of having been "protectors, friends and accomplices of Francisci". It was thought that Francisci had fallen foul of the new administration. In turn the police thought that the closure of this club unleashed another battle for control of the remaining clubs in Paris.

On 12 March 1982 Jean-Baptiste Andreani, now aged seventy-six and the leading figure in the gaming-club world, was arrested and charged with illegally changing foreign currency for gamblers. Police had raided Andreani's home the day after Francisci's death and found a stock of gold worth $3 million.

Francisci was sumptuously buried in his native village where he was regarded as a great benefactor. An airbus was chartered at a cost of £20,000 to fly 150 mourners to Corsica. Francisci may have been named Monsieur Heroin, but despite intense speculation there was never any real proof he was involved in the drug-trafficking.

Eddie Zemour was strongly fancied for the killing and was questioned at length by the police who believed he was trying to take over the Francisci empire and also retrieve a debt of several million US dollars. He provided an alibi and returned to the United States. In 1982 a film, *Le Grand Pardon*, was made about the rise of the Zemours with Eddie played by Roger Hanin, President Mitterrand's brother-in-law.

Perhaps Eddie had taken a step too far. He was shot on 8 April 1983 by a hired professional killer at his home in Keystone Bay, Miami, hit in the chest with five bullets from a rifle as he relaxed in pink silk pyjamas. He had been in Miami trying to gain a foothold into the lucrative Caribbean gambling market said to be controlled by the Mafia.

Three months later, on 28 July 1983, Gilbert Zemour himself was shot down near his home on the Avenue de Ségur as he walked his four miniature poodles. It appeared his killer, possibly the former hairdresser's assistant, Gilbert Hoareau, known as Gilbert the Lebanese, approached from behind and executed him in traditional gangland manner.

Hoareau was later killed in what was known as the "Lemonade War", a battle for control of Marseilles's nightclubs. On 6 October 1983 he was gunned down, hit by ten bullets in the Cours Joseph-Thierry in a motorcycle ride-by. He was there to "talk" with "Monsieur Paul", Paul Mondolini who would be killed in almost the same spot on 22 July two years later.

In an interview in *Paris Match*, Commissaire Roger Le Taillanter believed the end of the Zemours' tale came with the death of Gilbert. The question was how had they survived for some twenty years? The answer was with a combination of muscle, acumen and no doubt some political clout.

After attending the funeral of his brother the surviving Zemour, Theodore-André (known as Dédé), went in hiding far away from the scene and reportedly lived either in Palma, Majorca, or in the French Antilles where he had business interests.

The successors to the Zemours were the Clan Genova from Villemomble, an eastern suburb of Paris. They were headed by Claude, known as "Le Gros", who was noted for the tattoo of a butterfly on what the papers called a "sensitive part of his anatomy". Apparently at moments of passion it flapped its wings. The beginning of their end came when Eric Pasquet, known as "Petit Ricky", the Genovas' first lieutenant, kidnapped Ihmed Mohiedinne, known as "La Gelée", and tortured him in an attempt to make him give up the proceeds of an armed robbery at Saint-Ouen-l'Aumône. Mohiedinne was in turn the trusted lieutenant of a group known as the Frères Hornec: Jean-Claude, Mario, Gilbert and the youngest, Mark. Described as sedentary gypsies they ran bars and clubs around the Champs-Élysées and were alleged to have been involved in armed robberies, drugs and smuggling, and illegal one-armed bandits.

The Clan Genova paid dearly for this error of judgement. Petit Ricky and boxer Christophe Tizzo were trapped when the former left his gun in the boot of his car and they were shot dead in the rue de Charonne, not far from the Bastille. Bodies piled up on both sides until Claude Genova was shot in the back and killed on 22 August 1994 as he left a bar at the Concorde Lafayette near Porte Maillot where he had gone in an effort to settle the quarrel. Bits and pieces of the clan continued to operate until more or less the last two were shot dead in December 2000. They had been masterminding twelve prostitutes in the forest of Armainvilliers who had been servicing lorry drivers. The scheme had been run with some give and take on both sides. The girls were provided with social security numbers and a five-week annual holiday.

After the death of Claude Genova the Paris Milieu was now firmly in the control of the Frères Hornec. There was, however, still one fly in their ointment in the shape of the semi-retired long-standing member of the Milieu, the half-Spanish, half-Belgian François Vanverberghe, known as François le Belge, born in the Belle-de-Mai quarter of Marseilles in March 1946. He had survived the Marseilles gang wars of the 1970s and was said to have been a mastermind of the French Connection.

He was on the police slate at the age of sixteen after he stole a caravan and three years later he was an established pimp. In April 1973 he went to prison for thirty months when false papers and three guns were found in his flat. He was out for only a matter of days in 1975 before he received fourteen years for his part in the French Connection. He blamed his former ally Gaetan "Tony" Zampa for "balancing" (betraying) him. In January 1984 Zampa was found apparently hanged in his cell in Les Baumettes prison, Marseilles, where both men were being held. In January 1990, still in Les Baumettes, Vanverberghe was thought to have organized the killings of six members of the Marseilles Milieu and, more interestingly, the politician and doctor Jean-Jacques Peschard, friend of the then mayor of Marseilles, gunned down in a cul-de-sac after leaving a restaurant. Not that Peschard's earlier life had been without its excitement. His mistress, a nurse called Christine Barras who had been taking money to Switzerland on his behalf, had disappeared in December 1984. The police dug up the good doctor's garden but her body was never found.

It was a team associated with Vanverberghe, but without the great man himself, that went on trial in 1990 for a 1987 robbery when they tunnelled into the Caisse d'Epargne bank in Marseilles and took £1 million before escaping through the city's sewers.

Vanverberghe was again "balanced" in 1992, this time by another informer from the days of the French Connection, François Scapula, who was serving a twenty-year sentence. This time the Belgian was accused of smuggling forty-four pounds of heroin into the United States from Spain. After four years in prison, in April 1996 Vanverberghe was found not guilty and he returned to Paris after telling the press, "I had faith in my country's justice system. I have waited a long time for this moment. Now I can relax." Vanverberghe was later awarded £11,000 compensation and said he would donate it to the Abbé Pierre's Emmaus movement of self-supporting communities for dropouts. Although the Abbé rejected Vanverberghe's kindly gesture, it nevertheless took him one step further on the road towards being a folk-hero.

Vanverberghe's quarrel with the Frères Hornec was over the control of what the French call *machines à sous* – one-armed bandits. It was also thought that he was on the slide. In March 2000 he was sentenced to two months imprisonment for running prostitutes out of a bar in rue François Ier, near the Champs-Élysées. This was regarded as a downward step for the great man. Worse was that he had let the death of his godson François Boglietto in Aix in February the previous year go unpunished. When Vanverberghe's brother José had been killed in September 1989, his killer Bernard Bousquel had not lasted a week.

By now he had a declared income of around £500,000 a year, which he maintained was due to his success at gambling. In reality it came from the one-armed bandits, girls and nightclubs. He was thought to have owned around 150 bandits with an income of three to four and a half million francs a month.

Vanverberghe generally eschewed bodyguards, which made people nervous about sitting next to him, but he did take two men with him when he met the Hornec brothers to discuss an arrangement to split profits from the machines. It was thought things had been worked out but the end came during the afternoon of 27 September 2000. Vanverberghe was killed by gunmen in the basement of the Artois club off the Champs-Élysées while laundering money by buying winning tickets at a premium from gamblers on the afternoon's racing at St Cloud. His killers escaped on a motorcycle and no one was charged with his murder.

There were reprisals, however. One of the suspects, Boualem Talata, who had been arrested and released, was shot dead within the month. Talata's boss, Djilali Zitouni, was ambushed in July the next year near his home in Gennevilliers and shot in the head and neck. He died two hours later. On 15 October 2002 two of Vanverberghe's nephews were killed and that seemed to "settle accounts" as the Milieu calls it.

It is possible, however, that Zitouni was not the contractor of Vanverberghe's killing and that it was arranged by Corsican interests over the protection of a casino in the Nice area. Members of a Corsican gang, Brise de la Mer, were thought to have taken over Vanverberghe's interests in the Champs-Élysées area.

32

The Rise and Fall of the Moran Family

The rise and fall of the Moran family can be set against the background of the Melbourne drug wars of the early twenty-first century. By the end of the twentieth century, with the profits to be made from drugs, particularly amphetamines, crime in the Australian city changed radically. The rise of gang violence in Melbourne has stemmed, at least in part, from the high-risk policy adopted by the police in Victoria during the 1990s of manufacturing its own amphetamines in an attempt to break into the city's network of dealers.

The Victoria state police force's drug squad, far from being enlarged as was probably necessary to try to stem the tide of heroin flooding the markets, was divided into three units. The first was to investigate the Asian heroin syndicates, the second to investigate the Romanian drugs gangs and the third was to look into the local amphetamine market.

Amphetamines are relatively easy to produce and were being cooked in small laboratories. The profits were great and the dangers were few. A conviction for major trafficking in heroin could earn twenty years and upwards; for a similar amphetamine conviction the penalty was a quarter or a third of that. By 1990 Melbourne had become the amphetamine capital of Australia. Two years later producers, as opposed to distributors, were to be the main target of the police.

By the middle of the decade a system had been devised whereby the police would buy chemicals from wholesalers and, using controlled deliveries, they or trusted informers – if that is not an oxymoron – would sell on to the producers so providing evidence for prosecutions.

This was all well and good in theory. In the three years from 1998 nearly sixty clandestine laboratories were discovered. In 1999 a man regarded as Australia's biggest amphetamines manufacturer was arrested, as was a Melbourne character charged with conspiracy involving a shipping container of chemicals. But then the wheels began to fall off. There were allegations that chemicals were being stockpiled by the police. A secret bank account was opened and sometimes chemicals went missing. In December 2001 the drug squad was disbanded and replaced with a major drug investigation division. But the damage had been done.

By the end of the century there was a long-running turf war as the New Boys, who came from the suburb of Sunshine and who were led by Carl "Fat Boy" Williams and his close friend Andrew "Benji" Veniamin, clashed with the old guard known as the Carlton Crew. From 1998 there were over thirty gangland killings in Melbourne, many of which could be linked to the power struggle between the rival bosses. Williams had left school at the age of eleven and was soon selling amphetamines, moving steadily up the criminal hierarchy. His father George, who was thought by some to be the real brains behind the operation, pleaded guilty in 2005 to dealing in a commercial amount of amphetamines and was sentenced to four and a half years with a minimum of twenty months to be served.

Originally the disparate major underworld figures had seemed to get on well together, drinking and dancing in the city's clubs – Monday night would be Billboard night, Tuesday at Chasers and a third night at Sheiks – but then the drug trade, pride and that often fatal word "respect" reared their ugly heads.

Among the leading members of the Carlton Crew were the former receiver and safe-breaker Graham Kinniburgh, known as the Munster after a television character. He was a former member of a team known as the Magnetic Safe Gang. Ranged with him were his friend Lewis Moran and his two sons, Jason and Mark. The Moran family had a long and distinguished history. The patriarch was Old Des Moran, a leading starting-post bookmaker at Flemington and Moonee Ponds racecourses, and an associate of the great post-war thieves of the time including Wee Jimmy Wilson, Mickie Mutch and Arthur "Duke" Delaney. Old Des had married the backyard abortionist Belle, one-time mistress of the ex-police officer Stanley "Charlie" Wyatt, who also worked the badger game with her. Wyatt was literally the right-hand man of the abortionist Dr Fenton Bowen, who had rooms opposite the law courts and who ironically was called over if a defendant or witness was taken ill. Late in his career, Fenton Bowen, suffering from the shakes, was unable to perform the abortions himself but he saw the patients and then sent them into the back room where "Charlie did the business", recalls one lawyer. A little verse was written about them.

> You rape 'em
> We scrape 'em
> No foetus
> Can beat us

Belle's son Lewis Moran became inseparable from Kinniburgh, and it was he who brought him into the Carlton Crew. Jason Moran was Lewis's only biological child. Mark's natural father was Leslie "Johnny" Cole, a member of the virulent Ship Painters and Dockers Union. After the long-running war for control of the union many members left Melbourne and Cole went to Sydney, where early in September 1982 he was shot six times in the arm, leg, foot, knee and stomach when he was bringing his dogs back from their evening walk. He told the police he would "sort it out" himself but a few months later, on 10 November, while on his way home from the physiotherapist, Cole was shot and killed as he left his car at the garage of his very smart home on the Georges River, south of Sydney. Like so many before and after him he had turned the place into a virtual fortress with video surveillance and iron bars over the windows and a mesh fence. It did him no good. This time he was shot in the left shoulder and the heart and the masked gunman finished the job, Mafia style, with a bullet behind the left ear.

Cole's estranged wife, Judith, who had been a talented dancer as a child and teenager appearing on stage and on television, took up once more with Lewis Moran, her childhood sweetheart and now an illegal bookmaker. Together they had a son, Jason. As they grew up Mark was regarded as the more thoughtful and Jason the wilder brother who had learned to drive at the age of nine and made money parking cars for customers attending Melbourne's showground near where they lived.

When they left school neither of the half-brothers worked for long in the accepted sense although Mark trained as a pastry chef and Jason did a stint in an abattoir where he developed a drink problem.

Jason Moran's real work, however, was as a standover man and extortionist working in partnership with Alphonse Gangitano, a man who liked to be known as "The Robert de Niro of Lygon Street". On 7 February 1995 Gangitano killed the popular East St Kilda gangland figure, Gregory John Workman. The two had gone to a wake together and on to a party to raise bail for an alleged robber. Gangitano became abusive and he and Workman went outside. Two sisters saw the shooting and made detailed statements of seeing Gangitano almost literally with a smoking gun in his hand. The sisters went into a form of protective custody, living in a caravan, dining on takeaway food and collecting their clothes in a lay-by. Unfortunately from the viewpoint of the authorities it was not all that protective. They were contacted by Jason Moran who told them that if they turned up in court they and their families would certainly be killed. They were taken to see a lawyer and made statements withdrawing their evidence after which they absented themselves from Victoria, spending a year in Europe on a trip paid for by Gangitano. Inevitably the charges were dismissed and Gangitano's lawyer, George Defteros, put in a bill to the police for $69,975.35 (all figures are in Australian dollars). At the time it was thought highly probable that there would be revenge for Workman's death from St Kilda criminals but none came immediately.

Growing up, the man whom Jason Moran admired was his "uncle" Les Kane who had disappeared, presumed murdered, in October 1978. Jason later took up with Les Kane's daughter, Trisha, and they had three children. Although having limited earning capacity in the outside world – he was on the payroll of a jeweller's for a number of years – he was able to send his children to private schools. Despite his balding hair and paunch, he was seen as a wiseguy in the American tradition. "He was like a cat on the prowl, clicking his fingers as he walked. When he entered into a room he took control," said one lawyer admirer.

Judith Moran would later claim that her sons' criminal careers began when the pair were set up. She claimed they had been promised a good behaviour bond after a fight with an off-duty police officer in the Palace Disco in the seaside suburb of St Kilda, a twenty-minute tram ride from the city centre. The policeman, moonlighting as a bouncer, had, she said, called Mark a poofter, something which could not go unpunished. Despite the promise, Jason received five months and Mark four.

Other convictions for violence followed. In December 1995, for no clear reason other than they had been taking amphetamines, Jason Moran and Gangitano attacked customers in the city's Sports Bar with pool cues. When he was arrested Moran suffered a fractured skull. The trial judge declined to say anything more than that his arrest had been "remarkably heavy handed". Moran received a year's sentence, with a minimum of eight months to be served.

But between the Sports Bar incident and Moran's sentence there had been another assault. This time it was in Chasers nightclub in January 1996 when a row broke out between Trisha and another woman. Moran knocked the girl to the ground, punched and kicked her. In turn, he was on the end of another bad beating, possibly from Gangitano. For the Chasers assault he received eighteen months' imprisonment with half suspended for three years.

Opinions over the immediate cause of the gang war in the city vary. They may have stemmed from the amphetamine manufacturer's arrest and his consequent inability to control the distribution of the drug, which meant squabbling among men who had previously worked for him; or perhaps from the murder of Gangitano in his home in Templestowe on 16 January 1998. Possibly both.

The police believed that the scenario of the killing ran more or less as follows. Jason Moran was involved in an argument with Gangitano and shot him. Although he denied it, also present was Graham "The Munster" Kinniburgh, who saw what was happening and ran out through a security mesh on the front door, cutting himself in the process. Later, he went upstairs to see what the security video had recorded. On the sound principle that lies should be as close to the truth as possible, he told the police he had indeed been to see Gangitano, who was on the telephone speaking to his West Coast friend John Kizon, who was then having dinner with a barrister. Gangitano had asked Kinniburgh to leave as he was due to have a meeting with an unnamed man. Kinniburgh went to buy some cigarettes and returned half an hour later only to find his host dead. The coroner had no doubt that both he and Moran were implicated.

Moran posted a touching eulogy in the Melbourne paper the *Herald Sun*: "Words can't express how I feel. There will never be a man such as yourself. Whatever I asked of you was done 110 per cent. I will love you always. Your little mate Jase."

Less impressed with Gangitano was a genuine Melbourne hardman, Mark "Chopper" Read, who called him a "plastic gangster". Certainly Gangitano was afraid of Read who once walked into a nightclub with explosives strapped around his body. In 1991 Gangitano believed that a contract had been taken out on him to be executed by Read and retreated with his family to Italy. He only returned when Read was jailed in October 1992 following his conviction for the attempted murder of biker and drug-dealer Sid Collins in Tasmania.

Read may have had little time for Gangitano but he was well regarded by others, not least the bail justice Rowena Allsop. She knew both him and his great friend and subsequent leader of the Carlton Crew Mick Gatto, regarding the fallen leader as a man of parts unknown to those not close to him. In turn Ms Allsop came under some criticism for being quite as close to Gangitano as she had been. Only a few hours before his death they had been drinking together until his curfew came into effect for the night. Now prevailed upon to speak at his funeral, held at the underworld's favourite church St Mary's Star of the Sea, West Melbourne, dressed in turquoise and her voice trembling with emotion, she spoke of his wit, his love of Oscar Wilde and his passion for Dolce & Gabbana aftershave lotion.

The year after Gangitano's death the bodies began to pile up. On 13 October 1999 Jason Moran shot Carl Williams in the stomach in a Gladstone Park, Broadmeadows, over a failed amphetamine deal. Williams had been both undercutting the Morans and supplying them with substandard amphetamines. Mark Moran urged Jason urged to finish Williams off but, unfortunately for the pair and many others, he did not. Gallantly, the wounded man made no complaint and claimed in the teeth of evidence to the contrary that he did not know the identity of his attacker. But it took Williams less than a year to exact partial revenge.

Meanwhile, in February 2000 Jason Moran was found guilty of the affray at the Sports Bar. By then he and Trisha had a twin son and daughter. The court was told how he had settled down and was working on the docks. He may have been receiving a pay packet but neither the prosecution nor the judge accepted that he was actually working. This time the sentence was three years with a twenty-one month minimum.

On 15 June 2000 Mark Moran, pastry chef, designer drug-dealer, standover man and, it was alleged, the driver in a 1988 payroll robbery in which a guard was killed, was shot dead as he was getting into his car outside his luxury home in Essendon. He had been out during the night for half an hour and was shot as he returned home by men who were waiting for him – two blasts from a shotgun were followed by one in the head from a revolver. Moran's actual killers were thought to have been New Boys Dino Dibra and Benji Veniamin but really there were no prizes for guessing the contractor. Jason Moran lasted for some years longer than his half-brother.

In May 2003 Operation Purana, with a team of some sixty detectives, was set up to solve the Melbourne underworld murders and possibly to make pre-emptive strikes towards stopping the feuding. It did not get off to a good start. On 21 June that year Jason Moran was shot dead in front of his and other children in the car park of the Cross Keys hotel in Essendon North after they had been to an Auskick football clinic. Down with him went Pasquale Barbaro, his bodyguard. His killing had been slated for the previous week to coincide with the anniversary of the death of Mark, but it was said that one of the killers had failed to pick him out. Because the killing had been in front of his and other children it was regarded by some of the underworld as particularly shameful but over the years it has rather set a trend.

Jason Moran had previously survived one threat to his life when the robber Mark Anthony Smith, who had been convicted and jailed for a minimum of thirteen years for the murder of a man on a Craigieburn building site in 1987, failed to carry out the contract. As a reprisal Smith was shot in the neck on 28 December 2002. He survived and left Victoria.

Barbaro's death had some unlikely postscripts. Mark and Cheryl McEachran, frustrated by their inability to conceive a sixth child, snatched a three-week-old baby in a shopping centre. Their choice could not have been much more unfortunate. The baby was Montana, daughter of Barbaro's cousin Giuseppe, known as Joe, a drug-dealer with links to the upper echelons of the crime scene. They were jailed for a total of nineteen years and ordered to pay $20,000 to the child's mother. In turn the kidnapping served Joe Barbaro well. On his appearance for sentencing for dealing drugs, he told the court the kidnapping had changed his life. He now thought, "How could I have put another parent through that sort of agony?" He received a modest five-year minimum.

With the second of the Moran brothers gone, it was probably only a matter of time before a move was made on Kinniburgh. Over the decades, the modest, influential and shadowy Graham Allan Kinniburgh, once a member of the dying breed of safe-breakers, rose to become a kingpin of the city's crime scene. Kinniburgh, whose career spanned three decades, was one of the relatively few mobsters to have bridged the gap between the underworld and respectability and was well known for his discreet connections to Melbourne's establishment.

Born in a slum in Richmond, he was regarded in his early days as having a razor-sharp temper and the ability to back it up with his fists. He began his career as a fringe member of the shoplifting Kangaroo Gang, which pillaged jewellery shops all over Europe in the 1960s, and was then a member of the so-called Magnetic Drill Gang, which stole $1.7 million from a New South Wales bank, bagged a jewellery haul from a Lonsdale Street office, and raided safety deposit boxes in Melbourne. He was also thought to have been the organizer of a bullion snatch in Queensland.

Early in his criminal career he was charged with receiving stolen property from a burglary at the home of magnate Lindsay Fox. When the police raided Kinniburgh's home, he was found to have a unique pendant owned by Mrs Fox in a coat pocket as well as $4,500 in cash in a drawer. He offered the police the cash if they did not charge him but they declined. He was charged with both the burglary and the bribery but he had an identical pendant made in Hong Kong, so casting doubt in the minds of the jury that the pendant was, in fact, unique.

Over the years the lantern-jawed Kinniburgh refined his public image. He was seen with barristers and solicitors around the law courts and with owners and jockeys at Caulfield and other Melbourne tracks, where he was a genial and successful tipster as well as being privately regarded as a race-fixer. He was said to have been kind enough to help a jockey pay an $80,000 tax bill. Although he claimed to be a simple rigger he lived in the expensive suburb of Kew and could be seen in fashionable restaurants such as the Flower Drum in the city's Chinatown. He was, said one Melbourne barrister who socialized with him, "one of the three top crims I ever met".

In 1994, when his son married into one of the city's established families, the wedding was held at St Peter's Anglican Church and the reception was at the oldest of the Melbourne establishments, the Windsor. In a scene that could have been taken from *The Godfather*, intelligence police snapped not the bride and groom but the guests, so updating their files. Many of the guests wore Ray-Bans throughout the evening and Kinniburgh's speech was said to have resembled one by Marlon Brando. A few months before his death, his barrister daughter Suzie married the son of a former attorney-general.

In the month before he died Kinniburgh took to carrying a gun, something he had not done since his early days. Shortly before midnight on 13 December 2003, he was shot in the chest as he left his car outside his home and walked to his drive carrying a bag of groceries. It is thought he managed to get one shot off from his own gun.

It was said of the Carlton Crew's Dominic "Mick" Gatto, the semi-official newspaper epitaph writer and tribute payer to so many of the city's underworld figures, that no gangland killing could be regarded as such until he had inserted a flowery death notice in the *Herald Sun*. His tribute to the Munster is a fair example of his work:

> You were a true Chameleon, you could adapt to any situation, rubbing shoulders with the best of them and being able to talk at any level about any topic. I was so proud to be part of your life. This has left a void in my heart that can't be replaced. I love you "Pa" and I will never forget you.

Unkind people thought that Kinniburgh's ability to talk to the police on many topics may have helped to keep him out of prison in the years before his death. The week before he died he had held a series of meetings in the city's restaurants with the cream of the local villains. Indeed, according to the *Sunday Age*, the day before he was shot he had been seen having coffee in Lygon Street with a detective from the Carlton CIB. Others would have none of it, believing Kinniburgh, of all people, to be staunch.

Things climaxed early in 2004 when, on 23 March, New Boy Benji Veniamin, short with a shaven head and tattoos on his back and arms, regarded as dangerously erratic and now the bodyguard of Carl Williams, was shot in the head at lunchtime in a back room of La Porcella in Lygon Street. He had gone there for a meeting with Mick Gatto. Veniamin, who was said to have lively soft brown eyes and was thought to receive $100,000 a hit, arrived at the restaurant at 2 p.m. in a borrowed silver Mercedes, which he double-parked. At the time he was disqualified from driving and in the months before his death had racked up some forty speeding and parking tickets. Gatto, regarded as a great fixer and for whom a fee of $5,000 was required to sit with him, was at his usual table. The Royal Commission into the Building Industry had described this former heavyweight professional boxer as a standover man; he preferred "industrial consultant". They went into a back room and within minutes Veniamin was dead.

Later, it would be said that Veniamin was on the verge of giving up his criminal enterprises but was reluctant to do so in case it was thought he was a quitter. Quitter or not the police had him in their sights over at least five murders. He died after what has been described as "an altercation". As he waited for the police Gatto apologized to the restaurant-owner for the undoubted inconvenience caused by the shooting.

Now prices were rising on the street if not in La Porcella, which closed shortly afterwards to reopen as a Chinese restaurant. It was said the price on Gatto's head was $400,000. The word on the street was that Veniamin's employer, Carl Williams, would be killed before he arrived at the church to bury his friend. On this occasion, as indeed on so many others, the word was wrong. Over the years there were a number of attacks on Carl Williams and his demise was confidently and regularly predicted.

Now the deaths and attempted hits came faster. The next to go on 31 March 2004 was Lewis Moran, then on bail and a curfew after being charged with a variety of drug offences. He had been in custody for nine months before a successful application was made to have him released on the grounds he would act as a father figure for his grandchildren. The decision to kill Jason's father and Mark's stepfather was said to have been taken at the wake for Veniamin. Lewis Moran had been in the crosshairs if only because he had offered a mere $50,000 for the killing of Williams. It was only thirty hours after Veniamin was buried that Moran was shot in the Brunswick Poker Club on Sydney Road on 31 March. When two men, one with a handgun, the other armed with a shotgun, came into the main room of the club, Moran turned to his long-time friend Bert Wrout, with whom he was drinking, and remarked, "I think we're off here." The men shot and injured Wrout and, with Moran running in a panicked circle, killed him at close range. The contract was said to have been worth $140,000. Not all of it was paid.

Defended by Robert Richter QC, Mick Gatto went on trial in May 2005 maintaining that it was Veniamin who had attacked him and that as they struggled five shots were fired from Veniamin's gun, which Gatto had managed to turn on him. Expert witness Dr Dodd agreed that it was difficult to determine individual reactions to particular injuries and that even people shot in the brain could remain active for a brief time. This produced the unkind comment that since "Ol' Benji was brain dead from birth", this was a difficult call to make. Gatto was triumphantly acquitted and after the trial his wife Cheryl told journalists, "An innocent man has been vindicated and we couldn't be happier."

In February 2007 Noel Faure, the grandson of the 1920s Melbourne standover man Norman Bruhn, suddenly and unexpectedly pleaded guilty to the Lewis Moran murder. Although the gunmen who shot Moran and Wrout were masked, Noel Faure had been caught on CCTV and recognized by a tattoo of a bird on his hand. Said to be in poor health, via videolink from prison, he was jailed for life with a twenty-three-year minimum. In May 2008 ex-boxer Evangelos Goussis, already convicted of the murder of standover man Lewis Caine, was also found guilty of the Moran murder and the Wrout wounding. In February 2009 he received life imprisonment with a minimum non-parole period of thirty years.

Faced with the possibility of life without parole, a number of men whom the underworld had thought might be staunch began to roll over into the arms of the Director of Public Prosecutions in the hope that they might see the light of day before they were wearing incontinence pads. And most prominent among them was Carl Williams. On 7 May 2007, after a series of plea bargains, Williams pleaded guilty to the murders of the Morans and drug-dealer Mark Mallia, whose charred body had been found in a drain in West Sunshine in August 2003. He also pleaded guilty to conspiracy to murder former lawyer and Carlton Crew man, Mario Condello. He had previously been found guilty of the murder of another dealer, Michael Marshall. Justice Betty King sentenced him to life imprisonment with a minimum of thirty-five years, which meant his earliest release date would be in 2042. He was less than pleased, calling the judge "a puppet of Purana". Outside court Jason Moran's mother Judith was, for once in her life, too upset to comment. Williams's mother, Betty, thought the sentence unfair because Jason Moran had shot first and then tried to shoot him another three or four times. She told the press that her son had originally wanted to be a policeman. His wife Roberta, who served a short sentence in 2004 for drug-dealing, was reportedly thinking of converting to Islam but ultimately apparently rejected the faith. She said that she and her daughter would be standing by him even though it was reported there was potentially another Mrs Williams on the scene. Since Williams's imprisonment Roberta has become something of a B-list celebrity, modelling for men's magazine *Zoo Weekly* and making after-dinner speeches. Judith Moran wrote a book, *My Story*, describing what was called her "heartbreaking human story". Not all critics regarded it as the unvarnished truth.

Opinions vary whether the last surviving member of the Moran clan, Desmond Moran, known as "Tuppence", was the accountant and moneyman or whether, as Australians say, he was a kangaroo short in the top paddock and was never as involved in the underworld as his brother Lewis and nephews Mark and Jason. Chopper Read believes the former and that Lewis, the titular head, was merely an old drunk. Possibly Desmond had access to the millions made by the family in drug-dealing, starting-price bookmaking and the abortion racket, much of which was cleverly invested by lawyers. However, in view of what happened next, the kangaroo scenario was probably nearer the mark. Certainly he should never have told the press he was the last Moran standing; he paid dearly for that display of hubris.

At 8.50 p.m. on Tuesday, 17 March 2009, Desmond was shot at while in his car on the driveway at Langs Road, Melbourne. The bullet hit the steering wheel. Moran described the shooter, who wore a loose balaclava helmet which allowed more than a glimpse of his face, as "an inbred albino". Some weeks earlier Moran had been involved in a fight with a character from the racing world. At the time this was suggested to be the more likely cause of the shooting rather than a rekindling of the underworld ashes. There was, however, worse to come.

Around midday on 15 June Desmond was shot twice by masked gunmen at the Ascot Pasta and Deli in Ascot Vale. His sister-in-law Judith Moran arrived shortly afterwards, screaming his name. She was arrested and charged with his murder, something she denied. Read claims that before she was taken to the police station she went to talk to the ashes of her late husband saying, "I'm sorry, Lew." It was alleged that access to the Moran fortune was behind the killing. Also arrested and charged with the murder was Les Kane's other daughter, Suzanne, Jason's sister-in-law, along with her boyfriend, biker Geoffrey "Nuts" Armour and Michael Farrugia. They all denied the charge. In April 2010 all four were committed for trial. Then came a turnaround. In November, Farrugia pleaded guilty to manslaughter. The plea was accepted on the condition he would give evidence against his three co-defendants. In December, he was sentenced to a minimum of two years which, with time served, meant he was eligible for parole in August 2011.

Tuppence may not have been watching his back, but nor was Carl Williams concentrating properly. At 12.50 p.m. on Monday, 19 April 2010, he was attacked from behind with part of an exercise bicycle by a fellow prisoner in the maximum security Acacia unit of Barwon prison. He staggered to his cell where he died, apparently after suffering a heart attack. Later, it was claimed and denied that corrections officers had been playing indoor cricket instead of umpiring their charges.

It was not difficult to identify the suspected killer as thirty-seven-year-old Matthew Charles Johnson, who was duly charged, because the attack had been filmed by security cameras. Less easy to identify was the motive. Williams's two companions in the secure unit – Johnson and Williams's friend, Tommy Ivanovic – were men known to have been on generally good terms with him and had been sharing the accommodation for at least nine months. One suggestion has been that it was simply a jailhouse quarrel. A more sinister alternative is that the attack was a contract hit secured by interested parties outside the jail, possibly to prevent him from giving evidence in forthcoming high-profile cases involving alleged police corruption. If he coughed, Williams was said to be in line for a $1 million reward. The prosecution claimed Johnson had killed Williams because he did not like informers. The defence maintained it was a pre-emptive strike by Johnson who feared Williams was going to kill him with billiard balls wrapped in a sock.

When Judith Moran's trial for the murder of her brother-in-law began in February 2011 she was in the dock on her own and it became clear that the prosecution thought it had been all about money. Tuppence had access to funds that she thought were hers. He had been paying her $4,000 a month but after a row he had cut off the allowance. He was also thought to be about to change his will, cutting out the Moran tribe entirely. Trouble had also broken out at a benefit for Wrout in the Union Hotel, Ascot Vale, when Suzanne Kane told Tuppence, "You'll never be half the man your brother was." The first shooting in the driveway had been by Armour, as had the second and fatal one. Now Michael Farrugia said he had been recruited for what he thought was a debt-collecting expedition but, despite being told to wait in the car, he followed Armour and saw him shoot Tuppence with a Glock. When Armour returned to the car Judith Moran asked Armour if he had got him.

In her defence, Moran claimed that any thought of a quarrel with her de facto brother-in-law was just rubbish. After all, when he was ill didn't she make him soup and steak and kidney pies? Anyway, at the time of Tuppence's shooting she was at the cemetery giving the two angels on Mark's grave a wash and polish. It was the ninth anniversary of his death. Other problems seemed to have been reasonably deflected. Some wicked person had dumped the gun and car used in the shooting at her home and, in a panic, she had tried to get rid of them. All right, a call had been made on her mobile when she was meant to have been at the cemetery, but that must have been made by someone else. Nor had she said "Murder on" to Armour. She had actually said "Murderer", referring to the fact that Armour shot kangaroos for dog meat. In this she had some support from an expert witness on speech patterns.

By the time the jury reached the seventh day of its deliberations, Judith Moran and inexperienced jury-watchers must have thought that, at the very least, there would be a hung jury. But the trouble was that, while she could explain away each individual point – for instance, the remark to Armour or the disposal of the gun – the cumulative effect became overwhelming. The cognoscenti also knew that Melbourne juries like to take their time, and they duly convicted her. Trial observers had watched Moran under cross-examination and whenever the going got tough – which it did on a regular basis – her cheek began to twitch. Later it emerged that Suzanne Kane had pleaded guilty to being an accessory after the fact and had effectively been sentenced to time served. Nuts Armour had also pleaded guilty but true to the code of the underworld had declined to give evidence against his employer.

After the verdict there were stories that, when drunk, Judith Moran would boast that Lewis had arranged the offing of his predecessor, Les Cole, in Sydney as a gift to her.

Judith Moran and Armour had to wait until August 2011 to hear their sentences. Wearing a fetching, frilly collared, cream poncho she was now in a motorized wheelchair which, it was said unkindly, she used to run over the feet of those who annoyed her in prison. Not known as the harshest sentence-giver on the Victorian bench, Justice Lex Lasry sentenced her and Armour to twenty-six years with a minimum of twenty-one to be served before either was eligible for parole. Had she been younger and fitter it would have been more, he said. "Sir, you are wrong. I am innocent," she told him. She was now possibly the only person in the city who believed it. With the time she has spent in custody she will not be eligible for release until she is in her early eighties.

And so a gang war that began in the 1990s, and that over the years saw nearly forty deaths, left Mick Gatto as the last man standing.

33

The Moss Side Gangs

In the last 140 years, Manchester in the northwest of England has had its fair share of gangs, beginning with the fighting gangs of the 1870s such as the She Battery Mob, the Bengal Tigers and Buffalo Bill's Gang, all from around the Rochdale Road area, north of Cheetham Hill. By the 1930s there were street-gangs such as the Ikey Boys, the Dalfy Street Gang and the largely Italian Napoo Boys but again these were fighting and low-level street-crime gangs.

Perhaps the best known "gang" of the post-war years was the Quality Street Mob. Many old-time police officers have denied the existence of such a firm and of those who admit it existed many are keen to point out it was merely a loose collection of friends with criminal records who were involved in scrap-metal dealing, boxing and the second-hand car trade. It was not, however, until the 1980s that the predominantly black gangs from Moss Side and their rivals, the Doddington Close Gang, began to emerge.

In the 1850s Moss Side was known as Twenty Pits because the land was wet with pit-like indentations. As Manchester expanded the pits were drained and substantial houses of twelve or fourteen rooms were built. By the 1920s it was the home of teachers, bank clerks and "comfortable" traders. But, with the Depression, more and more of these began to take in lodgers to make ends meet. Some families provided board and lodging; others let out individual rooms. At first the tenants were from Europe and then in the 1950s from the West Indies. Finally, the Alexandra Park estate was built. As is so often the case, the road to a sink estate is paved with good intentions. Intended to be a neighbourhood community protected from traffic with little clusters of brick houses in cul-de-sacs, it was connected by what the planners described as "companionable footpaths". The planners, whose vision was hampered by rose-tinted spectacles, had not learned from earlier mistakes such as were made in Saffron Hill and the East End of London. It was an extremely difficult area to police – a warren of rat runs into which thieves and later drug-dealers could easily escape and hide. As the area deteriorated families moved out and gangs moved in. Vacated houses were vandalized and mob rule took hold.

As Moss Side expanded, a spillover estate was built in Cheetham Hill, Salford, in the 1970s with cul-de-sacs specifically designed to prevent escape; by the 1990s the estate was covered in graffiti. Many of Moss Side's black community moved to this much smaller, compact area. There was some drug-dealing in the pubs there, but it was nothing compared to the multimillion pound business in the sprawling council estates of Hulme and Moss Side. However, its smaller criminal community was more tightly knit and so more dangerous.

In the 1980s the gangs from Moss Side and Cheetham Hill agreed not to infringe on the other's territory but first a robbery and then a dispute over a young woman sparked trouble. By the end of the decade there was more or less a full-scale war when the Pepperhill Mob, based around the pub of that name in Bedwell Close on the Alexandra estate, began dealing only to find they were being made to hand over the profits – "taxed" – by the Cheetham Hill Gang. Instead of bowing to the knee, as the earlier Moss Side mob had done, they fought back. Then the Gooch Gang from the west side aligned itself with Cheetham Hill. When the Pepperhill pub was closed down, the associated mob changed its name to the Doddington Close Gang.

One version of the start of the war was the arrival of Delroy Brown from Birmingham, "dripping in gold and driving a BMW", who teamed up with the Pepperhill Mob. The story is that the fighting started not over drugs but over a girl. Brown was seen out with the girlfriend of a Cheetham Hill man serving five years for robbery. The information was relayed back and as a reprisal his car was held-up at gunpoint and taken from him. He retaliated and then four masked men visited his home in Moss Side.

The first recorded death came in 1987 when Ivan Preston, doorman of an illegal drinking club in Moss Side, was shot and killed. From then on it seemed easier for drug-dealers to kill those who stood in their way. Three more killings followed in quick succession.

The Gooch Gang suffered a serious blow when twenty-one members were caught in Operation China during which undercover police had filmed them selling drugs to members of the public. Sentences of up to eight years were handed down at Manchester Crown Court and the Gooch Gang was dead, only to rise Phoenix-like within six months as Young Gooch. In fact, reports of the death of the Gooch Gang were seriously exaggerated. It had merely metamorphosed into a prison gang putting pressure on prison officers and governors by demanding, in return for cooperation, privileges such as the exclusive use of gym equipment.

By 1990 Tony "White Tony" Johnstone had become a leading soldier. He usually wore body armour and by a curious coincidence his adopted mother, Winnie, was also the mother of Keith Bennett, still missing from the time of the Moors murders. Unusually, he was a white man in a black gang, but Johnstone became "The Man", carrying guns and driving Ford Cosworths which, with a comfortable speed of 120 mph, made police surveillance of the time difficult if not impossible. That year he led a group into the International Club in Longside where Delroy Brown was drinking and shot at him with a .38. The next step came when Brown ventured into Cheetham Hill territory and the PSV club in Hulme. There Stephen Jackson was shot in the testicles and Brown was dragged into a car park where a serious effort was made to cut his head off. He fled to Liverpool and hid in Toxteth, waiting for things to cool down. Jackson later received a ten-year sentence for dealing in cocaine. On his return from Liverpool, Brown had his car overturned after he attacked the wrong man and set his car on fire. The war escalated.

In 1991 there came a bizarre incident following the death of Carl Stapleton, who was found out of his ground and, as a punishment, stabbed eighteen times with a survival knife. A woman claimed she had seen a man getting out of a car at the murder scene, and consequently picked out Stephen Morrison as his attacker from an identification parade. Between the identification and the trial she was placed under police protection, but at the trial she said that she had made the identification simply because she fancied him. Another suspect in the murder who was never charged was Pierre Williams, who was convicted in 2008 of the murder of a family of three – a mother, daughter and son – in Fallowfield. He maintained that he had seen a hooded man leave the house shortly before he found the bodies. He had been in a long and abusive relationship with the mother.

In January 1993 one of the seemingly more horrific random killings took place in Moss Side when fourteen-year-old Benji Stanley was shot in the heart while he was queuing to get pies at the popular Alvino's Tattie and Dumplin' shop. The killer drove up in a silver Rover motor car and fired through the window at Benji. The assailant then walked into the shop and shot the boy again in the chest. All police investigations apparently showed the boy had not been part of any gang but at the time of his death he was wearing khaki clothing and a red bandana, the badge of one of the Moss Side gangs – red for Gooch, blue for Doddington. A sixteen-year-old boy who was with him when he was shot, and who was a gang-member, gave the police a version of the events that had led to the killing and a description of the gunman but later said he had made it up. It was later discovered that Benji not only had a £900 mountain bike but that he had over £24,000 in a building society account.

In August that year a truce was declared but it broke down in 1994 with the murder of Raymond Pitt, whose younger brother Tommy broke away from the Doddington Close Gang to create the Pitt Bull Crew. Meanwhile in Longsight, east of Moss Side, Julian Bell formed the Longsight Crew. Gangs splintered with fighting between the Longsight Crew and Gooch, the Longsight Crew and Pit Bull Crew, the Pit Bull Crew and the Doddington, and the Doddington and Gooch. Tit-for-tat gang shootings increased dramatically towards the end of the 1990s. In 1999 there were forty-one reported shootings in the area and there were eight deaths from the end of July.

It was not just drug-dealing that was a problem in Manchester; rival teams of armed robbers from Moss Side and Cheetham Hill were clashing over the same targets and the robberies themselves were becoming more and more violent. In 1989 Stephen Julian and Chinadu Iheagwara staged a robbery at the Coin Controls factory when a Security Express van was making a wages delivery. Iheagwara attacked one of the guards with a machete. As the man lifted his arms to defend himself he was knocked to the ground and tried to crawl under the van. Julian then shot the other guard in the groin, shearing off the top of his left thigh. Unfortunately the first guard had not crawled far enough and Julian then shot him in the ankle, almost severing it. His leg had to be amputated from below the knee. As the second guard tried to escape he was shot in the back. Amazingly both survived. The following year Julian and Iheagwara admitted other robberies at Manchester

Crown Court. Julian received a twenty-two-year sentence and Iheagwara two years less. After the robbery Julian had escaped to Jamaica with the help of Raymond Odoha and now he was wanted. He turned to "White Tony" Johnstone for help. It was now Johnstone who fell foul of the formidable Desmond Noonan.

At the time, Manchester's Irish gangs controlled the Ecstasy and amphetamine trades while the black gangs from Moss Side and Cheetham Hill dominated the heroin business. Desmond Noonan was part of a group that provided the black gangs with guns and other weapons.

Confusingly all the Noonan children, both male and female, of the Irish family from Whalley Range, Manchester, had first names beginning with the letter "D" – for their parents' home city of Dublin. Desmond and his younger brother Dominic became two of the most respected and feared gangland figures in Manchester in the 1980s and 1990s, garnering the Noonans the tag "one of the most notorious crime families in British history" along the way.

Desmond's criminal career began as a doorman in the early 1980s; his reputation as a fighter and his overall appearance gave him credibility on the club doors of Manchester. One of his earlier jobs was at Konspiracy, whose co-owner Marino Morgan's proud boast was that, "We have never paid protection. Konspiracy is ours. We run it – no one else does. The gangs come in but without Robocop on the door they are difficult to stop." Instead of Robocop on the door, it was Desmond Noonan, who wore body armour down to his groin, and was regarded as being nearly as good.

Part of his reputation came from his size, part from his willingness to mix it, and partly because he had just come out of jail following a sentence for conspiracy to pervert the course of justice by threatening to kill witnesses in a robbery trial.

Desmond then started to put his own men on the doors and, by the late 1980s, 80 per cent of Manchester's nightlife security was thought to be controlled by him and his family. Around this time Dominic Noonan was jailed for fifteen years for his part in an armed robbery at a bank in Cheetham Hill. During his imprisonment, while he was still in control of the crime family, brothers Damian and Derek Noonan were forging links with other notable Manchester gangs including the Cheetham Hill and Salford gangs.

In November 1990 Johnstone and three others robbed a security van at Monksbridge, Oldham, when a guard was kidnapped and some £360,000 was stolen. It could have been a great deal worse. A further £1 million was left in the van. Craig Bulger was convicted of dishonestly handling the money and when he later went to ask for his share, which amounted to £80,000, he was told by Desmond Noonan that there was only £40,000 left. He then told Noonan he was going to complain to Johnstone.

A week later, Johnstone was killed. According to the evidence of his friend Tony McKie, who became a prosecution witness, he and Johnstone were driving in a white Cosworth when they were flagged down by Desmond Noonan near the Penny Black public house at around 10.30 in the evening. McKie claimed that a Ford Orion was parked nearby with three men sitting in it. One of them was armed robber Paul Flannery, who was making his first outing after he had seriously injured his back diving through a window after mistaking police officers, who had come to arrest him, for members of a rival organization. According to McKie, Flannery nodded at Noonan and then opened fire. Johnstone tried to escape by climbing a wall and was shot in the back as he scaled it. The first trial ended in the jury being discharged and at the second, in the summer of 1993, Noonan, his brothers Damian and Derek, Flannery and a prison escapee called Michael Sharples, each of whom was able to call an alibi witness, were all acquitted. Part of the defence had been that McKie was trying to frame the defendants on behalf of the gang really responsible. Nor could

McKie explain how, while earning £250 a week working for his father's building company, he was able to acquire two Golf GTIs and a £20,000 Porsche. The acquittal effectively confirmed the status of the Noonan family.

Much of the trouble in the inner-city area has stemmed from the rise of the nightclub – now a long cry from those such as Owen Radcliffe's Cromwell where husbands and wives went to have dinner, dance and see a couple of wrestling bouts followed by a cabaret. The nightclubs were joined in the late 1980s by raves and acid house parties, along with the easy availability of Ecstasy and the necessary employment of doormen. The aim of drug-dealers was to have their own men on the door to enable their dealers to get in to the exclusion of others and so a form of protection grew up. A club would be protected from the trouble that would ensue if there was an open drug market, and the sponsor got a free run for the distribution of his product. When the Cheetham Hill-based Thunderdome Club decided to hire bouncers in 1990 from an out-of-town firm, the reprisals were swift. Three of the bouncers were kneecapped by masked men with shotguns in full view of more than 300 people. Seven were later arrested but the Crown Prosecution Service decided there was insufficient evidence to mount a successful case.

Over the next several years, Desmond Noonan faced a number of trials in connection with witness intimidation and jury-tampering, resulting in key witnesses refusing to testify against him and other members of the Noonan family. By the mid-1990s he was known as a notoriously violent enforcer who had links with a wide range of Britain's underworld.

In 1993 Dominic, sometimes Domenyk, Noonan was jailed for fourteen years after escaping from prison, carrying a loaded gun and conspiring to rob. He claimed that he had not escaped but that he had been kidnapped from prison. The prosecution said that he had been freed so he could take part in a £1.5 million robbery.

In 1994 there was also a fly-posting war in Manchester involving the family. It is not an industry for the faint-hearted, but it is worth hundreds of thousands of pounds a year in major cities where there are live music venues. It is also a trade that generates considerable ill feeling as posters are slapped over those of rival concerns and venues.

Controlling Manchester at the time were one-time blackmailer Jimmy Carr and his partner Marcel Williams. While putting up posters for the film *Four Weddings and a Funeral* late at night about a mile from the city centre, Carr and his then helper Chris Horrox were shot. Carr was badly injured but Horrox, who intervened, was killed. Carr said it was Marcel Williams who was the gunman.

In the trial of Marcel Williams for murder it was suggested that Desmond Noonan and Paul Carroll, head doorman of the Hacienda club, wanted a share of the fly-posting and a meeting was arranged in a McDonald's. Things were apparently sorted out but Carr believed Williams had turned him over and said so.

Williams called an alibi that he was at the home of his girlfriend and then Paul Flannery took the stand. Still wheelchair bound from his attempted escape from the police, he told the court of the meeting with Carroll and Noonan and he believed men from Salford had shot Carr and Horrox rather than the highly recognizable, dreadlocked Williams. In March 1996, amid allegations that Carr was gun-running, the jury took less than ten minutes to acquit. Flannery later sued the police over his injuries from his self-defenestration, claiming he had been dragged along the ground by officers. After a nine-year battle he was awarded £30,000 when the judge found the officers had indeed dragged him rather than carried him as they said.

The previous year Desmond was convicted of violently attacking twin brothers and was described by the court as psychotic. He was sentenced to thirty-three months' imprisonment.

By the end of the 1990s Desmond and Dominic Noonan had been linked to twenty gangland murders and dozens of robberies, and they had a stranglehold on most of the nightclub security in many of Britain's major cities.

In 2002 Dominic Noonan was released and when, in the next year, Damian was killed in a motorcycle accident in the Dominican Republic, he took over the running of the family businesses, which now included D. J. Noonan Security. Desmond had, by now, developed an addiction to crack cocaine.

In the three years before Desmond's death he and other members of the family had been the subjects of an extraordinary piece of film-making, *A Very British Gangster* by the Dublin-born Donal MacIntyre who, at considerable risk to himself, gained the confidence of the family and elicited a sometimes sympathetic picture of the brothers.

In the documentary Dominic recalled with some pride the night he cut off a dog's head, walked into a pub and placed it on the pool table as a warning to a rival gang. Just as the Krays are said to have done, he also provided what MacIntyre describes as "an alternative justice system". Many neighbours preferred to approach him for help rather than the police or other authorities.

Just how many murders the brothers were involved in is open to speculation. In the film MacIntyre asks Dominic, who legally changed his name to Lattlay Fottfoy, an acronym of the family motto "Look after those that look after you, fuck off those that fuck off you", how many people he had killed; there is an indication that the answer was twenty-seven. That is not necessarily correct. Many a gangster has exaggerated his tally to gain even more respect. It is, after all, something that can be denied if questioned by the police but, in the brothers' case, the police seem to think it approximates the total. Over the years the Urdu-speaking Dominic has certainly acquired over forty convictions and has spent over twenty years in prison. For his part Desmond said he had more guns than the police.

The film showed Dominic surrounded by a score of acolytes and one reviewer thought that he was:

> like some kind of modern day Fagan, dispensing advice through the grim voice of experience, to who knows what ends. Each of these young men clearly hero-worships him, and you can see a new generation of street toughs being raised right before your eyes. It's an extraordinary sight, unlike anything you've ever seen at the movies.

MacIntyre was also brave enough to ask Dominic if he was gay, something he admitted, generally a taboo subject for the higher class of gangster.

On the night of 18 March 2005, Desmond Noonan was drinking in the Parkside public house in Northern Moor, Wythenshawe. He had apparently being trying to buy drugs but had failed and had gone to see Derek McDuffus, a DJ and drug-dealer from South Manchester, better known as "Yardie". In the early hours of the following morning, Sandra Noonan received a phone call from her husband telling her that he had been stabbed and asking her to pick him up in the suburb of Chorlton. It was thought he had been taken there and dumped. By the time she arrived Noonan was lying unconscious in Merseybank Avenue. She called for an ambulance, but Noonan died of his wounds before arriving at Manchester Royal Infirmary.

On 22 April his funeral in south Manchester was reportedly attended by hundreds of local residents, with a sixteen-piece kilted pipe band playing as his body arrived in a black-plumed horse-drawn hearse at St Aidan's Roman Catholic Church, Northern Moor. Members of D. J. Noonan Security, in black jackets bearing the legend "We serve to protect", surrounded

Dominic as he walked to the church. To the fury of parents, two local schools with nearly 1,800 pupils were shut for the day.

A note was also passed around which read:

The Noonan family would like to take this opportunity to thank everyone for attending Dessy's funeral. This is a very sad time for family and friends. We wish to give Dessy a really good send off which is what he deserved. We have given permission for Channel 5 to film and take photographs of the procession. Anyone who knows Dessy knows that he would love all this attention.

The statement added: "Everyone is welcome to the Southern Public House, Nell Lane, after the funeral. The landlord has kindly offered all profits sold on bottles to go towards the cost of the funeral."

One of his family posted the following tribute:

MY DAD WAS A HERO TO THE PEOPLE THAT NEW HIM AND THE PEOPLE HE HELPED OUT OVER THE YEARS THATS MY DAD GONE AND I MISS HIM MORE EVERY DAY HES NOT HERE I WOULD DO ANYTHING TO SEE HIS FACE AGAIN COZ I JUST WANT TO SAY DAD I LOVE YOU BUT I CARNT BECAUSE SOMEONE HAS TOOK THAT CHANCE AWAY FROM ALL OF US HE MIGHT OF BEIN A BAD GUY BUT HE IS MY DAD AND HE ALWAYS GOING TO BE IN MY HEART EVERYONE THAT NOWS MY DAD WILL BE PROUD TO NO THAT HES AWAY FROM DANGER AND IS SAFE IN A PLACE THEY CALL PARADICE ALL I WONT TO DO IS SAY R.II.P DAD AKA DESMOND P NOONAN {DESSEI} WE ALL MISS YOU VERY MUCH X X XX

McDuffus was charged on 15 June and, after appearing at Preston Crown Court, was convicted of Noonan's murder, for which he received a life sentence with a minimum of fifteen years to be served. Despite a conviction in the mid-1990s for possessing heroin with intent to supply, he claimed he had never dealt drugs and had never met Noonan. His girlfriend, Shajahan Cooke, with whom he had three children, received eighteen months for attempting to pervert the course of justice.

McDuffus was subsequently placed in solitary confinement to protect him from possible retribution by the Noonan family. The authorities suspected that Noonan had been coercing local drug-dealers into supplying him with narcotics, and had left the pub intoxicated in search of a drug-dealer. It is believed McDuffus stabbed Noonan and threw him out of his home, following which he bled to death in the street. Witnesses at the trial claimed there had been bad blood between the pair because Noonan had previously stolen drugs from McDuffus.

In December 2005 Dominic, described by the trial judge as a "very dangerous man who is clearly a risk to the public", was sentenced to nine and a half years when he was convicted after a revolver and five .357 Magnum bullets were found under the bonnet of his Jaguar when he was stopped near Darlington in the previous May. At his trial he claimed they had been planted by criminals who then tipped off the police. He claimed he had become legitimate and was running a security firm employing over 400 people.

At the time his nephew, Desmond, was serving thirty months for his part in a riot on 13 February 2005 at Deerbolt Young Offenders Institution near Barnard Castle when inmates destroyed a prison chapel, drank the communion wine and dressed in the vicar's vestments after going berserk because, they claimed, they were homesick. They had shouted abuse at the vicar conducting Sunday service before throwing chairs at prison wardens, barricading themselves in and causing more than £40,000 of damage. The siege had lasted seven hours.

In November 2009 Desmond Jr was again jailed, this time for twenty months after being involved in two incidents with his brother, Damian Jr, outside the Syndicate nightclub in Blackpool and another at the Wellington pub in Salford. In the Blackpool incident part of the ear of the victim was bitten off. Neither victim would cooperate with the police and no witnesses were willing to give evidence. The evidence against Desmond, who admitted affray, was wholly based on CCTV evidence. His counsel explained that the death of his father Damian in the road accident in 2003 had been so traumatic that Desmond had been unable to deal with it.

Before passing sentence Judge Lever told Desmond: "There is not a judge in Manchester that doesn't know the name of this family, but I sentence scrupulously on the facts of the case. There is no premium on a family name in these courts."

Dominic was released from prison in 2010 halfway through his sentence. He claimed to have changed during his time in prison and was now a regular church attendant. He was confident his conviction would be overturned.

Within days, on 7 May, he was arrested on public order charges which were dropped – he was alleged to have banged a newspaper on the windscreen of a woman driver who had beeped at him in Gorton. She later realized the offender had been his driver. Despite the dropping of the charges he was returned to jail for a short time. Now it was said he was due to marry.

He was in the headlines again when it was reported that he was related, albeit tenuously, to "Starrish" Mark Duggan, whose shooting by police in Tottenham in July 2011 sparked the subsequent riots. Duggan was the nephew of Desmond Noonan's second wife. When the riots spread to Manchester there was video footage of Dominic talking to youths on the streets, and it was alleged that a hundred "Noonan Boys" youths, said to be allied to the family, had taken part. The final insult came when he was arrested and charged with dishonestly handling stolen alcohol and cigarettes. He did not enter a plea and was remanded in custody.

Away from the Noonans, if anyone thought the Gooch Gang was dead then they were swiftly disabused in April 2009 when twenty-nine-year-old Colin Joyce, its self-styled general who was said to make £700,000 a year from drug-dealing, was jailed by Mr Justice Brian Langstaff at Liverpool Crown Court. He was applauded by other gang-members in the dock as he defiantly told the court that the five-month trial had been a circus, and that no sentence could take away the "freedom and innocence from inside me".

In the run-up to their arrest, Joyce and his second-in-command, thirty-three-year-old Lee Amos, had previously embarked on an ambitious plan to expand their heroin- and cocaine-dealing across the city's suburbs, torturing street-dealers and targeting potential rivals. When a member of the relatively newly formed Old Trafford Cripz was shot in February 2007, the Gooch Gang took their revenge in an open air shoot-out in Pepper Hill Road, at the heart of Doddington territory.

The gang war reached a climax that year – a period in which 3,000 firearm incidents were recorded in fifteen months – shortly after Joyce and Amos were released from jail on licence from a nine-year sentence for firearms offences.

On 15 June 2007, Ucal Chin, a member of the Longsight Crew, was shot dead at the wheel of his red Renault Mégane by a gunman in a silver Audi that pulled up alongside him as he drove down a suburban street. Shortly before midnight on 27 June at Chin's wake at his home in Chorlton-on-Medlock, gunmen in three cars sprayed mourners with bullets killing his close friend and Longsight Crew associate Tyrone Gilbert. As they fled a balaclava snagged on a fence post, providing enough DNA evidence to link it to Aeeron Campbell, a known gang-member. Meanwhile, mobile phone data suggested that Joyce and Amos were in one of the cars used in the shooting.

The gang was arrested one by one but the breakthrough came when the police managed to turn six low-level workers to give evidence against their former employers in exchange for immunity and places in witness protection programmes.

At the trial, the judge was told that members of the Gooch Gang would shoot at people over minor disagreements while drunk in nightclubs and torture street-dealers who crossed them. They had an arsenal of weapons including machine-guns and Magnum-style handguns that they used "at the drop of a hat" to exact revenge and enforce drug debts.

Joyce was jailed for a minimum of thirty-nine years. Amos was given a life sentence for his involvement in the murder of Gilbert and ordered to serve a minimum of thirty-five years before parole. Six other gang-members were also convicted of possessing guns and drug-dealing for the gang, including a "Wild West" shoot-out with rival gangsters in Moss Side. In all eleven gang-members, all from Manchester, were convicted of twenty-seven of the twenty-eight charges.

Since the Gooch Gang arrests, Greater Manchester Police has recorded a 92 per cent reduction in gun-related crime leading at least one detective to speak optimistically about the "end of gang culture". That may be a wish too far.

34

The A Team

Born in north London to working-class Irish parents Florence and George in October 1954, Terence George Adams, a man who for years kept his head firmly below the parapet, was the eldest of eleven children. He and his two brothers, Sean, known as "Tommy", and Patrick, known as "Patsy", graduated from small-time protection, first at school and then in and around Islington, to a firm that had the highest possible rating of the British gangs of the late 1990s and early 2000s. The Adams family, known as the A Team and less frequently as the Clerkenwell Crime Syndicate, is said to have included some cousins, including the late Robert Adams who received fifteen years for his part in the failed Millennium Dome jewel robbery. In the 1980s and 1990s the A Team built up a multimillion-pound empire based on gun- and drug-running involving shipments from east Europe and Israel to Britain and Ireland. It was said, romantically and possibly even accurately, that they had gained their expertise listening to the tales and sitting at the feet of the survivors of the old Italian families in Clerkenwell.

The first the outside world heard of them was almost in passing when in 1985 Tommy Adams, born in 1958, was acquitted of handling some of the proceeds from the celebrated Brink's-Mat robbery. The next public appearance, so to speak, was in 1993 when Patsy was acquitted of involvement in an importation of 3.5 tons of cannabis estimated to be worth £25 million. His co-defendant received eleven years. He was also acquitted of another offence involving drugs, while claiming that a gun and a full suit of body armour belonged to his wife.

Over the years reports began to surface of a struggle between the Adams family and the Rileys, a family based in the Kentish Town area of London. There had been a major skirmish in January 1990 when there was a shooting in Huntingdon Street near the Angel, Islington. The whole matter was thought to have been finally resolved in March 1996 – substantially in favour of the Adamses, it was said – following a gun battle in Finsbury Square in the City.

Perhaps on the principle of giving dogs bad names, over the last twenty years a number of incidents have been laid at the Adams family's door without any real evidence to support them. These have included the blame for the death of Terry Gooderham, found shot, together with his girlfriend Maxine Arnold, in his black Mercedes in Epping Forest on 22 December 1989. Gooderham had been a stocktaker for a number of clubs and among the suggested reasons on offer was the disappearance of £150,000, said euphemistically to have been redirected.

Some laid the actual killing at the feet of the by now deceased Jimmy Moody, a former associate of the Richardsons, who was himself shot dead in an East End pub on 1 June 1993. But there again it has been argued that it might just as easily have been undertaken by an Adams associate, Gilbert Wynter, who walked with a limp after being hit by a police car in 1992.

It has also been alleged but never proved that Wynter had been involved in the murder of Claude Moseley, the former junior British high-jump champion, who was stabbed to death with a samurai sword, more or less slicing him in half, over a drugs deal in 1994. Whoever had been responsible, it was thought that Moseley had been lax in his accounting methods. A twenty-two-year-old received three months for contempt of court when he refused to testify against Wynter. The man, who was serving a five-year sentence for armed robbery, had originally made a statement claiming he witnessed the murder, which took place in his house while he was on the run from prison. The case against Wynter was dropped. "It is terrible that a man who can commit this kind of crime can get away with it because another man refuses to do his duty and give evidence. If a murderer gets away with it they are likely to kill again until men have the courage to give evidence," said Judge Coombe. But there again some will argue that the judge did not have to live and work in the area.

Wynter also freelanced, running the lucrative doorman trade and taking outside contracts. In 1998 Paul "Paddlefoot" Anthony received eighteen years for shooting Tony Smith in the crowded Emporium nightclub off Regent Street. Two weeks before Christmas 1997 the forty-three-year-old father of two went to the club to join a private party. Anthony, together with another taller man who was never arrested, appeared and shot him three times from a range of six feet. The first two shots hit him in the chest, leaving a hole the size of a fist. He collapsed on the floor and instinctively pretended to be dead. Anthony, however, wanted to make sure and stood over him to fire a third shot. The bullet went through Smith's cheek and out through the palate of his mouth. Amazingly, he survived. Another man was also hit. Anthony fled and, when a bouncer set off in pursuit, the second man opened fire again.

The shooting had all the hallmarks of a drug-gang execution but the police were initially baffled. Mr Smith had absolutely no criminal connections and the case was even presented in court as "motiveless". In fact, Wynter had ordered the hit with a figure of £300 as the price quoted and, perhaps ill advisedly, he chose Anthony, a known drug addict. On the night of the killing Anthony had been smoking crack in the Costello Park Hotel in Finsbury Park with a girlfriend.

However, now the police believe that Anthony and the "taller man" deliberately chose to shoot the wrong man when they found out – to their horror – who was intended to be the real target. They dared not shoot this formidable figure for fear of inevitable reprisals. On the other hand, they could not go back to Wynter having refused to carry out the hit. The only solution was to kill somebody else and they all but succeeded. The suggestion is that the correct target was a member of a powerful west London family whom Wynter believed had the better of him in a drug deal.

In 1988 one supposed member of the A Team, Wayne Hurren, was jailed for twenty years for armed robbery after he had shot a boy in the street. In the mid-1990s a story circulated that he had been kept for his own safety in various segregation units throughout the country but was now about to be released and had turned informer against the Adams family. If this was indeed at some point true, he seems to have changed his mind.

Hurren came into the limelight again in August 1995 when he told the *Daily Mirror* that he had shot two men dead and ordered the killing of a third while in jail. He was, he said, wiping the slate clean before he came out of prison.

The first of his victims had been in 1986 when he killed robber Gary Hutchings, whom he shot in Islington over a domestic matter. The second had been in August of the same year when he killed Frank Moody, the doorman of the Willows public house in Bermondsey. This was for an alleged slight to his cousin whom Moody had punched, knocking her teeth out. On trial in 1999 for plotting to kill David Foley, it was alleged he had organized this killing from prison. Foley, who was said to have beaten Hurren's wife, was killed outside the Northumberland Arms in King's Cross in July 1994. In March 1999 Hurran was found not guilty on the direction of the trial judge. However, Hurren admitted to some sixty-five robberies committed, he said, in London and on the south coast. He received twenty years.

The Adamses, rightly or not, were thought by members of the underworld to be a group to be feared. One noted thief, asked if he would say anything off the record about them, said he wanted to say, on the record, that he had nothing to say.

Another had said earlier: "They are today's equivalent of the Krays and the Richardsons. Say a man owes you £15,000 for a legit piece of business, then he goes to the Adamses and says he doesn't want to pay. They say they'll get you off his back for £5,000 and they do."

Some have not been happy with their style in allegedly using black criminals to do the dirty work. Others, however, speak well of their generosity: "When I had just come out I was introduced to Tommy and he simply said, 'I've heard about you' and pulled out all the money he had on him and told me if I needed more I was to see him. When I counted it out it came to £300."

In 1991, the old-timer and former Billy Hill and Richardson man, "Mad" Frank Fraser, was shot outside Turnmills nightclub, owned by the Adamses, near Farringdon station. The *Observer* even reported him as dead but the bullet went in one side of his face and came out the other, and he was only detained in hospital a matter of hours during which time he told inquiring police that his name was Tutankhamen. With no evidence to support it the shooting was suggested to have been by Patrick Adams, said to be the most violent of the brothers, over a drug dispute. However, Fraser claimed he had been shot by a rogue policeman, arguing, not wholly logically, that since he did not even smoke he could not have been involved in anything to do with marijuana. The underworld and newspapers believed the A Team was behind the shooting. The family did not deign to make any comment.

Patsy Adams was also said to have assaulted Fraser's son, David, cutting off part of his ear during a drug deal. In the late 1990s, he was reported to spend much of his time abroad. In 2001 the *Independent* believed that he was "living in exile in Spain in a walled villa bristling with security cameras a few miles south of Torremolinos".

Another old-timer, Freddie Foreman, was also said to have been at the sharp end of Adams family's attention. It was suggested, but later found to be false, that his son had been attacked by Adams – associated men in Spain. Foreman received messages of support and loyalty from the London and Essex underworld including, it was said, the Riley brothers and the Arifs from south London. A meeting was arranged at a club in the Finchley Road where an accommodation was reached.

It was shortly after the Fraser shooting that John McVicar, the former East End hardman turned sociologist and writer for *Punch*, was again told of the folly of writing stories about the family. He had, apparently, previously been visited in 1987 and this time the messenger had shrugged and warned him, "John, it saddens me to say it, and I hope it won't go further, but if I were you I'd purchase some insurance, get in some target practice and be very, very careful of big trail bikes in your immediate vicinity."

In September 1998 Tommy Adams, suspected of establishing connections to other international criminal organizations including numerous Yardie gangs as well as gaining an $80 million credit line from Colombian drug cartels, was reported to have left the dock laughing when he received seven and a half years for conspiracy to import cannabis worth £8 million. One suggestion for his conviction was that he had been freelancing and, with no family help forthcoming, it was a lesson not to act without the authority of his older brother. A family meeting was said to have taken place in Belmarsh prison, where he was on remand, when the facts of life were explained to him in words of one syllable. Two of Tommy Adams's old schoolfriends, Michael Papamichael and Edward Wilkinson, received six and nine years respectively.

Adams was also ordered to pay £6 million in fines or serve a further five years. The figure was reduced to £1 million by the Court of Appeal, mainly because the police and Crown Prosecution Service were unable to find a single bank account that would back up their estimation of his wealth. The £1 million was paid by his wife Androula in two instalments of £500,000 in cash at a police station. No one seems to have enquired too closely from where these payments came.

Now, the newspapers turned on the family. "Britain's Biggest Crime Family" wrote the *Daily Express*. There were suggestions that the family had originated the "two on a bike" hit in which the pillion passenger shoots the victim. At best they can only have imported it to England because it had been a trademark of Griselda Blanco's Miami hitmen decades earlier.

The cognoscenti had known of the family for years, however, and had wondered why the police had taken no steps to crush the team in its infancy. Since they had not, the Adamses had acquired the reputation of being untouchable. The Krays had that kind of reputation before their arrest at the end of the 1960s when it was said that if a complaint was made against them, the Kray twins would know about it by the time the complainant walked out of the police station. Perhaps the police did have a grander plan. In October 1996 it was believed that, following the unwelcome attentions of MI5 under orders to liquidate the Adams empire, the family was selling up. Six nightclubs, including two in Chelsea and Islington, were said to have been sold and they had disposed of their interests in others pubs and restaurants. In early 1997 it was said that the senior members of the family had moved to Spain.

Clearly, however, the family was going through a difficult patch at the time. Their enforcer, Gilbert Wynter, had simply disappeared in March 1998 and at the end of November a close friend and associate, the talented conman Anthony Passmore, went down for a massive fraud. Then within days the secretive, diminutive, Iranian-born forty-eight-year-old Saul "Solly" Nahome, a Hatton Garden diamond buyer who was said to be the family's money adviser, was shot dead outside his £300,000 Finchley home by a black gunman who escaped on a motorcycle. Now it was alleged Nahome had been recruited by the syndicate to launder money through the jewellery business, a restaurant in Smithfield and a West End nightclub. He was also said to have tucked away at least £25 million in offshore accounts. The secret of the money's whereabouts may have died with him. He is believed either to have died at the hands of the family when they found out he had stolen money from them, or that he might crack if, as was thought likely, the police were investigating him. It might also have been on the orders of Bertie Smalls's friend, Mickey Green, for similar false accounting. A third suggestion was that he might have been killed by another north London gang seeking to unhorse the family and that all-out war might follow. It did not. Nahome's brother, also a jeweller, loyally denied Solly had any links with the underworld.

But what had happened to Wynter? One version of his disappearance was that he had decamped to the Caribbean. Another version, which is more likely as he has not been seen for over ten years, is that he was murdered, and that it was his vanity that did for him. His behaviour was attracting too much attention, and it was decided that he had to be killed. He was summoned to Islington, where a van was waiting. It was raining heavily and Wynter, anxious not to get his expensive suit wet, borrowed an umbrella and was still protecting himself from the rain as he got into the van backwards, not seeing the men who were to kill him until it was too late. "If he hadn't been worried about his suit he would have seen who was inside and realized what was up," said a gangland observer. "He won't be seen again." A common story is that Wynter was strangled and buried in the foundations of the Millennium Dome.

Wynter's former girlfriend, Dee, said he spoke a lot about God but also, backing things each way, used African oils to keep him from harm. His mother, said to be a sort of Obeah princess, was believed to have also disappeared around the same time.

Immediately there were suggestions that a gang war would follow Wynter's disappearance and that Patrick Adams had been seen at Heathrow amid speculation that he had returned from Spain to exercise some control on matters. Certainly in the weeks that followed no gang war broke out. Instead, the family became involved in the financing of a very smart and fashionable nightclub in the East End.

In 1999 one of the family's close friends, Christopher McCormack, was acquitted of causing grievous bodily harm to the financier David McKenzie. It had been alleged at the Old Bailey that McKenzie had borrowed money, said to be around £1.5 million, from Terry Adams and the man was summoned to a house in Finchley, north London. Describing Terry Adams, McKenzie said: "Everyone stood up when he walked in. He looked like a star . . . a cross between Liberace and Peter Stringfellow. He was immaculately dressed in a long black coat and white frilly shirt. He was completely in command."

McKenzie told the court that later an attack took place at the Islington home of John Potter, Terry Adams's brother-in-law. It was accepted there had been an attack in which McKenzie's ribs were broken and he suffered knife wounds to his face. His nose and left ear were left flapping. Tendons in his wrist were cut. The jury, who deliberated for a day, accepted John Potter's version of the incident that the attack had been carried out by a complete stranger. Allegations that McKenzie's blood was on Christopher McCormack's jacket were explained by the fact that he had broken up a fight between the financier and another man at an earlier meeting and that was when it had become stained.

Wannabe gangsters have always traded on the names of their betters to gain a bit of respect. It was the thing to do in the 1960s to say you were a friend of the Krays but the

Adams brothers were reputed to have more or less franchised the family name, renting it out for £250,000 to those who needed to impress. It may seem an enormous amount but apparently to have the backing of London's most feared family was regarded as well worth it and is an indication of how much a major drug deal can bring in.

Reports of the family's permanent exile proved premature when in 1999 the Crown Prosecution Service (CPS) found to its horror that a clerk in its service, Mark Herbert, son of a retired Scotland Yard detective, had sold a list of thirty-three informers to the Adamses.

The prosecution at the Old Bailey claimed that while Herbert had been moonlighting as a bouncer in a southwest London nightclub to supplement his £14,000 a year CPS salary, he had also been passing on information. It featured tip-offs about twelve forthcoming arrests including that of an alleged enforcer for the family. When that man was arrested there was no sign of evidence at his home and he was acquitted. Herbert had also passed over details of two brothers from south London who were said to be in dispute with the family and to have contracts worth £250,000 on their heads.

In 1998 Herbert had been a junior clerk working on a team investigating the brothers. He told the jury that he had passed on the information because he was fearful for his life and that of his fiancée. In fact, he had received £1,000 for the information, which he had accessed from computers. He was sentenced to six years' imprisonment. His co-accused, fellow nightclub bouncer Kevin Sumer, who was alleged to be the conduit pipe, told the court that he had simply been humouring Herbert when agreeing to show the lists to the Adams family. As far as he was concerned the lists were bound for the police. The prosecution had alleged that a bag passed to his friend Billy Isaacs contained the lists. In fact, said Sumer, the bag contained wedding photographs. He had no idea that Isaacs knew the Adams family. He was acquitted. It was thought that Herbert would be kept in some form of segregation both to protect him and also to prevent him passing on more information he might have memorized.

In September 2000 the *News of the World*, in its survey of Britain's wealthy criminals, listed Tommy Adams as the second wealthiest behind Liverpool's drug-dealing Curtis Warren. Warren's wealth or at least earnings were probably matched, if not overtaken, by those of Andrew Billimore, a former guide at Ely Cathedral who, when he received twenty years at Norwich Crown Court in September 2000, was thought to have grossed £640 million. This was the figure calculated by detectives after a remand prisoner said that Billimore had told him he was bringing in cocaine from the Netherlands at £20,000 a kilo and from Colombia at £4,000 less.

Despite efforts to keep out of the public eye the Adams family continued to make the news. From the 1970s a number of British criminals have died on what they mistakenly thought was the sanctuary of the south coast of Spain. They have included the bank-robber turned informer John Moriarty and horse and greyhound doper Charlie Mitchell, who defected from the Krays. The name of Scott Bradfield was added to the list when his dismembered body was found in two suitcases dumped close to the Spanish holiday resort of Torremolinos. The twenty-eight-year-old suspected drug-dealer had been beaten to death before his arms and legs were cut from his body. These were found crammed into a pink Samsonite case that had been dumped in an abandoned olive grove behind a conference centre alongside a motorway. Attempts had been made to set fire to the case, which was discovered by the fire brigade on 26 October 2001 when they were called to the site.

A second plastic suitcase, containing Bradfield's head and torso, was found the following day on another piece of wasteground near the Torre Quebrada casino in nearby Benalmadena. He was identified by his fingerprints and dental records. Bradfield was the prime suspect for the murder of

James Gaspa, who died after he was shot in the abdomen with a single bullet from a handgun. His body was found slumped in the garden of a house in Islington, north London, on 8 May 2000. Bradfield, seen with Gaspa at his home on the day before the murder, fled to Spain.

Bradfield was about to be arrested and extradited from Spain. He has been linked to north London criminals, including the Adams organization, and it was thought he might be turned by the police and give evidence back in Britain. Another possibility is that Bradfield was attacked by rival drug-dealers as a warning to potential competitors.

Terry Adams was finally arrested in April 2003 in an operation which included such unlikely bedfellows as the MI5 and the Inland Revenue. Detectives found art and antiques valued at £500,000, £59,000 in cash and more than £40,000 worth of jewellery in his home near Arkley. He managed to drag out the trial until 2007. By then it was a question of plea bargains and keeping his sick wife Ruth out of jail. He had done what he could to delay the trial by changing his lawyers at the last minute and claiming that he was too stupid to understand the charges. In March that year he pleaded guilty to a single count of conspiracy to conceal criminal property and a further eight counts were left on the file. He was sentenced to seven and a half years' imprisonment. In the May he was ordered to pay £4.8 million in legal fees; he was also required to pay £800,000 in prosecution costs. Three days later he was ordered to file reports setting out his income for the next ten years.

The Adamses were again back in the news in June 2009 after sixteen-year-old Ben Kinsella, brother of former *EastEnders* actress Brooke Kinsella, was stabbed to death – eleven times in five seconds – in Islington when he was celebrating the end of his GCSE examinations. There were reports that an Adams family member had vowed to hunt down the killers, not for any business reasons, but because the family took exception to such a killing on their turf. Whether the reports were correct, eighteen-year-old Jade Braithwaite promptly handed himself in to the police. He was followed into the dock by Michael Alleyne and Juress Kika, small-time dealers who dealt drugs netting around £100 a day. They all received life sentences for the killing.

On 23 June 2010 a young woman stepped out of a black Range Rover in the car park of Spring Hill open prison near Aylesbury. In the car park with her were two men in a Porsche Cayenne 4x4. They had come to collect Terry Adams, released that morning after serving half his sentence. There would be, however, substantial restrictions on his ability to operate. Under recent legislation he would be facing a series of requirements such as a reporting order designed to compel so-called career criminals to disclose any cash and assets worth over £500. Adams, along with others in similar positions, would have to submit his bank statements to the authorities on a regular basis.

That year the police may have thought they had a breakthrough when body-builder Stephen Marshall claimed he had worked for the Adams family. He admitted he had dismembered and scattered the remains of one victim Jeffrey Howe after killing him in Southgate, north London, in what was known as the "Jigsaw murder". On 22 March 2009 a leg had been found in plastic bags in a road in Cottered, Hertfordshire. A fortnight later Howe's forearm was found in another part of Hertfordshire and after that his head was found in Leicestershire and most of the rest of him in other parts of Hertfordshire. Once he had been identified it was a simple matter to trace Marshall and his prostitute girlfriend Sarah Bush. They had moved into Howe's home and killed him to steal his identity. A witness at the trial told the jury that Marshall, who had worked as a club doorman, told her that he had disposed of four bodies between 1995 and 1998. His barrister said Marshall had thought it sensible not to ask questions of his employers. He was sentenced to life imprisonment with a minimum of thirty-six years. In May

2011 it was announced the police would be looking at further evidence in the murders of Wynter and Nahome.

In early August that year Terry Adams was reported to have been arrested for allegedly breaching orders requiring him to notify the Serious and Organized Crime Agency about payments to an undeclared account.

Bibliography

Introduction

Germain, G.-H., *Souvenirs de Monica* (Montreal: Editions Libre Expression, 1997).

1. Marm Mandelbaum

Eldridge, B., *Our Rival the Rascal* (Boston: Pemberton, 1897).

Lyons-Burke, S., *Why Crime Does Not Pay* (New York: J. S. Ogilvie, 1913).

Morton, J., *Gangland: The Early Years* (London: Time Warner, 2004).

Walling, G., *Recollections of a New York Chief of Police* (New York: Caxton Book Concern, 1887).

2. The Foster and Stander Gangs

Bennett, B., *Famous South African Murders* (London: Werner Laurie, 1938).

Marsh, R., *Famous South African Crimes* (Johannesburg: Struik Timmins, 1991).

Turrell, R. (ed.), *The Mind of the South African Murderer (An Anthology of Justice Ministers' Reports, 1907–1945)* (South Africa: SARob Books, 2000).

3. The Ashley–Mobley Gang

Bucuvalas, T. *et al.*, *South Florida Folklife* (Jackson: University Press of Mississippi, 1994).

Caudle, H. M., *The Hanging at Bahia Mar* (Fort Lauderdale: Wake-Brook House, 1976).

Luckhardt, A. L., *O. B. Padgett, A Florida Son* (Los Gatos: Smashwords, 2009).

Stuart, H. C., *The Notorious Ashley Gang* (Stuart: St Lucie Printing, 1928).

University of Miami, Special Collections, James Horace Alderman Collection, 1929, ASMO443.

4. Johnny Torrio and Al Capone

Bergreen, L., *Capone* (New York: Simon & Schuster, 1994).

Schoenberg, R. J., *Mr Capone* (London: Robson Books, 1993).

5. The Lewis–Jones Gang

Anon., *The True Story of the Last Crime and Capture of the "Lewis Gang"* (Baltimore: United States Fidelity and Guaranty Company, n.d.).

6. Rocco and Bessie Perri

Dubro, J. and Rowland, R. F., *King of the Mob* (Markham: Viking, 1987).

——, *Undercover* (Markham: Octopus, 1991).

Edwards, P. and Auger, M., *The Encyclopedia of Canadian Organized Crime* (Toronto: McClelland & Stewart, 2004).

Nicaso, A., *Rocco Perri: The Story of Canada's Most Notorious Bootlegger* (Toronto: John Wiley & Sons, 2005).

Schneider, S., *Iced: The Story of Organized Crime in Canada*, (London: John Wiley and Sons, 2009).

7. The Purples

Cohen, R., *Tough Jews, Fathers, Sons and Gangster Dreams* (New York: Vintage, 1999).

Kavieff, P. R., *The Purple Gang* (New York: Barricade, 2000).
Rockaway, R. A., *But – He Was Good to His Mother* (Jerusalem: Gefen, 1993).
Rudensky, M., *The Gonif* (Woodbridge: Apollo, 1971).

8. British Protection Rackets

Bean, J. P., *Sheffield Gang Wars* (Sheffield: D&D Publications, 1981).
——, *Crime in Sheffield* (Sheffield: Sheffield City Libraries, 1987).
Colquhoun, R., *Life Begins at Midnight* (London: John Long, 1962).
Lucas, N., *Britain's Gangland* (London: Pan, 1969).
Thomas, D. and Grant, R., *Seek Out the Guilty* (London: John Long, 1969).

9. Ma Barker and Her Boys

Edge, L. L., *Run the Cat Roads: A True Story of Bank Robbers in the Thirties* (New York: Dembner, 1981).
Haley, J. E., *Robbing Banks Was My Business: The Story of J. Harvey Bailey, America's Most Successful Bank Robber* (Canyon: Palo Duro Press, 1973).
Maccabee, P., *John Dillinger Slept Here* (St Paul: Minnesota Historical Society Press, 1995).
Purvis, M., *American Agent* (Garden City: Doubleday, Doran, 1936).
Wallis, M., *Pretty Boy: The Life and Times of Charles Arthur Floyd* (New York: St Martin's Press, 1994).

10. John Dillinger

Giradin, G. R. with Helmer, W. J., *Dillinger: The Untold Story* (Bloomingdale: University of Indiana Press, 1994).
Maccabee, P., *John Dillinger Slept Here* (St Paul: Minnesota Historical Society Press, 1995).
Nash, R., *Dillinger: Dead or Alive?* (Chicago: Henry Regnery, 1975).
Poulson, E., *Don't Call Us Molls* (New York: Clinton Cook, 2002).

11. Murder Inc.

Johnson, M. H. and Miller, K. E. Q., *Harlem Godfather: The Rap on My Husband, Ellsworth "Bumpy" Johnson* (New York: Oshun, 2008).

Turkus, B. B. and Feder, S., *Murder Inc., The Story of the Syndicate* (Cambridge, MA: Da Capo Press, 2003).

12. Prostitution in Soho – The French Gangs

Fabian, R., *Fabian of the Yard* (Toronto: Harlequin, 1954).

Morton, J., *Gangland Soho* (London: Piatkus, 2008).

13. The Messina Brothers

Lucas, N., *Britain's Gangland* (London: Pan, 1969).

Morton, J., *Gangland Soho* (London: Piatkus, 2008).

Watts, M., *The Men in My Life* (London: Christopher Johnson, 1960).

Webb, D., *Crime Is My Business* (London: Frederick Muller, 1953).

—, *Deadline for Crime* (London: Frederick Muller, 1955).

—, *Line-up for Crime* (London: Frederick Muller, 1956).

14. The Sabinis

Greeno, T., *War on the Underworld* (London: John Long, 1960).

McDonald, B., *Gangs of London* (Preston: Milo, 2010).

—, *Elephant Boys* (Edinburgh: Mainstream, 2000).

Morton, J., *Gangland* (London: Warner, 1993).

—, *Gangland Soho* (London: Piatkus, 2008).

Thorp, A., *Calling Scotland Yard* (London: Allan Wingate, 1954).

15. Mimile Buisson and the Front Wheel Drive Gang

Attia, N., *Jo Attia Mon Père* (Paris: Gallimard, 1974).

Auda, G., *Les Belles Années du Milieu* (Paris: Éditions Michalon, 2002).

Borniche, R., *Flic Story* (New York: Doubleday, 1975).

Boudard, A., *Les Grands Criminels* (Paris: Pré aux Clercs, 1989).

Buisson C., *Fille de Gangster* (Paris: Fil d'Ariane Editeur, 2004).
Goodman, D., *Villainy Unlimited* (London: Elek, 1957).
Guillon, E., *Abel Danos, Le Mammouth* (Paris: Fayard, 2006).
Marcantoni, F. with Garde, S., *Monsieur François (Le Milieu et Moi de A à Z)* (Paris: Le Cherche Midi, 2006).
Marcilly, J., *Histoire Secrete du "Milieu"* (Geneva: Tome 3, Eds Famot, 1978).
—, *Vie et Mort d'un Caïd, Jo Attia* (Paris: Fayard, 1977).
Montarron, M., *Histoire du Milieu* (Paris: Plon, 1969).
Pierrat, J., *Une Histoire du Milieu* (Paris: Eds DeNoël, 2003).

16. Billy Hill, "Boss of Britain's Underworld"

Hill, B., *Boss of Britain's Underworld* (London: Naldrett Press, 1955).
Jansen, H., *Man of a Thousand Cuts* (London: Alexander Moring, 1958).
Morton, J. and Parker, G., *Gangland Bosses* (London: Time Warner, 2005).
Murphy, R., *Smash and Grab* (London: Faber and Faber, 1993).

17. Jack Spot

Jansen, H., *Man of a Thousand Cuts* (London: Alexander Moring, 1958).
Morton, J. and Parker, G., *Gangland Bosses* (London: Time Warner, 2005).
Murphy, R., *Smash and Grab* (London: Faber and Faber, 1993).

18. The Painters and Dockers War

Morton, J. and Robinson, R., *Shotgun and Standover* (Sydney: Pan Macmillan, 2011).

19. The Great Bookie Robbery

Morton, J. and Robinson, R., *Shotgun and Standover* (Sydney: Pan Macmillan, 2011).

20. Jimmy "The Gent" Burke and the Lufthansa Robbery

Pileggi, N., *Wiseguy: Life in a Mafia Family* (New York: Simon & Schuster, 1966).

Volkman, E. and Cummings, J., *The Heist: How a Gang Stole $8,000,000 at Kennedy Airport and Lived to Regret It* (New York: Franklin Watts, 1986).

21. Bertie Smalls and the Wembley Mob

Ball, J. *et al.*, *Cops and Robbers: An Investigation into Armed Bank Robbery* (London: Penguin, 1979).

Mills, L., *Crimewatch* (London: Penguin, 1994).

Morton, J., *Gangland* (London: Warner, 1993).

Slipper, J., *Slipper of the Yard* (London: Sidgwick & Jackson, 1981).

Taylor, L., *Inside the Underworld* (Oxford: Basil Blackwell, 1984).

22. The Kray Twins in Soho

Morton, J., *Gangland Soho* (London: Piatkus, 2008).

Pearson, J., *The Profession of Violence* (London: Grafton, 1985).

23. The Dixie Mafia

Humes, E., *Mississippi Mud* (New York: Simon & Schuster, 1994).

Morris, W. R., *The State Line Mob* (Nashville: Rutledge Hill Press, 1990).

Nicholson, C., *Dream Room: Tales of the Dixie Mafia* (Dallas: Durban House, 2009).

24. The Cocaine War

Eddy, P. and Walden, S., "Natural Born Killers", *Sunday Times Magazine* (23 November 1997).

Smitten, R., *The Godmother* (New York: Pocket, 1994).

25. The Birth of the Prison Gang

Brook, J. L., *Blood In, Blood Out: The Violent Empire of the Aryan Brotherhood* (London: Headpress, 2011).

Grann, D., "Annals of Crime 'The Brand'", *New Yorker* (16 February 2004).

26. The Scottish Godfather

Ferris, P. and McKay, R., *The Ferris Conspiracy* (Edinburgh: Mainstream, 2001).

McKay, R., *The Last Godfather* (Edinburgh: Black & White, 2004).

27. Brink's-Mat and After

Knight, R. *et al.*, *Gotcha! The Untold Story of Britain's Biggest Cash Robbery* (London: Pan, 2003).

Pearson, W., *Death Warrant: Kenneth Noye, The Brink's-Mat Robbery and the Gold* (London: Orion, 2006).

28. Martin Cahill, "The General"

Morton, J., *Gangland 2* (London: Warner, 1994).

Williams, P., *The General: Godfather of Crime* (Dublin: O'Brien Press, 1995).

—, *Gangland* (Dublin: O'Brien Press, 1998).

29. Two Bandit Queens and a King

Clarke, J. and Neville, R., *The Life and Serious Crimes of Charles Sobhraj* (Basingstoke: Pan Macmillan, 1980).

Devi, P. *et al.*, *Phoolan Devi: The Autobiography of India's Bandit Queen* (London: Little, Brown and Co., 1996).

Thompson, T., *Serpentine* (New York: Doubleday, 1979).

30. The Triads in Soho

Black, D., *Triad Takeover* (London: Sidgwick & Jackson, 1991).

Bresler, F., *The Trail of the Triads* (London: Weidenfeld & Nicolson, 1980).

Morton, J., *Gangland Soho* (London: Piatkus, 2008).

Newark, T., *Empire of Crime* (Edinburgh: Mainstream, 2011).

Thompson, T., *Gangs* (London: Hodder & Stoughton, 2004).

31. The Zemours and Their Friends

Borel, S., *Mon Père Francis le Belge* (Paris: Éditions Jean-Claude Lattès, 2005).

Dubois, C., *Paris Gangster* (Paris: Parigramme, 2006).

Le Taillanter, R., *Les Derniers Seigneurs de la Pègre* (Paris: Juillard, 1985).

Leclerc, M., *De l'Antigang à la Criminelle: Un Grand Flic ouvre ses Dossiers* (Paris: Plon, 2000).

Morton, J., *Gangland International* (London: Warner, 1999).

—, *Gangland Today* (London: Time Warner, 2003).

Ploquin, F., *Parrains et Caïds: Le Grand Banditisme dans l'Oeil de la P.J.* (Paris: Éditions Fayard, 2005).

32. The Rise and Fall of the Moran Family

Anderson, P., *Shotgun City* (Prahran: Hardie Grant, 2004).

Moran, J., *My Story* (Milford Point: Random House, 2005).

Rule, A. and Silvester, J., *Underbelly* (London: Blake, 2003).

33. The Moss Side Gangs

Morton, J., *Gangland 2* (London: Warner, 1994).

Walsh, P., *Gang War* (Preston: Milo, 2003).

34. The A Team

Morton, J., *Gangland Today* (London: Time Warner, 2003).

—, *Gangland Soho* (London: Piatkus, 2008).